Interactive Media
Design & Development
with Adobe **CS6**

Revealed

Interactive Media
Design & Development with Adobe CS6

Revealed

Sherry Bishop
Annesa Hartman

DELMAR
CENGAGE Learning·

Australia • Brazil • Japan • Korea • Mexico • Singapore • Spain • United Kingdom • United States

DELMAR
CENGAGE Learning®

Interactive Media Design and Development with Adobe CS6 Revealed
Sherry Bishop and Annesa Hartman

Vice President, Career and Professional Editorial:
  Dave Garza

Director of Learning Solutions: Sandy Clark

Senior Acquisitions Editor: Jim Gish

Managing Editor: Larry Main

Product Managers: Jane Hosie-Bounar, Nicole Calisi

Editorial Assistant: Sarah Timm

Vice President Marketing, Career and Professional:
  Jennifer Baker

Executive Marketing Manager: Deborah S. Yarnell

Associate Marketing Manager: Erin DeAngelo

Senior Production Director: Wendy Troeger

Production Manager: Andrew Crouth

Senior Content Project Manager: Kathryn B. Kucharek

Developmental Editor: Barbara Clemens

Technical Editor: Sarah Mosser

Director of Design: Bruce Bond

Cover Design: Riezebos Holzbaur/Tim Heraldo

Cover Photo: Riezebos Holzbaur/Andrei Pasternak

Text Designer: Liz Kingslein

Production House: Integra Software Services Pvt. Ltd.

Copy Editor/Proofreader: Dave Belden

Permissions Research: Kathleen Ryan

Indexer: Alexandra Nickerson

Technology Project Manager: Jim Gilbert

Adobe® Premiere Pro®, Adobe® Premiere® Elements, Adobe® After Effects®, Adobe®, Audition®, Adobe® Encore®, Adobe® Bridge, Adobe® Photoshop®, Adobe® InDesign®, Adobe® Illustrator®, Adobe® Flash®, Adobe® Dreamweaver®, Adobe® Fireworks®, Adobe® BrowserLab, Adobe® Edge, and Adobe® Creative Suite® are trademarks or registered trademarks of Adobe Systems, Inc. in the United States and/or other countries. Third party products, services, company names, logos, design, titles, words, or phrases within these materials may be trademarks of their respective owners.

Adobe product screenshots reprinted with permission from Adobe Systems Incorporated.

Library of Congress Control Number: 2011945479

ISBN-13: 978-1-133-69327-7
ISBN-10: 1-133-69327-X

Delmar
5 Maxwell Drive
Clifton Park, NY 12065-2919 USA

Cengage Learning is a leading provider of customized learning solutions with office locations around the globe, including Singapore, the United Kingdom, Australia, Mexico, Brazil, and Japan. Locate your local office at: **international.cengage.com/region**

Cengage Learning products are represented in Canada by Nelson Education, Ltd.

To learn more about Delmar, visit **www.cengage.com/delmar**

Purchase any of our products at your local college store or at our preferred online store **www.cengagebrain.com**

Notice to the Reader
Publisher does not warrant or guarantee any of the products described herein or perform any independent analysis in connection with any of the product information contained herein. Publisher does not assume, and expressly disclaims, any obligation to obtain and include information other than that provided to it by the manufacturer. The reader is expressly warned to consider and adopt all safety precautions that might be indicated by the activities described herein and to avoid all potential hazards. By following the instructions contained herein, the reader willingly assumes all risks in connection with such instructions. The publisher makes no representations or warranties of any kind, including but not limited to, the warranties of fitness for particular purpose or merchantability, nor are any such representations implied with respect to the material set forth herein, and the publisher takes no responsibility with respect to such material. The publisher shall not be liable for any special, consequential, or exemplary damages resulting, in whole or part, from the readers' use of, or reliance upon, this material.

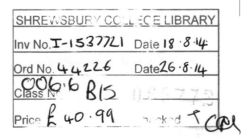
Printed in the United States of America
1 2 3 4 5 6 7 16 15 14 13 12

Revealed Series Vision

The Revealed Series is your guide to today's hottest multimedia applications. For years, the Revealed Series has kept pace with the dynamic demands of the multimedia community, and continues to do so with the publication of 13 new titles covering the latest Adobe Creative Suite products. Each comprehensive book teaches not only the technical skills required for success in today's competitive multimedia market, but the design skills as well. From animation, to web design, to digital image-editing and interactive media skills, the Revealed Series has you covered.

We recognize the unique learning environment of the multimedia classroom, and we deliver textbooks that include

- Comprehensive step-by-step instructions
- In-depth explanations of the "Why" behind a skill
- Creative projects for additional practice
- Full-color visuals for a clear explanation of concepts
- Comprehensive online material offering additional instruction and skills practice
- Video tutorials for skills reinforcement as well as the presentation of additional features

With the Revealed series, we've created books that speak directly to the multimedia and design community—one of the most rapidly growing computer fields today.

—The Revealed Series

About This Edition

This brand new book in the Revealed Series embraces an integrated approach to teaching interactive media design and development—guiding you as you develop your interactive media project, and prompting you with design and accessibility considerations along the way. What kind of interactive media project you end up with is entirely up to you. The goal is to complete a portfolio ready project that is a unique, creative representation of your abilities.

CourseMate

A CourseMate is available to accompany *Interactive Media Design and Development with Adobe CS6 Revealed*, which helps you make the grade! This CourseMate includes:

- An interactive eBook, with highlighting, note-taking, and search capabilities
- Interactive learning tools, including:
  - Chapter quizzes
  - Flash cards
  - Instructional video lessons from Total Training, the leading provider of video instruction for Adobe software. These video lessons are tightly integrated with the book, chapter by chapter, and include assessment.
  - And more!

Go to login.cengagebrain.com to access these resources.

AUTHORS' VISION

Writing a book about interactive media is like taking a photo of a horse race. Both subjects are elusive targets racing so fast that it's difficult to capture a clear picture. At best, you end up with a representative snapshot of a moment in time.

It is impossible to express my admiration and appreciation for each person that has poured time and talent into this project. Jim Gish, Senior Acquisitions Editor, believed in the book from the beginning and made sure Annesa and I had the necessary resources. Attending Adobe MAX was certainly the highlight of the research process. Thank you, Jim.

I can't imagine beginning a book without Jane Hosie-Bounar, our Product Manager, and Barbara Clemens, our Developmental Editor, at the helm. Their titles do not begin to describe their roles. They are tireless, dedicated, and talented professionals. I have been so blessed to know and work with both of them over the years.

Of course, Annesa was an incredible co-author. Our differences and similarities provided a nice blend of experiences, teaching styles, and philosophies. As fellow Master Gardeners, we share the love of digging into interactive media technologies and the love of digging in the dirt. Thank you, Annesa!

Dave Belden, our multi-talented copy editor and proofreader, provided fresh insights on the technical side. His keen eye for detail and suggestions for improvement were much appreciated, providing valuable insight in regard to the accuracy of content specifics. We were also very fortunate to have a fresh talent in the design field, Sarah Mosser, critique each chapter to make sure we stayed true to current design theory and techniques. Entering the project at the end of the editorial process, she was the icing on the cake for us. Thank you, Sarah.

I count my friend Barbara Waxer an invaluable resource and contributor on copyright issues. Additional information on locating media on the Internet and determining its legal use is available in her Revealed Series book *Internet Surf and Turf Revealed: The Essential Guide to Copyright, Fair Use, and Finding Media*. Speaking of copyright issues, Kathleen Ryan patiently contacted the websites we used as examples to obtain permission for their inclusion. This component adds much to the content of the book and would not have been possible without her. Thank you to each of you that allowed us to use images of your websites.

Kathryn Kucharek, Senior Content Project Manager; Suwathiga Velayutham, Project Manager; and Nicole Calisi, Product Manager; worked tirelessly on the layout and kept the schedule on track. We thank them for keeping up with the many details and deadlines. The work is beautiful.

Typically, your family is the last to be thanked. My husband, Don, supports and encourages me every day, and has now for forty-two years! His wise counsel guides me over the bumps in the road along the way during our journey together. Our children and grandchildren are the joys of our lives. Thank you to each of them for their love and support.

—Sherry Bishop

Truth be told, I often wondered if this book would see fruition. It was realized after 11 drafts of an outline, a visit to Adobe Max 2011, a round of academic reviews, numerous calls and emails with my co-author, and lots of revision in an attempt to keep up with the fast moving nature of the topic itself. The behemoth result would not have happened without the dedication, kindness, and talent of Sherry Bishop – thank you co-author! Also, along with us on this journey and deserving of much appreciation are Jane Hosie-Bounar and Barbara Clemens. Many thanks for your commitment to every detail of this book, as well as the rest of the dedicated Cengage team who has believed in my work since the first book I published with them 10 years ago. The demonstrations in this book are also inspiration from my dear friends Dan and Ruth Marx, Ethan Lipton and His Orchestra, River Theater Company, and my garden— much appreciated! And, finally, thank you to my dear beau, Dave Marx; with your support the "not so good" is always balanced with "pretty darn awesome!"

—Annesa Hartman

Introduction to *Interactive Media Design and Development with Adobe CS6, Revealed*

Welcome to *Interactive Media Design and Development with Adobe CS6—Revealed*. This book, brand new to the Revealed Series, will guide you through the process of creating a professional-looking, accessible interactive media project. Use this book both in the classroom and as your own reference guide.

This text is organized into 10 chapters. In these chapters, you will examine the interactive media design and development life cycle from start to finish, exploring planning, budgeting, design, development, and implementation processes along the way.

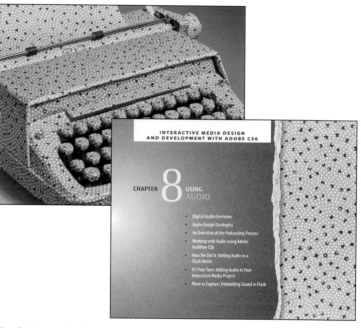

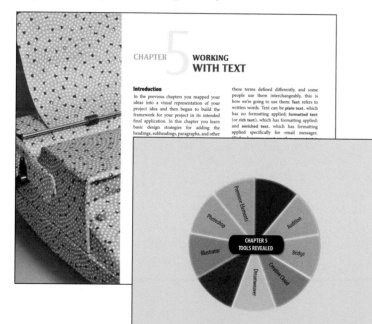

Tools Revealed

A Tools Revealed figure begins every chapter. This figure gives you an at-a-glance look at what software you'll use in the chapter.

Comprehensive Chapter Introductions

This book provides a wealth of material at the beginning of every chapter, comprehensively covering such topics as:

- Managing and planning a project
- Considering design and development goals and challenges
- Building a framework for your project
- Working with text, visuals, animation, audio, and video
- Fine-tuning and completing your project

How We Did It

Our unique *How We Did It* sections use a website called Gardener's Walk to show you, step by step, how we accomplished the design and development of our interactive media project. References to large colorful images help you understand the process, but you can also visit the site either through CengageBrain or by going to gardenerswalk.com.

This book combines in-depth conceptual information with instructions on how to go about achieving the particular goal of the chapter, whether it's planning your project or implementing your ideas.

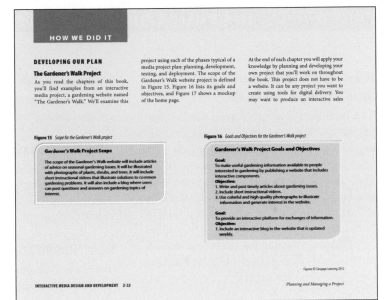

It's Your Turn

Each *It's Your Turn* gives you the chance to flex your creative muscles as you work on developing your own interactive media project. *It's Your Turn* material includes an introduction explaining what you're expected to accomplish, followed by step-by-step suggestions for achieving your goals.

More to Explore

Every chapter ends with a *More to Explore* section, with suggestions for further research on concepts and tools that will help you design, develop, and implement your interactive media project.

INSTRUCTOR RESOURCES

What Instructor Resources Are Available with This Book?

The Instructor Resources are Delmar's way of putting the resources and information needed to teach and learn effectively into your hands. All the resources are available for both Macintosh and Windows operating systems. These resources can be found online at: **http://login.cengage.com**. Once you login or create an account, search for the title under 'My Dashboard' using the ISBN. Then select the instructor companion site resources and click 'Add to my Bookshelf.'

Instructor's Manual

The Instructor's Manual includes chapter overviews and detailed lecture topics for each chapter, with teaching tips.

Sample Syllabus

The Sample Syllabus includes a suggested syllabus for any course that uses this book.

PowerPoint Presentations

Each chapter has a corresponding PowerPoint presentation that you can use in lectures, distribute to your students, or customize to suit your course.

Data Files for Students

There are no accompanying Data Files for this textbook. Users develop and work with their own Data Files to create unique, individual portfolio-ready projects. The Gardener's Walk website project provided with the book can be viewed at gardenerswalk.com. You can also find additional resources on CengageBrain.

Solutions to Exercises

There are no Solution Files provided with this book. All Solution Files should be unique to the student based on his or her interactive media project. For a sample completed project, go to gardenerswalk.com

Test Bank and Test Engine

ExamView is a powerful testing software package that allows instructors to create and administer printed and computer (LAN-based) exams. ExamView includes hundreds of questions that correspond to the topics covered in this text, enabling students to generate detailed study guides that include page references for further review. The computer-based and LAN-based/online testing component allows students to take exams using the EV Player, and also saves the instructor time by grading each exam automatically.

BRIEF CONTENTS

CONTENTS

CHAPTER 1: INTRODUCING INTERACTIVE MEDIA DESIGN AND DEVELOPMENT

CHAPTER 7: ADDING ANIMATION

CHAPTER 8: USING AUDIO

Read This Before You Begin

Interactive Media Design and Development with Adobe CS6 aims to provide the next generation of digital content creators with a comprehensive understanding of the elements of interactive media design and development and their implementation in a project from start to finish. This book is intended to reach those who have studied the fundamentals of individual Adobe programs, such as Photoshop, Dreamweaver, Flash, Audition, and Premiere and are ready to master how the tools in these programs come together to complete an interactive project with the most up-to-date principles and guidelines for working with interactive media.

Specifically this book includes:

- Individual chapters that cover the basic elements of interactive media—text, visuals, animation, audio, and video—with "How We Did It" author examples, and hands-on "It's Your Turn" and "More to Explore" sections.
- Comprehensive guidelines for planning and managing an interactive media project.
- A solid overview of interface design principles and usability, accessibility and copyright considerations.

- Strategies for testing and marketing your project.
- Steps for conceptualizing and creating your own project from start to finish.

Intended audience/prerequisites:

- Individuals who have a basic understanding of the Adobe Creative Suite product line and want to understand how these tool sets work together in the interactive media content creation arena.
- Students who want to complete a capstone/final project for their portfolio.
- A supplemental resource for individuals who manage or direct interactive media related projects, or will do so in the future.
- A supplemental resource for individuals who desire a solid understanding of the latest tools, processes, and terminology related to interactive media design and development.

To use this book, successfully you should have some experience with the Adobe Creative Suite products. If you don't feel comfortable with the Adobe Creative Suite products, consider completing some of these textbooks before you begin this one:

Adobe Dreamweaver CS6 Revealed by Sherry Bishop
Adobe Flash CS6 Revealed by Jim Shuman
Adobe Photoshop CS6 Revealed by Liz Reding
Adobe Illustrator CS6 Revealed by Chris Botello

Once you've mastered the fundamentals, *Interactive Media Design and Development* will be the perfect book for you.

There are no accompanying Data Files or detailed step-by-step instructions with Solution Files for this textbook. Rather, the focus is on encouraging readers to develop and work with their own Data Files to create unique, individual portfolio-ready projects. The website project that is developed throughout the book is a live demonstration website at gardenerswalk.com. You can view the source code for each page in the site to understand fully how each page is built. The code for the style sheets is available on CengageBrain at www.cengagebrain.com.

CHAPTER 1

INTRODUCING INTERACTIVE MEDIA DESIGN AND DEVELOPMENT

- Digital Interactivity Then and Now
- Keeping Up with the Interactive Media Consumer
- The Need for Integration
- Identifying the Interactive Media Designer/ Developer Skillset
- How We Did It: Managing Assets with Adobe Bridge
- It's Your Turn: Keeping Your Assets Organized
- More to Explore: The History of Computers

INTRODUCING INTERACTIVE MEDIA DESIGN AND DEVELOPMENT

Introduction

As you learned in the preface, this book aims to give you an overview of the terminology, processes, media types, and technologies necessary to design and develop interactive media. It is a great resource for those who want to know what it takes to produce interactive content, such as a mobile app, an immersive website, or online game, in today's market. In addition to presenting important concepts, this book guides you, start to finish, through the process of creating a project of your own.

But before we do that, let's take a moment to examine how interactive media has evolved to this point and where it's heading. We'll review the skills you need to produce interactive media content. Then we'll get some hands-on experience using Adobe Bridge as a first step in understanding the concept of integration in interactive media design and development. By the end of this chapter, you'll understand the importance of integrating each media piece to give your users a seamless, intuitive, and exciting interactive experience.

Throughout this book, you will use selected Adobe software programs, features and tools. In this chapter you'll get experience with Adobe Bridge, a media content manager. Your interactive media projects might include Flash animations, Premiere videos, Photoshop images, or Illustrator graphics. Bridge helps you easily organize and manage these media **assets**, or resources, from across all Adobe products, in one place.

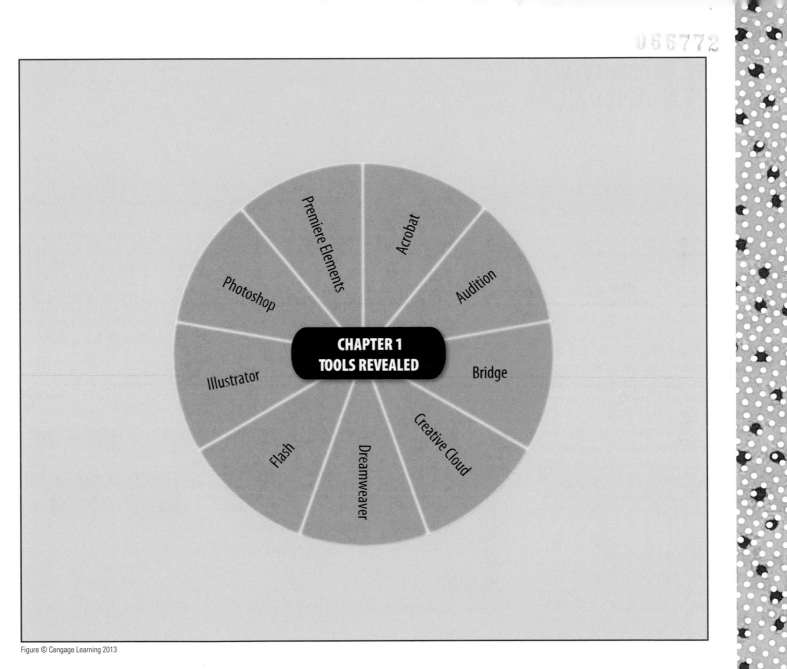

CHAPTER 1
TOOLS REVEALED

Premiere Elements

Acrobat

Photoshop

Audition

Illustrator

Bridge

Flash

Creative Cloud

Dreamweaver

Figure © Cengage Learning 2013

Digital Interactivity
THEN AND NOW

How It Was

It might be difficult to imagine the world without interactive content at your fingertips. Imagine a time when teenagers passed their days at the local arcade, phone booths stood on every street corner, and computers were called mainframes. **Mainframes**, firmly established in the 1960s and 70s, were large, cabinet-like machines that housed a central processing unit and memory, and were used to process financial or statistical data, like the U.S. Census. At that time, students studying computer programming would code their data using punch cards, submit their punch cards to a mainframe's card reader, and wait over dinner or overnight to receive a printout of their final results. Can you imagine? What if, each time you wanted to change the typeface in your word processing document, you had to wait a few hours or more?

The Graphical User Interface

Luckily for us, things have changed fast. Around 1974, with the discovery of microprocessor technologies, computers went from being monstrous machines, slowly crunching data, to something that could fit neatly on a desktop. But it wasn't until 1983 when Apple Computer introduced Lisa, the first home computer with a graphical user interface, that the average consumer could really embrace computer technology. A computer became more than just a terminal to type in text prompts. With a **graphical user interface (GUI)** a computer's interface became visually oriented, with windows, pull-down menus, clickable buttons, icons and images, all of which the user manipulated using a mouse pointer. The GUI offered the first inkling of what we today call interactivity. See Figure 1.

In turn, the introduction of the GUI prompted the growth of software companies that created processes that could translate complex data into visual form, both on

Figure 1 *From mainframe to mobile*

© Spectral-Design/Shutterstock.com; © Feng Yu/Shutterstock.com; © Jojje/Shutterstock.com; © Oleksiy Mark/Shutterstock.com; © Graeme Dawes/Shutterstock.com

screen and on the printed page. For example, in the early 80s, Adobe created the font translation technology PostScript, and the first WYSIWYG (What-You-See-Is-What-You-Get) desktop publishing program, MacPublisher. With GUIs, technologies like PostScript, and programs like MacPublisher and later Aldus PageMaker, a new world of possibilities opened up for traditional graphic designers, one that has become the digital publishing industry of today.

The Web and Desktop Publishing

Then came the commercialization of the Internet, and digital content began moving from individual computers to being shared worldwide. The idea of the **Internet**, an infrastructure of networked computers, began in the early 1960s and was successfully implemented through ARPANET. **ARPANET** was a government-financed research project to test the networking of four major computer systems at universities in the southwestern United States, including the University of California at Los Angeles, Stanford Research Institute, the University of California Santa Barbara, and the University of Utah.

But it wasn't until the early 1990s that the Internet became intuitive and easy enough for anyone to use. This came with the introduction of a new protocol for information distribution developed by Tim Berners-Lee, which became known as the World Wide Web (WWW or the Web). The **Web**, as we know it today, is based on **hypertext**, a system of embedding links in text to connect to other, related, text. The language for the development of hypertext is called **hypertext mark-up language**, or **HTML**. The Web was made even more accessible with the development of the first graphical browser, **Mosaic**, developed by Marc Andreessen in 1993.

In 1996, as the Web made its commercial entrance, Adobe became a publicly-held company and its PostScript technologies and page layout programs continued to define the desktop publishing industry. Adobe built applications, such as Illustrator and Photoshop, for creative professionals to take advantage of evolving, graphically oriented technologies. As processor speeds and the availability of the Web increased, Adobe created applications where designers and developers could begin to work with moving pixels – video and animation.

Multimedia and Interactive Media

Adobe was also faced with rising competition from Macromedia, the developer of Director, one of the first multimedia authoring tools used to make CD-ROMs and information kiosks. By 1997 Macromedia had also released the still-popular HTML authoring tool Dreamweaver (now owned by Adobe). Macromedia also developed the first technologies to offer more complex multimedia experiences for low-bandwidth web users, which would eventually become the Flash Player and its corresponding authoring tool, Flash.

Around this time, the term "interactive media" made an appearance. Suddenly, opportunities for designers and developers in digital communication jumped to higher levels of innovation than ever before. This speed has meant that the definition of "interactive media" is in constant flux, and established principles on how to create and produce content for the interactive environment are still in their infancy. Students who want to venture into this area of design and development find it a challenge to decipher exactly what an interactive media curriculum might entail. Is interactive media design and development the same as interaction, experience, or interface design and development? In our research, these terms often overlapped and converged—a sign that perhaps this type of study is still too new for norms.

For the purpose of this book, however, the term "interactive media design and development" seems most fitting. There are other related terms around the concepts of "interactivity" and "media," but for now, we will define **interactive media design and development** as the design and development of content that is presented in a digital environment, can encompass many multimedia elements—text, images, animation, video, audio—and is an experience one can interact with, participate in, or simply view.

Keeping Up with the Interactive
MEDIA CONSUMER

Evolution of Consumers

As digital interactivity has evolved, so have consumer expectations. What differentiates interactive media from print and other digital-based media content is that it can be consumed in various ways. There are three types of interactive media consumers—passive viewer, active user, and participant—and a single content consumer can be any of these types throughout an interactive experience. See Figure 2.

Passive Viewer: passively consumes services and information. For example: reading a Wikipedia article; comparing products on consumerreports.org; or surfing craigslist.

Active User: actively handles web content through interactive functions. For example: purchasing something on amazon.com; playing an online game; or downloading an app.

Participant: a contributor or author of content. For example: posting a YouTube video; editing a Wikipedia article; or contributing to or monitoring a shared community space.

The skills needed to create content for these varied interactive media consumers differ from those required in the mature, static desktop

Figure 2 *Three types of interactive media consumers*

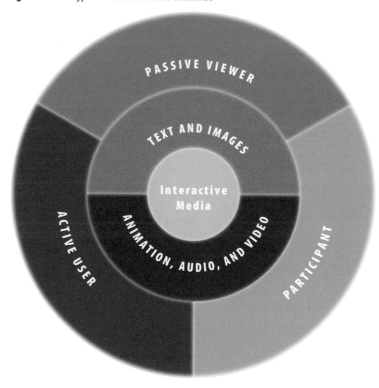

publishing and print arena. (You'll learn more on interactive media skills later in this chapter). These skills differ because, while desktop publishing has established guidelines for effectively engaging its end user, the guidelines for planning, managing, and creating an interactive media project are in constant flux.

Industry Growth and Opportunity

This book will help you navigate your journey as you begin to design and develop media for today's demanding media consumer. The opportunities are endless. It's an area of design where new benchmarks and standards develop as the systems with which we view and interact with content evolve. Systems now engage the user with all the senses— touch screens with gesture recognition, voice activation, immersive 3D animated graphics, motion capturing, and probably not too far beyond, digital scent. **Digital scent** technology can digitize scent so that we receive smell through the Internet. **Gesture recognition** enables humans to interact directly with a computer screen via the motions or gestures of one's fingers or a pen-like stylus rather than a mouse.

One reason interactive media is more prevalent in our culture today is that the technologies used to view, interact with, and produce these experiences are now readily available and relatively inexpensive. The days of needing exclusive access to 3D animation applications that ran only on high-end Silicon Graphics machines is long past. Software programs used to build the amazing special effects seen in movies and TV can now be bought off the shelf at a fraction of the cost of only a decade ago. And, the computers and peripheral hardware necessary to run these programs are easy to come by— most consumer-grade PCs now come fully equipped with ample processer speeds, RAM, video and sound cards, high resolution monitors, and accessible high-speed Internet connections.

As more households invest in these technologies, companies specializing in building content for these devices scramble to keep up. The gaming industry, for example, has grown exponentially. Game industry journalist Nich Maragos wrote in 2006 that "According to a study from ABI Research, the video game industry is expected to double in sales from 2005's $32.6 billion to $65.9 billion in 2011." With the rising popularity of online, mobile gaming, and sophisticated, affordable video game consoles like the Microsoft Xbox 360, Nintendo Wii and portable 3DS, this prediction has been surpassed and the industry is continuing its meteoric rise. Gartner Research reported that worldwide spending in the "gaming ecosystem" reached $67 billion in 2010, and will reach $112 billion by 2015.

The Need for
INTEGRATION

Interactive Media Software

One thing for sure is that as consumers demand more from their interactive media applications, the demand for more streamlined solutions and workflow processes for producing interactive media content is also greater. Software developers are looking to meet these demands in various ways. Some are creating solutions to help do-it-yourselfers with WYSIWYG editors and plug-and-play content templates. Others are going the open source route, creating robust content management systems, such as WordPress, Joomla!, and Drupal, where you can pull together asset modules (such as navigation menus, forms, login and search components) into accessible web page templates that can customize and track a user's experience, as shown in Figure 3.

In this website, the basic template was designed by JoomSpirit (joomspirit.com), and assembled by Annesa in the Joomla content management system. The pull-out navigation system, animated Flash banner, mail form, and Facebook link icons are all premade elements within the system. As a website creator, you only need to enter your site information and it's ready to go.

Because these applications are open source, they are available for use by the designer or developer at little or no cost. **Open source** describes software for which the original source code is freely available and may be redistributed with or without modification.

Companies like Adobe, Inc. which provide professional, industry-standard media creation tools, are finding new ways to create applications with similar interfaces, making it easy to import and export content from one application to another.

Growth of Integration

The theme that underlies both open source software and common software interfaces is integration. In a broad sense, **integration** is the act or process of forming, coordinating, or blending something into a functioning or unified whole. Unlike the creation of print products, such as a poster or business card design, where only one or two software programs are necessary to complete the final result, interactive media content development involves the use of many programs. If you explore online job descriptions for digital content developers (or graphic, web, interactive, animation, instructional, multimedia developers—the titles are endless), you will inevitably find a list of programs you need to know—and, not just to know them, but how they integrate with each other. To help you begin to understand this idea of integration, the lesson at the end of this chapter provides a tour of Adobe Bridge. Bridge is the Adobe organization software application designed to facilitate the workflow of content among Adobe programs.

It is also interesting to note that integration has become easier with the increasing popularity of cloud computing. **Cloud computing** is a networked, browser-based system that lets you share and create content, using storage space on the Internet instead of your own computer system. With cloud computing you can conveniently create, collaborate, and

Figure 3 *A website created in Joomla*

Courtesy of River Theater Company.

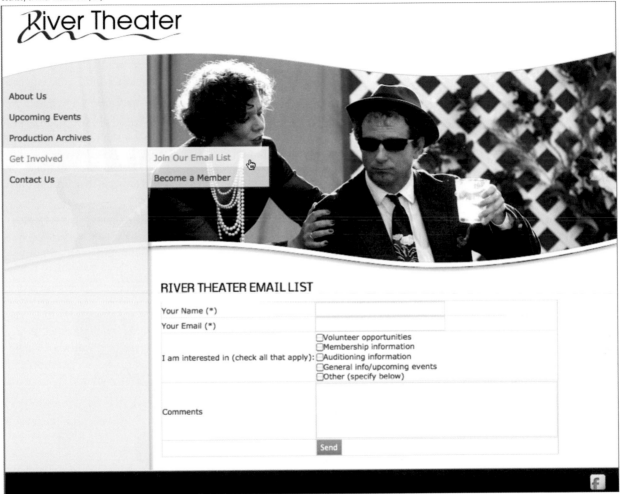

move media among different devices, mobile or desktop. See Figure 4.

Despite the apparent rivalry between Windows and Macintosh users, content integration is also becoming easier between computer platforms. A majority of the common programs used by designers are available for both the Mac and Windows platforms, including the Adobe and Microsoft program suites. You will notice in this book that we have provided screen shots taken from both Windows and Mac.

The Adobe Creative Suites

In this book we introduce the process of producing an interactive media project from start to finish using the Adobe Creative Suite software programs. The Creative Suite products are used more than any other product suite in the graphic design industry. (This is not to say there aren't many other valuable tools and resources that you can explore and use, and when they're available, we'll give examples.) To help you understand the context of what each of the Adobe programs can contribute and how they work together in interactive media production, some background is essential.

The **Adobe Creative Suite (CS)** is a collection of interactive media applications made by Adobe Systems for both the Macintosh and Windows platforms. The first version of the CS collection was released in September 2003. In 2005, Adobe acquired Macromedia (their closest competitor) and integrated their products with their own, including Flash, Fireworks, and Dreamweaver. In the past

these applications had been sold separately, but Adobe has now combined them into various suites or editions based on the needs of various interactive design disciplines— print, web, video, and broadcast.

For more information on these Creative Suite collections and the software bundled with each edition, see the Adobe website at adobe.com/products/creativesuite.html. To demonstrate the design and development of the various media types within this book, we use specific tools and features within the Adobe applications. We hope you will walk away with a clearer understanding of how the Adobe products integrate to bring together the assorted elements of an interactive media project.

Flash Catalyst is designed to produce interactive Flash-based projects without writing code. We demonstrate the use of Flash Catalyst as an option to create a mock-up for our demonstration website project called the Gardener's Walk. (You'll learn more on this in Chapters 2 and 3). See Figure 5.

Dreamweaver is a web authoring and editing software application for creating standards-based websites and designs for the desktop, smartphones, tablets, and other devices. We use Dreamweaver to build the interface and navigational structure of our demonstration project.

Photoshop is the premiere program for working with pixel-based imagery and photographs, with extensive photo editing

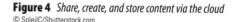

Figure 4 *Share, create, and store content via the cloud*
© SoleilC/Shutterstock.com

capabilities, painting and drawing tools, and special effects. We use Photoshop to optimize, edit, and output the photos for our demonstration project.

Illustrator helps create distinctive vector artwork with sophisticated drawing tools, brushes, and special effects. We use Illustrator to create the initial mockup of the project interface and all illustrations in our project design.

Premiere Pro, and its lighter version **Premiere Elements**, are the Adobe video editing applications, with robust editing options, transitional effects, and multiscreen output options. We use Premiere to edit and output the video resources in our project.

Audition handles audio production tasks, such as editing, mixing, and recording. We use Audition to edit the sound files that are used in our project.

Flash is an authoring and animation program for producing interactive content that is viewable through the Adobe Flash Player. We use Flash to create the animated photo gallery movie within our project.

Acrobat is designed to deliver content in **Portable Document Format (PDF) format,** an open standard (publicly available) file format that provides an electronic image of text or text and graphics that looks like a printed document. PDF documents are widely used because you can view, print, search and electronically transmit them with ease. We use Acrobat to produce accessible and printable versions of our project content, and downloadable resources.

Figure 5 *Gardener's Walk demonstration project used throughout this book*

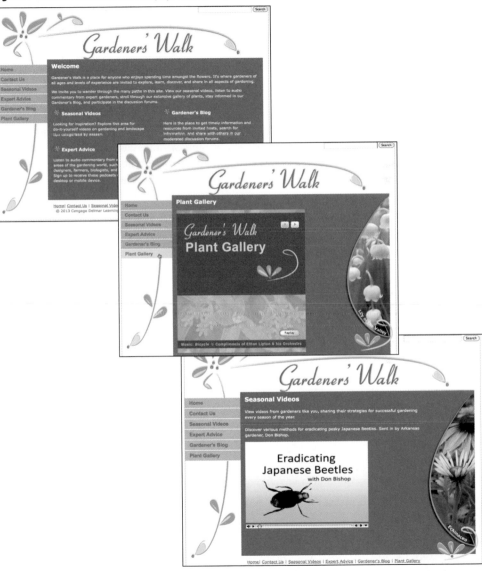

Figures © Cengage Learning 2013

Introducing Interactive Media Design and Development

Identifying the Interactive Media
DESIGNER/DEVELOPER SKILLSET

Skills You'll Need

The skills you need as an interactive media designer or developer are different from the skills you need as a traditional graphic designer or developer. Let's examine some of the important skills that the interactive media designer or developer needs—especially those that separate the professional from the novice.

- **Develop a broad knowledge of tools and methods:** Take a more generalized approach to learning new tools and methods. In short, go for it, whatever it is! Don't limit yourself to a specialized area until you are established in the field. Learn as many tools as possible for design of both front-end visuals and back-end programming. And play with them a lot!
- **Know end users:** Observe and evaluate how people interact with media, and the methods and tools they prefer. Don't underestimate the knowledge you can glean by profiling how others utilize digital technologies in their day-to-day lives.
- **Have current and accurate knowledge of standard tools and methods:** Identify and use the technological applications, tools and methods you need to develop the most effective end product. This means having a keen eye to what's standard, most reliable, and yet new and up-and-coming in the industry and how these applications, tools and methods work together to produce the envisioned result for the client and end-user.
- **Know current usability and accessibility standards and practices:** Develop a strong foundation in what is current in the areas of usability and accessibility in digital content creation. Meeting usability and accessibility standards and practices are critical for ensuring your content meets its widest audience. We will look at these concepts in more detail in Chapter 3.
- **Develop excellent graphic design skills:** Build a foundation in basic graphic design principles. Anyone can use the numerous WYSIWYG web page and desktop publishing apps and premade templates to construct their own digital creations. But interactive media specialists go beyond construction. They must be designers and architects. They must be able to design media that is truly awe-inspiring, navigationally sound, highly usable, adaptable, and promotes its message with intention and clarity. For example, Figure 6 shows a great adaptation of a static printed page (a traditional business card) to an interactive business card for a mobile phone that can adapt to new forms of technology and user experience.
- **Develop a flexible project vision:** Develop the skill of navigating between the big picture vision of a project and its minute details. It's akin to being a cinematographer. Depending on the situation, it's the ability to quickly adjust your "lens" to step back, absorb, and critically observe the panoramic view of a project, while in the next instance being able to zoom in and tweak one particular aspect of a scene. You need to be able to stop your project workflow on a regular basis and ask the bigger questions; for example, to move from "Would this paragraph be more legible if I use 1.5 leading vs. 1.0 leading?" to "Am I still on track with the original objectives of this project's design?"

This list of skills is a tall order, so it is no surprise that many in this field work in teams, where each member of the team has a particular skillset that complements the others. The aim of this book, however, is to guide in broad strokes the workflow of an interactive media project by a single designer—you! It's an opportunity to explore the essential parts of producing an interactive media project from start to finish. We aim to give you an understanding of what it takes to communicate intelligently about every aspect of the media creation process. Once you experience, from a generalized approach, the varied aspects of what interactive media design and development can entail, you may find that it will guide you to identify and promote your unique talents. See Figure 7.

Figure 6 *Adapting a printed card (A) into an interactive design (B)*

Figure © Cengage Learning 2013. Photo Courtesy of Dan Marx, Ph.D.

Figure 7 *What you need to be a successful interactive media designer*

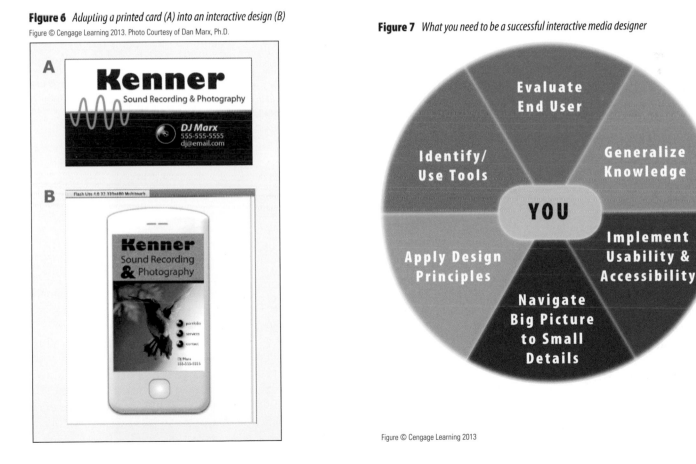

Figure © Cengage Learning 2013

MANAGING ASSETS WITH ADOBE BRIDGE

Let's take a few minutes to explore Adobe Bridge, the program that kept track of the assets we used in the development of the demonstration project we use throughout this book, the Gardener's Walk. **Adobe Bridge** acts as the media content manager across all Adobe products and serves as a good example of how to organize assets that you will integrate across these products when producing an interactive media experience. In Bridge, you can open and preview any file format that Adobe recognizes such as JPGs, SWFs, PNGs, and PDFs. Although the most common use of Bridge is to organize and view media, it has many powerful features that you will find useful.

Finding Adobe Bridge

Adobe Bridge comes packaged with the Adobe Creative Suite. There are several ways to access the program: by opening it directly from your Applications or Program Files folder on your computer's hard drive, or within Adobe Illustrator, Photoshop or InDesign, from the Bridge icon on the Application bar (see Figure 8) or by choosing File > Browse in Bridge within the programs. InDesign is not covered in this book, but it's the Adobe desktop publishing program for print and digital page layouts. A streamlined version of Bridge called Mini Bridge is also available in Photoshop and InDesign; it appears as a panel that opens directly within the Photoshop or InDesign programs. See Figure 9.

Figure 8 *Opening the Adobe Bridge application from the Application bar*

Figure 9 *Selecting a file to view in Mini Bridge*

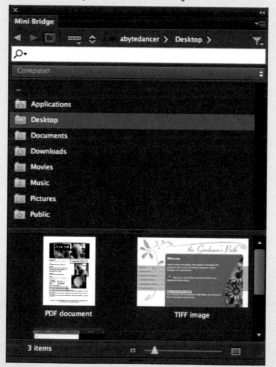

Figures © Cengage Learning 2013

Set up your files and use Adobe Bridge

1. Create a folder named **Chapter 1** to store your original files in the drive and folder that you will use to complete the projects in this book. There are no data files supplied with this book. You will create or locate your own files to complete each project.

2. For practice with using Bridge, place at least five photographs in your Chapter 1 folder. You can use photos that you have taken with a digital camera, print photos that you have scanned, or images that are in the public domain. **Public domain** images are images that are available to use legally without permission or restrictions.

3. Open Adobe Bridge, verify that you are in the Essentials workspace, then use either the breadcrumbs trail across the top of the Bridge window or the Folders panel to navigate to and select the Chapter 1 folder.

4. Click to select the first file in your folder. See Figure 10.

Figure 10 *Opening and viewing files using Adobe Bridge (Mac)*

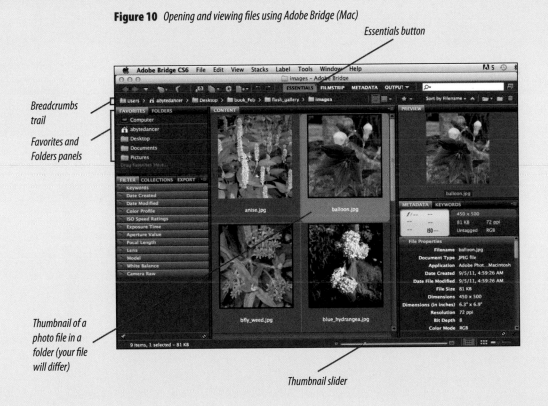

Essentials button

Breadcrumbs trail

Favorites and Folders panels

Thumbnail of a photo file in a folder (your file will differ)

Thumbnail slider

Figure © Cengage Learning 2013. Photos courtesy of Sherry Bishop and Annesa Hartman.

Use the Thumbnail slider on the bottom right of the Bridge window to adjust the size of the thumbnails, as shown in Figure 11.

5. Click **View** on the Menu bar, click **Review Mode** (or press **[Ctrl][B]** (Win) or **[⌘] [B]** (Mac)), to display the contents of your folder in a carousel arrangement, and use the keyboard arrow keys to shuffle through the images.

6. Click the **Loupe tool** ◯ in the lower-right corner of the window, then move the mouse pointer over the image to magnify a selected area so you can examine the detail more closely. See Figure 12. Press **[Esc]** to exit Review Mode, click to deselect the files, then click the first one again.

Figure 11 *Using the Thumbnail slider to adjust thumbnail size*

Thumbnails of files in a folder (your files will differ)

Thumbnail slider

Figure 12 *Viewing files in Review Mode*

Thumbnails displayed in Review Mode

Magnified area of image

Loupe tool

Figures © Cengage Learning 2013. Photos courtesy of Sherry Bishop and Annesa Hartman.

Introducing Interactive Media Design and Development

7. Open the **Metadata panel** and click File Properties if necessary to view the file size, dimensions, and resolution. See Figure 13.

   The Metadata panel is a rich source of information about a file, including the camera settings used (descriptive information that cannot be changed) and copyright information (additive data that can be changed). You can view and edit the copyright information in the IPTC (International Press Telecommunications Council) Core section of the Metadata panel.

8. Click the **Keywords panel** (if the Keywords panel is not already open, click **Window** on the Menu bar, then click **Keywords panel** to open it), then click the **New Keyword button** in the bottom right corner of the panel.

   Keywords let you search for and quickly locate files.

9. Type an appropriate keyword in the Keywords text box, press **[Enter]**, then click to place a check mark in the checkbox next to the new keyword. The check mark applies the keyword to the file. See Figure 14.

10. Close Adobe Bridge.

Figure 13 *Viewing file Metadata*

Figure 14 *Adding a keyword to search for assets*

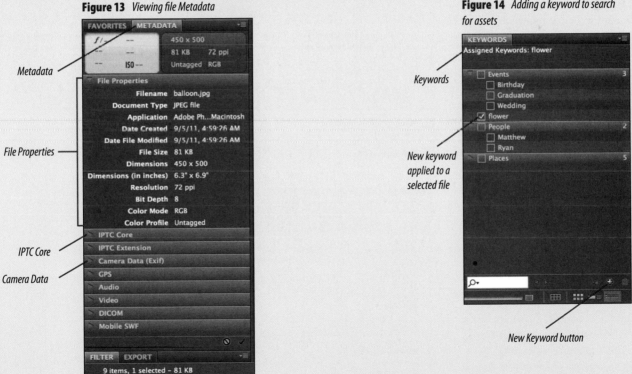

Metadata

File Properties

IPTC Core

Camera Data

Keywords

New keyword applied to a selected file

New Keyword button

Figures © Cengage Learning 2013

Introducing Interactive Media Design and Development

INTERACTIVE MEDIA DESIGN AND DEVELOPMENT   1-17

KEEPING YOUR ASSETS ORGANIZED

Adobe Bridge can help you manage and easily access your assets, but to get the most from this program and your work processes, it's useful to take the time to keep your interactive media project folders and file structures organized, and to maintain consistent and intuitive naming conventions. Well-organized content allows you to find what you need more quickly, and ensures that linked document items stay intact. It also avoids excessive troubleshooting when something is missing, demonstrates a level of work ethic that attracts employers, and is useful in collaborative environments. Are you someone with a collage of icons strewn across the desktop, or someone who neatly saves items in colorfully labeled folders? Try the following exercise to improve your computer content organizational skills.

1. Consider an interactive media project you might like to produce. What content items can you envision you would need for the project? For example, if you want to design an interactive how-to presentation, you might have images, videos, and HTML pages.

2. Next, create a tree diagram that categorizes and identifies the folders that would contain these various content items (see Figure 15 for an example). A **tree diagram** is a visual way to define hierarchical relationships. In our example, each box in the diagram can represent a computer folder and/or files. You can create a tree diagram by sketching it on a piece paper,

by using the SmartArt features in Microsoft Word or PowerPoint, or by downloading a free trial of Annesa's favorite visual brainstorming and outlining program, Inspiration, from inspiration.com.

3. After you have created your tree diagram, replicate the structure in the Documents area on your computer. See Figure 16.

Figure 15 *Organizational structure of an example interactive media project*

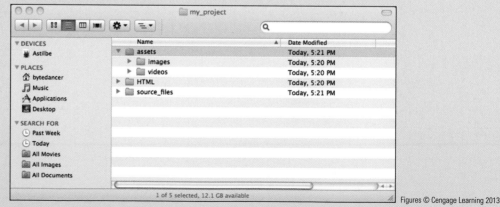

Figure 16 *Example project file structure*

Figures © Cengage Learning 2013

THE HISTORY OF COMPUTERS

The history of digital computing, the Internet, and the rise of graphic and interactive media applications is not only fascinating, but also provides useful context for what we experience in the interactive media industry today, and might experience in the future. Explore some of the historical information below, or do your own online searches on the topic:

- About Adobe: History of Innovation: adobe.com/aboutadobe/history/

- The History of Computers: inventors.about.com/library/blcoindex.htm
- A Brief History of the Internet: walthowe.com/navnet/history.html
- A Biased History of Interactive Media: smackerel.net/smackerelclassic.html

Even More to Explore

To explore some of the topics discussed in this chapter in more depth, see the References section at the end of the book. For links to additional web resources, visit the Even More to Explore link under Book Resources on Cengage Brain.

CHAPTER 2 PLANNING AND MANAGING A PROJECT

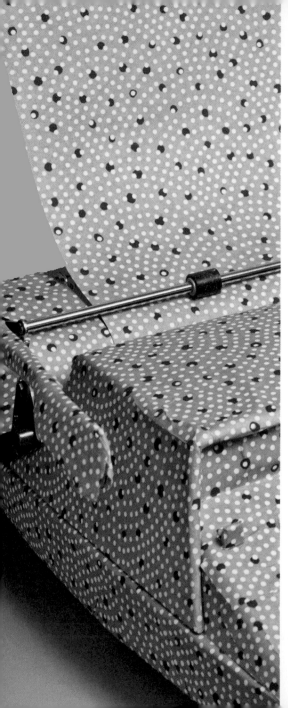

PLANNING AND MANAGING A PROJECT

Introduction

In the previous chapter you learned a brief history and definition of interactive media design, as well as an overview of the skill set and tools needed to be an interactive media designer. In this chapter you learn how to design and manage a project plan for a proposed interactive media project, which spans the time from the project's inception to the delivery of the final product. You learn the phases that make up a project plan and what you need to accomplish during each phase. You then identify tools that can help you to define, analyze, track, and complete each phase of the plan.

As you progress through the book, you'll see that we use a demonstration project to illustrate the concepts we present. The demonstration project outlines the creation of a website, but you might prefer to create a different type of project, such as a video game, a mobile phone app, a demonstration video, or a series of podcasts. Think about your interests and try to imagine how you could develop a project that would fit those interests. You may want to create a project with skills you have and that you would like to develop further, or you may want to tackle a project that will require you to learn new skills. After reading through the concepts and referring to the examples, you'll be ready to put together your own interactive media project plan.

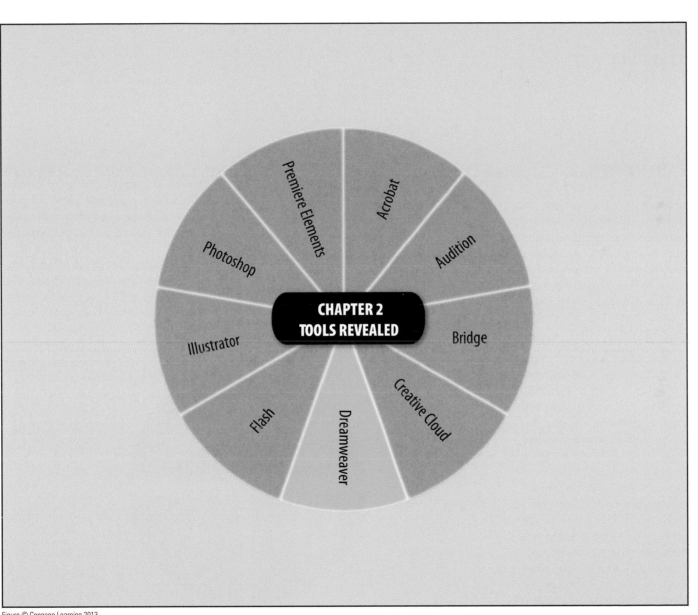

CHAPTER 2
TOOLS REVEALED

Acrobat

Audition

Bridge

Creative Cloud

Dreamweaver

Flash

Illustrator

Photoshop

Premiere Elements

Figure © Cengage Learning 2013

Managing
A PROJECT

Why is project management important?

Project management is the process of planning, organizing, and managing resources to complete a defined project. Before you begin an interactive media project, it's important to formulate a realistic plan for implementing and completing it. Proper planning is critical to the completion of any successful media project.

A plan can be simple or complex, depending on the scope of the project. A project's **scope** refers to the range the project encompasses after you have defined all of the project goals and objectives—what will be included and perhaps what will be excluded. For example, the scope and plan to create a fifteen-second radio spot would be quite different from a plan to develop a twenty-page interactive website. Each would require different types of source files, different programs to create and edit the files, and different skill sets to produce the work. Defining the scope is important to avoid a common project management problem called scope creep. **Scope creep** means making impromptu changes or additions to a project without corresponding increases in the schedule or budget. Proper

project control and communication among team members and clients can minimize scope creep and achieve the successful and timely completion of a project.

Identifying Project Components

Although a short radio spot project and an interactive website project differ considerably in scope, they will have the same basic components: clearly defined goals, stated objectives to accomplish each goal, available resources, a budget, and a timeline, as shown in Figure 1. A **goal** is a specific ambition that is measurable and attainable. An **objective** is a specific action whose purpose is to accomplish a goal. To ensure a successful project, it is essential that you define clear goals and create a list of all the objectives necessary to accomplish those goals.

Figure 1 *Project management components*

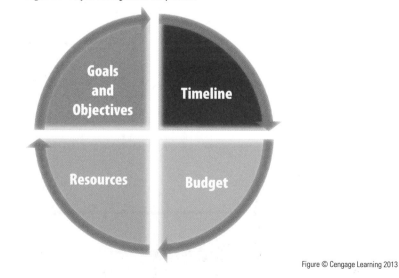

For example: a goal of the Weather Channel website might be to display the current local weather conditions on demand when requested by a website user. Objectives to accomplish this goal might include (1) obtaining the user's ZIP code, (2) connecting to the corresponding databases, and (3) displaying the weather information in a variety of forms such as maps, charts, and graphics. **Resources** would include your computer system, technical expertise, available staff, and access to materials and content. A **budget** is a list of itemized expenditures necessary to complete the project. A **timeline** is a chronological representation of dates and times from the project inception to the project completion.

These components can often conflict with each other, so as the project manager, you may need to adjust one or more of them. For instance, a shortage of time, resources, or funding can constrain goals and objectives. Or an unexpected increase in funding can allow you to expand your goals. If a project is running short on time, perhaps another person (resource) can be temporarily added to the team to help meet a deadline. Striking a balance among them is the job of the project manager.

Finalize your plan after conferring with both your clients and other team members to make sure that the purpose, scope, goals, and objectives are clear to everyone. Establish the **deliverables**, or products that will be provided to the client at the project completion, and a timeline for their delivery. Be realistic in setting a project completion date; beware of promising more than you can deliver, sooner than you can deliver it. At strategic times during the development process, present your work in progress to your team members and your client for feedback and evaluation. Analyze all feedback objectively, incorporating both the positive and negative comments to help you make improvements to the project and to meet the client's expectations and goals.

Locating Project Management Tools

There are countless tools available to help you manage every aspect of a project. You may plan to use application software already available to you, rather than purchasing specialized project management software. But if you're looking for dedicated project management applications, consider their features in relation to their cost. Some features you might want to consider are:

- how and where the information will be stored (on your computer or offsite)
- what collaboration tools are included (discussion forums, whiteboards, scheduling)
- whether it can be used remotely
- how it allows you to track the project

Also worth considering: Can you access the tool using your mobile devices? How secure is it? Is there training available? How is the data backed up and how often? Is it customizable?

Some project management tools use the Cloud to store files online. The **Cloud** refers to storage space on computers you access over the Internet, as opposed to storage on your own computer system. Whenever you send emails using a web-based service like Google, or upload your photos to a photo sharing site, you are using the Cloud for storage. **Zoho,** shown in Figure 2, is a suite of web-based applications available at zoho.com. The applications range from collaboration applications such as Chat, Discussions, Mail, Meeting, and Projects; business applications such as Books, Invoice, Marketplace, and Reports; and productivity applications such as Calendar, Planner, and Writer. Pricing is available based on the number of users and number of available features you need, but available at no cost for personal users.

Other project management alternatives include Microsoft Project and Microsoft SharePoint. **Microsoft Project** lets you plan, schedule, assign resources, and track the progress of any project. It shares a similar interface with Microsoft Office products, so you'll find it easy to learn if you're comfortable with Office. **Microsoft SharePoint** lets you set up websites that you can use for managing documents and publishing reports. Go to microsoft.com/project to learn more about Microsoft Project, and sharepoint.microsoft.com to learn more about Microsoft SharePoint.

Figure 2 *Zoho website*

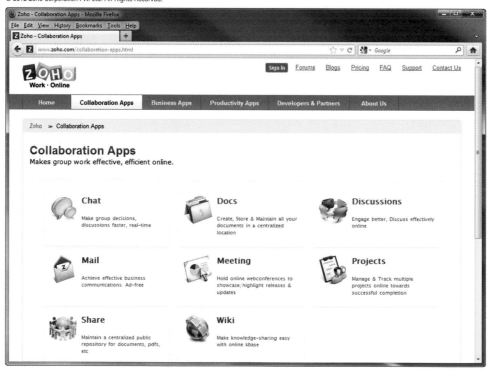

Some project management tools, such as the Bamboo Project Management Suite, work together with Microsoft SharePoint. **The Bamboo Project Management Suite** includes features to automate and manage notifications to team members, calendaring tools, and visual presentation tools. For a complete list of features they offer, go to store.bamboosolutions.com, shown in Figure 3.

If you plan to use tools that you already have, rather than purchasing project management or collaboration tools, you can use a Microsoft Office program such as Microsoft Excel to create and track your budget. The office.microsoft.com website offers numerous budget templates you can download. Microsoft Outlook is great for scheduling meetings and deadlines, viewing co-workers' schedules, and sending group messages. Microsoft Access is a database tool that you can use to store information about project resources, client contacts, and billing. Access lets you easily organize and search for information, print reports, and share data. You can also create Web databases and share them with anyone via the Internet.

Figure 3 *Bamboo Project Management for SharePoint*

Defining and Developing
A PLAN

Beginning the Process

Although many people are eager to begin new projects by jumping right into them, it's wise to first take time to determine exactly what you plan to do and how you plan to do it. Without defined goals and objectives, it's difficult to move forward on a straight path to successful project completion. Understanding the phases of project development by all team members is critical.

Defining the Project

Before you can begin to plan a project, you must have a clear definition of the project's purpose and scope. It is essential to meet with your potential client and ascertain exactly what they want. Sometimes this is not as simple as it seems. The more communication you have with your client, the better you will understand their needs and expectations.

To help define the project scope, create a checklist of questions you need to answer about the client and the project. These can include:

- What are the goals and objectives for the project?
- Who is the target audience?

- Is it a specific audience or a broad audience?
- How can the project be designed so it will appeal to the target audience?
- How will the project be designed so it can be viewed on multiple devices?
- What content will be appropriate for the target audience?
- What content is relevant to the purpose of the project?

- Does the client have a plan in place for updating the project?
- Can the project be completed within the client's time limitations?
- Can the project be developed within the client's budget?

The more questions you can answer about the project, the better prepared you'll be when you begin to develop the content. Table 1

TABLE 1: WEBSITE PLANNING QUESTIONS TO ANSWER	
Who is the target audience?	People of all ages who are interested in gardening
How can I tailor the site to reach that audience?	Include timely gardening tips; use colorful plant photographs
What are the goals for the site?	To make useful gardening information available to people interested in gardening; to provide a site for exchange of information
How will the information be gathered?	The authors will provide photographs from their personal collections and gardening tips learned from their experience as Master Gardeners
What are the sources for media content?	The authors or public domain repositories
What is the budget?	No out-of-pocket expenses will be charged by either author to the project
What is the timeline?	1 month from inception to initial launch
Who is on the project team?	The two authors
How often should the site be updated?	After each page is approved and finalized
Who will update the site?	The two authors
Which devices will be targeted in the site design?	Desktop, tablet vertical, tablet horizontal, mobile phone vertical, and mobile phone horizontal

© Cengage Learning 2013

lists some basic questions we considered while defining the scope of the Gardener's Walk site. Our answers helped us formulate our ideas and write a statement of purpose. A **statement of purpose** clearly states the reason why the project is being developed. The purpose is different from the scope, which states what will be included after the goals and objectives are met. See Figure 4 for the statement of purpose for the Gardener's Walk website project.

You can use similar questions and answers to create a user profile for the project you plan to complete. A **user profile** describes the characteristics of the target audience. A user profile might also include how users would interact with the project components, what they would be looking for, and what their expectations would be. The statement of purpose and the user profile will help you define your goals and objectives. Figure 5 shows the user profile for the Gardener's Walk website.

If the project is a website, stating the user's vision for what they expect to see and do on the site will help you to create a site usability test. In a **site usability test**, you ask unbiased people, who are not connected to the design process, to use and evaluate the site. Projects other than websites would also benefit from usability tests. For instance, for a video game you would ask people to play the game and provide feedback on how easy or difficult the interface was to understand or how easy or difficult the game was to play. For a mobile phone app, you would ask for feedback on how useful and intuitive the features are.

Once you have defined your project, it's time to begin development.

Understanding Development Phases

For any project, the first phase should always be to formulate the client's goals and objectives, and then create your project plan

Figure 4 *Statement of purpose for the Gardener's Walk project*

Gardener's Walk Statement of Purpose

The purpose of the Gardener's Walk website will be to provide seasonal information of interest to gardening enthusiasts.

Figure 5 *User profile for the Gardener's Walk project*

Gardener's Walk User Profile

The potential users of the Gardener's Walk site are people of all ages who are interested in reading about gardening issues. They have access to a computer and the Internet and enjoy viewing botanical images and reading about plants. They may be looking for answers to questions they have about their gardens. They might be interested in sharing information with other gardeners.

Figures © Cengage Learning 2013

with these in mind. Communicate with the client to get a clear idea of their needs and expectations. It's also important to get input from all project stakeholders. **Stakeholders** include anyone with an interest in the project. Stakeholders might include the project manager, the project team, the client, project sponsors, users, and testers.

Next, set up the basic structure, or the "bones" of the project, and create the content. After you have a working version, you begin to test and modify the content until you feel it is complete enough that you can present it to the client as a prototype. A **prototype** is a model built to help conceptualize, test, or evaluate a project. After the client approves the final version, you publish the project and put in place the system that will be used to update it. For example, a website project would have a preliminary site or prototype of the site for a client to browse through; a video game would have a working model that a client could play to see and experience the game levels; and a mobile phone app would have a prototype that a client could download and use to test the features. Figure 6 illustrates these phases of project development.

Let's look at each of these development phases in more detail.

Developing a Plan

"Prior planning prevents poor performance." Have you heard that old saying? There's a lot of truth to it. Planning is the most important phase of any successful project. Planning is

actually a continuous process that can overlap other project phases.

An interactive media project may be one you have solicited as a solo designer or one that has been assigned to you as an employee

within a large company. A project may involve a large team of people working in various roles to complete the work, or it may be the responsibility of just one person to plan and execute the project. Regardless of the number

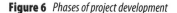

Figure 6 *Phases of project development*

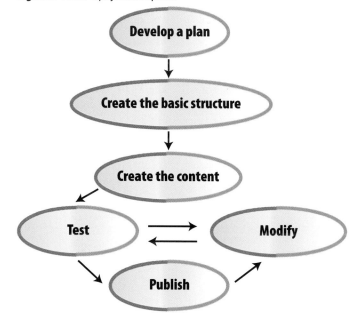

Planning and Managing a Project

of people involved, the same processes must be followed.

Project plans can vary from detailed to general. For example, recording every detail step-by-step from the largest to the smallest is referred to as the "waterfall" method. This method provides good results, but can be tedious to implement. At the opposite end of the spectrum is the "plan as you go" (or the "by the seat of your pants") method, which is usually not very efficient. The ideal approach is somewhere in between these two extremes.

After your initial meeting with the client, review the answers to your questions. From the responses, create the statement of purpose and scope, the timeline for all due dates, the budget, a task list with work assignments, and a list of resources needed. Also include a list of deliverables, such as page prototypes and art for approval. Include due dates for each deliverable in the timeline.

As you specify the deliverables, be as specific as possible, because your choices will affect both your budget and the timeline. Will you design original Flash or video content? Will you create original art, or will you use stock photos and public domain or royalty-free images? **Stock photos** are high-quality photographs that are sold for commercial use. You can either pay a fee for a defined use of the site (such as number of downloads in a set time frame) or you can pay for each individual image that you download. Getty Images, Shutterstock, and iStockphoto are examples of websites where you can find good quality stock photos. If you see a shopping cart on a site's home page, you can be sure that there is a charge for some or all of the images on the site. As you learned in Chapter 1, public domain images are free to use without restriction, either personally or commercially. **Royalty-free images** are images that can be used legally with certain restrictions, such as attaching a credit to the owner.

After you've developed a complete plan, you can begin creating your project.

Developing a Fluid Plan

It's not unusual for a project developer to encounter new information or unforeseen problems during development and have to "go back to the drawing board." When this occurs, the timeline can be adversely affected. Open and clear communication with the client regarding goals, objectives, time required, and total cost is critical to prevent dissatisfaction. Together, you should develop a procedure to address technical problems and delays that may arise so it's clear who is responsible for the resulting additional expense.

Forming the Structure and
ADDING CONTENT

Creating the Basic Structure

Once you complete the planning phase, you determine the structure of the project by creating a wireframe or storyboard. For a website, an illustration called a **wireframe** portrays the flow of content in an interactive experience. Like a flowchart, a wireframe is an illustration that shows the relationships between each component of a website. Don't confuse this meaning with another meaning: a 3D illustration of a character you create for a Flash animation. The term

storyboard is often used when referring to animation or video projects, but can also be used for website projects. Wireframes or storyboards are helpful when you're planning an interactive media project, because they allow you to visualize how each component links to the others. They're also an important tool to help the client see how the screens in the project will look and work together. Make sure that the client approves the wireframe or storyboard before you begin constructing the product.

You can create very simple **low-fidelity** wireframes using a pencil or pen, using a graphics program such as Adobe Illustrator or Adobe Fireworks, or using a presentation program such as Microsoft PowerPoint. To create more complex **high-fidelity** wireframes that simulate site navigation and user interaction, use a high-fidelity wireframe application such as OverSite, ProtoShare, Microsoft Visio, or Adobe Proto. You'll learn more about wireframes in Chapter 3.

Figure 7 *Wireframe for the Gardener's Walk website*

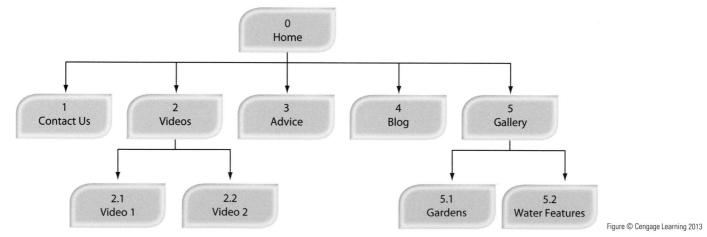

Figure © Cengage Learning 2013

The wireframe serves as your blueprint as you construct your project. The basic wireframe shown in Figure 7 diagrams all of the pages that are planned for this book's demonstration project, the Gardener's Walk website. The home page appears at the top of the wireframe and five pages are linked to it. The home page is called the **parent page**, because it's at a higher level in the web hierarchy relative to all of the pages linked to it from a lower level. The pages linked to a page from a lower level are called **child pages**.

So a page can be both a parent page and a child page if it has links to pages on both a higher and lower level in the website heirarchy. The number at the top of each page placeholder represents the file number. Each arrow pointing down represents a link from the page above it to the page below it. A horizontal line represents the level that the pages below it share. More detailed wireframes include all document names, images, text files, and link information. Once you have established your link structure and begin to link the pages together, check the links regularly to verify that they work according to the wireframe plans. Verifying links is an ongoing process.

In addition to creating the wireframe for your project, you should also create a folder hierarchy on your computer for all of the files that you'll create for the site. Start by creating a folder for the site with a descriptive name, such as the name of the company. This folder, known as the **local site folder**, will store all of the pages and files for the site. Traditionally, this folder has been called a root folder and many people still use this term; in this book we'll call it the local site folder. Next you create a subfolder, often called **assets** or **images**, in which you store all of the files that are not pages, such as images and audio files.

After you create your folder structure, you're ready to set up the site. When you set up the site using Dreamweaver, you use the Dreamweaver Site Setup dialog box to assign your site a name and to specify the local site folder. After you've set up your site, the site name and any folders and files it contains appear in the Files panel. Using the Files panel to manage your files ensures that the site links work correctly when the website is published.

If you're creating an interactive media project other than a website, your basic structure will be slightly different. For example, if you're going to create a video, you'll use a storyboard to outline how many scenes you'll have, the content of each scene, how long each scene will be, what camera techniques, transitions, and sounds you'll use, and so forth. You would also include any introductory scenes containing the title of the video, any concluding scenes with a list of credits, and your plans for locations, actors, and props. A storyboard might also include any playback controls for users to pause, stop, play, and rewind the video, as well as controls for displaying closed captioning.

Creating the Content

There are many design and development issues to consider before you actually begin creating the content. Refer to your user profile to decide such issues as the writing level, the use of color, and the level of technology required to navigate the site. In choosing your page elements, carefully consider the file size of each page. Images and Flash content contribute to making a page attractive and interesting, but can increase the file size. A page that takes too long to download could cause users to leave your site.

You also need to identify what system or systems will be used to view or display the content. Because Internet users now access content from a variety of devices, you can no longer design content that can only be viewed on a desktop monitor. You now need to design for tablets and mobile phones, in both horizontal and vertical orientation.

Dreamweaver has a feature that lets you view web pages in three different simulated environments simultaneously, as shown in Figure 8. In this Multiscreen view, you can view your page using the default settings for a desktop, tablet, or phone, or you can create custom settings. You can see in Figure 8 that more work needs to be done on the Gardener's Walk home page to make it usable on a tablet or mobile phone. You can ensure this compatibility by using CSS3 and media queries. **CSS** stands for **Cascading Style Sheets**, the most efficient and acceptable way to format web pages with a consistent presentation across the site. You'll learn more about CSS in Chapters 3, 4, and 5. **Media queries** are a part of CSS3, the latest version of CSS,

Figure 8 *Viewing the home page with Multiscreen Preview in Dreamweaver*

The style sheets for the phone and tablet pages need to be revised to fit the content to these screens.

The page content fits the screen for a desktop.

Figure © Cengage Learning 2013

Planning and Managing a Project

and include attributes that specify which styles to use for each defined device. So a desktop monitor would use one style sheet and a mobile phone would use another style sheet, with both accessing the same content. The difference is the way the content is displayed.

Content Development Tools

Now that you've learned about project management tools, let's talk about tools to help you create content. Chapter 3 contains detailed descriptions of each of the Adobe software tools that we used in constructing this book's demonstration project.

If you're creating a website, Adobe Dreamweaver is an excellent tool. Dreamweaver incorporates the most up-to-date technology such as CSS3, HTML5, and a grid framework to help you design attractive, functional, and accessible pages. Dreamweaver has several page layouts, shown in Figure 9, that you

Figure 9 *New Document dialog box In Dreamweaver with the Blank Page options*

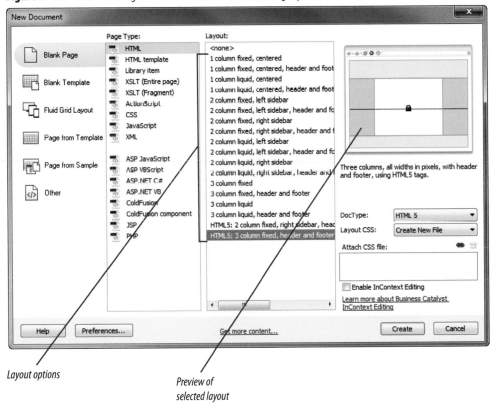

Layout options

Preview of
selected layout

can modify to create new pages, or you can choose to create new pages from scratch.

Dreamweaver also features a new Fluid Grid layout, shown in Figure 10. Notice that there are three layouts, each with a different width and number of columns for displaying page content. When the content is viewed, the code detects the device being used and displays the appropriate layout. While these layouts are a huge advantage over writing your own code, they are rarely coded exactly to fit your needs. Knowledge of HTML and CSS will allow you to modify the code as necessary.

However, it is not necessary to create all of your templates from scratch or from existing pages. You can also use templates from outside sources such as the Internet. You'll find numerous templates for web page components, as well as themed sites such as individual business types, charities, events, and blogs. Some websites offer free templates for downloading and some offer them for sale. Go to your favorite search engine and search for "website templates." For example, Template Monster, at templatemonster.com,

Figure 10 *New Document dialog box in Dreamweaver with the Multiscreen Project option*

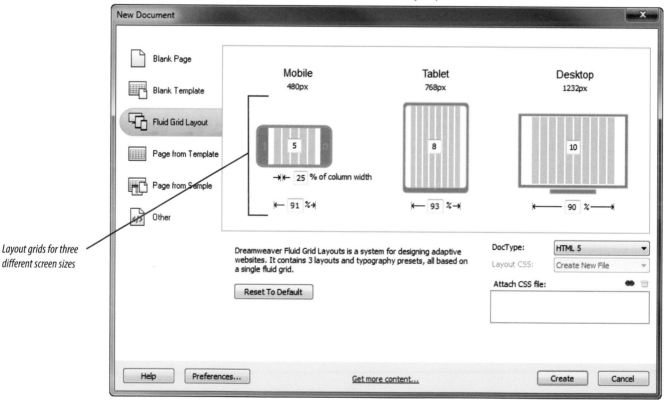

Layout grids for three different screen sizes

shown in Figure 11, offers many types of templates for purchase, as well as several types of Flash and video templates.

Other tools, such as the Google Web Toolkit, include free and open source options for developing browser-based applications. **Free software** can be downloaded at no charge. **Open source software**, as you learned in Chapter 1, is software distributed at no cost and the application source code is made available for users to read and modify to fit individual needs. The disadvantage of open source applications is a lack of product support and a lack of warranty. Open source, however, has led to a spirit of sharing technology and encouraging innovation, and has a large community of enthusiastic supporters. For more information on free or open source software, go to the Free Software Foundation at fsf.org or the Open Source Initiative at opensource.org.

At the other end of the spectrum from open source software is proprietary software.

Proprietary software is owned by an individual or company. You must purchase a license to use it, and you cannot legally copy or distribute it. The terms of use govern how many computers you can install it on, such as a desktop and a laptop. An example of proprietary software is Adobe Flash, a tool used for creating Flash animations, and Unity Pro, a game engine for creating Windows, Mac, and Web applications. Upgrades are available with Unity Pro to also produce games for iOS and Android.

Figure 11 *TemplateMonster website*

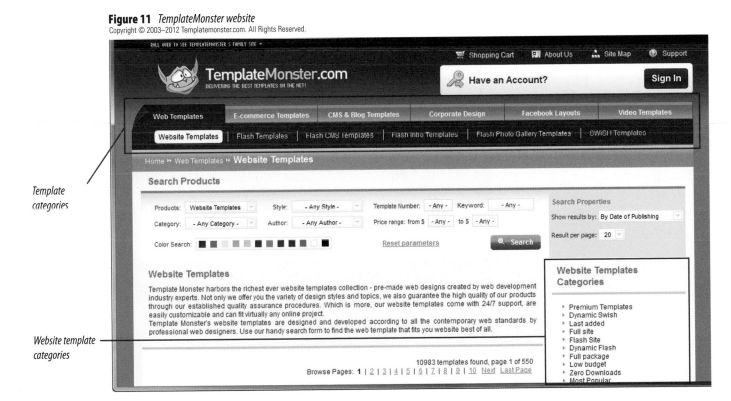

Template categories

Website template categories

Finalizing and Publishing
A PROJECT

Testing and Modifying

After you have created enough content to test, you should begin the testing process. For a website, test to make sure all the links work and the pages look good in all targeted devices. It's also important to test your pages using different browsers. The four most common browsers are Microsoft Internet Explorer, Mozilla Firefox, Google Chrome, and Apple Safari. Test your site using different versions of each browser, because older browsers may not support the latest web technology.

Testing is a continuous process and it's a good idea to start testing as soon as you have a working version. **Adobe BrowserLab** is an online service that you can access through Dreamweaver to test your site with multiple browsers. It provides online viewing, diagnostic tools, and comparison tools. The great thing about BrowserLab, shown in Figure 12, is that you don't have to have the various browsers installed on your computer. You'll need an Adobe ID to access the service; there is no charge to create the Adobe ID, but there could be a charge for using Adobe BrowserLab.

Figure 12 *Home page viewed using Adobe BrowserLab*
Copyright © 2012 Adobe Systems Incorporated. All rights reserved.

List of browsers selected to use for testing

List of available browsers you can use

The home page open in a simulated Firefox window

Dreamweaver has a variety of site reports that can help you identify important design and accessibility issues, such as pages without page titles or images without alternate text. You'll find them on the Site > Reports menu, and you can run them on a single page, selected files, a folder, or the entire site, as shown in Figure 13.

After you have designed your site usability test, you are now ready to implement it. Remember that your testers are project stakeholders who can provide valuable feedback. A comprehensive usability test includes pre-test questions, participant tasks, a post-test interview, and a post-test survey. This provides much-needed information as to how usable the site is to those unfamiliar with it. Typical questions include:

- What are your overall impressions?
- What do you like best about the site?
- What do you like least about the site?
- How easy is it to navigate the site?

You can refer to your user profile to formulate tasks for the site usability test. For more information, go to w3.org and search for "site usability test."

Data Security: Storage, Backup, and Version Control

No matter what kind of project you're creating, a storage and backup plan is one of the most important decisions you have to make. A regular backup is crucial to keeping your data secure. In the event of data loss

due to hardware failure or some other event, you must have a way to recover your data. Sometimes it is possible to recover data from a failed system, but don't count on being able to do so. Chances are you'll have to rely on a backup, or copy, of your data. At other times, you may not have actually lost data, but you may want to access your data from a historical period in time, to undo changes you have made to your files. It's sometimes far easier to revert to an earlier version of your data. The most secure backup plans include **redundant backups**, which back up the same data to different locations.

Backup locations can include removable hard drives, which are a good choice as long as they are kept in a secure, fire-proof location. Removable hard drives are relatively inexpensive and can store massive

amounts of data. You can use Windows to back up your files to a backup system such as a Seagate backup drive. A regular backup system is another option that many businesses use. **Regular backup systems** offer additional security because they back up data automatically, according to a schedule you set. You can customize a backup application to back up your entire system or just part of it. You can back up files locally, online, or both. An example of an online backup system is Mozy at mozy.com. Barracuda at barracudanetworks.com, provides both local and online backup options.

Another important aspect of data security is data **version control**, or keeping track of and protecting the latest versions of your data. In a team environment with multiple content contributors, it's important to be able to

Figure 13 *Reports dialog box in Dreamweaver*

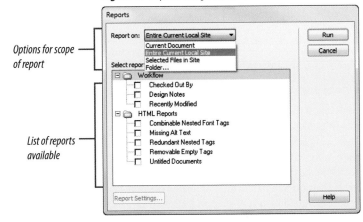

identify and locate the most current project documents, and it can become confusing if more than one person can open and write to common files. Microsoft SharePoint Services allows you to store, track, and restore files. You can restore to a previous version of a document if a mistake has been made or if the earlier version has not been improved with a later version. Dreamweaver has a preference you can set in the Site Setup dialog box to require content contributors to "check out" a file before they can work on it. Similar to checking out a library book, it prevents others from working on the same file simultaneously. Other can only access it after you have checked it back in.

Adobe has a workgroup collaboration tool called Adobe Version Cue. **Adobe Version Cue** provides a way to collaborate with team members, manage security, back up data, and use metadata to search files. **Metadata** includes information about a file such as keywords, descriptions, and copyright information.

Adobe Bridge, the media management tool you learned about in Chapter 1, also uses metadata to organize assets.

Publishing Your Project

Publishing a mobile phone app means to upload it to a site such as the iTunes App Store, Android Market, or Nokia Store where it can be purchased and downloaded. Publishing a game means to self-publish it or to submit it to professional game publishers such as Nintendo or Electronic Arts. Publishing a website site refers to the process of transferring all of the site files to a **web server**, a computer that is connected to the Internet with an IP (Internet Protocol) address, so that it's available for viewing on the Internet. There are several options for publishing a site. For instance, many **Internet Service Providers (ISPs)** provide space on their servers for customers to publish sites, and some commercial websites like Go Daddy or Yahoo! offer reasonable rates for web hosting

and setup. Before you can publish a site, you must have a domain name. Many hosting sites, such as Go Daddy, will register a domain name for you as part of their services. You can also go directly to networksolutions.com to register a domain name. After you make arrangements with an ISP, you'll be given a login and password, along with file and folder locations that you can use to access the site.

After you have your server set up and ready to go, transfer your files using the FTP process. **FTP (File Transfer Protocol)** is the process of uploading and downloading files to and from a remote site. Although publishing happens at the end of the process, it's a good idea to set up web server access during the planning phase. In Dreamweaver, you use the Files panel to transfer your files using the Dreamweaver FTP capability, as shown in Figure 14.

Compensation Issues

Before you begin working on any project, be sure to finalize all compensation agreements and contracts. Many projects run over the estimated time and expenses, so it's important to have an understanding in place when this occurs. In addition, some projects miss the scheduled delivery date that was promised to the client. If you find that you spent more time on the project than you expected, determine if it was because you underestimated the amount of work it would take, ran into unforeseen technical problems, or because the client changed the requirements or increased the scope of the project as it went

---

Testing Strategies

It's far better to begin testing your site as you have content completed rather than waiting until the end of the process. Some tests, like the site usability test, are designed to be executed near the end of the project. Others, like missing alternate text, should be done on a regular basis so you can correct errors as you go. You'll learn more about usability and usability testing in Chapter 3. These same principles apply to other types of media projects such as games or mobile apps. Define content pieces that can be tested separately as they are completed; then, as related pieces are completed, test to see how they work interactively. Games should be tested as blind tests with gamers who do not know you and do not receive any help from you to play the game.

---

along. If you underestimated the project or ran into unexpected difficulties from causes other than the client, you usually cannot expect the client to make up the difference without a prior agreement. No client wants surprises at the end of a project, so it's best to communicate frequently and let the client know the status of all site elements as you go. Good planning up front will eliminate many of these problems.

If the client changes the project scope, make sure you discuss the implications of this with the client. Ideally, you've made the client aware of any schedule or budget changes when they occurred so that your cost estimate will only grow by a predictable, agreed-upon amount.

There are two main compensation methods: bidding the job or charging by the hour. Appropriate amounts for either method are influenced by the going rates of your potential competitors with similar skills. Over the history of the Internet, website development prices have been driven down by the availability of new technology and the increasing number of designers with the expertise to create websites. Factors that contribute to your pricing for developing a website could include:

- the number of pages
- the amount of Flash used
- extra components required
- custom graphics
- content management systems
- quality of the design level

Figure © Cengage Learning 2013

Extra components would include such features as shopping carts, site searches, and calendars. Your client may also ask you to secure the domain name for the site, host the site, and maintain the site. These would all be added to your total estimate for the project.

Projects other than websites use similar methods for compensation. A video, a game, or a mobile app might have a defined end: the delivery of the completed project to the client. However, the client might ask that you also guide the project through publication and distribution. Naturally, this would add to the project cost.

Once you've decided whether you'll provide services by the job or by the hour, provide clients with an estimate of the project cost in writing and ask them to sign it to indicate their acceptance. Explain how and when they'll be billed and what the terms of payment will be. A firm understanding about compensation before beginning the work will save you many headaches when it's time to be compensated. Bill promptly, as the law of diminishing returns applies to customer satisfaction: customers are the most happy to pay for the work as soon as the work is completed. Prompt billing leads to fewer unpaid invoices.

Figure 14 *Using the Dreamweaver Files panel to transfer files*

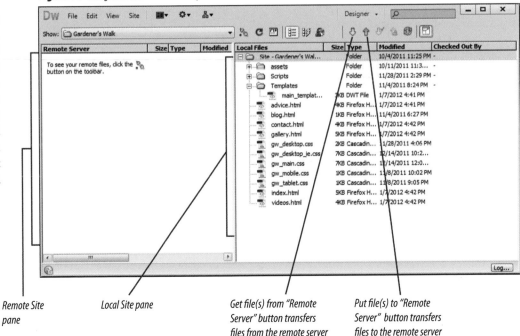

Remote Site pane

Local Site pane

Get file(s) from "Remote Server" button transfers files from the remote server

Put file(s) to "Remote Server" button transfers files to the remote server

DEVELOPING OUR PLAN

The Gardener's Walk Project

As you read the chapters of this book, you'll find examples from an interactive media project, a gardening website named "The Gardener's Walk." We'll examine this project using each of the phases typical of a media project plan: planning, development, testing, and deployment. The scope of the Gardener's Walk website project is defined in Figure 15. Figure 16 lists its goals and objectives, and Figure 17 shows a mockup of the home page.

At the end of each chapter you will apply your knowledge by planning and developing your own project that you'll work on throughout the book. This project does not have to be a website. It can be any project you want to create using tools for digital delivery. You may want to produce an interactive sales

Figure 15 *Scope for the Gardener's Walk project*

Gardener's Walk Project Scope

The scope of the Gardener's Walk website will include articles of advice on seasonal gardening issues. It will be illustrated with photographs of plants, shrubs, and trees. It will include short instructional videos that illustrate solutions to common gardening problems. It will also include a blog where users can post questions and answers on gardening topics of interest.

Figure 16 *Goals and Objectives for the Gardener's Walk project*

Gardener's Walk Project Goals and Objectives

Goal:
To make useful gardening information available to people interested in gardening by publishing a website that includes interactive components.
Objective:
1. Write and post timely articles about gardening issues.
2. Include short instructional videos.
3. Use colorful and high quality photographs to illustrate information and generate interest in the website.

Goal:
To provide an interactive platform for exchanges of information.
Objective:
1. Include an interactive blog in the website that is updated weekly.

Figures © Cengage Learning 2013

presentation, a video, a series of instructional learning objects, or an interface for a game or mobile application. Although Adobe applications will be used throughout the book for most of the examples, you can use any tools that are available to you. We'll discuss optional tools you can consider as alternatives.

Before you begin your project, you should:

- write a statement of purpose
- create a user profile
- define project goals and write objectives to meet those goals
- identify the project scope
- create a budget
- develop a timeline for meeting your project goals and deliverables

After completing this book, you'll have a project that can be used as a part of your professional portfolio.

Figure 17 *Mockup of home page for the Gardener's Walk project*

DEFINING AND DEVELOPING YOUR INTERACTIVE MEDIA PROJECT PLAN

1. Choose a project that you would like to use to work through the book. Your choice might be determined by the software that you have available and enjoy using or would like to learn more about. You might choose to create a website, a video, a mobile application, a series of podcasts, or any project that is created using interactive media. Remember that a website is used for the project example in the book, so many of the instructions will relate more to website development than other interactive media projects. If a step does not apply to your project, either modify it to fit your project or skip it.

2. If you're working with a team, decide who will be the project manager.

3. Write a statement of purpose for your project.

4. Write at least two goals that fulfill your statement of purpose, with a minimum of two objectives each.

5. If you're working with a team, use Microsoft Outlook to make a contact for each team member. Include information such as phone numbers and email addresses, then decide on the next meeting time and location and set up a meeting using Microsoft Outlook.

6. Use a word processing application such as Microsoft Word to list at least ten questions for you to answer about the project's scope.

7. Answer each question and then use your answers to create a user profile.

8. Review your statement of purpose, goals, and objectives to see if you need to revise them to meet the needs of your users as defined in your user profile.

9. Use your goals, objectives, and user profile to write several sentences that define the scope of your project.

10. Use a word processing or spreadsheet program to make a list of the deliverables that would be required to complete your project.

11. Estimate a realistic due date for each deliverable and record it with each deliverable.

12. If you're working with a team, record the name of the person responsible for each deliverable.

13. Using your goals, objectives, and list of deliverables, set up a timeline that illustrates the completion of each item in your project plan. Your ending date will probably coincide with the ending date of your class if you are using this book in a classroom setting. To create your timeline, use a word processing, spreadsheet, or image editing program of your choice.

14. If you're working with a team, designate who will be responsible for ensuring that each item is completed according to the date on the timeline.

15. Make a list of every expense that you expect to affect the price of your project. If this is a project you're doing for learning purposes only, you may not have any estimated expenses, but record a value for your time, mileage, and so forth.

16. Assign an estimated cost to each item.

17. Use a spreadsheet program such as Microsoft Excel to create a budget that shows each itemized expense, the estimated cost of each expense, and the percentage of the total expenses that each represents.

18. Make a list of the assets required and formulate a plan to obtain those you don't have.

19. Locate at least two possible sources for images. Include at least one public domain source for images.

20. Describe how you will publish your project when it's completed.

21. Write a paragraph explaining how you will evaluate and test your project. Include a usability test and explain how it will work.

22. Write a paragraph explaining how you will present your work to your client (or your class).

CHOOSING PROJECT MANAGEMENT TOOLS

You learned about some of the project management tools available today. For this assignment, explore some of these tools in depth and make a recommendation for your tool of choice to manage a large project involving several team members, some of whom are working remotely. For example, Figure 18 shows some of the management tools available from Microsoft Windows Azure. Windows Azure is a Microsoft cloud platform that is used to build cloud applications through Microsoft-managed datacenters. For more information, visit the Windows Azure website at windowsazure.com.

1. Compare and contrast the cost and features of at least three project management tools.
2. Provide the names and URLs of any websites you use.
3. Based on your findings, choose one of these tools to recommend and explain why you chose it.

Figure 18 *Microsoft website*
© 2012 Microsoft

Even More to Explore

To explore some of the topics discussed in this chapter in more depth, see the References section at the end of the book. For links to additional web resources, visit the Even More to Explore link under Book Resources on Cengage Brain.

CHAPTER 3 IDENTIFYING DESIGN AND DEVELOPMENT CONSIDERATIONS

- Getting Your Ideas Out There
- Reaching Your Audience
- Identifying Usability Solutions
- Identifying Accessibility Solutions
- Using Basic Design Principles
- Useful Online Evaluation Tools and Resources
- How We Did It: Building a Comp in Adobe Illustrator
- It's Your Turn: Conceptualizing Your Project Design
- More to Explore: Evaluating the Usability of a Mobile App

IDENTIFYING DESIGN AND DEVELOPMENT CONSIDERATIONS

Introduction

In the previous chapter you learned how to design, manage, and implement a production plan for a proposed interactive media project. In this chapter, you identify ways to visually mock up your project ideas and reach your target audience. Next, you identify the design and development considerations for the project; including usability, accessibility, and design principles. Last, you gather the tools you'll need. In this chapter, however, keep in mind that the design and development considerations are just an overview of concepts and terminology. In subsequent chapters, you'll learn specific guidelines about each content element (text, images, animation, audio and video). After reading through the concepts and referring to the examples in this chapter, you'll have the skills to start conceptualizing your own digital media project.

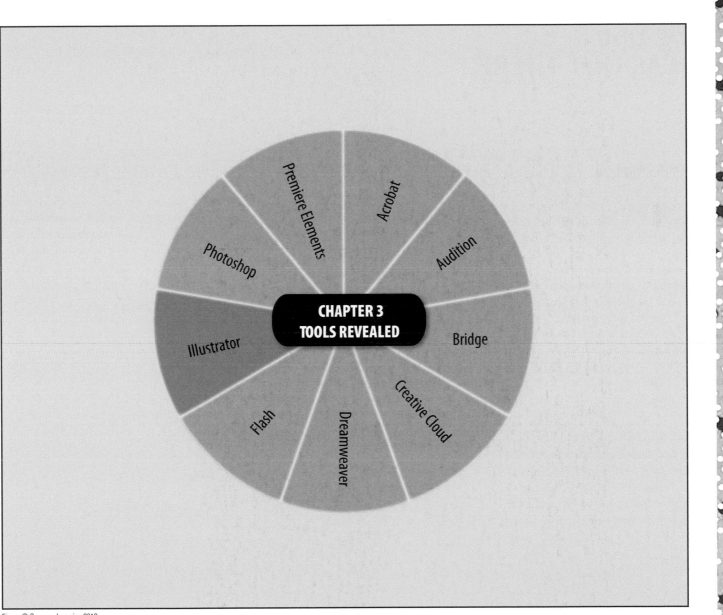

**CHAPTER 3
TOOLS REVEALED**

Acrobat

Audition

Bridge

Creative Cloud

Dreamweaver

Flash

Illustrator

Photoshop

Premiere Elements

Figure © Cengage Learning 2013

Getting Your IDEAS OUT THERE

Wireframes and Comps

One of the most difficult steps in a creative process is to successfully render an idea that is fully formed in your mind into a tangible, visual form. It might begin with a lot of scribbling of random notes, drawing sketches, or talking it out with a friend or colleague. Eventually all those loose ideas that kept you up at night begin to take shape. Visualizing your project is an essential step in your planning process. You must take on the role of an information architect, whose goal is to identify the most effective ways to meet the project objectives and satisfy its intended audience.

We began the visualization process for our Gardener's Walk website by creating a comp. A **comp**, short for "comprehensive layout" or "comprehensive," is a rough, static layout of a project's individual screens or pages showing the relative positioning of user interface (UI) elements (e.g. buttons, text and graphics).

We started our comp by sketching some initial designs on paper (see Figure 1), and then transferring those sketches into Illustrator (shown in Figure 2). In the How We Did It section of this chapter, we'll show you how we used Illustrator to create our comp.

In creating a comp, you don't need to have the actual content you'll use for the design. Instead you can use image placeholders and *lorem ipsum* text. An **image placeholder** is a graphic you use in your document until final artwork is ready to be added to the page.

Figure 1 *Sketches of Gardener's Walk interface design*

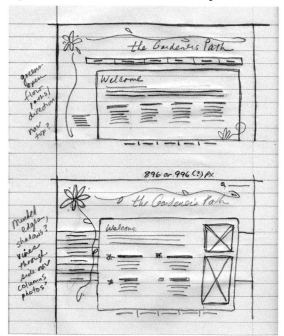

You can download images to use as placeholders by searching for them on the web, or you can make your own by drawing a simple rectangle with an X through it. Some programs, such as Dreamweaver and InDesign, provide image placeholders that you can access directly from their menu commands. **Lorem ipsum** or **Greeking text** is "dummy" (placeholder) text that helps you approximate the look of text in your layout until the actual copy is ready. There are many lorem ipsum generators online that can create the number of words, characters, or paragraphs you need. Our favorite is the Blind Text Generator at blindtextgenerator. com/lorem-ipsum.

Figure 2 *Illustrator Comp for the Gardener's Walk website*

Identifying Design and Development Considerations

At the comp phase we spent a lot of time considering our design choices for the project's visual look and feel. Does the green background provide sufficient contrast with the text? Do we like a more forest green or a sea green? Is orange a complementary accent color? Is there too much or too little white space? Should the navigation bar, or nav bar for short, be on the top or the side of the page? Is the font legible?

We then imported our static Illustrator comp into Flash Catalyst 5.5 to build an interactive wireframe of how the rest of the pages and features in the site would interact with each other and with the overall interface design. As you learned in Chapter 2, a wireframe illustrates the relationship and flow of content within an interactive experience. With Catalyst we added button interactions that allowed us to take our ideas from static visions to a working prototype without having to build every detail of the project. However, just before this book's printing, we learned that Adobe discontinued development of Flash Catalyst. Luckily, there are many other comp creation and wireframing tools that you can use. See Table 1.

TABLE 1: WIREFRAMING TOOLS			
Tool	Description	Website	Approximate Cost
Lumzy	A quick mock-up creation and wireframing tool	http://www.lumzy.com	Free
Cacoo	An online drawing tool for creating diagrams and wireframes that can be multiple users can share and edit.	https://cacoo.com/	Under $100/month depending on number of users
Lovely Charts	A diagramming program available for desktop, online, or the iPad.	http://lovelycharts.com/	Under $80 depending on platform; Under $50/yr. online
Tumult Hype	A timeline-based tool for creating user interactions (buttons, user-triggered animations); creates wireframes with functional navigation	http://tumultco.com/hype/	Under $50
OverSite	A wireframing solution with a wireframe editor and ability to test site interaction.	http://taubler.com/oversite/	Under $70
ProtoShare	A program designed for collaborative website and application development wireframing.	http://www.protoshare.com/	Monthly or yearly (from $500/yr) depending on number of editors
Adobe Proto	Part of the new Adobe touch apps for tablets; lets you design interactive wireframes for websites and mobile apps.	http://www.adobe.com/products/proto.html	Cost: Under $10.
MindManager	A fully-featured program for collaborative visual mapping and wireframing.	https://www.mindjet.com/products/mindmanager/#mmFeatures	Under $250; trial download available

© Cengage Learning 2013

For the final phase of our "taking shape" process, we conducted a user test of the wireframe by asking colleagues for their feedback on whether or not the site met our original objectives. If we had a client for this project, the wireframe would also serve as a model of how we implemented the client's vision, as well as a useful way to share our solution with the client for feedback. In addition, it served as a working model and visual aid for any contributing programmers, content writers, and artists with whom we collaborated in developing the final project's framework and media assets. (You'll learn more on that process in Chapter 4.)

We realize that the way in which you "get your ideas out there" might vary from ours—the creative process works in mysterious ways—but essentially the end results should be the same. Your visualization process should:

- Help clarify the mission and vision of your project
- Determine its content and functionality
- Identify how the user will navigate through the experience and find information
- Map out how the project might accommodate growth and change, and adapt into different formats

Now, let's take some time to get into more depth on some design and development considerations. These will assist you in fully realizing your comps, wireframe, and ultimately your final project, so that it can successfully reach its widest audience. These considerations include *how* to reach your audience, as well as usability, accessibility and basic design principles.

Reaching Your
AUDIENCE

Questions to Consider

Understanding the audience for your project is a critical part of the planning process. With that understanding, you can most effectively identify your project's design. For our Gardener's Walk site, our intended audience is obvious: gardeners, but more specifically all levels of gardeners—novice to expert. Through our design we want to attract and engage our audience and provide a "mood" for our site. For the interface, we chose a clean, open look with touches of green, photos of our own flowers and vegetation, and clear navigation tools. As our own clients for this project, we asked ourselves questions about our intended audience to help us define the site's aesthetics and mood.

You might ask yourself or your client questions like the following to help define the mood of your interactive media project. Considering these questions might also lead to more questions and brainstorming that can help further define the scope of your design.

- What is the age group of your target audience? For example, if the audience is children and their parents, you would then need to consider how to balance the look of your project to appeal to both groups.
- What are the technical limitations of your target audience? For example, if you're building an interactive training program for a company, does the company have a firewall set up that could hinder the use of certain technologies?
- What colors will appeal to your audience and fit within the theme and content of the project? For example if the content is geared toward teenagers, you might go for a more edgy, trendy look than if it was to be advertised to senior citizens.
- What would be three or four adjectives that you would use to describe how you envision the look of your site? For example, do you want it to be contemporary, traditional, earthy, colorful, corporate, flowery, bold, minimalist, or avant-garde?
- How do you see your content displayed? With text? With graphics and video? Will it include sound? Or will it be a combination of all these things?

Needs Assessments and User Scenarios

To further refine your project design, you might also consider taking the time to do a needs assessment of your audience and/or create user scenarios. A **needs assessment** is the process of determining and addressing the actual needs of your end user, rather than relying on assumption or personal preference. A **user scenario,** also often referred to as a user profile, is a written or drawn storyboard that indicates who a typical user of the interactive experience might be.

Identifying Design and Development Considerations

For large corporations, implementing a needs assessment and creating user scenarios provide justification for a project before any decisions are made. In the long run, the answers can save money, avoid scope creep, and lessen headaches. Amazon.com is a good example of a company that has leveraged what it has learned from its extensive strategic planning (including needs assessments) to position itself as one of the most admired companies in the world. To view the entire Amazon Strategic Plan, see the website link available in the References section in the back of this book.

Extensive needs assessments and usability testing for interactive media projects (such as the complete overhaul of amazon.com's online presence) are best conducted by someone who has a background in human-computer interaction (HCI). **HCI** is the study of how human beings interact with computers. The research that's come out of the HCI field has provided the foundation for many of the usability and accessibility guidelines that you'll learn about in the next sections of this chapter.

Asking your audience what they want from your interactive media experience, and evaluating their responses, are both imperative parts of the planning process. But keep in mind that the audience doesn't always know what it wants. There's no guaranteed way of determining what types of people might find and navigate through your interactive experience. Consider Hello Kitty, a fictional character of a white, female, bobtail cat (adorned with a pink bow) produced by the Japanese company Sanrio. Launched in 1974, this cute little icon was first aimed at the pre-adolescent female market, but has grown into an international brand beloved by adults and children alike. In fact, Japanese businessmen are known to emblazon Hello Kitty stickers on their briefcases. The point is that you just never know!

Skillfully navigating unknown variables, such as differences between your expected audience and your actual audience, is where the job of an experienced interactive media designer or developer really comes into play. As you learned in Chapter 1, the interactive media designer/developer should have a thorough knowledge of design principles. The better your grasp of these, the better you're able to guide your decisions (and your client's!) to reach your intended audience— as well as audiences that you might not have originally considered. By applying these concepts, guidelines and principles to your project, you'll be able to reach the widest audience possible.

Example User Scenarios for the Gardener's Walk site

Here are a couple of simple scenarios that reflect the Gardener's Walk target user group.

Rachel – Novice Gardener

Rachel has dabbled in gardening for many years, but has recently moved from Arkansas (hardiness zone 8) to Vermont (hardiness zone 5). She needs a good resource to reach out to other gardeners in her area and view expert advice on gardening issues categorized by season.

Owen – Advanced Gardener

Owen is an active gardener who has an affinity for flowering perennials. He's looking for a resource where he can talk with other gardeners, post photos of his prized flowers, and perhaps share in the form of podcasts or videos some of his "lessons learned" as a long-time gardener.

Identifying Usability
SOLUTIONS

Usability Guidelines

Broadly, **usability** refers to how easy a product is to learn and use. Usability guidelines help designers and developers create products that are effective (that they do what they're intended to do), efficient (that they accomplish their goals in the best way possible) and that satisfy user needs. The goal of effective usability design is to be invisible. It's the difference, for example, between surfing a website and becoming frustrated that you can't find what you need, and being so fully engaged that you don't notice how it's put together.

One of the most comprehensive sets of usability guidelines for interactive media content development is the Research-Based Web Design and Usability Guidelines commissioned by the U.S. Government. You can download a full copy of this document and access other great resources from usability.gov. Another recommended resource is Jakob Nielsen's Ten Usability Heuristics (useit.com/papers/heuristic). **Jakob Nielsen,** a familiar name in the web design community, is a leading web usability researcher and consultant.

Let's discuss some usability guidelines that are important to consider in developing the wireframe of your project:

- **Use Standard GUI Controls.**
  As you learned in Chapter 1, GUI stands for Graphical User Interface. Standard GUI controls for online applications and websites include button and command links, such as scroll bars, radio buttons, checkboxes, and drop-down menus. Over time these controls have become part of a common "vocabulary" in interactive applications and most users now understand how to use

them. If you alter standard controls or make them overly complicated, you can confuse end users. So if you're someone who likes to push the envelope artistically, don't push it when it comes to the look and functionality of standard GUI controls or hyperlinked elements. For example, don't underline text unless it's a hyperlink, and be sure buttons look like buttons. Ask yourself: Does the button appear clickable, without having to place a blinking neon-colored arrow near it saying "Click here"? Figure 3 shows the difference between a standard control and a nonstandard control.

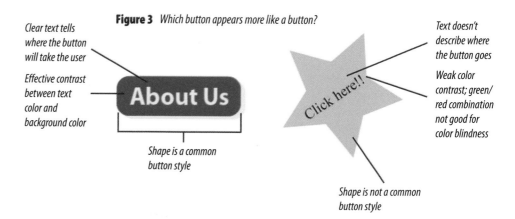

Figure 3 *Which button appears more like a button?*

Clear text tells where the button will take the user

Effective contrast between text color and background color

Shape is a common button style

Text doesn't describe where the button goes

Weak color contrast; green/red combination not good for color blindness

Shape is not a common button style

Figure © Cengage Learning 2013

Identifying Design and Development Considerations

■ **Keep Page Elements Consistent**

As Nielsen puts it, use the "same name of the same thing in the same place." In other words, keep your page elements consistent across all the pages of a website or all the sections of a video or other project, as shown in Figure 4. If you put the section title in the upper left corner of one page, put it in the same location on all the other pages. That way, users know where to look for it. If you change a standard element, you run the risk of confusing users. According to Nielsen, you should remember the double-D rule: "Differences are difficult."

■ **Write for On-screen Viewing**

When you're writing screen-based text, consider both writing style and format. Your writing style in a PhD dissertation would differ considerably from your writing style in text for on-screen viewing. Studies have shown that people scan when

Figure 4 *Examples of consistent elements across two web page designs*

Buttons in same location and order on both pages.

Standard GUI control in same location.

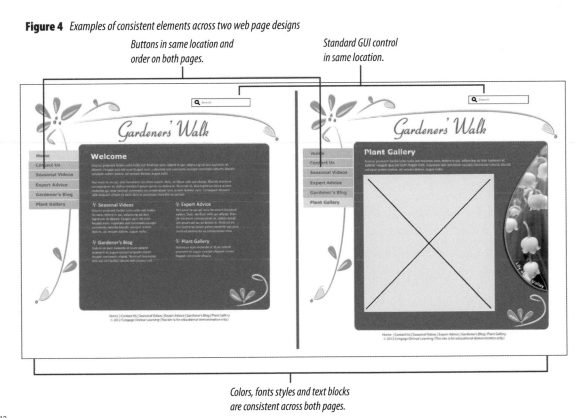

Colors, fonts styles and text blocks are consistent across both pages.

Figure © Cengage Learning 2013

Identifying Design and Development Considerations

they read on the Web. With that in mind, when you write for the Web you want to use natural language and keep sentences succinct and to the point.

Formatting is extremely important for on-screen text. Use chunks of information, bullet points, highlighting, or other visual cues to draw attention to important information. Apply margins and line spacing that are appropriate for the font and column width you're using.

Avoid long blocks of text both vertically and horizontally, and choose fonts designed for screen-based viewing. See Figure 5.

■ **Strive for an Aesthetic and Minimalist Design**
Have you ever walked into a department store and felt overwhelmed by all the bright lights, shiny signage, and abundance of merchandise? An on-screen design with too much text and too many

graphic elements can leave your users feeling the same way. Visually guide your users through your interface design using consistent page elements so they can accomplish what they are there to do with minimal effort.

■ **Offer User Control**
Provide clearly marked exits, as well as options to undo, go back, mute, and bookmark. If possible, give users content

Figure 5 *Examples of effective and ineffective on-screen formatting*

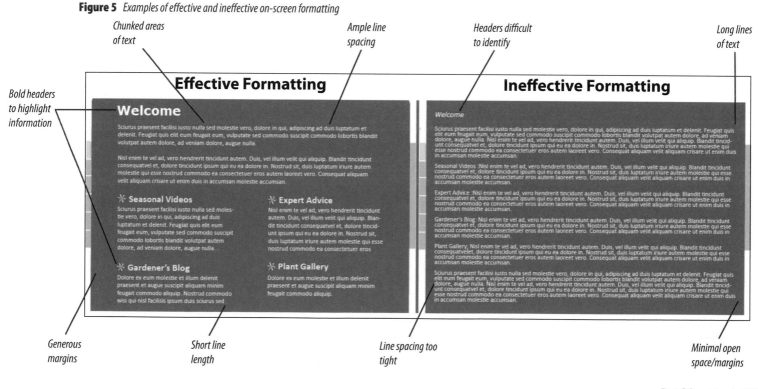

Identifying Design and Development Considerations

controls for repetitive actions, such as shortcut keys. Also let them utilize built-in browser features such as turning off images, changing the screen contrast, or accessing screen readers. Figure 6 shows several controls in the Firefox browser.

■ **Help Users Recover from Errors**

Understanding how to help users recognize, troubleshoot, and recover from an error within your interactive experience is where user testing becomes helpful. User testing can identify possible roadblocks in your design so that you can rework them to minimize user error. If a user does make an error, provide helpful feedback. For example, if someone fails to fill out a required form field, instead of an error message that says something cryptic like "validation unauthenticated," try something more specific, like "Oops! You forgot to enter your email address. Please close this message and enter your email address." Also, always provide clearly marked contact information and help documentation for users who run into problems they can't easily solve themselves.

Remember that the guidelines discussed here are just that—guidelines. As technology changes the way humans interact with new forms of digital content delivery, these guidelines will inevitably grow and evolve. That's why it's so important to stay current in this ever-changing, interactive media landscape.

Figure 6 *Example of end user content controls in Firefox*

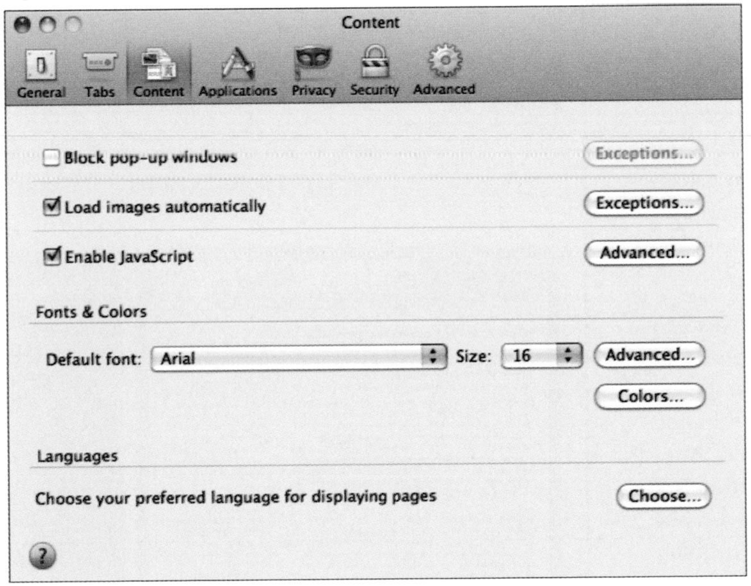

Figure © Cengage Learning 2013

Identifying Accessibility SOLUTIONS

Accessibility Guidelines

Hand-in-hand with usability is accessibility. Usability, as you've learned, refers to how easy a product is to learn and use, while **accessibility** describes the availability of that product to as many people as possible. According to the U.S. Department of Justice *Guide to Disability Rights Laws*, an accessible system "is one that can be operated in a variety of ways and does not rely on a single sense or ability of the user." For example, media designed to be read on the Internet should also have an audio equivalent, providing an alternative way for an end user to get the information and thus reducing access barriers.

It's imperative that interactive media designers have a thorough understanding of web accessibility guidelines as well as the impact of Federal accessibility regulations required for their clients. For example, United States Federal agencies are required by Section 508 of the Rehabilitation Act of 1973 to make their electronic and information technology accessible to people with disabilities. For a full definition of the U.S. Section 508 Law, visit the official Section 508 website at

More About Accessible Websites

Jim Thatcher is a web accessibility consultant with a website that is full of useful resources. The site itself is also an excellent example of accessibility and usability standards. It offers an area where you can find out more about the site's specific accessibility features. It also offers the option to invert the site's foreground and background colors. Studies have shown that visually impaired individuals have less eye strain when reading lighter text on a darker background.

You can find it at jimthatcher.com. See Figure 7.

Figure 7 *Section 508-compliant site example: JimThatcher.com*
Courtesy of Jim Thatcher

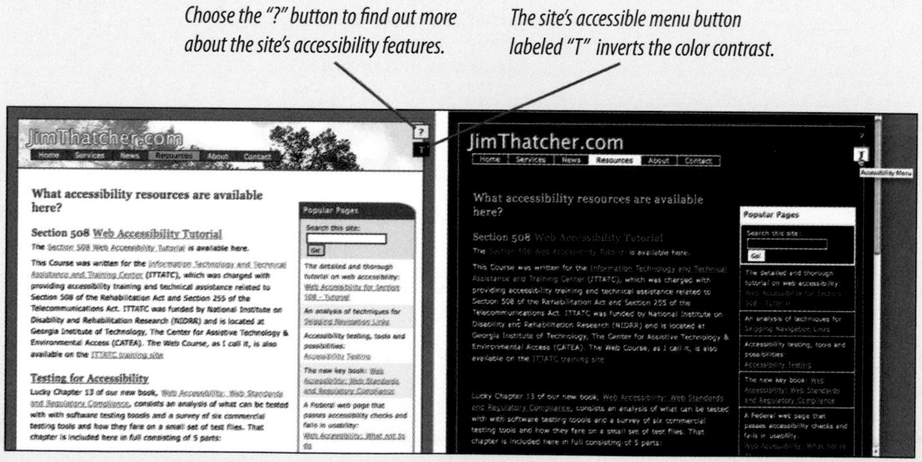

Choose the "?" button to find out more about the site's accessibility features.

The site's accessible menu button labeled "T" inverts the color contrast.

section508.gov. Private institutional websites need not comply with Section 508, unless they receive Federal funds or are under contract with a Federal agency.

However, any content that will appear on the Web should follow the World Wide Web Consortium's (W3C) Web Content Accessibility Guidelines (WCAG). As we work through the various content sections of our interactive project, we'll provide suggestions for how best to implement these guidelines.

WCAG (version 2.0) has 12 guidelines that are organized under four principles, which state that Web content must be perceivable, operable, understandable, and robust. Here is WCAG 2 at a glance, as indicated on the W3C Web Accessibility Initiative (WAI) website (w3.org/WAI/WCAG20/glance/):

Perceivable

- Provide text alternatives for non-text content.
- Provide captions and other alternatives for multimedia.
- Create content that can be presented in different ways, including by assistive technologies, without losing meaning.
- Make it easier for users to see and hear content.

Operable

- Make all functionality available from a keyboard.
- Give users enough time to read and use content.
- Do not use content that causes seizures.
- Help users navigate and find content.

Understandable

- Make text readable and understandable.
- Make content appear and operate in predictable ways.
- Help users avoid and correct mistakes.

Robust

- Maximize compatibility with current and future user tools.

While usability and accessibility are often described as separate concepts, we encourage you to think of them as one universal principle. Ben Shneiderman, a pioneer in the field of HCI, defines this as universal usability. **Universal usability** strives to enable all citizens to *succeed* using communication and information technology in their tasks. The key word here is *succeed,* not just access. When you apply basic accessibility guidelines, a user can better access digital content, but why not reach beyond that and provide an environment where all content can be accessed not by a few, but by a majority?

Browser Accessibility Options

Some accessibility options are already built into most browsers. For example, these browsers allow you to:

1. Increase or reduce the text size of any site by repeatedly pressing Control + or Control - (Windows) or ⌘ + or ⌘ - (Mac) on your keyboard.
2. View a page without styling: In Firefox, choose View > Page Style > No Style, and in Internet Explorer, choose View > Style > No Style.
3. Have text read aloud by searching for browser add-ins or operating system features, such as Speak It for Firefox or NaturalReader for Internet Explorer.
4. Disable images. In IE go to Tools > Internet Options, select the Advanced tab, then scroll down to the Multimedia category and uncheck Show Pictures. In Firefox choose Tools > Options, and under the Content tab uncheck Load Pages Automatically (Windows) or Firefox > Preferences > Content (Mac).
5. Adjust general accessibility options by going to Tools > Internet Options, and choosing the Advanced tab in IE. In Firefox, go to Tools > Options, and choose the Advanced tab.

Identifying Design and Development Considerations

Using Basic DESIGN PRINCIPLES

Building Blocks of Design

In addition to having a solid foundation in creating usable and accessible content, an interactive media designer or developer also needs a good working knowledge of basic design elements and principles. While this book can't provide comprehensive coverage of these (we recommend a course in art, design, and color theory for that), we can define and give you examples of some important design terms to help you form your project vision. Basic design elements and principles are the building blocks you use to create an aesthetically pleasing and user-friendly visual design.

Elements of Design

The elements of design are line, shape, color, value, and texture. These are the design elements that you use to create any illustration. One way to get an idea of how the elements of design work together is to examine the structure of a vector illustration, shown in Figure 8. The figure, derived from a logo created by Annesa, demonstrates the design elements that make up the parts of an illustration.

A **line** is an edge or boundary in a drawing or design. A **shape** is a closed line that encloses an area. See Figure 9.

Figure 8 *Design elements that make up an illustration*

Figure 9 *Examples of open lines and closed lines (shapes)*

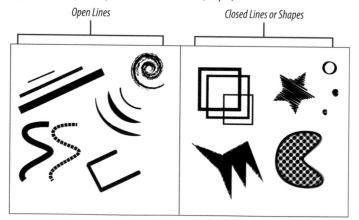

Identifying Design and Development Considerations

Color describes the visual property of what we see when an object encounters light. We categorize these properties as red, green, blue, purple, and so on. Every device that can reproduce color has its own color range (or limit), which defines its color space or **gamut** (pronounced GAM-uht). The human color device—our eyes—can see many more colors than a computer can display, or printer can reproduce, as shown in Figure 10.

Value is the relationship of the light and dark parts in an image, sometimes referred to as tone, shade, or brightness. See Figure 11.

Texture describes an object's surface—how it might feel if we were to touch it. Texture informs us of our surroundings, and tells us about the nature of objects—whether they're smooth, rough, soft, or hard. Textures in our environment are created by how light hits a surface, creating highlights and shadows. In graphics programs like Illustrator and Photoshop, the textures you create are simulated, meaning the texture is flat by touch but tricks the eye into thinking it is not. See Figure 12.

Figure 10 *Range of color one can see within various gamuts*

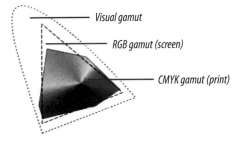

—— *Visual gamut*

—— *RGB gamut (screen)*

—— *CMYK gamut (print)*

Figures © Cengage Learning 2013. Figure 11: Photo courtesy of Annesa Hartman.

Figure 11 *Example uses of value effects created in Photoshop*

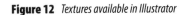

Gradient Map   *Threshold*   *Gradient Overlay*   *Gradient Fill*   *Desaturate*

Figure 12 *Textures available in Illustrator*

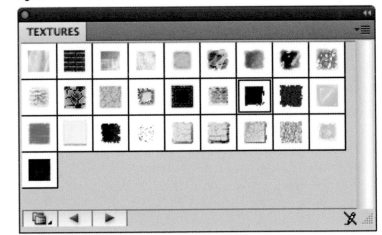

The Principles of Design

We see examples of design principles everywhere; we merely need to take notice, observe closely, and then translate those principles to our own creative visions. Nature surrounds us with perfect examples of design principles. Let's look at each of the principles as they relate to what we see in nature.

Balance can be symmetrical, asymmetrical, or radial. Symmetrical balance is like a mirror image, as shown in Figure 13. Asymmetrical balance occurs when several smaller items on one side are balanced by a large item on the other side, or smaller items are placed further away from the center of the screen than larger items, as shown in Figure 14. With the use of value, darker items may need to be balanced by several lighter items. Radial balance occurs where all elements radiate out from a center

Figure 13 *Demonstration of symmetrical balance in nature*

Figure 14 *Demonstration of asymmetrical balance in nature*

Identifying Design and Development Considerations

point in a circular fashion, drawing your eye into a central focal point, as shown in Figure 15.

A gradation, or a change from one color to another, can vary in its size, tone, and direction to produce linear perspective. Gradation can add interest and movement to a shape. A gradation from dark to light, for example, will cause the eye to move along a shape and add dimensionality, as shown in Figure 16.

Repetition is a useful design principle, especially when the repeated elements include a degree of variation, as shown in Figure 17. Repetition with variation can add visual interest; without variation, repetition can become monotonous. In interface design, repetition might include the use of an icon and its text equivalent. Examples include an image of a home for a home button and also the text "home" near it; and a repeat of

information in two different formats, not only for variation, but for accessibility as well.

Contrast implies the juxtaposition of opposing elements. For example, you might juxtapose

opposite colors on the color wheel—like blue and orange or red and green. You can also use contrast with tone or value, such as light to dark, or with direction, such as

Figure 15 *Demonstration of radial balance in nature*

Figure 16 *Demonstration of gradation in nature*

Figure 17 *Demonstration of repetition in nature*

horizontal to vertical. In interface design, carefully consider where to place your areas of maximum contrast, so as not to create confusion or visual overload. See Figure 18.

Harmony is the visually satisfying effect of combining similar, related elements, such as adjacent colors on a wheel, or similar shapes. In interface design, you can add harmony in how text and visuals flow, link together, or align on the screen. See Figure 19.

Dominance provides interest, counteracting both confusion and monotony. Dominance can be applied to one or more of the elements of design to give emphasis to important information. In interface design, you might provide dominance using visual cues, like a rollover effect, to draw users' attention to a navigation menu. See Figure 20.

Figure 18 *Demonstration of contrast in nature*

Figure 19 *Demonstration of harmony in nature*

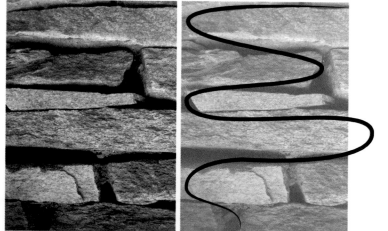

Figure 20 *Demonstration of dominance in nature*

Figures © Cengage Learning 2013. Photos courtesy of Annesa Hartman.

Identifying Design and Development Considerations

Unity is the artful combining of related design elements with the idea being expressed. Unity in an interactive design can refer to how you combine elements (such as color, visuals, and writing style) to most effectively reach your target audience and express the mood of your design. See Figure 21.

Figure 21 *Demonstration of unity in nature*

Figure 22 *Business card designs without and with CRAP applied*

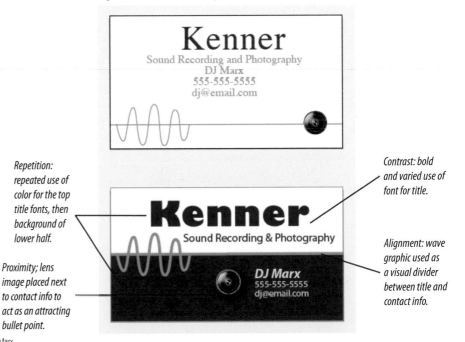

Repetition: repeated use of color for the top title fonts, then background of lower half.

Proximity; lens image placed next to contact info to act as an attracting bullet point.

Contrast: bold and varied use of font for title.

Alignment: wave graphic used as a visual divider between title and contact info.

Figures © Cengage Learning 2013. Figure 21 Courtesy of Jane Hosie-Bounar. Figure 22 Courtesy of Dan Marx.

Useful Online Evaluation
TOOLS AND RESOURCES

Usability Resources

- **Jakob Nielsen's Alertbox: Current Issues in Web Usability:**
  useit.com/alertbox/
  Sign-up to periodically receive a short newsletter on the latest trends in website usability.
- **10 Tips for Good Web Writing** by Jennifer Kyrnin for About.com: webdesign.about.com/od/writing/a/aa031405.htm
- **Write Plainly** webinar from Howto.gov: www.howto.gov/training/classes/plain-writing-principles-and-the-new-law
- **Writing Web Content** downloadable PDF at Usability.gov:
  usability.gov/pdfs/chapter15.pdf
- **Using MS Word Readability Statistics for Web Writing**:
  kerryr.net/webwriting/tools_readability.htm

- **8 Readability Web Tools to Test Your Writing Quality** by Saikat Basu from makeuseof.com:
  makeuseof.com/tag/writing-reader-friendly-check-8-readability-testing-web-tools/

Accessibility Resources

- **The World Wide Web Consortium**
  The World Wide Web Consortium (W3C) provides the Web Content Accessibility Guidelines (WCAG) 2.0 as the standard for designing sites that are accessible to users of all abilities. Accessibility levels are grouped into three priority-level checkpoints. All websites must complete all of the Priority 1 checkpoints, such as providing a text equivalent for every non-text element. These guidelines are published at w3.org.

- **WebAIM:** To read the rationale behind creating accessible sites, go to webaim.org to find information about the POUR principles (Perceivable, Operable, Understandable and Robust) of making a website accessible.
- **Jim Thatcher (jimthatcher.com):** Jim Thatcher is a web accessibility consultant with a website full of useful resources.
- **Juicy Studio (juicystudio.com):** A resource with many useful tools for assessing the accessibility and usability of a site. Go to the Quality Assurance section and review the local, external and downloadable tools. Some of Annesa's favorites are the Readability Test, CSS Analyser, Luminosity Colour Contrast Ratio Analyser, and The Web Developer Extension.

- **Colour Contrast Check (snook.ca/technical/colour_contrast/colour.html):** This tool lets you specify foreground and background colors and determine if they provide enough contrast "when viewed by someone having color deficits."

Design Element and Principle Resources

- **Kuler:** Color theme generator; easily pick colors that work well together: kuler.adobe.com

- **Color Schemer:** Color generator; enter an RGB or HEX value, or click on a color palette to find colors that work well together: colorschemer.com/online.html
- **Design Better with CRAP** by Dustin Wax from Lifehack.com: lifehack.org/articles/communication/design-better-with-crap.html

- *The Non-Designer's Design Book* by Robin Williams.
- *Exploring the Elements of Design* by Poppy Evans and Mark A. Thomas, Cengage Learning.

BUILDING A COMP IN ADOBE ILLUSTRATOR

In this lesson, we'll create the comp for our demonstration project, the Gardener's Walk website. We'll use basic Illustrator features to build the comp. We used the steps below to accomplish our goals. Feel free to follow these steps using your own assets and adjust as necessary for your envisioned project. Keep in mind that developing a comp is a fluid process—your project's structure will evolve as you explore the placement of elements on the interface design. It's a good idea to save various versions of your work along the way, so you can refer to them later when deciding on the look of the final comp.

Set Up the Document

1. Open Adobe Illustrator and set the workspace to Essentials.

2. Create a new document; in the New Document dialog box, enter a name for your project, and set the document profile that will best suit the format of your project (print, web, mobile and devices, etc.)

3. If you know the exact dimensions of your project, set them in the Width and Height area; see Figure 23.

   We set our project to the Web document profile, with the initial custom width of 960 × 560 pixels. We also chose Pixels as the measurement unit option.

4. Choose **View** > **Rulers** > **Show Rulers**.

5. Choose **View** > **Guides** > **Show Guides**, if not already selected.

6. Choose **View** > **Guides** > **Lock Guides** (if it does not already have a check mark).

   Unlocking the guides lets you more easily move the guides around as you work.

TIP We also turned on Smart Guides. (Select View > Smart Guides to place a check mark next to it if necessary).

Smart Guides have a visual snap-to-guide feature that allows you to more easily align and transform objects relative to other objects.

7. From the vertical and horizontal rulers along the sides of the document, drag guides onto your document as necessary to help identify a basic grid structure for your project. See Figure 24.

Figure 24 *Adding guides to the document*

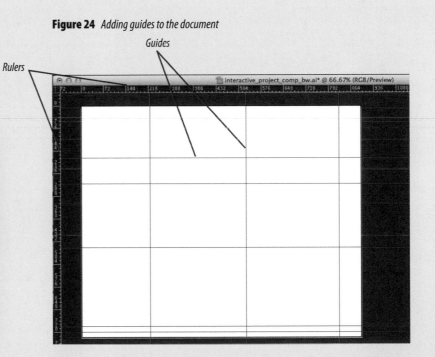

Figure 23 *Setting options for the new project*

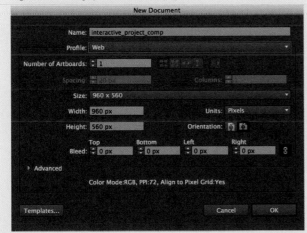

Identifying Design and Development Considerations

TIP If the selected color for the guides is difficult to see, go the File > Preferences > Guides and Grid (Windows) or Illustrator > Preferences > Guides and Grids (Mac) and change the color of the guides.

8. If the Layers panel is not visible, choose **Window** > **Layers**, then in the Layers panel expand Layer 1.

    All the guides you created are now located on this layer and are listed.

9. Rename the layer **guides**.

    It's a good idea to keep the objects, including guides, well organized in the Layers panel, so you can find them quickly as your document grows. See Figure 25.

10. Save your document.

11. If the Illustrator options box appears, keep the default settings and click **OK**.

Create the Placeholders

1. Click the **Create New Layer button** in the Layers panel (see Figure 26) to create a new layer, and name it **placeholders**.

    We'll use this layer to contain placeholders representing the various parts of our design. Using placeholders will let us focus on the placement of each element and worry about color and imagery later.

Figure 25 *Organizing items in the Layers panel*

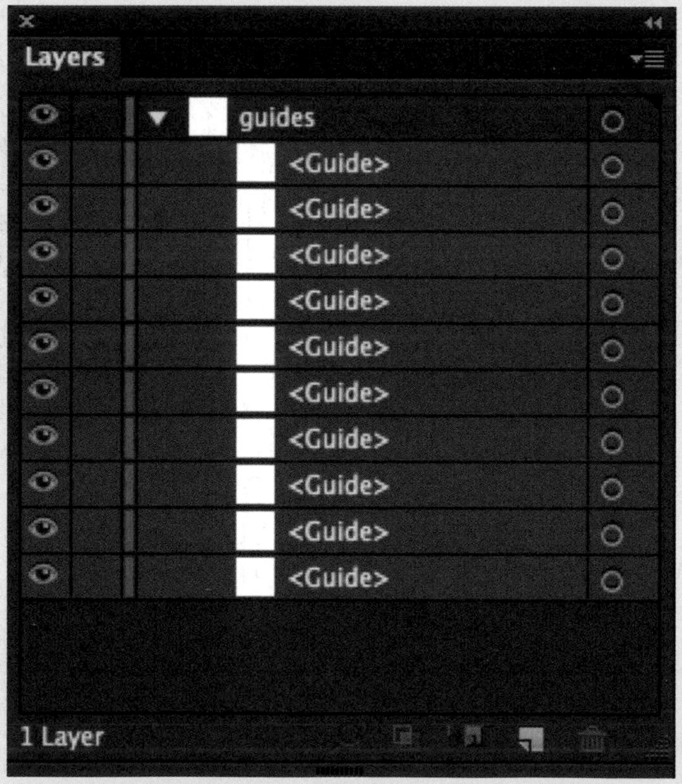

![Layers panel showing "guides" layer expanded with multiple <Guide> entries. "1 Layer" shown at bottom.]

Figure 26 *Creating a new layer*

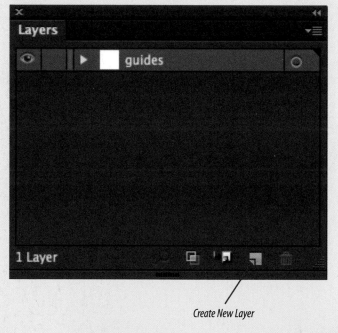

Create New Layer

Identifying Design and Development Considerations

2. Choose **Window** > **Swatches** to open the Swatches panel if necessary, then select a grey-toned swatch. See Figure 27.

3. Select the **Rectangle Tool** in the Tools panel, as shown in Figure 28.

4. Using the guides to keep objects aligned, draw rectangular blocks to represent each element.

Figure 29 shows our initial comp for the Gardener's Walk site. We used light gray tones to represent graphics and a darker gray to represent the text area.

Figure 27 *Selecting a gray-toned swatch*

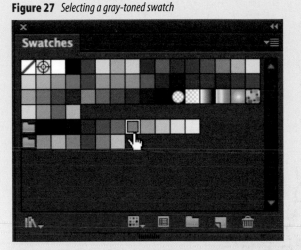

Figure 28 *Selecting the Rectangle tool*

Figure 29 *An initial comp for the Gardener's Walk site*

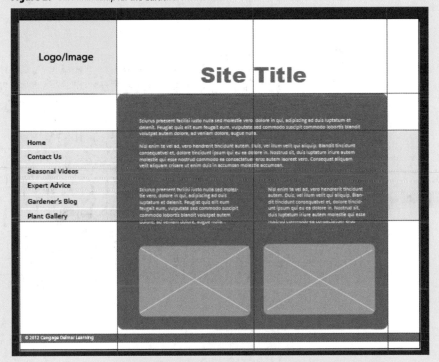

5. Select the Type tool (see Figure 30) and label the various placeholders.

6. Add lorem ipsum text in the text-based placeholder areas.

   See the section on Getting Your Ideas Out There, earlier in this chapter, for more info on lorem ipsum text.

Exploring Variations on the Layout

To help visualize the many options that are possible in your design, it's a good idea to explore variations of your comp. Illustrator lets you do this using multiple artboards, each with different sizes and orientations. Artboards are wonderful for creating items that are related in design, like a set of marketing materials that might include a business card, a letterhead, and a brochure, or a series of different pages in a web site. Then you can easily maneuver the design elements across all items in the set.

1. Click the **Artboard tool** in the Tools panel, shown in Figure 31.

Figure 30 *Selecting the Type Tool in the Tools panel*

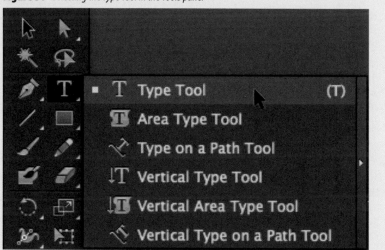

Figure 31 *Choosing the Artboard tool*

Figures © Cengage Learning 2013

Pre-Made UI Elements

Instead of drawing each user interface (UI) elements on your comp, you can download a UI Kit compatible with Illustrator or other drawing programs. For example, Jank0AtWarpSpeed provides free components that can be imported into Illustrator (www.jankoatwarpspeed.com/post/2009/12/24/sketching-wireframing-kit.aspx). You can also find a UI Kit resource list at smashingmagazine.com. Search the site for "50 Free UI and Web Design Wireframing Kits."

The document area is surrounded by a transformation box indicated with a dashed line and a tab titled Artboard 1 in the upper left corner. You are now in Edit Artboards mode. See Figure 32.

2. Click the **Move/Copy Artwork with Artboard button** in the Control panel, shown in Figure 33.

Figure 32 *Document in Edit Artboards mode*

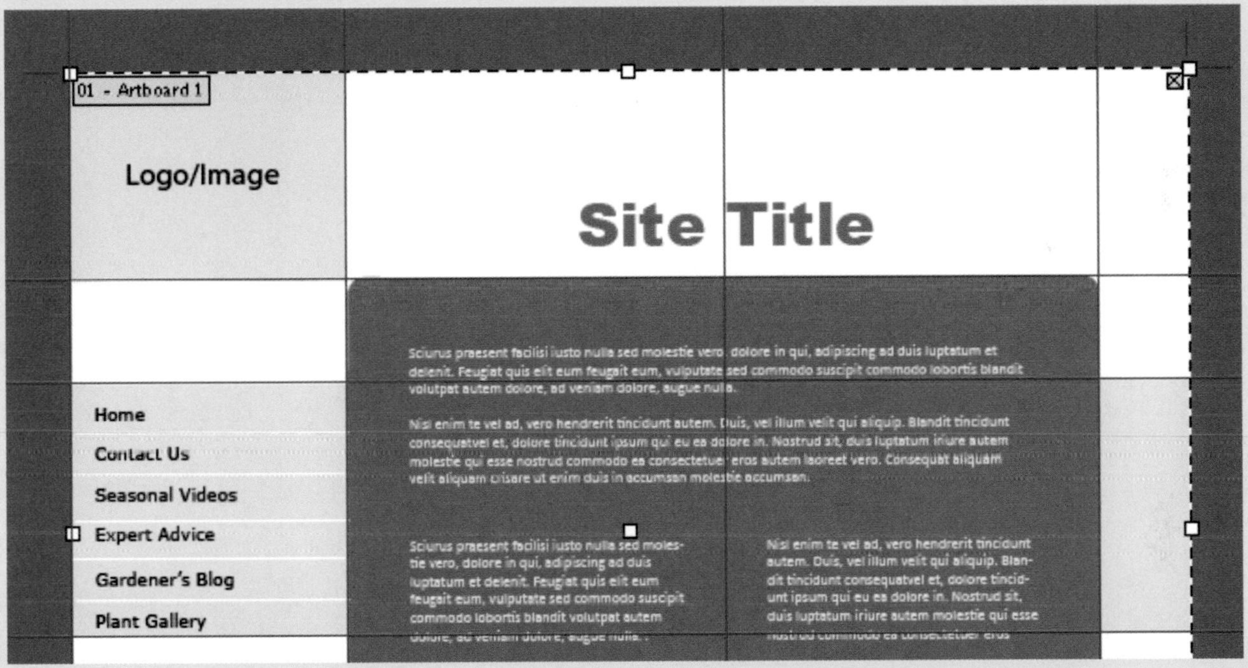

Figure 33 *Selecting the Move/Copy Artwork with Artboard button*

TIP If don't see this option along the top of the document, be sure the Artboard tool is selected in the Tools panel.

3. Click on the artboard, press and hold down [Alt] or [Option] (Mac) or [Alt] (Win), then drag a copy of the artboard vertically downward, as shown in Figure 34.

Figure 34 *Copying the artboard*

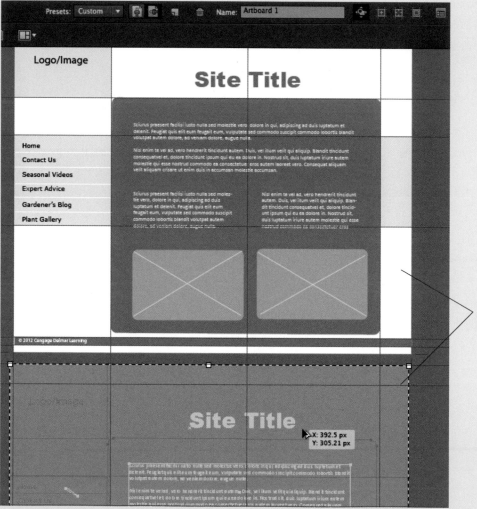

[Alt]-dragging a copy of the artboard

Figure © Cengage Learning 2013

4. Save a version of your file under a different name, and then use the second, duplicate artboard as the basis for exploring variations on your project design.

Figure 35 shows three artboards with variations of the Gardener's Walk home page design.

Figure 35 *Varied comps of the Gardener's Walk home page design*

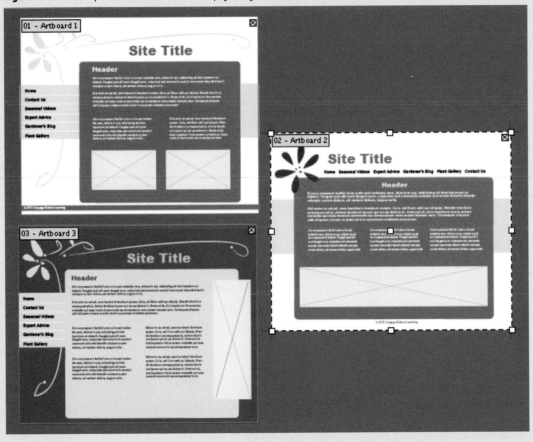

Figure © Cengage Learning 2013

IT'S YOUR TURN

CONCEPTUALIZING YOUR PROJECT DESIGN

Now it's your turn to spend some time conceptualizing your interactive design project. Here are some steps to get you started.

1. Ask yourself and/or your client about your site's intended audience; this will help identify its aesthetics: its mood, theme, or style.
2. Create a few user profiles, representing members of your target audience, to help narrow down the elements your project will require to meet their needs.
3. Start sketching your design. Your creative muse might suggest a different approach, but we started with hand-drawn sketches to quickly bring our initial ideas to life. Consider keeping a sketchpad near the bed, or with you while you travel, to be ready to scribble down your thoughts at any opportune moment.
4. Create a comp of your project's main page. Use your sketches to construct a template of your interface design in a drawing program such as Illustrator, InDesign or Fireworks. Be sure to set the document to the intended size of your project. Use basic shapes, guides, and grids to help align the basic pieces of the design—navigation bars, location of logo or header, main content, and image areas. Use placeholders for images and lorem ipsum text. Review the usability, accessibility, and design principles to inspire your design, and follow the steps for how we created a comp in the How We Did It section of this chapter.

5. Share your final comps with your client or a sample of your intended users. Document any feedback you receive and revise your design, if necessary.

Figure 36 *Final Gardener's Walk web page comps*

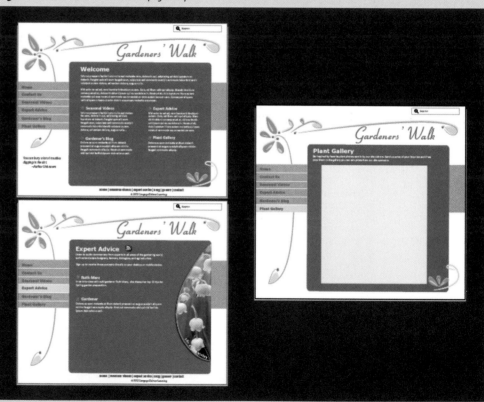

See Figure 36 for a view of the final comps of three of the Gardener's Walk web pages with color and visual elements added.

Identifying Design and Development Considerations

EVALUATING THE USABILITY OF A MOBILE APP

A smart way to hone your skills to make a usable, accessible, and pleasing interface design is to evaluate what's currently on the market. Choose two or three popular mobile apps and evaluate them by considering the following criteria:

1. On a scale from 1-5 (5 being "very intuitive") how would you rate the app's overall ease of use? Consider your experience navigating the app. For example, are standard GUI controls used? What is it like to enter information into form fields, if any? Can you easily recover from an error?

2. On a scale from 1-5 (5 being "highly accessible") how would you rate the accessibility options available with the app? Consider, for example, if there are alternative ways to access the information: Are there text descriptions of images, perhaps the option to use voice commands? Is the text readable and understandable?

3. On a scale from 1-5 (5 being "very user-friendly") how would you rate the app's aesthetic design? Consider, for example, your impressions of the color choices, the use of white space, and the positioning of buttons, text, and images. Can you identify where there is an effective use of design elements and principles?

Even More to Explore

To explore some of the topics discussed in this chapter in more depth, see the References section at the end of the book. For links to additional web resources, visit the Even More to Explore link under Book Resources on Cengage Brain.

CHAPTER 4 — BUILDING THE FRAMEWORK

CHAPTER 4 BUILDING THE FRAMEWORK

Introduction

In the previous two chapters you discovered the process and considerations for planning your interactive media project. You then mapped your ideas into a visual representation of your project idea. In this chapter you learn to lay the foundation for your framework. A **framework** consists of the basic files and folders that form the structure and organize the content in a project. For a website, a framework begins with the local site folder, and includes the style sheets that will be used to format and place the content on the pages, the template files that will be used to create the pages, and a folder to store the site assets such as images and media files. Another type of project would include similar elements,

with a main folder to store the project files as they are created and subfolders to store the source files used to create the content, such as video clips and sound files. Your wireframe gives you the information you need to build your framework. Frameworking is the initial step in the development phase.

You then begin to build your project's framework in your chosen application. As you build your framework, you create placeholders for the various content pieces in your project. In this chapter, we'll build the framework for our website, the Gardener's Walk, which we planned in Chapter 2. If your project is an interactive media project other than a website, you'll follow similar steps to build your framework.

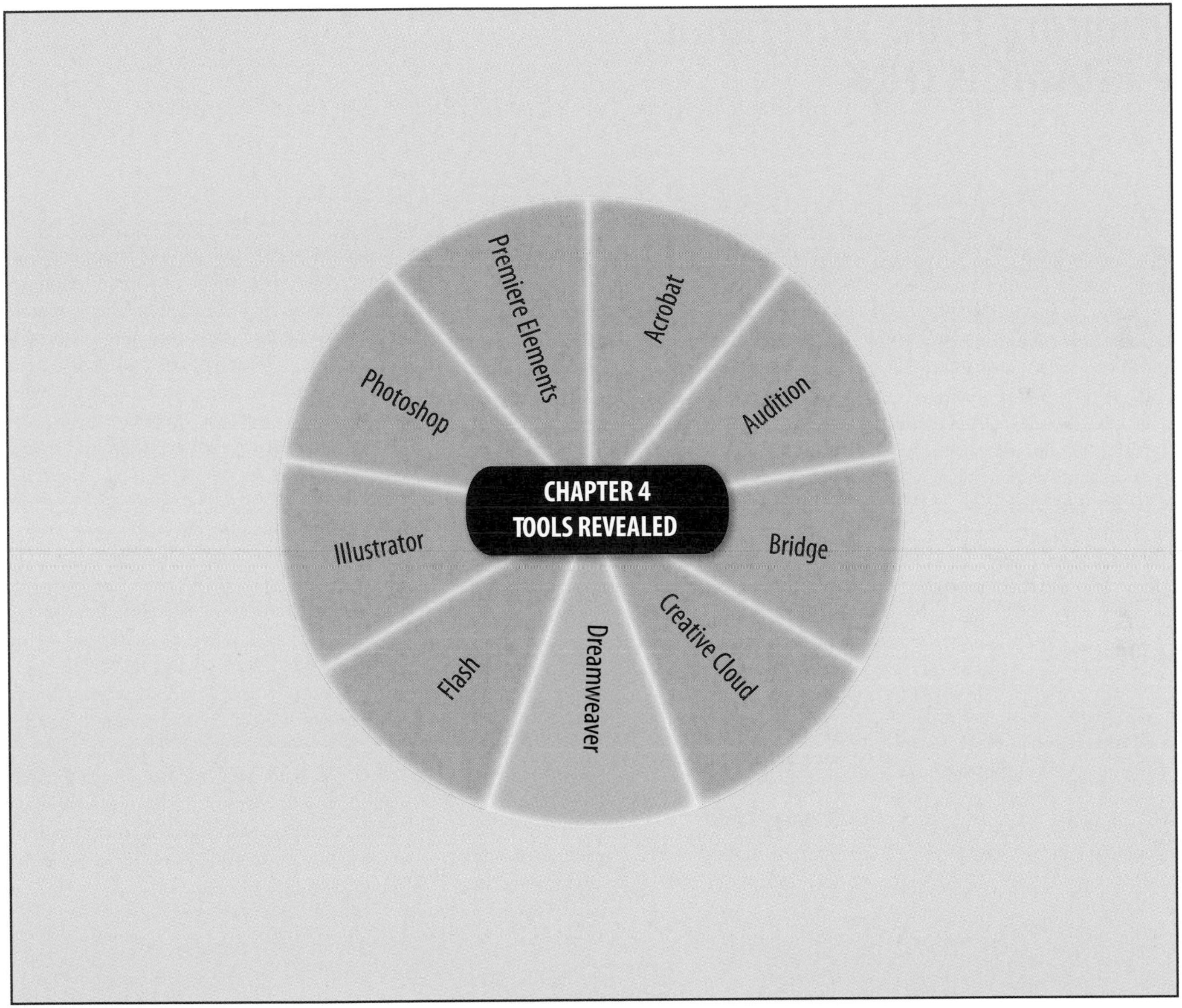
CHAPTER 4
TOOLS REVEALED
Premiere Elements
Acrobat
Audition
Bridge
Creative Cloud
Dreamweaver
Flash
Illustrator
Photoshop

Figure © Cengage Learning 2013

Transitioning from Wireframe
TO FRAMEWORK

Introduction

The technologies used to deliver interactive media content have changed dramatically. These changes include increased access and processing speed, the wide availability of wireless networks, higher display resolutions, and a variety of new mobile devices. How do you know where to start as you set up the basic framework and design for a new interactive media project? One of your first decisions is to select the appropriate tools to create the pieces of your project and then choose the right tools to put them together.

Choosing the Right Tools

There are a tremendous number of tools available to designers today, regardless of the type of interactive project you're creating. These include web authoring tools, content management systems, 2D animation programs, 3D animation programs, web apps and widgets that can be integrated for interactivity, and of course, the HTML markup language itself. HTML5 has introduced exciting new ways to add interactivity.

Authoring Tools

The World Wide Web Consortium states that "any software, or collection of software components, that authors can use to create or modify web content for use by other people, is an **Authoring Tool**." (w3.org/standards/agents/authoring) Authoring tools are available in a wide range of prices and features, just as there are sites with wide ranges of quality, complexity, and usability. Some authoring tools include software that generates web content by using wizards or by letting the user edit pre-designed templates. **Wizards** are interfaces that allow you to choose from lists of choices or fill in blanks to customize pre-designed content.

Web App Tools

For most of the personal computer applications we're accustomed to, the program and data files are stored locally on our computer system. Web apps such as Gmail (Google's approach to email) are stored on a remote computer and accessed through web browsers, so you can run them and access your data from any location using any device connected to the Internet. Web apps tend to be smaller than traditional applications, because they're usually written to perform a specific task. With web apps there's no need to check for updates, since the latest version is always available when you access it. Web apps have exploded in popularity because they're easy to access, easy to use, and exist for almost every interest. However, web apps do depend on the availability of a browser to run. Mobile apps, in contrast to web apps, are downloaded onto a mobile device and do not necessarily require a browser to run. One example might be a currency calculator app. You can search for web apps to add to your website or you can develop them yourself. To develop your own web apps or mobile apps, you'll need to know some programming.

Content Management System (CMS) Tools

Content management systems are applications used to process, store, and retrieve information. Three examples are WordPress, Joomla, and Drupal. **WordPress** is a general purpose CMS that began as open-source blogging software. It's estimated that as many as 10% of current websites are built using WordPress. WordPress sites can be self-hosted sites or managed sites. Self-hosted sites require a server running PHP and a database; plus you'll need some familiarity with database operations. PHP stands for **PHP: Hypertext Preprocessor**. (The first word of the acronym is the acronym.) PHP is an open source, server-side scripting language used to create websites. Managed sites are free, easy to set up, and published to WordPress.com. **Drupal** is a free and open source content management system used for project components such as blogs, RSS feeds, and menus. It requires a web server that can run PHP and a database application. **Joomla!** is an open source content management system used to create small and medium-sized websites.

Widgets

Widgets are tools that can add interaction to an interactive media project. A **widget** refers to a part of a **GUI** (Graphical User Interface) that enables the user to interact with the application and operating system. Some of the technologies used to create widgets are HTML, CSS, and JavaScript. An example of a widget might be a button, a menu, a progress indicator, or a site search feature. You can download widgets from the Internet or you can use the Adobe Widget Browser to locate and download widgets from the Adobe Exchange, such as CSS3 gradients, CSS3 buttons, and CSS3 columns, as shown in Figure 1. To use Adobe Widget Browser and the Adobe Exchange, you must first create an Adobe ID and sign in. There is no charge to create an Adobe ID. After creating your ID, you then install the Adobe Widget Browser so you'll have access to the widgets posted on the site. Widget Browser is integrated into the Dreamweaver interface, but you

Figure 1 *Adobe Widget Browser on the Adobe Exchange*

can use the Widget Browser regardless of whether you're using Dreamweaver as your authoring tool. For more information, visit adobe.com.

HTML5

HTML5 is the latest version of **HTML**, the authoring language used by web browsers. As the Internet and its content have evolved, HTML has been updated to adapt to new needs. To take advantage of HTML5 and its new tags, such as the <video> tag, keep your browsers updated to their latest versions to ensure they support HTML5. When you construct your pages, you'll want to use HTML5 so you can take advantage of the newer technology support it offers, such as better typography and streaming video. HTML5 also introduced new tags that support semantic markup, such as the <nav> tag used for navigation links. **Semantic markup** refers to coding that conveys meaning to other computer programs such as search engines. **Semantics**, or the meanings of words, when used with **syntax**, or the actual words and sentence structure, allows the computer to no longer just "read" words, but "understand" the meaning behind the words. The new HTML5 tags that create a search form are shown in Figure 2, along with the search form they generate on a web page. Some of the other semantic HTML5 tags include:

- <header> Defines the header area, or the top of a page or section
- <footer> Defines the footer area, or the bottom of a page or section
- <article> Defines an article

Figure 2 *HTML tags to create a search form*

Sample code for search form

Search form

Building the Framework

- <aside> Defines content aside from the main page content
- <audio> Defines sound content
- <canvas> Defines graphics
- <figure> Defines a group of media content and their caption (graphics, video, or sound files and their supporting files or code)
- <section> Defines a section
- <video> Defines a video or movie

To read more about HTML5 tags, go to the HTML5 Tag Reference at w3schools.com/html5/html5_reference.asp. HTML5 will be the new standard for HTML, XHTML, and the HTML DOM (Document Object Model). **DOM** is a W3C standard interface for programs and scripts that defines how they can be used to manipulate a document. Although it is still a work in progress, most modern browsers support it.

Adobe Tools for Creating Interactive Content

Adobe products are considered to be the industry standard by professional designers. Dreamweaver and Flash are robust authoring tools for creating web and mobile content. With the Adobe InDesign CS5.5 release, new functions were introduced for publishing interactive content, so the program became a tremendous interactive media creation tool. With the addition of the Digital Publishing Suite, you can create, upload, and publish interactive content on the Adobe Creative Cloud. Adobe Creative Suite 6.0 Design Premium, which includes these applications, along with many others, is relatively expensive. However, you can purchase

Developing Interactive Media with HTML5 and Flash

In November 2011, Adobe announced it was ceasing development of Flash for mobile devices, due to increasing demand for solutions that use HTML5. Nearly across the board, HTML5 has won the hearts of mobile operating system makers as a solution that creates less processor-intensive content, which is necessary in the mobile environment.

However, while universal support for HTML5 is clearly moving forward, it is yet to become a final standard for web and mobile device development. Time will tell. With the future in mind, Adobe is working on a web motion and interactivity program called Adobe Edge that promises to offer features similar to what Flash provides, but within the HTML5 format. See Chapter 7 for more information on Adobe Edge.

In the meantime, Adobe Flash still plays an important role in interactive media development and Adobe will continue to support Flash as a premiere tool for developing animated content for streaming video and gaming.

applications separately or purchase a yearly or monthly subscription for the suite. Table 1 lists some of the Adobe tools that you should consider as you begin transitioning from wireframe to framework. When you look at the prices, remember that upgrades or subscriptions are less expensive than purchasing a new application. Remember also to check the Adobe Creative Cloud for monthly subscription prices.

Additional Tools for Creating Interactive Media

There are a number of other tools and classifications of tools you'll want to know about, listed in Table 2. Some are professional tools with a high price tag, but others are inexpensive or free tools that are full-featured and robust. You choices will depend on your development needs and your budget.

Applying the Tools

As you begin your work, how do you make sure you're incorporating the most current technology and standards? Fortunately, there are vast repositories of information you can access and most are free It's still overwhelming, however, to locate, sort through, and analyze the available information. Here are some useful resources that can help you with research as you decide how to frame your content:

TABLE 1: ADOBE TOOLS FOR CREATING INTERACTIVE CONTENT		
Adobe Product Suites	**Used For**	**Approximate Cost**
Adobe Creative Suite • Design Premium • Design Standard • Web Premium • Production Premium • Master Collection	Creating and producing print, digital, interactive, and mobile projects	Over $1,000 for each suite, with the Master Collection over $2,000
Adobe Digital Publishing Suite	Creating and distributing content for tablet devices	• Single Edition: Under $500 • Professional Edition monthly: Under $500 per month • Enterprise Edition or Professional Edition Annual: Contact Adobe for pricing
Individual Adobe Suite Products	**Used For**	**Approximate Cost**
Adobe After Effects	Creating motion graphics and cinematic visual effects	Under $1,000
Adobe Air	Developing and deploying standalone cross-platform Internet applications	Free
Adobe Audition	Producing audio content for audio and video productions	Under $500
Adobe Dreamweaver	Web authoring and web editing	Under $1,000
Adobe Edge	Web motion and interaction design tool	Preview is free
Adobe Fireworks	Producing optimized graphics for any device	Under $300
Adobe Flash Builder	Developing iPhone, iPad, Android, Blackberry Playbook, web, and desktop applications	Under $1,000
Adobe Flash Professional	Producing interactive content	Under $1,000
Adobe Flex	Building mobile applications for iOS, Android, Blackberry Tablet OS, browser, and desktop	Free, open source
Adobe Illustrator	Creating vector artwork	Under $1,000
Adobe InDesign	Designing page layouts and integrating interactive content	Under $1,000
Adobe Photoshop	Editing digital images	Under $1,000
Adobe Premiere Elements	Editing video content – lighter version	Under $100
Adobe Premiere Pro	Editing video content	Under $1,000

■ The World Wide Web Consortium

In addition to providing the Web Content Accessibility Guidelines (WCAG) that you learned about in Chapter 3, the World Wide Web Consortium (W3C) is your best resource for keeping up with web standards in general, including CSS, mobile web applications, HTML5, and XML.

■ w3schools.com

This website has a multitude of information on HTML, XML, browser scripting, server scripting, web services, multimedia, and web building. It also has a "Try it Yourself Editor" that lets you create content and view it in a browser. The most popular tutorials are also published as books. There are quizzes available and an online certification program.

■ Google Tech Talks

Google Tech Talks, at youtube.com/user/GoogleTechTalks, are a series of talks hosted by Google on various topics and made available for viewing on YouTube. You can search the videos for a specific topic, such

TABLE 2: ADDITIONAL TOOLS FOR CREATING INTERACTIVE MEDIA		
Application	**Used For**	**Approximate Cost**
Avid Pro Tools 10	Audio recording and editing	Under $1,000
Blender	Web animation	Free, open source
CoffeeCup Visual Site Designer	Basic web design for Windows	Under $100
CrazyTalk Animator	Web animation	Under $100
Drupal	Content management system	Free, open source
Firebug	In-browser web development	Free, open source
Google Blogger	Blog publishing, photo and video sharing	Free
iOS Software Development Kit	App development for release through the Apple App store	Free, but requires enrollment in the iOS Developer Program ($99/year) to release software
Joomla!	Content management system	Free, open source
MacJournal	Blog publishing for Mac	Under $100
MarsEdit	Blog publishing for Mac	Under $100
Microsoft Expression Web	Web development	Under $1,000
Panic Coda	Web development	Under $100
Toon Boom Studio	Web animation	Under $500
Windows Live Writer	Blog publishing for Windows	Free
WordPress	Content management system	Free, open source

© Cengage Learning 2013

as "building a game for the web" using the Google channel as shown in Figure 3.

■ evri.com

For the most current news in technology, consider trying the new Evri for iPad app, shown on the Evri website in Figure 4 at evri.com. This free app is a newsreader with channels you can use to tailor the app to display the topics of most interest to you. **Channels** are groupings of common content, similar to folders, with descriptive names such as "CSS" or "Dreamweaver."

■ Blogs

Blogs are great sources for technology discussions. **Blogs** are websites where the website owner regularly posts commentaries and opinions on various topics. Blogs have become extremely popular ways to post web content. Blogs such as WordPress have made it easier for people with limited technical skills to publish online. Google Blog Search lists blogs that publish a site feed such as an RSS feed. **RSS** stands for Really Simple Syndication and is the standard for the syndication of web content. **Syndication** used in this context means to make website content available for other websites. Websites use **RSS feeds** to distribute news stories, information about upcoming events, and announcements. Google indexes the site feeds for new postings and lets you use date ranges to search for specific posts. There are a host of technology blogs, including the popular Slashdot at slashdot.org, Engadget at engadget.com, and Boing Boing at boingboing.net.

Figure 3 *Google Research on YouTube*
© 2012 Google

Enter search terms to search video list

Figure 4 *Evri website technology topics*
Courtesy of evri.com

■ Demonstration and Training Videos

YouTube allows individuals to post original videos online to share with others. The types of videos available include music, entertainment, sports, film, animation, comedy, science, and technology. Use the Search text box to find the many tutorials for using web applications. To upload a video, you must first create an account, but you don't need an account to view videos. Total Training at totaltraining.com is a website that provides training videos for most major software applications.

■ Technical magazines

Magazines are another great source of information on current web technology trends. Wired, at wired.com, is both an online and print subscription-based magazine. Smashing Magazine, at smashingmagazine.com, is a free magazine with RSS feeds and a bi-weekly newsletter.

■ Delicious.com

Delicious is a social bookmarking website where you can store your bookmarks online so you can access them from any computer. Instead of creating folders to store common website links, you can use keywords to describe your sites. Delicious will direct you to them by using the common keywords you have assigned to each site. You can also view bookmarks that have been saved by others sorted by the most recently saved or the most popular. The most difficult thing about using this site is leaving it.

■ Books

Books, whether print or online, are still useful tools for learning new applications. For example, *Smashing WordPress: Beyond the Blog* by Thord Daniel Hedengren is an excellent guide for learning to use WordPress, the open source program for publishing blogs. When visiting bookstores online, you can search topics by a specific order, such as sales rank, to give you an idea which books have the most current appeal to the largest number of people. In large brick and mortar bookstores, you can spot the best sellers on the shelves by the number of books that are stocked. Look for a series that you find easy to read and understand. Once you've read one book in the series, the similar layout used in the rest of them will feel comfortable and familiar, making learning easier. Two good examples of popular series include the Revealed Series and the Exploring Series, both published by Delmar, Cengage Learning.

■ Adobe website

The Adobe website has an abundance of information about designing digital media. Information is presented on Adobe TV, in articles, through blogs, and with RSS feeds. Adobe Community Forums at forums.adobe.com is an interactive online environment where you can post questions or share ideas or tips for using Adobe products.

TABLE 3: TOUCH APPS FOR CREATING CONTENT WITH OR FOR TABLETS		
Application	**Used For**	**Approximate Cost**
Adobe Photoshop Touch	Combine, enhance, and share images	Under $10.00
Adobe Proto	Create wireframes and prototypes	Under $10.00
Adobe Ideas	Design content for Illustrator and Photoshop	Under $10.00
Adobe Debut	Present and mark up designs from Photoshop, InDesign, and Illustrator	Under $10.00
Adobe Collage	Combine images into moodboards	Under $10.00
Adobe Kuler	Create and export color themes	Under $10.00
Brushes	Painting, original artwork	Under $10.00 from iTunes
Inkpad	Create vector images	Under $10.00 from iTunes
Codify	iPad-based game development	Under $10.00 from App Store
iBooks Author	Create Multi-Touch books for iPad	Free from Mac App Store

© Cengage Learning 2013

Building a Framework for
INTERACTIVE MEDIA PROJECTS

Introduction

The basic processes for building a framework from your storyboard or wireframe are the same, regardless of the type of project. Yet each framework method must fit the type of project, the software required, and the type and degree of interactivity required. We're going to start by providing short overviews for three different types of interactive project frameworks. Then we'll provide detailed steps to create a framework for a website.

Framework Considerations for a Mobile App

The article "iPhone Apps Design Mistakes: Over-Blown Visuals," posted in Smashing Magazine, reported that an average of 3% of the people who download an app are still using it after 30 days. The primary reason for this is probably due to poor design of the interactive components. In an effort to create a distinctive look, designers mistakenly use non-standard designs that are inconsistent with other apps. By creating design elements that are recognizable from other apps, such as navigation buttons or a search text box, you make it easy for buyers to use their new app without spending too much effort.

Use a storyboard or wireframe to design your navigation flow from screen to screen, and refer to it as you build your framework. Remember to program ways for users to interact with the app that are specific to mobile devices, such as using your fingers instead of a mouse. A mobile device is a different kind of computer from a desktop computer: users can tilt and rotate it. Think about how users will use your app with their devices and anticipate their technological needs. The Course Technology Cengage Learning app for iPhone is pictured in Figure 5.

Framework Considerations for an Interactive Game

There are several ways to classify games: games for learning vs. games for entertainment; and linear vs. non-linear. A **linear game** moves from one sequence to the next. A **non-linear game** allows movement back and forth between sequences. One type of non-linear game is an RPG. **RPG** stands for role-playing game. An RPG is a fantasy game

Figure 5 *Course Technology Cengage Learning app*

such as Dungeons and Dragons where the players assume the roles of characters in the game.

Tailor your game design to the type of game you want to create and the target age of your users. Once you've arrived at an idea for your game, developed your plot, and identified your characters, design the controls and actions that will lead the user through the game. Organize your assets, such as music, audio, and artwork, so they'll be ready to incorporate into your game. Research your options for game development software and evaluate each one, comparing the required coding skills with your own. Evaluate the cost of the software and decide which program fits your skill level and budget, then use it to develop your prototype.

Adobe Flash Professional, shown in Figure 6, is an excellent choice to use to begin creating your animations, especially if you're familiar with other Adobe products and are comfortable with the common interface elements. When you have enough of the game completed, gather some willing participants to test and provide feedback.

Framework Considerations for an eMagazine or eBook

Adobe InDesign, shown in Figure 7, is the Adobe Publishing Suite program used to create interactive eBooks and eMagazines for viewing on tablets. Interactive magazines are a

Figure 6 *Adobe Flash Professional CS6 interface elements*

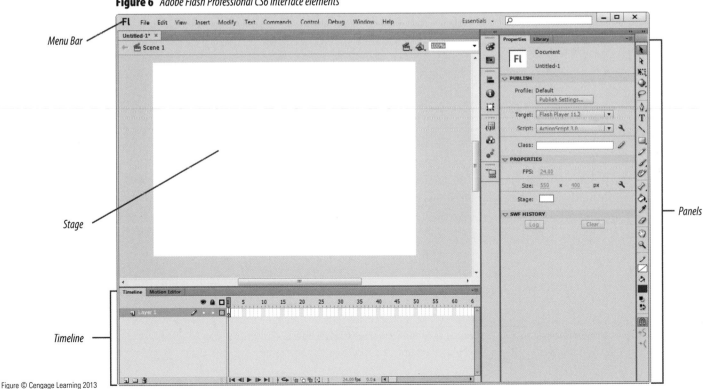

Menu Bar

Stage

Timeline

Panels

Figure © Cengage Learning 2013

major leap for the publishing world. Let's say, for example, that you are reading an online magazine on your tablet. The hard copy version of the magazine has an ad for a car; you can look at the photo and read the text describing the car. An interactive ad created with InDesign might let users click the car, rotate it, perhaps even open its doors and look inside.

When you use InDesign to create an interactive document, you create folios, or collections of digital publishing articles. A folio can consist of one article or many articles, each one using horizontal or vertical orientation. Each book or magazine requires a specific viewer, or device for reading the content. Books use single-folio viewers and magazines that are published with multiple issues use multi-folio viewers. Developers can upload single-folio viewers to the Apple App Store or Android Market to make them available for users to download. Multi-folio viewers are uploaded to the Adobe fulfillment server.

Designing content layouts on a screen is similar to designing content layouts for a print magazine or a book. You divide the content into articles for magazines, and into chapters for books. For magazines, you add placeholders for advertising using tools such as the Rectangle Frame Tool. To design a complex interactive document, you would

Figure 7 *Adobe InDesign CS6 interface with Digital Publishing workspace selected*

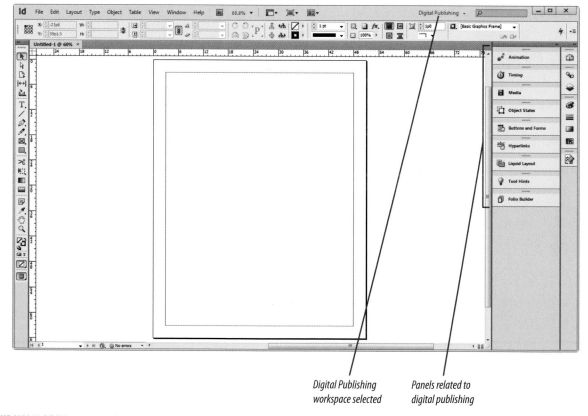

Digital Publishing
workspace selected

Panels related to
digital publishing

Building the Framework

need to know not only InDesign, but also Illustrator and Flash.

Building the Framework for an Interactive Website

Building the framework for a website begins with creating a local site folder to store your files, then using this folder to set up, or define a site, with a program such as Dreamweaver. Setting up a site includes designating a folder to store images and other media files, setting up access to a web server, and creating pages that will be used for the main navigation system.

Using Links to Navigate

What makes the World Wide Web so useful (and addictive) is that you can search for and find content about almost any topic you can dream of. You browse content on the Internet by clicking **links**, also known as **hyperlinks**, to navigate between web pages and websites. All interactive projects rely on links to connect the project pieces and to let the user control the order in which they view web pages, page through magazines, play a game, listen to podcasts, or choose scenes to watch in a video. Links are the backbone of interactive media, providing the principal way of navigating content. The explosion of Web 2.0 and social networking have provided new ways to link content and people together though blogs, wikis, mobile apps, and video sharing. It is important, therefore, to understand how links work.

There are two types of links: internal links and external links. We will talk about them now as they relate to websites, but the same principles apply to other interactive projects. **Internal links** are links to web pages within the same website, and **external links** are links to web pages in other websites or to email addresses. Both types of links have two separate parts that work together. The first part of a link is the text, image, or button that is displayed on a web page. This is the page element that you see and click to go to, or open, a specified location. The second part of a link is called the **path**, which is located in the HTML code for the link. The path tells the browser where to go to find the linked content.

Creating External and Internal Links

External links use **absolute paths** in the HTML code, including the protocol (such as http://) and the complete **URL** (Uniform Resource Locator), or address, of the destination page. When necessary, the web page filename and folder hierarchy are also part of an absolute path. See Figure 8. You would type "www.coxandkingsusa.com/india.html" in the address text box in a browser navigation bar to go directly to this page in the Cox and Kings website. If you were linking to this page from a site other than the Cox and Kings website, the HTML code for this link would look something like this, depending on the text on the page that was used for the link: <a href="http://www.coxandkingsusa.com/india.html">India and Beyond</a>.

Internal links use relative paths in the HTML code. A **relative path** is a type of path that references web pages or media files within the same website. Relative paths include the filename and folder location of a file. So if you were browsing inside the Cox and Kings website used as the example in Figure 8 to go to the india.html page, your path could look something like Figure 9. Notice the series of

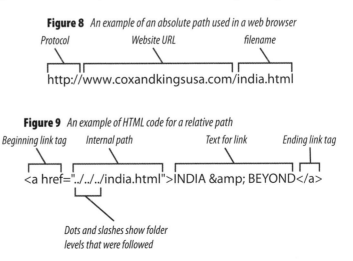

Figure 8 *An example of an absolute path used in a web browser*

Protocol   Website URL   filename

http://www.coxandkingsusa.com/india.html

Figure 9 *An example of HTML code for a relative path*

Beginning link tag   Internal path   Text for link   Ending link tag

<a href="../../../india.html">INDIA & BEYOND</a>

Dots and slashes show folder levels that were followed

Figures © Cengage Learning 2013

dots and slashes. These indicate folder levels in the site that the user followed to find the destination file. If the india.html file was in the same folder as the page with the link, the path would simply be "<a href="india.html">India and Beyond</a> with no dots or slashes.

You can use text, images, or buttons to create links. In our project, we used ordered list items formatted to look like buttons to create internal links to the Gardener's Walk website pages. The method will be helpful when we create additional style sheets to modify the design for mobile devices, because it will be easy to make the "buttons" larger or smaller with style sheets.

Separating Form from Content with CSS

Cascading Style Sheets, or CSS, are files that contain rules that define how page elements appear on a page. One of the big advantages of using CSS to format content is the ability to separate page content from the way in which it's presented. This lets you make changes to either the content or the formatting without one affecting the other. This is a huge timesaver when you begin to edit content, allowing you to focus on the content itself rather than how it looks on the pages. The most efficient way to use CSS is to store each CSS rule in an external style sheet. One style sheet can then determine the formatting for multiple pages, resulting in a uniform look.

You can separate the content on your pages using **CSS layout blocks**. These blocks are created with div tags and the CSS include code for determining the placement, size, and appearance of each block. They also include code for determining the appearance of the content within each block. You'll learn more about CSS in Chapter 5.

Coding for the Semantic Web

We mentioned the Semantic Web when we talked about HTML5. To this point, search engines have depended on keywords in meta tags to construct relevant searches. With semantics to help them, they will be more accurate in how they understand the content.

A common feature of interactive media content is the non-linear experience it provides. This means that users can move through the content in various ways, using different paths to navigate the site and search for data.

The concept of the semantic web provides the foundation to create this flexible navigation for the end user; for example, clearly labeled page sections such as "header" and "footer" indicate the position of the content on the page. The position of the content implies the type of information and relative importance. We are used to seeing page elements such as a banner and menu bar at the top of a page in the header section. We think of contact links, copyright information, and terms of use at the bottom of a page in the footer section. This means that when placing content on pages, we need to use tags that convey the most meaning. One example is to use the <em> tag, which means "emphasis," rather than the <i> tag, which means "italic" to show emphasis. Another example would be to use font size attributes such as <small> or <medium> rather than using font size attributes expressed in pixels. Assigning a text size in this way makes the text more scalable when viewed on different sized screens. The HTML5 <header> tag groups content by designating it as information appearing at the top of a page or section of a page. The <footer> tag groups content appearing at the bottom of a page.

Cascading Style Sheets are used to define the appearance of semantic tags. For instance, you can specify the attributes of the <h1> heading tag by choosing Selector Type: Class (can apply to any HTML element) in the New CSS Rule dialog box, as shown in Figure 10, then specifying a font, font size, font weight, etc., for all text formatted with the <h1> tag. CSS and semantic coding work together to enhance the meaning of the page content and provide well-designed pages that are attractive and consistent throughout the site. An ideal digital media piece would incorporate semantic coding with external style sheets to format all content. This approach would enable browsers to interpret the content presented; it would also make it easier for interactive media designers to write and edit, thus enhancing the overall experience for site users. For more information on the Semantic Web, go to semanticweb.org.

Building Your Framework for the Mobile Web

You read briefly about designing for the Adaptive Web in Chapter 2. It's critical to understand the importance of developing the framework for an interactive media project that will be platform and device agnostic. **Platform agnostic** means that the content should be accessible and attractive regardless of the mobile operating system (iOS, Android, Windows Phone 7). **Device agnostic** means that the content should be accessible and attractive whether it's being viewed on a desktop monitor, a tablet, or a mobile device. This is not only important for app developers, but for all interactive media designers.

Figure 10 *New CSS Rule dialog box*

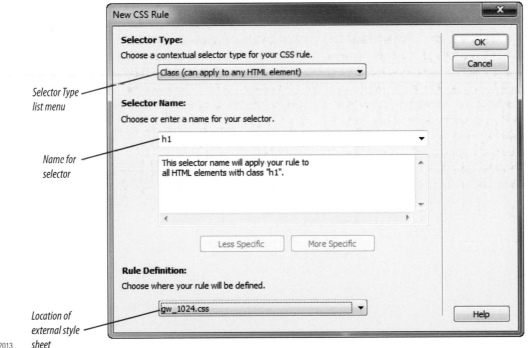

Selector Type list menu

Name for selector

Location of external style sheet

When software is developed for a specific platform, processor, or device, it's referred to as **native software**. An application that only runs on one platform or device is called a **native app**. Wouldn't it be wonderful if all applications could be used on any platform or device? Using any size screen? Using a touch screen, navigation buttons, or a cursor? We're making progress solving these issues with tools such as CSS, XML, and cross-browser JavaScript frameworks. A good example of an adaptability plan is SCORM. SCORM stands for "Sharable Content Object Reference Model." **SCORM** is "a set of technical standards for e-learning software products. SCORM tells programmers how to write their code so that it can 'play well' with other e-learning software." (scorm.com/scorm-explained) So if an educational textbook publisher decided to create a series of online study guides and tests, they would use SCORM to help them create the material so it could be used by schools and students using a variety of learning management systems.

Increasing the Results for Search Engine Optimization

Google, Yahoo! and Microsoft (Bing), in that order, are the three most popular general search engines today, with Google being the giant among the three. Google accounted for over 65% of the market in 2011 according to comScore (comscore.com). There are other types of search engines, including job search engines like Monster.com or child-oriented search engines like Yahoo! Kids (kids.yahoo. com). How does the subject of search engines relate to developing a project framework?

As you develop your framework, incorporate meta tags to help search engines find your pages.

> **QUICK TIP**
>
> Keeping your browsers up to date is a quick, free way to help you keep up with current technology.

Search engines gather information using various parts of web content. This information is then used to index the pages so they can be listed in search results. Page titles are one of the most common tags used by most search engines to index pages. The <title> tag is found in the head content of a web page, which is the part of a web page that does not appear in the browser. (The content that appears in the browser window is found between the <body> tags.) Each page should have a clear, concise, descriptive page title, and remember that titles *do* appear in browser title bars. The code for a title would look something like this:

```
<title> Welcome to the
Gardener's Walk website!
</title>
```

Keywords are also used by most search engines and are listed inside <meta> tags in the head content. **Keywords** are descriptive words that do not appear in the browser or the title bar. They simply reside in the head content and are separated by commas. Code for keywords would look something like this:

```
<meta name = "keywords"
content = "Gardener's Walk,
garden, gardener, plants,
flowers"/>
```

Another tag that search engines use is the description, which also resides in the head content. A **description** is a short paragraph that describes the content and features of the website. Like keywords, the description does not appear in the browser. Code for a description would look something like this:

```
<meta name = "description"
content = "The Gardener's Walk
is a website that provides
seasonal information for
gardening enthusiasts of all
ages."/>
```

Using Meta Tags Effectively

Meta tags are HTML codes that reside in the head section of a web page and include information about the page, such as keywords and descriptions. It's important to anticipate the search terms your potential customers would use and include these words in the keywords, description, and title. List the most important keywords first to make sure they're listed in those search engines that limit the number of keywords that they'll index. Keep your keywords and descriptions short and concise to ensure that all search engines will include your site. Many designers use focus groups to learn which words potential customers or clients might use. A **focus group** is a marketing tool that asks a group of people for feedback about a product, such as the impact of a television ad or the effectiveness of a website design.

Meta tags are also used with images, photographs, videos, audio files, and almost any other digital content.

USING DREAMWEAVER TO DEVELOP A FRAMEWORK

Beginning Construction

After you complete the planning phase for an interactive media project, it's time to develop the framework. Before you begin creating files, you should create the main folder and subfolders that will be used to store the files. After you have your file structure in place, you then create your files, saving them in the appropriate folders.

In this lesson, we'll review the steps we used to create our demonstration project, the Gardener's Walk website. If you're going to create a different kind of interactive media project, the steps to set up your file structure and file framework will be slightly different. We'll be using Adobe Dreamweaver to demonstrate the steps, but another type of project will require different software. We're assuming that you're already comfortable with opening and saving pages in Dreamweaver, editing HTML code and Cascading Style Sheets, and assigning page titles, keywords, and descriptions.

Selecting the Location for the Website's Local Site Folder

We began by creating a folder that will be used to store the folders and files created for the website. Remember the accepted file and folder naming conventions when you name your files and folders. Refer to the sidebar "Choosing Names for Folders and Files" for more information. Next, we tell Dreamweaver to set up the local site folder using this folder. The **local site folder** is the location where you store all of the pages or HTML files for the site. Traditionally, this folder has been called the **root folder** and many people still use this term; in this book we'll refer to it as the local site folder.

Setting Up a Website

The next step is to set up the website. When you set up a site in Dreamweaver, you use the Dreamweaver Site Setup dialog box to assign your site a name and specify the local site folder. After you've set up your site, the site name and any folders and files it contains appear in the Files panel, the panel you use to manage your website's files and folder. Using the Files panel to manage your files ensures that the site links work correctly when the website is published. You can also use the Files panel to add or delete pages.

Choosing Names for Folders and Files

When you choose a name for a web page or website folder, use a short, simple descriptive name that reflects the contents of the page or folder. For instance, if the page is about your company's services, name it services.html. You should also follow the general rules for naming web pages, such as naming the home page index.html. Most file servers look for the file named index.html or default.html to use for the initial page for a website. Do not use spaces, special characters, or punctuation in filenames or folders that you will use in your site. Use underscores rather than spaces for readability; for example: use balloon_flower.jpg rather than balloon flower.jpg. To be totally compatible with all file servers, use only letters, numbers, or underscores in file or folder names. Many designers also avoid the use of uppercase letters.

Setting Up Web Server Access

The next part of the process is to set up access to the server where the website will be published. When you set up web server access, you're laying the groundwork for publishing your site, which happens when your site is finished and ready to share with others. **Publishing** a website refers to the process of transferring all the local site files for the site from your computer to a web server, a computer that is connected to the Internet with an IP (Internet Protocol) address so that it's available for viewing on the Internet. A website must be published so that Internet users can access it.

There are two ways to make your site available to others. One way is to configure your home computer as a web server, if you have the necessary hardware and software. You would then designate a folder on your computer as your remote site folder, and transfer your finished site files there. If you don't have your own web server, you can use a web service provider, and transfer your files to the remote folder your service provider designates. After the files are transferred to a web server, they are known as the **remote site files**.

Even though publishing happens during a later phase, it's a good idea to set up web server access when you set up the framework. It's useful to set up both the **live server**, which is where the website will reside, and a **testing server**, which is a server that is only used for testing the website. Use the Files panel to transfer your files using the Dreamweaver FTP capability. **FTP (File Transfer Protocol)** is the process of uploading and downloading files to and from a remote site.

Setting Up a Default Images Folder

You also should designate the location where you'll be organizing and storing your website assets, or non-HTML files. You can give this folder any name that makes sense to you, but "assets" or "images" are names that are commonly used. Just remember to follow proper folder naming conventions, such as avoiding the use of spaces. Once you've created this folder, designate it as the default images folder and Dreamweaver will automatically save imported images in that location. Depending on how many **dependent files**, or files that are necessary to create the pages, you have, you may choose to organize your asset files by placing them in subfolders.

Creating the Home Page using CSS

Now that you have your folders set up, you're ready to begin constructing the home, or index page. You can either open an existing page to save as the home page or you can create a new, blank page from scratch or by using one of Dreamweaver's predesigned layouts. These predesigned layouts are a great shortcut to create new pages with existing columns, headers, and footers, each defined and formatted using div tags and Cascading Style Sheets. However, the CSS properties rarely meet your design specifications. They're intended only to serve as a starting point. Notice the instructions in each CSS Layout block to help you understand how to modify the layout. We'll explore CSS in more depth in Chapter 5.

Our plan is to create a page layout that can be modified to display on a desktop, a tablet (in portrait and landscape orientations), and a mobile phone (in portrait and landscape orientations). This will require using separate style sheets for each screen size. We'll begin with the desktop style sheet and use 1024 pixels for the maximum width of the content area.

Adding Meta Tags for the Title, Keywords, and Description

You'll recall that a page title, keywords, and a description are important to include in your pages because they're used by search engines to locate and index your pages. To add meta tags in Dreamweaver, use one of the Meta commands in the Common category on the Insert Bar. Spend some time writing your titles, keywords, and descriptions to be sure that they accurately reflect your site content and match search terms that potential users would use to find your site.

Modifying the CSS Layout Block Properties

After you choose a layout and use it to create a page, you then modify the properties of each style to create your custom design. When you're satisfied with the appearance, you can then use the index page as a basis for all other pages in the website or you can create a template from the index page. **Templates** are pages with editable and protected regions that are used to create pages with consistent design elements and common content, such as a banner and menu bar.

Once you have your page created, you can go to work customizing the layout blocks to your specifications. Each layout block is a separate div tag, with a corresponding rule name preceded by a period. This rule's properties define the appearance and position of the div, such as the width, background color, and font. The placeholder text inside each div should be replaced with your content. You can replace the content first or you can customize the styles first. The following steps show a few examples for how to begin this process. You can key the steps with your own practice website, or just read through them and use them as a guide for the It's Your Turn section.

Creating Animation with Adobe Edge

Although Adobe Flash is regarded as the premier tool used for creating animation, with the development of HTML5 and CSS3, we have new ways available to us for creating motion and animation. HTML5 includes new tags for animation and video, such as the <video> tag with attributes such as autoplay, controls, loop, and src and the <audio> tag. With CSS3, there are new styles for enhancing the appearance of page objects, such as rounded corners and gradients. **Adobe Edge**, a new program introduced by Adobe in August, 2011 as preview software, combines the new capabilities of HTML5, CSS3, and JavaScript but uses a program interface similar to Flash. Like Flash, it lets you manipulate text, shapes, and images using a stage, timeline, playhead, symbols, frames, and layers. Unlike Flash, Edge codes in JSON (JavaScript Object Notation), a subset of JavaScript, rather than ActionScript. This means that Edge creates animation that is coded entirely with HTML and JavaScript, so browsers that support HTML5 will not need a plug-in to play the animations. Edge also incorporates web fonts using font services such as Typekit or FontSquirrel. This means that users will not have to have fonts installed on their systems to view type in files created in Edge. The correct fonts will be downloaded seamlessly.

Select the location for the website's local site folder

1. Open Dreamweaver.
2. Open or expand the Files panel if necessary to view the contents.

3. Click the **drive or folder** that currently appears in the pop-up menu in the files panel. See Figure 11.
4. Click to select the **drive or folder** (or subfolder) in the list where we will store our folders and files for the website. Dreamweaver will store all

of the folders and files you create inside this drive or folder.

5. Verify that the drive or folder where you want to store the site is selected in the Files panel, right-click (Windows) or Ctrl-click (Mac) the **drive or folder**, then click **New Folder**.

Figure 11 *Selecting a drive in the Files panel*

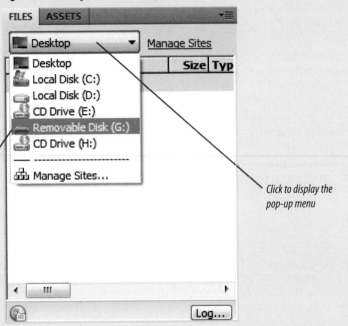

Click to select the drive or folder that you will use to store your files (your drive or folder may differ)

Click to display the pop-up menu

6. Type **gardeners_walk** or **(your_folder_name)** to rename the folder, then press **[Enter]**.

The folder is renamed with the site name. The name of the folder for the demonstration project site is gardeners_walk, as shown in Figure 12. We have not created a website yet. We've just created the folder that will serve as the local site folder after we set up the site.

The folder color is currently yellow (Mac users will see blue folders), but after you set up a site, it will change to green. Notice the difference between Figures 12 and 13. In Figure 12, only the site folder has been created, not the website, and the color of the folder in the Files panel is yellow. In Figure 13, the project website has been created, so the local site folder is green.

TIP You should not use uppercase letters or spaces in a folder or file name that will be published on the Internet. You can, however, use underscores to help visually separate the words.

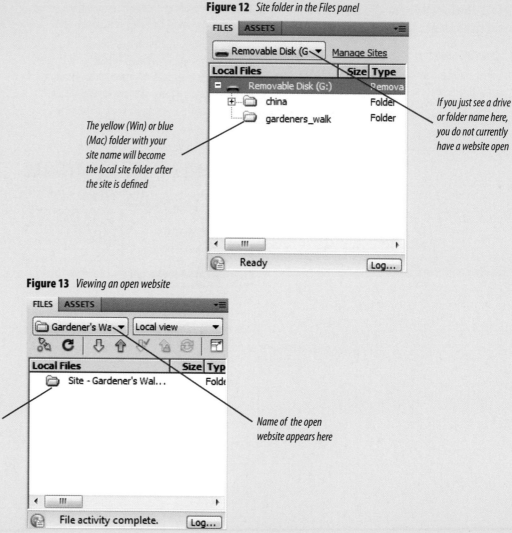

Figure 12 *Site folder in the Files panel*

The yellow (Win) or blue (Mac) folder with your site name will become the local site folder after the site is defined

If you just see a drive or folder name here, you do not currently have a website open

Figure 13 *Viewing an open website*

Green folder and the word "Site" indicate that this is a website folder

Name of the open website appears here

Figures © Cengage Learning 2013

Set up a website

1. Click **Site** on the Menu bar, then click **New Site**.

2. Click **Site** in the category list in the Site Setup for Unnamed Site dialog box (if necessary), then type **Gardener's Walk** or (*your site name*) in the Site Name text box.

TIP You can use uppercase letters and spaces in the site name because it's not the name of a folder or a file.

3. Click the **Browse for folder button** 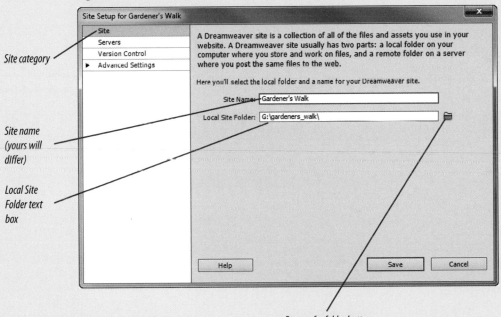 next to the Local Site Folder text box, click the **Select list arrow** (Win) or the **navigation list arrow** (Mac) in the Choose Root Folder dialog box, navigate to and click the **drive and folder** where the website files will be stored, then click **gardeners_walk** or (*your project folder*).

4. Click **Open** (Win) or **Choose** (Mac) in the Select Root Folder dialog box, click **Select** (Win), then compare your screen to Figure 14.

Figure 14 *Site Setup dialog box*

Site category

Site name (yours will differ)

Local Site Folder text box

Site Setup for Gardener's Walk

Site
Servers
Version Control
▶ Advanced Settings

A Dreamweaver site is a collection of all of the files and assets you use in your website. A Dreamweaver site usually has two parts: a local folder on your computer where you store and work on files, and a remote folder on a server where you post the same files to the web.

Here you'll select the local folder and a name for your Dreamweaver site.

Site Name: Gardener's Walk

Local Site Folder: G:\gardeners_walk\

Help   Save   Cancel

Browse for folder button

Figure © Cengage Learning 2013

Building the Framework

Set up web server access

1. Click **Servers** in the Category list, then click the **Add new Server button** ➕, as shown in Figure 15.

2. Click the **Connect using: list arrow**, choose the method you will use to publish the website, as shown in Figure 16, enter any necessary information in the Site Setup dialog box based on the settings you chose, then click **Save**.

TIP Your network administrator or web hosting service will provide you with the necessary information to publish your website. If you don't have this information now, you can complete this step later.

Figure 15 *Adding a server for remote access*

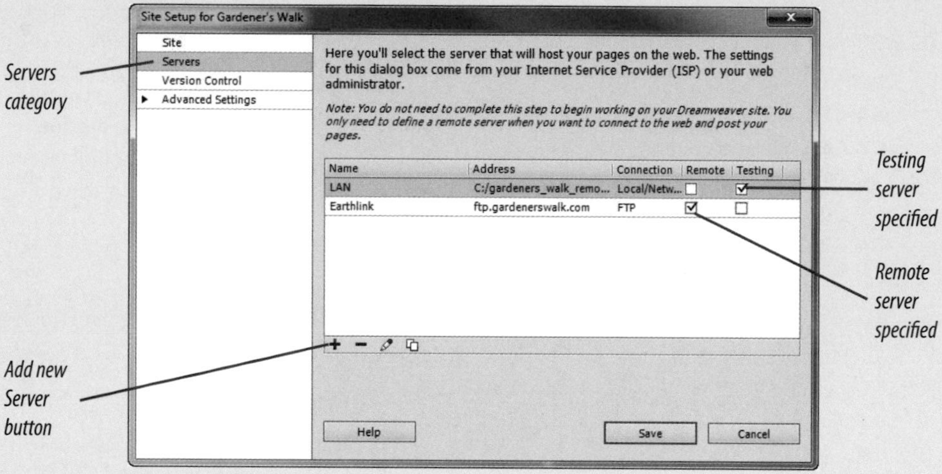

Servers category

Add new Server button

Testing server specified

Remote server specified

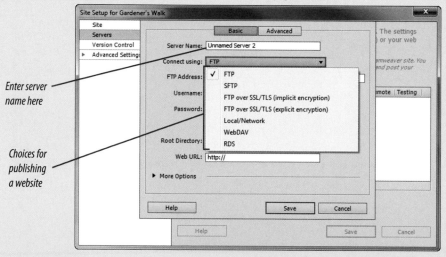

Figure 16 *Entering publishing information for the project website*

Enter server name here

Choices for publishing a website

Figures © Cengage Learning 2013

Set up a default images folder

1. Click **Advanced Settings** in the category list in the Site Setup dialog box, then click **Local Info**, if necessary.

2. Click the **Browse for folder button** 📁 next to the Default Images folder text box.

3. If necessary, navigate to your site folder, then click the **Create New Folder button** 📁 in the Choose Image Folder dialog box.

4. Type **assets** or (*the name for your default images folder*), press **[Enter]**, click **Open** (Win) or **Choose** (Mac), then click **Select** (Win) or **Choose** (Mac) in the Choose Image Folder dialog box.

5. Compare your screen to Figure 17, click **Save**, then click **Done** to close the Manage Sites dialog box (Win).

Create the home page using CSS

1. Click **File** on the Menu bar, click **New**, click **HTML5: 2 column fixed, right sidebar, header and footer** in the Layout column in the New Document dialog box.

2. Click the **Layout CSS list box**, click **Create New File**, as shown in Figure 18, then click **Create**.

   Choosing Create New File will save all of the CSS code used on the page in an external file, rather than as part of the page code.

Figure 17 *Site Setup dialog box with Default Images folder specified*

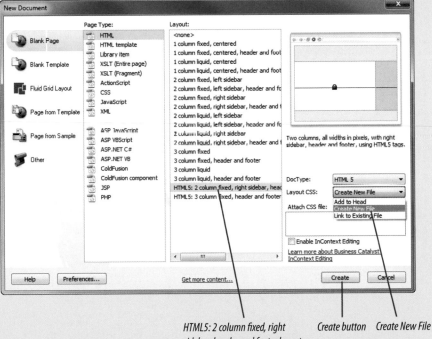

Local Info category

Default Images folder text box

Browse for folder button

Figure 18 *New Document dialog box*

HTML5: 2 column fixed, right sidebar, header and footer layout

Create button

Create New File

3. Replace the default file name of the CSS file that will be created with a name of your choice, unless you prefer to use the default name, then click **Save**.

   A new page is created, along with the style sheet file that contains the page formatting. The new page is divided into separate containers that were created with div tags. These div tags were formatted in the CSS file with preset dimensions, background colors, font sizes, and font styles. To customize your page, you edit the CSS settings for the div tags using settings of your choice. Note that the CSS file is listed in the Files panel and in the CSS Styles panel. We used the filename gw_main.css to designate that this style sheet is the style sheet that's used for the global styles for every page in the site. As we modify the settings, we'll add style sheets that enable the pages to be viewed on screens with different width displays.

4. Save the file as **index.html**.

   If you follow these steps, your new page will look like Figure 19. Each of the blocks serve as temporary placeholders for the text, images, and links that will be placed on this page.

Figure 19 *Index page with CSS layout block placeholders*

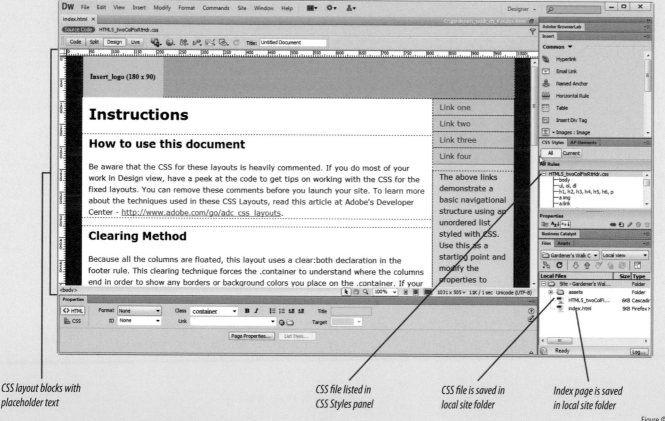

CSS layout blocks with placeholder text

CSS file listed in CSS Styles panel

CSS file is saved in local site folder

Index page is saved in local site folder

Figure © Cengage Learning 2013

Modify CSS layout block properties

1. Replace the placeholder text with your own notes about your page content, as shown in Figure 20.

   Don't worry about the background colors or font sizes, styles, or detailed content for now.

You're just making notes at this point for placing the content later.

TIP The Dreamweaver placeholder text has a lot of great information to guide you in customizing the page. It's a good idea to read it before you remove it.

2. Save your file, expand the CSS Styles panel if necessary, then scroll down and click the **.sidebar1** rule to select it.

TIP You may have to click the Plus sign next to the style sheet name in the CSS Styles panel to view the rules.

Figure 20 *Replacing the placeholder text on the index page*

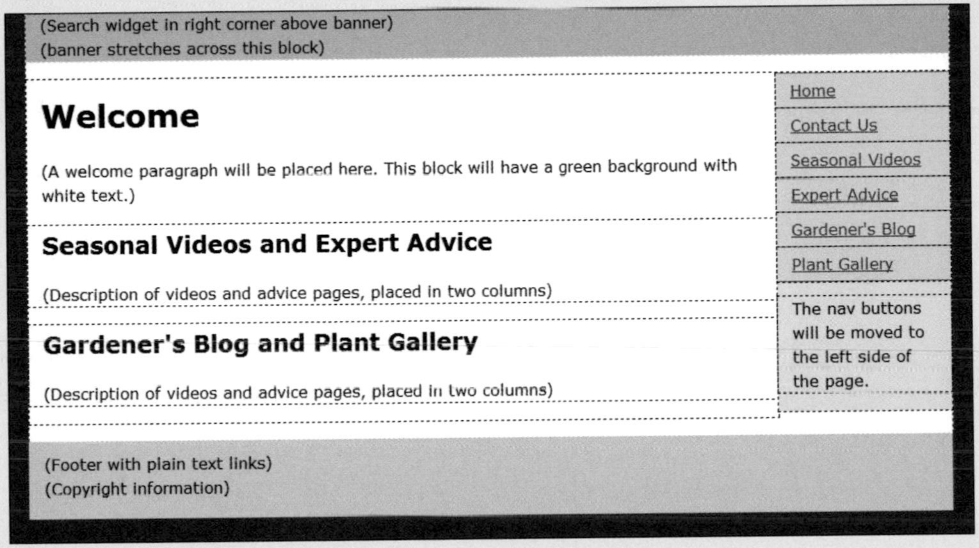

(Search widget in right corner above banner)
(banner stretches across this block)

Welcome

(A welcome paragraph will be placed here. This block will have a green background with white text.)

Seasonal Videos and Expert Advice

(Description of videos and advice pages, placed in two columns)

Gardener's Blog and Plant Gallery

(Description of videos and advice pages, placed in two columns)

Home
Contact Us
Seasonal Videos
Expert Advice
Gardener's Blog
Plant Gallery

The nav buttons will be moved to the left side of the page.

(Footer with plain text links)
(Copyright information)

3. Click the **Edit Rule button** 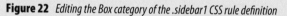, as shown in Figure 21.

4. Click the **Box Category**, change the Float from right to **left**, as shown in Figure 22, then click **OK**.

5. Scroll up in the CSS Styles panel if necessary, click the **.container rule** to select it, then click the **Edit Rule button** 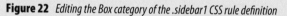.

Figure 21 *Using the Edit Rule button to edit a rule*

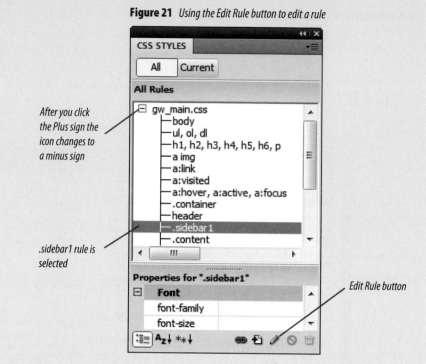

After you click the Plus sign the icon changes to a minus sign

.sidebar1 rule is selected

Edit Rule button

Figure 22 *Editing the Box category of the .sidebar1 CSS rule definition*

Box category

Float: left

Building the Framework

6. Click the **Border Category**, then change the Border Style to **solid**, the Border Width to **thin**, and the Border Color to **#6FB345**, as shown in Figure 23, then click **OK** to close the CSS Rule Definition dialog box.

7. Double-click the **body rule** in the CSS Styles panel, click the **Edit Rule button** ✎, click the **Type** category, change the type color to **#FFFFFF**, click the **Background** category, change the background color to **#FFFFFF**, as shown in Figure 24, then click **OK**.

8. Double-click the **content rule** in the CSS Styles panel, change the Background color to **#4A8217**, then click **OK**.

9. Double-click the **footer rule** in the CSS Styles panel, click the **Type** category, change the type color to **#4A8217**, click the **Background** category, select and delete the existing background color, then click **OK**.

10. Click the **Block** category, change the **Text-align** property to **center**, then click **OK**.

Figure 23 *Editing the Border category of the .container CSS rule definition*

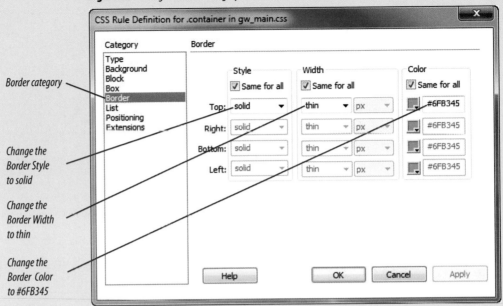

Border category

Change the Border Style to solid

Change the Border Width to thin

Change the Border Color to #6FB345

Figure 24 *Editing the body rule background color*

CSS Rule Definition for body in gw_main.css

Category
Type
Background
Block
Box
Border

Background

Background-color: ☐ #FFFFFF

Background-image: ▼ Browse...

Change the Background color to #FFFFFF

11. Edit the rest of the layout blocks to position your placeholder content on the page where you want it, then use Live view to see your content as it will appear in a browser.

12. When you're satisfied with your changes, save and use the **Preview/Debug in browser** button 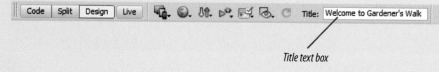 to preview the file in the browser. See Figure 25 for an example.

Add meta tags for the title, keywords, and description

1. Use the Title text box to add a page title, as shown in Figure 26.

TIP You can't see the Title text box on the Document toolbar if you are in Live view.

Figure 25 *Viewing the page with modified div tag settings*

(Search widget in right corner above banner)
(banner stretches across this block)

Home
Contact Us
Seasonal Videos
Expert Advice
Gardener's Blog
Plant Gallery
Quote?

Welcome

(A welcome paragraph will be placed here. This block will have a green background with white text.)

Seasonal Videos and Expert Advice

(Description of videos and advice pages, placed in two columns)

Gardener's Blog and Plant Gallery

(Description of videos and advice pages, placed in two columns)

(Footer with plain text links)
(Copyright information)

Figure 26 *Adding a page title in the Title text box*

Code | Split | Design | Live   Title: Welcome to Gardener's Walk

Title text box

2. Click the **Head list arrow** in the Common category on the Insert bar, then click **Keywords** to open the Keywords dialog box shown in Figure 27.

3. Add appropriate keywords for your site, then click **OK** to close the dialog box.

4. Click the **Head list arrow** in the Common category on the Insert bar, then click **Description** to open the Description dialog box shown in Figure 28.

5. Add an appropriate description for your site, then click **OK** to close the dialog box.

Figure 27 *Entering keywords in the Keywords dialog box*

Keywords

Keywords:

Gardener's Walk, gardener, garden, walk, gardening

OK

Cancel

Help

Keywords are separated by commas

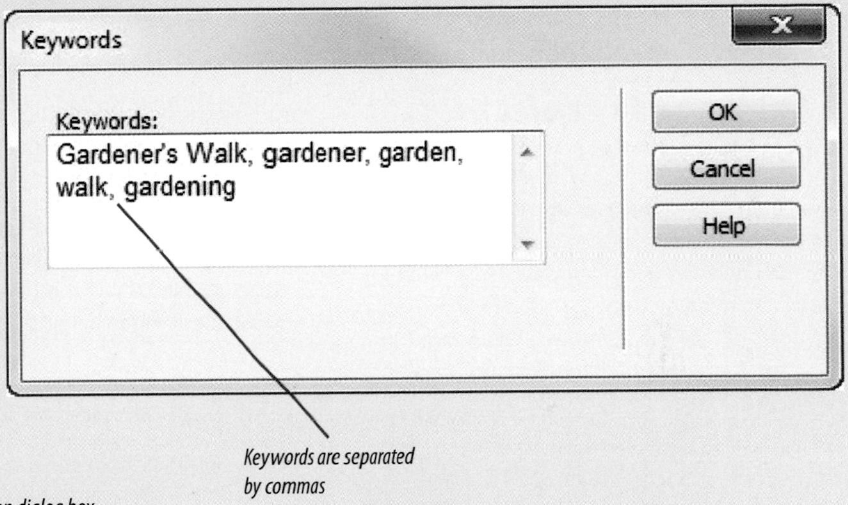

Figure 28 *Entering a description in the Description dialog box*

Description

Description:

Gardener's Walk is a website that provides seasonal information of interest to gardening enthusiasts.

OK

Cancel

Help

Description is entered in complete sentences

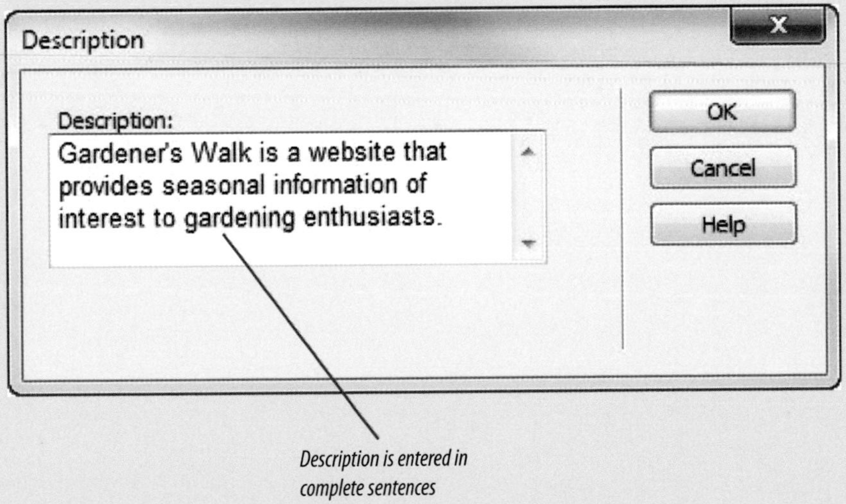

Figures © Cengage Learning 2013

BUILDING YOUR PROJECT FRAMEWORK

Now that you've read about how to create the framework for your project, and seen an example of how a website framework could be built, you're ready to begin your own project framework. Use the wireframe you created in Chapter 3 as your guide to create the content placeholders. If you're creating a project other than a website, you will generally follow these steps, modifying them to fit your needs.

1. Decide where to store your project and create your main project folder with any necessary subfolders.
2. Using software that's appropriate for creating your project, create the first main page.
3. Use content placeholders as guides for placing your content later.
4. Use styles to format the placeholder content containers, if appropriate.
5. Assign meta data that can be used to optimize search engine results.

FINDING WIDGETS TO ADD INTERACTION

You've learned about using widgets to allow the user to interact with the application and the operating system. Widgets are packaged pieces of code, or **code snippets**, that others have written and made available for downloading. We talked about Adobe Browser Lab as a great source to find widgets, and another option is jQuery. jQuery is a JavaScript library that contains DOM objects that are CSS3 and HTML5 compliant.

1. Use the Internet to research widget examples and then choose one that you might like to try in your interactive media project. One example you might try is a widget that will add a search feature to your project. Two places to start your search are the Adobe Browser Lab and jQuery.com. Another is Google Web Elements, at google.com/webelements/. Google Web Elements are code snippets published by Google that are available for you to add to your website.

2. Visit two websites and search the page source code to determine if they've used widgets in their site. Explain the purpose of one widget on each site. For example, the Neighbor's Mill Bakery & Café website shown in Figure 29 uses several widgets. Search the source code to locate them.

3. Write a paragraph that explains the function of the widget you chose and how you think it would add

Figure 29 *Neighbor's Mill Bakery & Café website*
Courtesy of Mike and Karin Nabors

to your users' interactive experience. Cite the source where you located the widget.

4. Decide where you'll place your widget in your project and make a note to yourself for when your content is developed enough to insert it.

Even More to Explore

To explore some of the topics discussed in this chapter in more depth, see the References section at the end of the book. For links to additional web resources, visit the Even More to Explore link under Book Resources on Cengage Brain.

CHAPTER 5 WORKING WITH TEXT

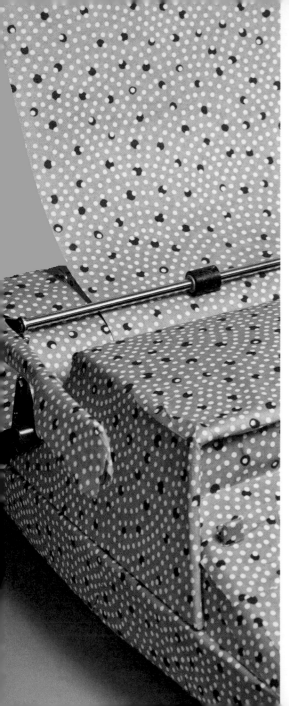

CHAPTER **5** **WORKING WITH TEXT**

Introduction

In the previous chapters you mapped your ideas into a visual representation of your project idea and then began to build the framework for your project in its intended final application. In this chapter you learn basic design strategies for adding the headings, subheadings, paragraphs, and other type elements to your project. You then create or import the text and format it to achieve the desired type appearance.

Throughout the book, we'll use the terms "text" and "type." Although you may find these terms defined differently, and some people use them interchangeably, this is how we're going to use them: **Text** refers to written words. Text can be **plain text**, which has no formatting applied; **formatted text** (or **rich text**), which has formatting applied; and **enriched text**, which has formatting applied specifically for email messages. (Today, however, most email message text is formatted with HTML.) **Type** is the term you use when you're including text characteristics such as font name, size, color, or style. Most applications use the term "type" in the menus and dialog boxes that are used to format text.

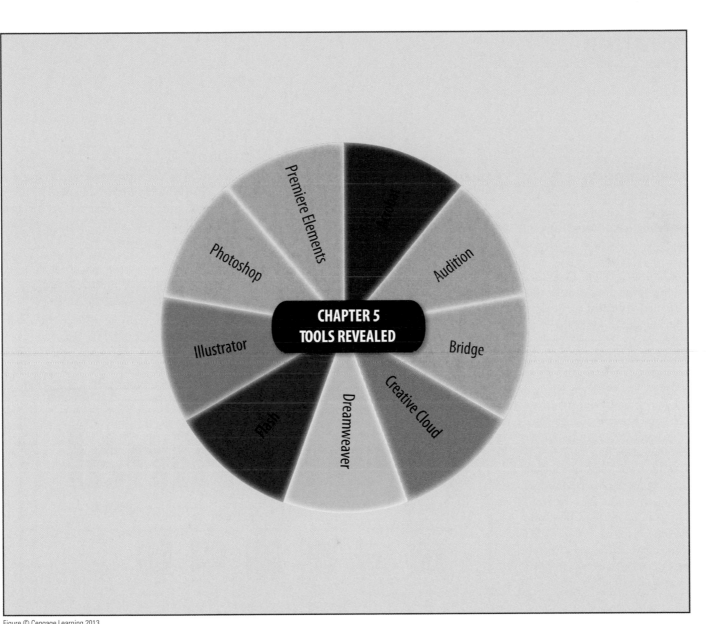

**CHAPTER 5
TOOLS REVEALED**

Premiere Elements

Photoshop

Illustrator

Flash

Dreamweaver

Creative Cloud

Bridge

Audition

Incorporating TEXT

Reviewing Basic Terminology

Let's begin by examining more of the basic terminology used when talking about text and type. **Typography** is the art of placing and arranging type. It includes choosing properties such as typefaces, styles such as bold and italic, size, color, alignment, spacing, and other formatting choices that affect text appearance. **Typefaces** are designs, like Times New Roman or Arial, that type designers create. Many people refer to typefaces as fonts, but technically these aren't interchangeable terms. Typefaces often come in **font families**, groups of similarly designed type sets. **Fonts**, as opposed to typefaces, are the complete character sets of a single style of a particular typeface. To illustrate: Times New Roman is a typeface, but Times New Roman Italic is a font. Font files contain the characters that make up the typeface design. Before widespread computer use, the word "font" referred to the metal slugs that were used to print the type. Font sizes are expressed in **points**; for example, a character that is 72 points is one inch tall and a character that is 36 points is one-half inch tall.

Locating Fonts

Today there are a multitude of fonts available. Your computer operating system includes a font library; individual applications include sets of fonts; and websites such as fonts.com, shown in Figure 1, offer fonts for downloading. The fonts.com website alone has over 167,000 fonts available. It's one of many web font

Figure 1 *Fonts.com website*
Copyright 2001–2012 Fonts.com

embedding services, which also include TypeFront, Google Font API, and Typekit. Sites like these allow you to use professionally designed fonts on your websites by offering them free of charge, by licensing arrangement, for purchase, or by subscription. For reviews of ten of these services, refer to the Smashing Magazine listing in the Reference section at the end of this book.

The fonts we used on the Gardener's Walk site are in the public domain. When you use a font or image from the public domain, it's wise to document the way in which you obtained it. Print the page you used when you downloaded the font so you'll have a record of the date and the site you used. For example, we downloaded the Aspire font in the site banner from the FontSpace website.

Unless you use license-free fonts (freeware), fonts are protected by copyright law. Just as you would if you wanted to use someone else's image, you should obtain permission to use a font from its creator. Even though a font is already installed on your computer, you can't assume you can freely embed it in a document, especially a document that will be used commercially. To find the copyright information about a font, you can select the font's filename, and right-click Properties (Win) or Ctrl-click > Get Info (Mac). Figure 2 shows the properties of the Rage Italic font, with the creator's name and

Figure 2 *Viewing font properties*

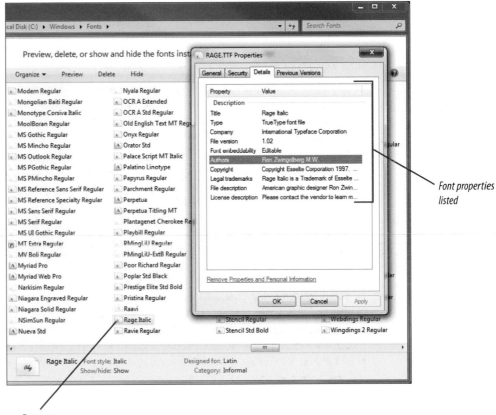

Font properties listed

Font name

copyright information displayed. (You may not see copyright information on every font in your system.) When you save a file with an embedded font, you may receive a font embedding notification, such as the one from Adobe Illustrator shown in Figure 3.

It's tempting to use unique fonts, but there are times when it's best to stick with standard fonts. If you're creating a document for printing, any font that's installed on your computer system and accessible through the application menu will print correctly, as long as the printer can read the font. If you're going to create a PDF, the font will be embedded in the document. If you're formatting text that will be published on a website, you'll want to stick to standard fonts that will likely be installed on most computers, unless you're using embedded fonts. Otherwise, you run the risk of the fonts not displaying correctly in users' browsers. When designing mobile, tablet, or phone apps, it's also a good idea to avoid setting manual font properties and stick to the built-in theme fonts.

Dreamweaver uses lists of default font families as one way to format text, such as "Arial, Helvetica, sans-serif." You can create your own font lists by using the Edit Font

Figure 3 *Adobe Illustrator font embedding notification*

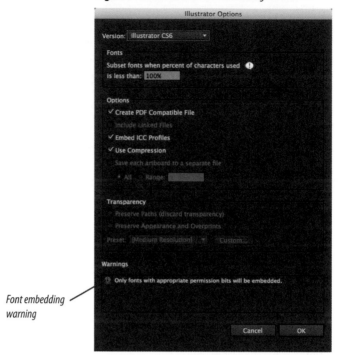

Font embedding warning

Typekit, Adobe, and the Adobe Creative Cloud

Adobe Systems purchased Typekit in 2011, giving Adobe users access to cloud-based fonts through the Adobe Creative Cloud. The **Adobe Creative Cloud**, an initiative introduced in 2011, is a virtual space that lets users download desktop and tablet applications, access creative services, and publish and share their work. The Adobe Creative Cloud serves as the hub for viewing, sharing, and syncing files created by Adobe Touch Apps (applications designed to run on tablets) and the Adobe Creative Suite. Users pay a subscription fee for this service. Benefits include access to the Adobe Creative Suite tools, which are technologies for delivering interactive publications on tablets, design services (such as Typekit), and forums for connecting with other creative people. Go to the Adobe website, adobe.com, to learn more about the Adobe Creative Cloud.

List dialog box, shown in Figure 4. When a page's HTML code includes the font list "Arial, Helvetica, sans-serif," a browser will look for the first font (Arial). If it doesn't find the first font, it will look for the second font (Helvetica). And if it doesn't find the second font, it will default to a sans-serif font. A sans-serif font is one of two classifications of fonts: serif and sans-serif. You'll learn more about these font classifications in the next section, "Using Type."

Font Compatibility Issues

When a document is created on one computer and then opened on a different computer, sometimes the application will be unable to find the necessary fonts, which are then known as **missing fonts**. Many applications, such as InDesign and Photoshop, will highlight or otherwise inform you that they can't find the requested font. When this happens you have two choices: you can either choose to substitute the missing font with a different font; or you can note the name of the missing font, download it, and install it. Some programs will automatically substitute missing fonts with default fonts.

Font compatibility is a common problem in classroom situations when students are transporting their files from home computers to school computers and vice versa, or when documents are transported back and forth between home computers and work computers. Transferring files between a Windows operating system and a Macintosh operating system can also result in missing fonts, as can software updates. Fonts that are available in one version may not be available in an older or newer version.

When you're concerned about being able to display a font correctly on all computers, one option, besides using standard fonts, is to create outlines from the type. This converts the text to vector graphics, essentially creating shapes from the individual characters so they'll be "drawn" using mathematical equations rather than displayed as type. You can then fill the outlines with gradients or patterns, as shown in Figure 5. If you decide to convert

Figure 4 *Edit Font List dialog box*

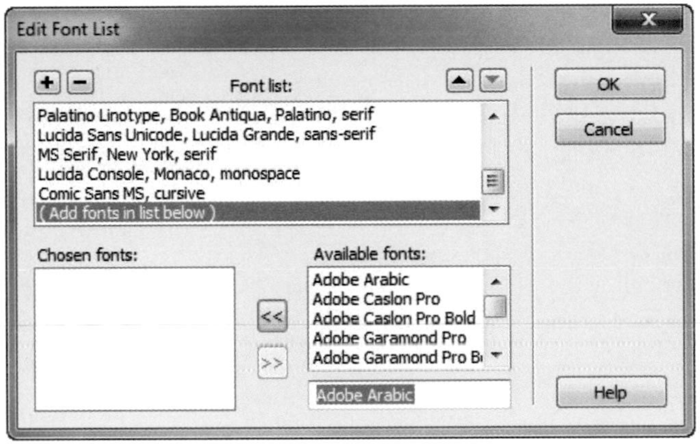

Figure 5 *Comparison of editable text and text converted to outlines*

type to outlines, be sure to save a copy of the original text first. Outlines aren't editable and if you find a spelling or typographical error, you won't be able to correct it unless you can access your original text.

Using Basic Text Tools

Many of the basic tools used to edit and format text are similar across many applications, such as Microsoft Office and most Adobe applications. **Editing** refers to changing content, and **formatting** refers to changing the appearance of content. For example, using a spell check command is an editing function, and changing a font color is a formatting function. Most text editors include a Find and Replace command that allows you to quickly edit documents by locating multiple instances of text and changing them, all with one command. The Dreamweaver Find and Replace dialog box is shown in Figure 6. This dialog box includes options for entering search parameters such as where you want to search, what you want to search, and several options such as Match Case. You can also save your query to use for a later search.

Most text editors also have a tool that creates text hyperlinks, especially useful for text in web pages or PDF documents. A **PDF (Portable Document Format) document** is one that's been saved using a special file format that allows it to be read on any computer using a free application called **Adobe Reader**. You can create PDFs using an application called **Adobe Acrobat**. You can also create them from files native to many other applications,

such as Adobe Photoshop or Microsoft Word. Figure 7 shows the Create Link dialog box in Adobe Acrobat. Links are created in Acrobat with the Link tool on the Advanced Editing toolbar. You'll learn more about PDFs in Chapter 7.

Figure 6 *Find and Replace dialog box in Dreamweaver*

Figure 7 *Create Link dialog box in Adobe Acrobat*

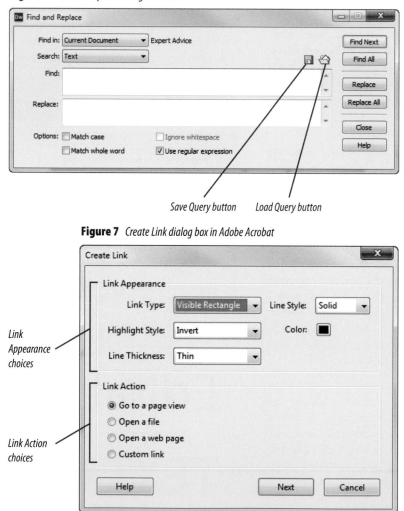

Save Query button   Load Query button

Link Appearance choices

Link Action choices

Figures © Cengage Learning 2013

Most applications that include text editing capabilities have character and paragraph settings for formatting text. Figure 8 shows the Character panels and Figure 9 on the next page shows the Paragraph panels in Adobe Photoshop, Flash, Illustrator, and InDesign. Notice the similarities in the panels; the common interfaces in Adobe products make it seamless to switch back and forth between applications. Also, once you've mastered one Adobe program, you have a good head start toward learning the others. (Dreamweaver doesn't have a Character or Paragraph panel, because formatting is primarily applied through the CSS Styles panel or Property inspector.)

Figure 8 *Character panels in Photoshop, Flash, Illustrator, and InDesign*

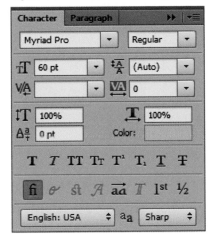

Photoshop

Flash

Illustrator

InDesign

Figure 9 *Paragraph panels in Photoshop, Flash, Illustrator, and InDesign*

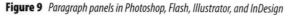

Figure 9 *Paragraph panels in Photoshop, Flash, Illustrator, and InDesign*

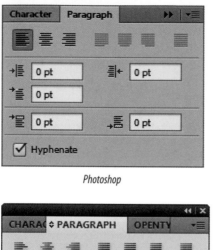

Photoshop

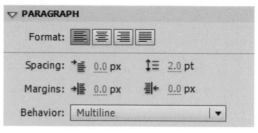

Flash

Illustrator

InDesign

Overview of Available Text Tools

Without question, the industry leader for graphic and web design software is Adobe Systems Inc. Font formats have evolved radically over time, and Figure 10 illustrates some of the key events since 1982. Adobe has contributed heavily to the shape of the digital typeface and graphic design industry. Their development of PostScript changed how computers handled text. **PostScript** is a page description language that stores glyphs as outlines or shapes, rather than as fixed-resolution bitmaps. This is similar to the different ways image files are created. **Bitmap images** are created pixel by pixel; **vector images** are created using mathematical formulas. **Glyphs** are character shapes on a page or screen. PostScript-derived glyphs can be reliably created at any resolution, so fonts will print clearly no matter what point size is specified. The three most common font formats are TrueType, OpenType, and PostScript. TrueType was created by Apple; OpenType was created by Adobe and Microsoft; and Postscript was created by Adobe. We'll compare these font formats in the next section, "Using Type."

All of the Adobe products include text or type commands. Some products, such as Acrobat and InDesign, are more robust than others for creating print or web-based text documents. Most of the Adobe products now use the Adobe Text Engine, an Adobe tool for creating high-quality typography in all of the major languages in the world. Adobe Type Manager Light is a free font utility from Adobe that you can use to view and print

PostScript fonts. It generates high-quality screen fonts from either Type 1 or OpenType formats. You can download Adobe Type Manager Light from the Adobe website.

To type web page text, most people use a word processing program like Microsoft Word. When you create text using a word processor, rather than typing the text directly in a web editor such as Dreamweaver, it's important

that you *not* format the text. Instead, apply all formatting using CSS in the web editor. Remember, though, that you don't need to use a full word processing program to create your text. Because you aren't concerned with formatting, a simple text editor like Windows Notepad or WordPad is sufficient. These two programs are included in the Windows operating system. The equivalent application for Mac users is TextEdit.

Figure 10 *Important dates in the evolution of the digital typeface and graphic design industry*

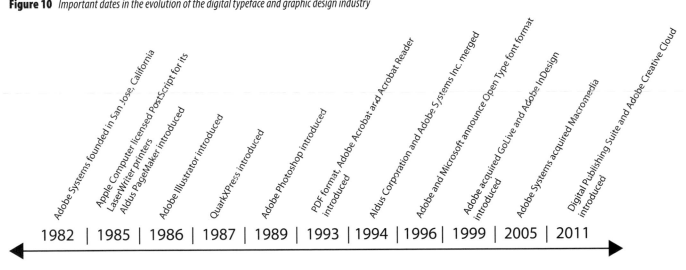

Using TYPE

Font Classifications

Fonts are classified in two ways: sans-serif and serif. **Sans-serif fonts** are block-style characters often used for headings and subheadings. The orange paragraph headings in this book are set in a sans-serif font. Examples of sans-serif fonts are Arial and Verdana. **Serif fonts** are more ornate, with small extra strokes, or "tails," at the beginning and end of each character. Serif fonts are considered easier to read in printed materials because the strokes help to lead your eye from character to character. That's why most printed documents with a lot of text, such as newspapers, use serif fonts. Examples of serif fonts are Times New Roman and Georgia. Notice how the sizes of the example fonts in the previous sentence appear different from the rest of the paragraph type. All of these fonts are the same font size, but typefaces display in varying sizes depending on the typeface design.

Most designers feel that a sans-serif font is preferable for screen content, especially if the type size is less than 12 points, because the extra "tails" are not as clear when the text is viewed on a backlit screen. If the screen content will be printed, however, such as a bank statement, you might want to use a serif font.

Regardless of which font or font classification you use, a good rule of thumb is to limit a website to no more than three fonts. Using more than that can be distracting and look unprofessional. It's fine to mix serif and sans-serif fonts when you want to add emphasis to headings or subheadings and set them apart from the body copy. In printed materials, such as business cards, you could use a sans-serif font for the name and title, but a serif font for the address and contact information.

Sometimes we choose fonts based on our personal style or personality—we like to use fonts and font settings that are pleasing to our eye. But more importantly, fonts help us to express the message we want to convey to our users.

> ### QUICK **TIP**
>
> The PBS website has a short, fun quiz that you can take to find out which font best expresses your personality. Go to pbs.org/independentlens/helvetica/type.html to read a short history of type and then use the link at the bottom of the page to take the quiz. We both matched the font Helvetica.

Font Formats

Fonts are also classified by their formats. Just as there are different ways in which a computer or printer renders a digital image (i.e., as bitmapped pixels or vectored outlines), the same is true for fonts. A font's format provides the instructions for how a digitized font is printed on paper, presented on screen, or both. You learned in the last section about PostScript-derived glyphs; with PostScript, the document will always look crisp and clean when you print it. To some extent, each of the these font formats uses PostScript:

- Type 1
  Type 1 is a digital font type that is resolution independent and can translate a font from the screen to a high-quality font in print. Adobe originally designed and manufactured Type 1 and maintains its standards. However, other companies have designed and released their own fonts using the Type 1 format. Type 1 fonts are commonly used by graphic designers whose work is primarily for print, such as magazine layouts.

- TrueType
  TrueType is the standard for digital fonts. TrueType was first developed by Apple Computer Corporation and subsequently licensed to Microsoft Corporation. Both companies have made independent

extensions to this format for Windows and Macintosh operating systems. Some can be used on both systems. TrueType fonts, like Type 1 fonts, have the ability to translate fonts for print and for screen, and are commonly used by graphic designers whose work is for both print and screen, such as web content that also appears in a print magazine.

- OpenType
OpenType fonts are the most sophisticated of the three font technologies. OpenType fonts were developed through a joint venture by Adobe and Microsoft and are based on TrueType fonts. TrueType fonts are cross-platform compatible, can support expanded character sets and languages, have more glyph variations, and provide better control over type layout and design.

It's easy to identify a font's format on an Adobe application menu. On a font list, you'll see a small icon to the left of the font name that indicates the font type, as shown in Figure 11. To view a font list, use the menu command Type > Font or Window > Type > Character.

In addition to the three principal font types, **Web Open Font Format (WOFF)** was developed by the Mozilla Foundation, in concert with several other organizations, to use for text on the World Wide Web. WOFF was proposed to the W3C in 2010 to be a standard format for all web browsers to use. It works using the same structure as TrueType and Open Type, but can also include metadata such as licensing

information. Because WOFF is a compressed format, it allows WOFF-formatted content to download faster. Currently, the following browsers support the WOFF format:

- Firefox Version 3.6 and up
- Internet Explorer Version 9 and up
- Google Chrome Version 5 and up
- Safari Version 5.1 and up

WOFF fonts are embedded in web pages with the CSS3 property @font-face, which allows the browser to access and deliver the font when the page is viewed in a browser.

QUICK TIP

You can convert fonts to a WOFF format using Font Squirrel, a free online service at fontsquirrel.com/fontface/generator.

Figure 11 *Viewing Font format icons in a Font menu*

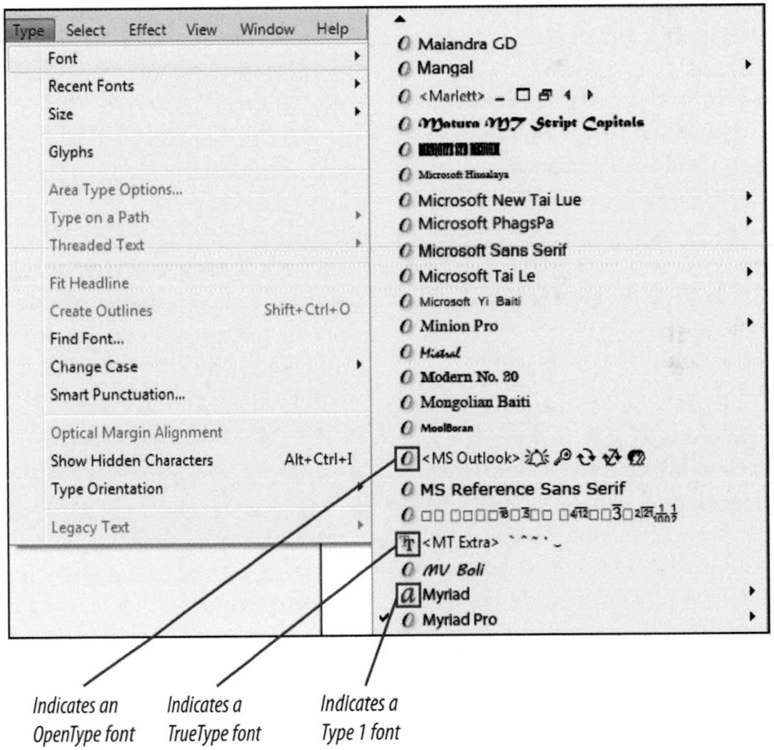

Indicates an OpenType font
Indicates a TrueType font
Indicates a Type 1 font

Figure © Cengage Learning 2013

Writing
SCREEN-BASED TEXT

Writing Text for the Web

As you learned in Chapter 3, there are two factors to consider when generating screen-based text: the writing style and the format. Because users expect short passages of text they can read quickly, you should put careful thought into writing clear, concise text that's easy to read. Use natural language, but avoid slang or jargon. **Jargon** is language that is specific to particular groups or professions. **Slang** is similar to jargon, but considered very informal. Both slang and jargon can be misunderstood by users unfamiliar with their meanings. Your goal is to provide content that's understandable to your target audience.

It doesn't matter how attractive or informative your text is if it isn't readable. Readability is determined by the complexity of your sentences, the average number of sentences per paragraph, and the average length of your words. To reach the largest audience for most documents, Microsoft Word documentation states that you should keep your reading level between the seventh and eighth grade levels. According to Alexander Macris, most widely-circulated newspapers are written on the ninth grade level, best-selling novels are written on the seventh grade level, and romance novels are written on the fifth grade level.

If you paste your page text into Microsoft Word, you can easily evaluate it with two tests: the Flesch Reading Ease Test and the Flesch-Kincaid Grade Level Test. To do this, open the Word Options dialog box, click Proofing, make sure Check grammar with spelling is checked, then click the Show readability statistics check box to select it. After you use the Check Spelling and Grammar command, the Readability Statistics dialog box will display the results for your document. See Figure 12. The following are several websites that test for on-screen and web text readability:

- Readability Test Tool at read-able.com
- Analysis of the MS Word Readability statistics as applied to web writing at KerryR.net, kerryr.net/webwriting/tools_readability.htm
- Guidelines for writing for the web are provided by the U.S. Department of Health and Human Services, usability.gov/guidelines/index.html. See Figure 13 for a list of the topics covered.
- 10 Tips for Good Web Writing by Jennifer Kyrnin, About.com, webdesign.about.com/od/writing/a/aa031405.htm.

Since other forms of interactive media, such as mobile apps and games, don't usually contain long text passages, these tests aren't

Figure 12 *Readability Statistics dialog box in Microsoft Word*

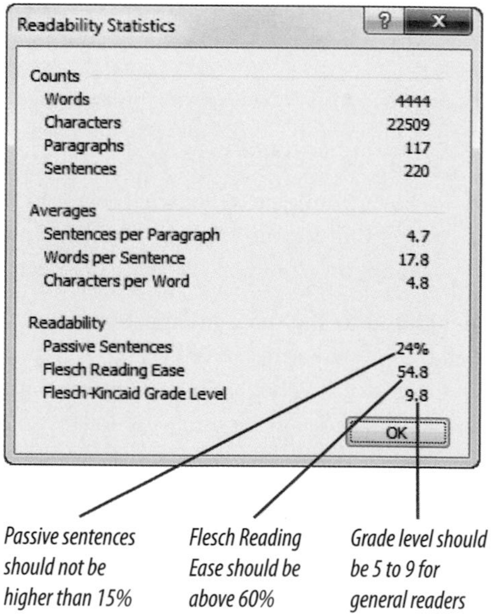

Passive sentences should not be higher than 15%

Flesch Reading Ease should be above 60%

Grade level should be 5 to 9 for general readers

as useful. However, clear, concise instructions and intuitively labeled screen elements (buttons, text boxes, and menu items) are essential to helping users get the most from your product.

Guidelines for Web Writing

When you write text for the Web, follow these accepted guidelines to make it as readable and usable as possible:

Use attention-grabbing headings and blurbs

Headings should generate interest and give the user motivation to continue reading through the content. The font, font size, and font style should contribute to conveying the relative importance of the headings. **Blurbs** are short extensions of a headline that provide a few more details to draw the user's attention and emphasize the content.

Use bulleted and numbered lists

Bulleted and numbered lists help to emphasize important information, making it easier to read and absorb by chopping up large blocks of text.

Use embedded links

Embedded links let users click a link to access additional content, rather than having to copy and paste to enter a URL in a browser address box.

Provide plain text link navigation equivalents

Navigation links are usually created using Flash, rollover buttons, or widgets to provide visual interest and excitement to the user's experience. **Rollover buttons** are sets of buttons that change appearance when the user points to, presses, or clicks them. When you create navigation elements with anything other than plain text (a set of Flash buttons, for example), it's important to provide plain text equivalents in case users don't have the technology necessary to view the content. Many sites add these plain text links across the bottom of each page.

Styling Text for the Web

You learned about the importance of using Cascading Style Sheets (CSS) for formatting, specifically CSS3, the latest W3C standard. In Chapter 4 you used CSS to create div tags to place content on the project index page and you changed some of the div properties to customize the page to fit the content. Not only do CSS save web authors time, but they also help keep web pages consistent and make them accessible for users. External style sheets are especially useful because you can use them to format all the pages on a website, whereas internal style sheets only format a single page. Remember also to take

Figure 13 *Usability.gov website*
Usability.gov website – www.usability.gov

advantage of style sheet properties to style for the Semantic Web, remembering to use values such as "small" or "large" for font properties rather than a specific pixel value, as you learned in Chapter 4.

CSS are made up of sets of formatting attributes called **rules**, which define the appearance and placement of page content. Style sheets are classified by where the code is stored: in a separate file (**external style sheet**), as part of the head content of an individual web page (**internal or embedded style**), or as part of the body of the HTML code (**inline style**). External CSS are saved as files with the .css file extension and stored in the website's directory structure. External style sheets are the preferred method for creating and applying styles. CSS are also classified by their selector type. A **Class type** can be used to format any page element. An **ID type** and a **Tag type** are used to redefine an HTML tag. A **Compound type** is used to format a selection. You define the type of rule when you create it, as shown in Figure 14. As you create styles, the code is generated in the style sheet. An example of code for an external style sheet is shown in Figure 15.

Using CSS saves an enormous amount of time. Being able to define a rule and then apply it to page elements across the site means that you can make hundreds of formatting changes quickly. Style sheets also create a more uniform look from page to page and they generate much cleaner code. **Clean HTML code** is code that does what it's supposed to

Figure 14 *New CSS Rule dialog box*

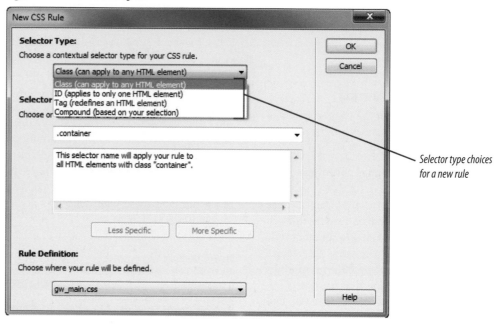

Selector type choices for a new rule

Figure 15 *Example code from a CSS file*

```
1   @charset "utf-8";
2   body {
3       margin: 0;
4       padding: 0;
5       color: #FFFFFF;
6       font-family: Verdana, Arial, Helvetica, sans-serif;
7       font-size: 100%;
8       line-height: 1.4;
9       background-color: #FFFFFF;
10  }
11  .right_image {
12      float: left;
13      height: 400px;
14      width: 43px;
15  }
```

Figures © Cengage Learning 2013

Working with Text

do without using unnecessary instructions, which can take up memory.

Not only do style sheets create uniformity and cleaner code, but most importantly, they separate the development of content from the way the content is presented, making pages more compliant with current accessibility standards.

Most sites today are delivered on multiple devices, so it's smart to define separate style sheets for mobile content. Separate style sheets will ensure that the content will appear correctly when it's accessed on multiple devices. You can also define separate style sheets for printed content.

Other strategies for styling your written content include the following:

■ **Use templates for consistency across the pages**
Templates provide a way to present content in a consistent way with repeating objects like navigation bars in the same location on each page. They also provide a way to update the content quickly without making it necessary to open and edit each page separately.

■ **Use good contrast between the text and background**
Good contrast for text is a basic accessibility issue, and it's easy to attain. Dark text on a light background or light text on a dark background makes text more readable for all users.

■ **Choose fonts designed for screen-based viewing**
Until the WOFF format becomes the standard text formatting method for web pages, choose fonts that display clearly on screen and that are reasonably available using the major browsers.

■ **Include a link to a printer-friendly page for content that may be printed**
If you expect your users will want to print page content (e.g., for directions to your building), it's helpful to create a printer-friendly page. **Printer-friendly pages** duplicate formatted content so it will print correctly, without omitting the ends of lines or printing extraneous pages. Consider also omitting unnecessary content, such as navigation bars, to help save time, paper, and toner.

■ **Use leading, tracking, and kerning to space text**
Leading refers to the space between two lines of type. It's measured in points from baseline to baseline. You can adjust leading to increase readability or to make a type passage stand out on a page.

Tracking refers to the space between characters in a block of text. Increasing a tracking value spreads the characters f a r t h e r a p a r t; decreasing tracking moves them closertogether. **Kerning** is similar to tracking, but refers to the spacing between two characters. Sometimes a wider or narrower character needs to be moved closer or farther away from the character next to it.

Working with Text Using Adobe DREAMWEAVER, ILLUSTRATOR, AND FLASH

Introduction

Every application handles text in a different way, depending on its purpose. For example, you use Adobe Dreamweaver to create websites and web pages; you use Adobe Flash to create animation for the Web; and you use Adobe Illustrator to create vector images for print or online projects. You use InDesign to create electronic publications such as apps, eMagazines and eBooks. Of the Adobe applications, InDesign is the closest to a text editor, but all are capable of generating and formatting text. The way you enter, position, and style text is slightly different with each application. Let's look at the way you work with text using each one.

Working with Text in Dreamweaver

To add text to web pages using Dreamweaver, you can either type the text, use the File > Import command to import a Word document, or paste text onto a page. It's easier to start with text that isn't formatted. If it has been formatted, use the Property inspector to remove all prior formatting. Once you have "clean" text to work with, use style sheets to apply all formatting; don't use manual formatting, such as indented or centered

Figure 16 *W3C CSS Validation Service*
Courtesy of w3.org

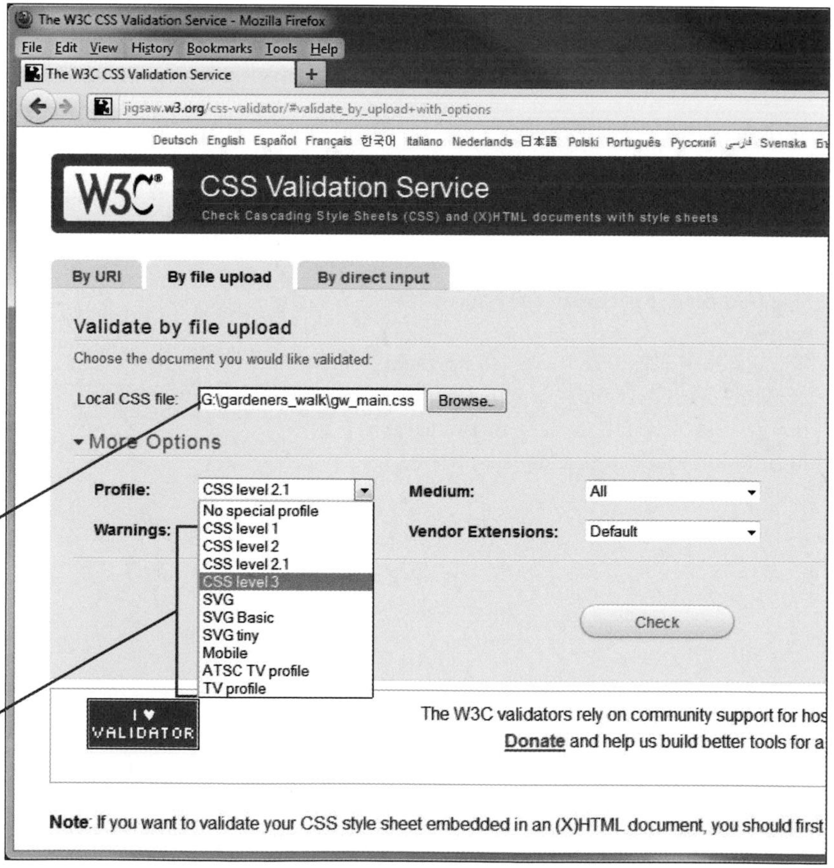

Location of local file to validate

Validation options

paragraphs, or lists. Remember that CSS3 is the current standard for style sheets. Once you've used style sheets to format your content, you can upload your file to validate that your code is compliant with CSS3 standards by using the CSS Validation Service at jigsaw.w3.org/css-validator/#validate_by_upload+with_options as shown in Figure 16. After you click the Check button, you'll receive the results of the validation, as shown in Figure 17. Pages that have been validated can display either of the two icons shown in the results to prove that they are CSS3 compliant.

Let's go over a few examples of creating a new rule, creating a new style sheet file, editing a rule, applying a rule to text, and attaching a style sheet file to an HTML page.

Figure 17 *W3C CSS Validator results*
Courtesy of w3.org

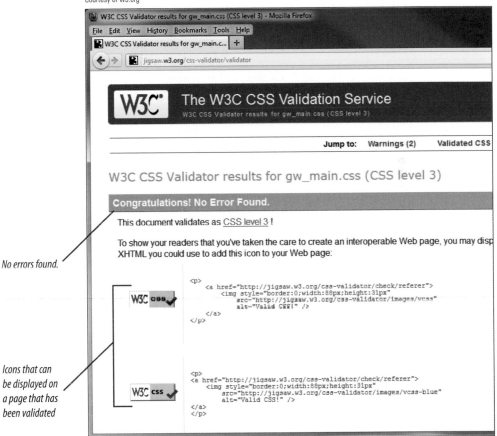

No errors found.

Icons that can be displayed on a page that has been validated

Create a New CSS Rule in Dreamweaver

To create a new rule, and unless you're going to type the code into an existing style sheet file, open an HTML page in your website in Dreamweaver, then follow the steps below:

1. Click the **New CSS Rule button** 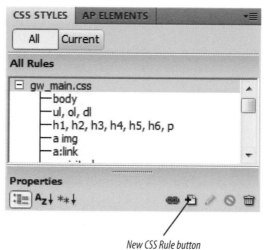 on the CSS Styles panel, as shown in Figure 18.

2. Choose a **Selector Type**, choose or enter a **Selector Name**, then choose where your rule will be defined, as shown in Figure 19.

   The selector types are Class, ID, Tag, and Compound. You can use a **Class type** to format any page element. You can use an **ID type** or **Tag type** to redefine an HTML tag. A **Compound type** is used to format a selection. You can choose an existing rule or tag to create your rule, or you can type a new name in the Selector Name text box. Use the Rule Definition list arrow to choose whether your rule will be added to an existing style sheet, a new style sheet, or in the document page code.

   (continued)

Figure 18 *New CSS Rule button*

New CSS Rule button

Figure 19 *New CSS Rule dialog box*

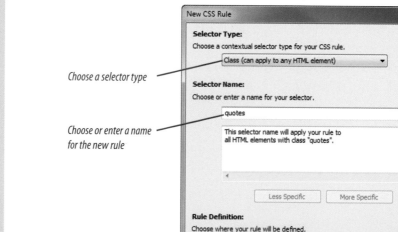

Choose a selector type

Choose or enter a name for the new rule

Choose where your new rule will be defined

Figures © Cengage Learning 2013

Working with Text

Figure 20 *CSS Rule Definition dialog box*

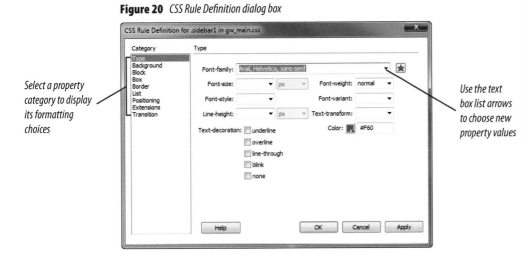

Select a property category to display its formatting choices

Use the text box list arrows to choose new property values

Figure 21 *New Document dialog box*

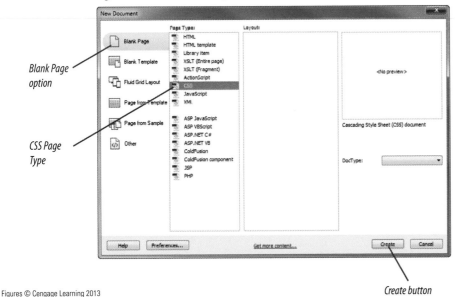

Blank Page option

CSS Page Type

Create button

3. Click **OK**, select a Category to display its formatting choices, then enter your new values, as shown in Figure 20.

   You don't have to specify every Type property and value for a new style. For instance, if the Font-family property is left undefined, it will be automatically inherited from the parent container. **Inheritance** is a CSS governing principle that allows for the properties of a parent container (like body or div tags) to be used to format the content in a child container (another div tag, table, etc.).

4. Click **OK** to close the CSS Rule Definition dialog box.

Create a New Style Sheet File in Dreamweaver

To create a new style sheet file, you can simply type a new name in the Rule Definition text box in the New CSS Rule dialog box. Another option is to use the Dreamweaver menu.

1. Click **File** on the Menu bar, then click **New**.

2. Click **Blank Page** in the New Document dialog box if necessary, click **CSS** in the Page Type column, then click **Create**, as shown in Figure 21.

Edit a Rule in Dreamweaver

To edit a rule, refer to the following steps:

1. Select the **rule name** in the CSS Style panel, then click the **Edit Rule button** 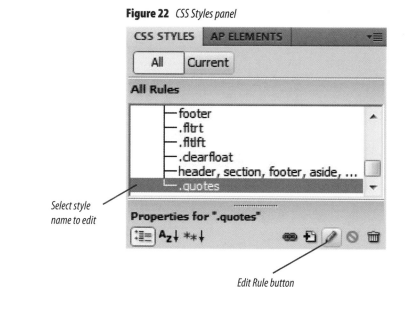, as shown in Figure 22.

TIP You can also double-click the rule name to open the Rule Definition dialog box.

2. Select the appropriate **Category name** in the CSS Rule Definition dialog box for the property you want to modify, enter the **new property value**, then click **OK**.

Or

1. With the insertion point in a text block that has a rule applied to it, click the CSS button on the Property inspector to display the CSS Property inspector, if necessary.

2. Click **Edit Rule** on the CSS Property inspector, as shown in Figure 23.

3. Select the appropriate **Category name** in the CSS Rule Definition dialog box for the property you want to modify, enter the **new property values**, then click **OK**.

Or

1. Type your changes in Code view.

   If you're using an external style sheet, the changes will be made to all text with that style on every page in the website.

Figure 22 *CSS Styles panel*

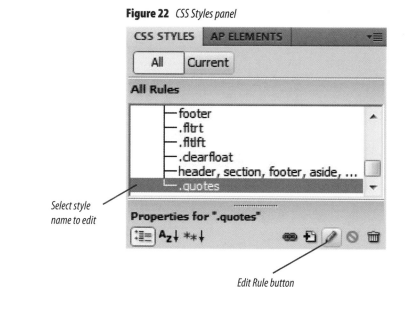

Select style name to edit

Edit Rule button

Figure 23 *Using the CSS Property inspector to edit a CSS rule*

Clicking the CSS button displays the CSS Property inspector

Click to edit rule

Figure 24 *Using the CSS Property inspector to apply a rule*

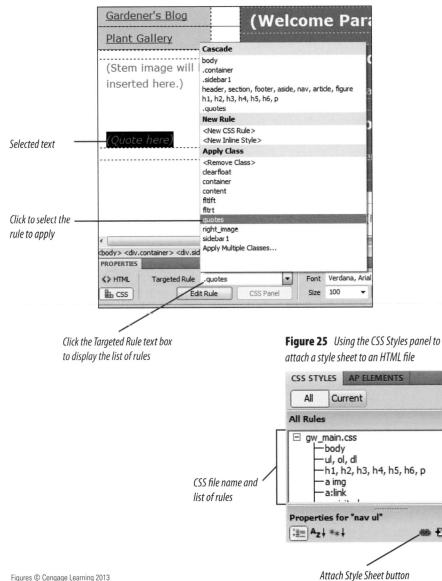

Selected text

Click to select the
rule to apply

Click the Targeted Rule text box
to display the list of rules

Figure 25 *Using the CSS Styles panel to attach a style sheet to an HTML file*

CSS file name and
list of rules

Attach Style Sheet button

Apply a Rule to Text in Dreamweaver

To use an existing rule to format text:

1. Select the text that you want to format with a CSS rule.

2. Click the **Targeted Rule text box** on the CSS Property inspector, then click to select the rule name, as shown in Figure 24.

Attach a Style Sheet File to an HTML File in Dreamweaver

To attach a style sheet file to an HTML file:

1. Open a page in Dreamweaver, then click the **Attach Style Sheet button** 🔗 on the CSS Styles panel, as shown in Figure 25.

2. Browse to select the name of the style sheet file you want to attach, then click **OK**.

   If the style sheet is successfully attached, you will see the name of the CSS file and its list of rules in the CSS Styles panel.

Working with Text in Illustrator

Illustrator offers a superb array of options for working with text and formatting type.

There are three methods for creating text in Illustrator: type at a point, type in an area, and type on a path. The method you choose to use depends on the aesthetic goal you have in mind. For example, if you would like to title an arc over an image, as seen in many logo treatments, you would use the type on a path method. You perform each of these methods by selecting the appropriate tool in the Illustrator tools panel, shown in Figure 26. You can also create type in each of these methods, either horizontally or vertically.

Let's explore these methods for creating text in Illustrator.

Figure 26 *Type tool and its expanded options*

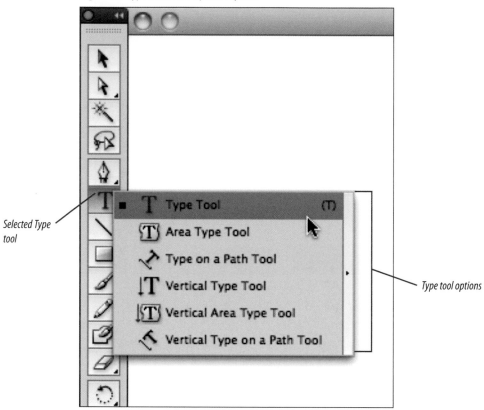

Selected Type tool

Type tool options

Figure © Cengage Learning 2013

Figure 27 *Insertion point indicates where you will enter new type*

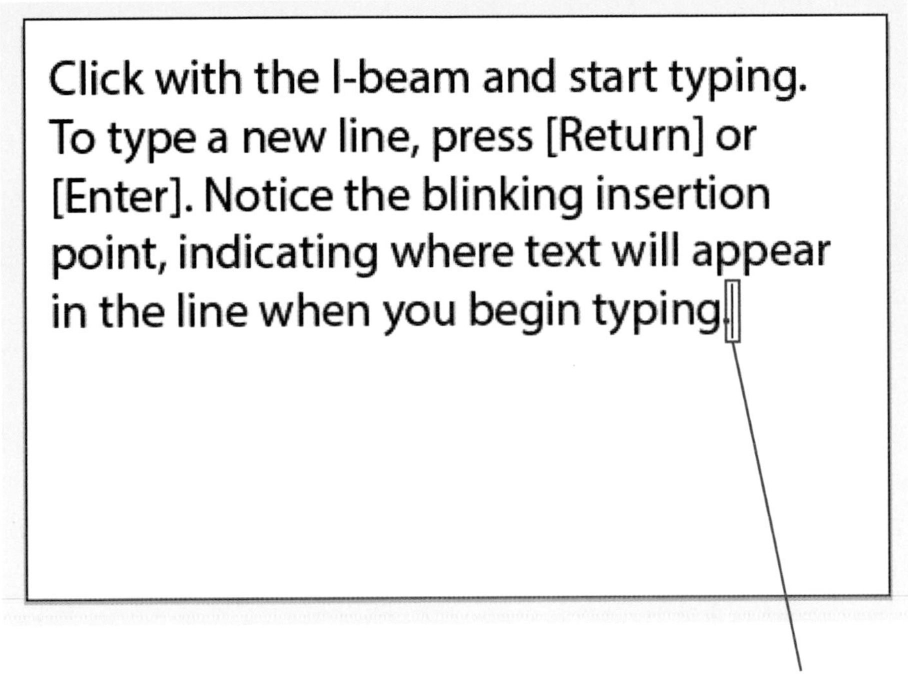

Click with the I-beam and start typing. To type a new line, press [Return] or [Enter]. Notice the blinking insertion point, indicating where text will appear in the line when you begin typing.

Blinking insertion point

Figure © Cengage Learning 2013

Working with Text

Type at a Point in Illustrator

Just as you would enter text in a basic word processing program, click at a point in a document with the Type tool, and start typing.

1. Create a new document in Illustrator.

2. Select the **Type tool** in the Tools panel.

   After you move the pointer over the document, the mouse pointer changes to an I-beam pointer; this is your starting mark. The small horizontal line toward the bottom of the I-beam, called the baseline, determines where the text rests.

3. Click anywhere in the document and start typing.

   Notice the insertion point at the end of the paragraph in Figure 27. This shows the point where you last entered text. New text will begin at this point when you begin typing unless you move the I-beam pointer and click in another location.

4. Press **[Enter]** or **[Return]** to start a new line. To add a letter, word, or line to an existing text block, click between any two letters and start typing.

5. To select the block of text so you can move it around, choose the **Selection tool** , or right-click (Windows) or Ctrl-click (Mac) the text, point to **Transform**, then click **Move**.

6. To go back and edit the text within the block, select the Type tool and click inside the text block to place the insertion point.

Type in an Area In Illustrator

Typing in an area creates text that flows within a defined area or shape. See Figure 28.

1. Press and hold the current **Shape tool** in the Illustrator Tools panel and choose the **Star Tool**, as shown in Figure 29.

2. Drag on the document to create the star shape.

3. Select the **Area Type tool** or **Vertical Area Type tool** in the Tools panel, click on the edge of the star shape (the shape's path), and in the Properties panel along the top of the Illustrator screen, select a font size, type, and color. See Figure 30.

(continued)

Figure 28 *An example of type flowing within a shape*

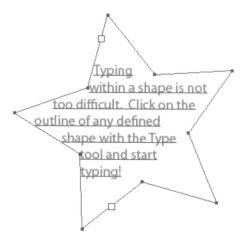

Figure 29 *Shape tools available in Illustrator*

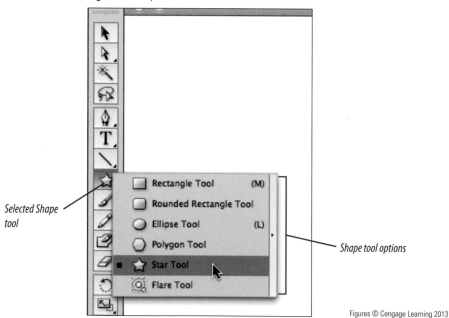

Selected Shape tool

Shape tool options

Working with Text

Figure 30 *Text formatting options using the Illustrator Properties panel*

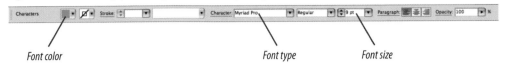

Font color   Font type   Font size

Figure 31 *An example of text along a spiraling path*

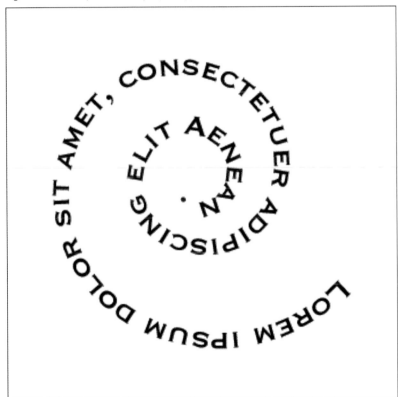

Clicking on the path converts the shape to a text container; the blinking insertion point indicates that you can begin typing.

4. Type some text and notice how the text fills only the shape area, either horizontally or vertically, depending on what area type tool you chose in Step 3.

   Note: If you type more than can fit in the defined area, a small red box with a plus sign appears at the bottom of the text block, indicating that part of the text is hidden. To fix this problem, you can either use a smaller font size or scale the text area to make it larger. To scale the text area, choose View > Show Bounding Box, then select the area and drag the transform handles.

Type on a Path in Illustrator

In Illustrator you can also create text that flows along an open or closed path. An example of an open path is a straight line. An example of a closed path is a circle. To do this, use the Type tool, Type on a Path tool, Vertical Type tool, or Vertical Type on a Path tool, depending on your preference. Figure 31 shows text typed along a spiraling path.

1. Create a line or shape in Illustrator.

2. Select the **Type on a Path tool** from the Tools panel. Click on the path (tool edge) of the shape or line, and begin typing.

(continued)

3. You might need to move text along its path and adjust its orientation. To move text along a path, first select the path with the **Selection tool**. A bracket appears at the beginning, middle, and end of the path. Place the mouse pointer over the middle bracket until an icon that looks like an upside-down T appears. Click and drag on the middle bracket to move the path. The brackets on each end of the type line adjust the distance between the beginning and end of the typed line. See Figure 32.

4. To adjust other path options, select the text and, from the Illustrator main menu, choose **Type > Type on a Path > Type on a Path Options**. See Figure 33.

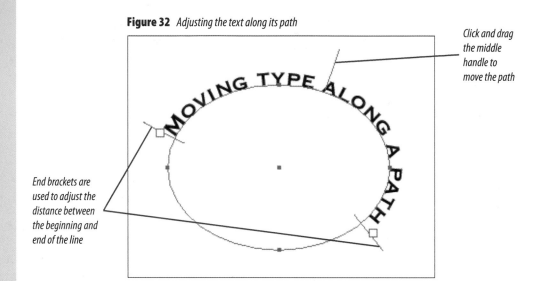

Figure 32 *Adjusting the text along its path*

Click and drag the middle handle to move the path

End brackets are used to adjust the distance between the beginning and end of the line

Figure 33 *Type on a Path Options dialog box*

Type on a Path Options

Effect: Rainbow ☐ Flip OK

Align to Path: Baseline Cancel

Spacing: Auto ☑ Preview

Working with Text

Working with Text in Flash

Text created in Flash is rendered within an optimized Flash movie. Your goal is to provide the best options for optimum text display. These options vary depending on whether you're building your text within an ActionScript 2.0 or ActionScript 3.0 file with Flash Player 10 or above. ActionScript 3.0 files support both Classic Text (the only option for ActionScript 2.0) and the **Text Layout Framework (TLF)** text properties. TLF, together with the Flash Player 10 text engine and AIR 1.5, aims to deliver multilingual, print-quality typography for the web.

There are three types of text in Flash—static, input, and dynamic. We'll explore static and input text in the step-by-step sections on the following page.

Static text displays text that doesn't change within your Flash movie (or SWF). It's embedded when you publish the movie. **Input text** allows you to create form fields in which users enter text that can either be sent back to them or to another receiving party (e.g., the owner of the website or the site administrator). Unlike static text, input text can also have an instance name applied to it so that it can be called through ActionScript.

Dynamic text displays text created in response to a variable. It can be imported at the run time of a SWF from another source, such as a text (.txt) file outside of Flash, or a database with continuously updated content like stock quotes or the weather report. Dynamic text can be updated outside of Flash, have HTML style properties defined within it, and can be made accessible to screen readers. Like input text, dynamic text can also have an instance name applied to it so that it can be called through ActionScript.

Another unique feature of text in Flash is that it can be represented in two ways: (1) as **font outlines** (characters broken down into shapes) that are embedded within a published Flash document (SWF) or (2) by **device fonts**, which is a font determined by a specific font name (Arial, Verdana, Comic Sans, etc.) or general font type like serif or sans-serif that must be located on the end-user's computer.

The advantage of embedded fonts is that the typographic design of a movie is uncompromised, maintaining the layout envisioned by the designer. The disadvantage is that they increase the size of the SWF file and, depending on the font style and size, can make the text less legible than if it were rendered with a device font. Device fonts are an alternative to embedded fonts and result in a smaller SWF file. They're also more legible at font sizes below 10 points. However, remember that if a user's computer doesn't have an installed font that corresponds to the device font, text may look different than expected. Flash includes three generic device fonts, and when you specify one of these fonts and then export the document, Flash Player uses the font on the user's computer that most closely resembles the generic device font:

- _sans (similar to Helvetica or Arial)
- _serif (similar to Times Roman)
- _typewriter (similar to Courier)

Create Static Text in Flash

When creating static text, you can place text on a single line that expands as you type (called label text) or in a fixed-width (horizontal) or fixed-height (vertical) field that expands and wraps words automatically (called block text). Follow these steps to learn how to create each type.

To create label text:

1. Open a new document in Flash, choosing a document type such as ActionScript 3.0.
2. Select the **Text tool** T in the Tools panel, and be sure the Classic Text and Static Text options are selected in the Properties panel. See Figure 34.
3. In the Properties panel, choose a font family, style, size, and color for the text, also shown in Figure 34.
4. Click once on the Stage and start typing.

   As you type, the text line grows longer, until you press [Enter] or [Return] to start a new line. This is called label text, as indicated by a circle in the upper-right corner of the box. See Figure 35.

Figure 34 *Selecting the Text tool and formatting options*

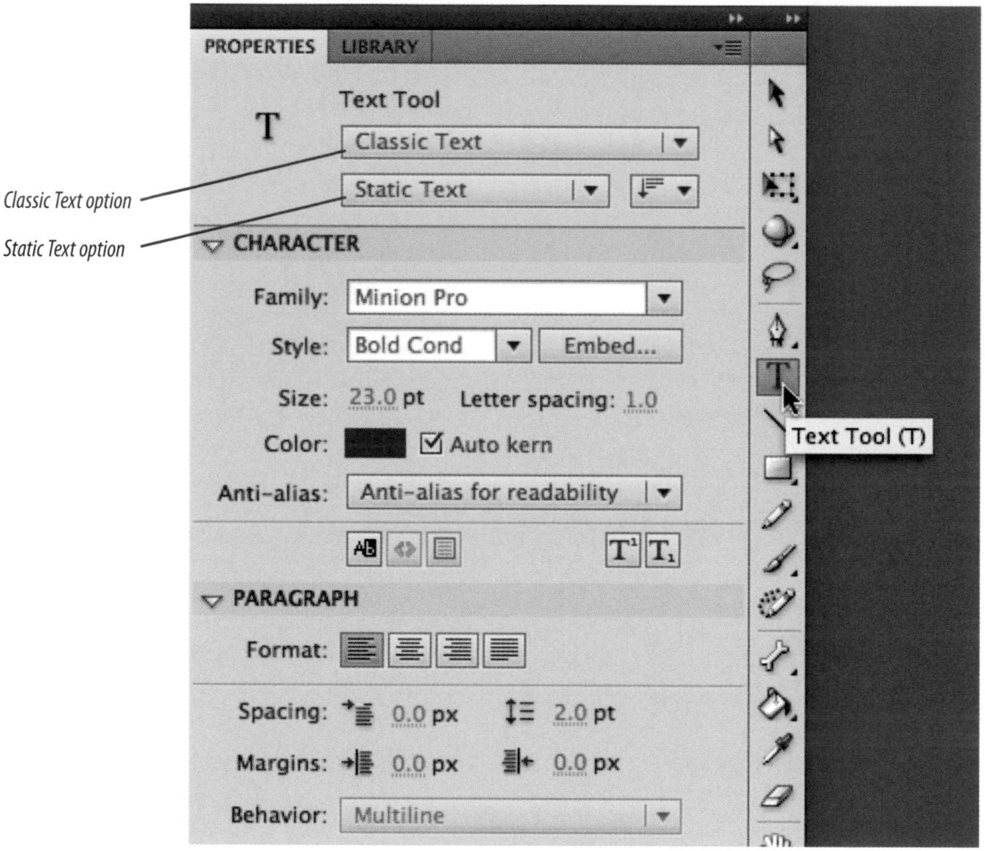

Classic Text option

Static Text option

Figure 35 *Viewing label text*

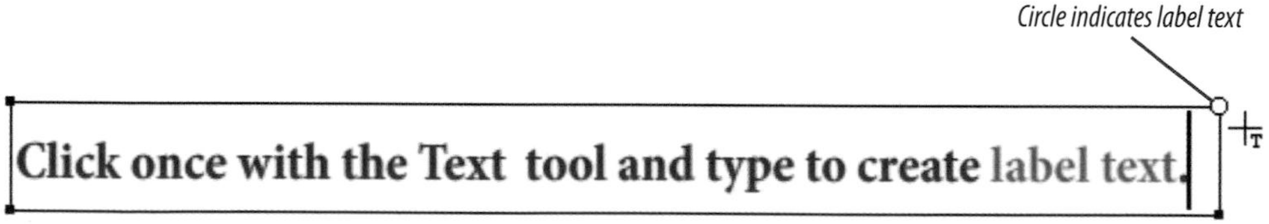

Circle indicates label text

Click once with the Text tool and type to create label text.

Figures © Cengage Learning 2013

Working with Text

Figure 36 *Viewing a text block*

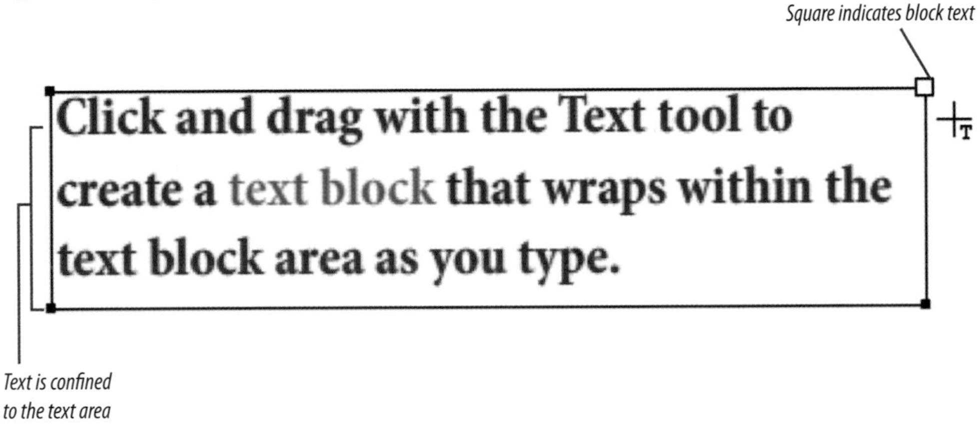

Square indicates block text

Click and drag with the Text tool to create a text block that wraps within the text block area as you type.

Text is confined
to the text area

Figure 37 *Placing the static text elements*

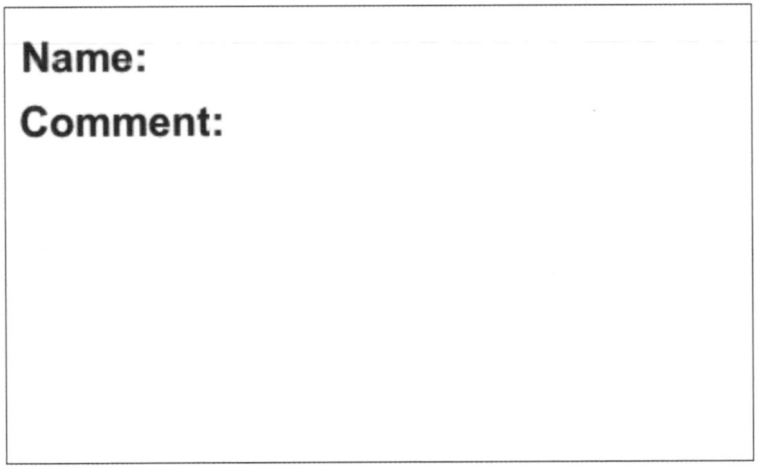

Name:
Comment:

To create block text (also referred to as area or paragraph text):

1. Select the **Text tool** T in the Tools panel, and be sure the Classic Text and Static Text options are selected in the Properties panel. Refer again to Figure 34.

2. Drag across the Stage to determine the width of the text area you would like. Start typing in the block; when you reach the end of the first line, the text automatically wraps to the next line. This is called block text, as indicated by the square in the top-right corner of the box. See Figure 36.

Create Input Text in Flash

To create a simple form interface using input text:

1. Create a new Flash ActionScript 3.0 document.

2. With the Static Text type selected on the Properties panel, click in your document with the Text tool and type **Name:** [leave space to enter name].

3. Click under Name: and type **Comment:**
   See the example in Figure 37.

4. Use the Text type drop-down menu in the Properties panel to switch from Static Text to Input Text.

5. Drag a text block after the Name: area on the document.

(continued)

6. Drag a text block after the Comment: area on the document.

   You'll know you're working in Input Text when the text blocks you created are surrounded by a dotted line, as shown in Figure 38.

7. To move the input text fields, choose the **Selection tool** at the top of the Tools panel, then drag the **field** to adjust placement as desired.

8. Drag the field's sizing handles to resize the field if necessary.

(continued)

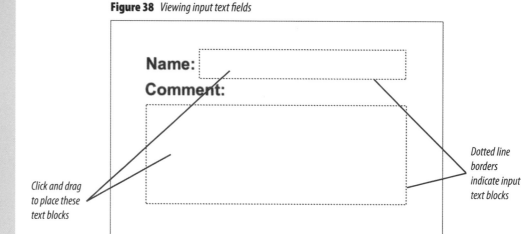

Figure 38 *Viewing input text fields*

Click and drag to place these text blocks

Dotted line borders indicate input text blocks

Working with Text

Figure 39 *Setting properties for input text fields*

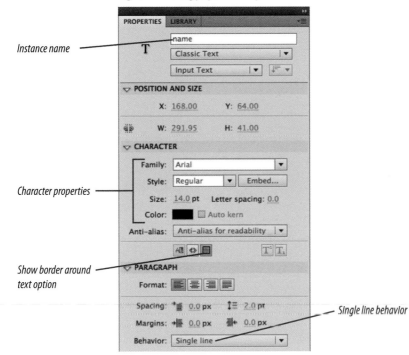

Instance name

Character properties

Show border around text option

Single line behavior

9. With the Selection tool, click the **Name: input text field** to select it, and in the Properties panel set the following, as shown in Figure 39:
   - Instance name: **name**
   - Character: Family: **Arial**, Style: **Regular**
   - Character: Size: **14 pt**
   - Character: Color: **Black**
   - Character: **The Show border around text option**
   - Paragraph: Behavior: **Single line**

10. Next, with the Selection tool, select the **Comments: input text field** and in the Properties panel, set the following:
    - Instance Name: **comments**
    - Character: Family: **Arial**, Style: **Regular**
    - Character: Size: **14 pt**
    - Character: Color: **black**
    - Character: **The Show border around text option**
    - Paragraph: Behavior: **Multiline**

11. From the main menu, choose **Control > Test Movie > In Flash Professional.** When the SWF opens, type your name and comments in the appropriate form fields to test the display of the inputted text. See Figure 40.

Figure 40 *Viewing information entered in input text fields*

Name: Annesa Hartman

Comment:

Wow! Working with input text is pretty cool. As I type the content flows within the comments box, because in the Properties panel the Behavior was set to Multiline.

ADDING AND FORMATTING TEXT WITH CSS

Introduction

After you've determined the framework that includes your basic design plan, you can begin placing and formatting the text. Most website content is in the form of text, so you want the text to get your message across in an attractive, efficient way. In this section, we'll place the text on the home page for the Gardener's Walk website and use CSS to format it. If you're going to create a different kind of interactive media project, your steps will differ. If you're using Flash or Illustrator, refer to the information in the previous section. We'll use Adobe Dreamweaver to demonstrate these steps. While you're working through them, you may choose to follow along with a practice site.

Adding Text

In the steps that follow, we'll add text to the home page in the content, sidebar1, and footer elements. You may recall that we set the text properties for these containers in Chapter 4. The white text in the content article is a property inherited from the body tag, which we modified in Chapter 4. After we type the text, we'll edit the formatting used for some of the headings.

Modifying Rules to Enhance Text Presentation

You can modify the properties and values of any HTML tags or div tags to format text. For example, you can change their position, color, font, and font size. Remember the theory of Cascading Style Sheets: properties and values of parent tags are inherited by all child tags unless otherwise specified. When possible, try to use external style sheets for all formatting so that any changes you make are applied globally across the entire project. We like the idea of using rounded corners (a new feature in CSS3) for the content div to help set off the main text, as shown in Figure 41.

Adding a Search Text Box

HTML5 has added an easy way to incorporate a site search feature with a simple search form. We decided to add a search form to the top of our home page by adding code where we want the search form to appear, also shown in Figure 41. There are several other search forms available that are free to download and use such as those included with Google Web Elements at google.com/webelements. You test a search form after you've published the site. To test the search form we used, go to the live site at gardenerswalk.com.

Testing for CSS3 Validation

After you complete additions to your pages, it's a good idea to submit the style sheet to the W3C CSS Validation Service. Correcting any errors as you go is much simpler than waiting until the project is finished. You can choose the CSS level you'd like to use for validation: CSS level 1, level 2, level 2.1, or level 3. To submit a style sheet for validation, you can enter a URL, upload the file, or input the code directly. You can request that the report submit both errors and warnings. Errors include code that will present a problem, while warnings include code that might present problems. You can also specify the medium that the code will be checked against, for example: handheld, print, Braille, and TV. The address for the CSS Validation Service is jigsaw.w3.org/css-validator.

Figure 41 *CSS3 rounded corners and search form added*

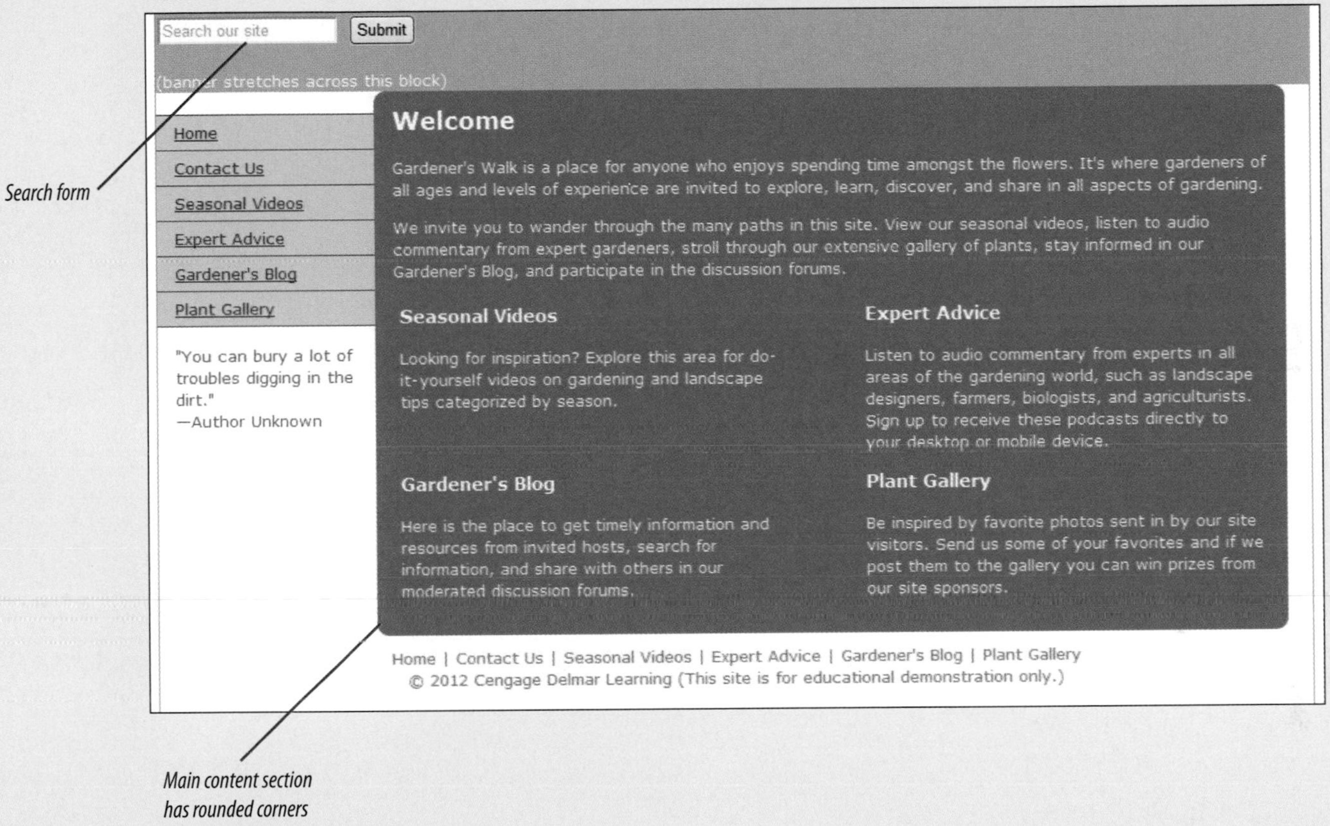

Search form

Main content section has rounded corners

Add text

1. Open the project home page in Dreamweaver and locate its page layout from your wireframe.

2. Using the wireframe for guidance, type or import text in the locations you've specified.

Since we wanted four paragraphs that describe our other pages to appear in two columns under the introductory paragraph, we deleted the two section tags under the introduction and inserted two divs in their place. But before we inserted the divs, we added two new class rules to the style sheet called "flt_lf_360" and "flt_rt_360" which we'll use to style them. Dreamweaver added placeholder text in the divs, as shown in Figure 42. Refer to Figure 43 to see the text after it is placed in the divs. The settings used for the two divs are as follows:

.flt_lt_360	.flt_rt_360
ID: left_column	ID: right_column
Box Width: 360px	Box Width: 360px
Padding: 5px	Padding: 5px
Box Float: left	Box Float: right

3. Use the Property inspector to experiment with heading formats, as shown in Figure 44.

We adjusted the spacing between paragraphs by adding bottom margins to the appropriate CSS rules.

4. We changed the body tag's font-size property value to "small."

Figure 42 *Two divs add two columns of text*

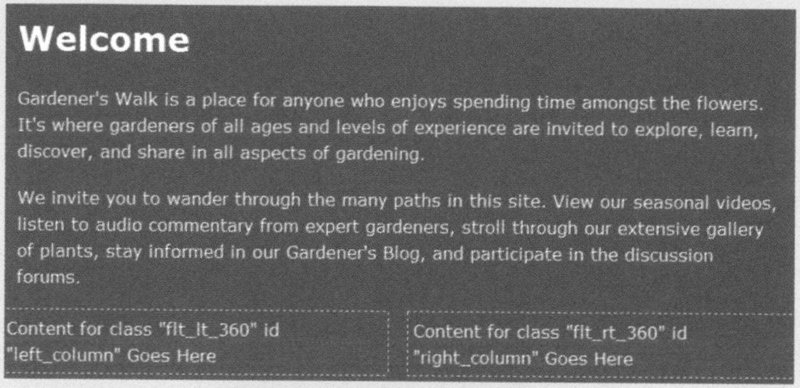

Figure 43 *Two divs with content placed*

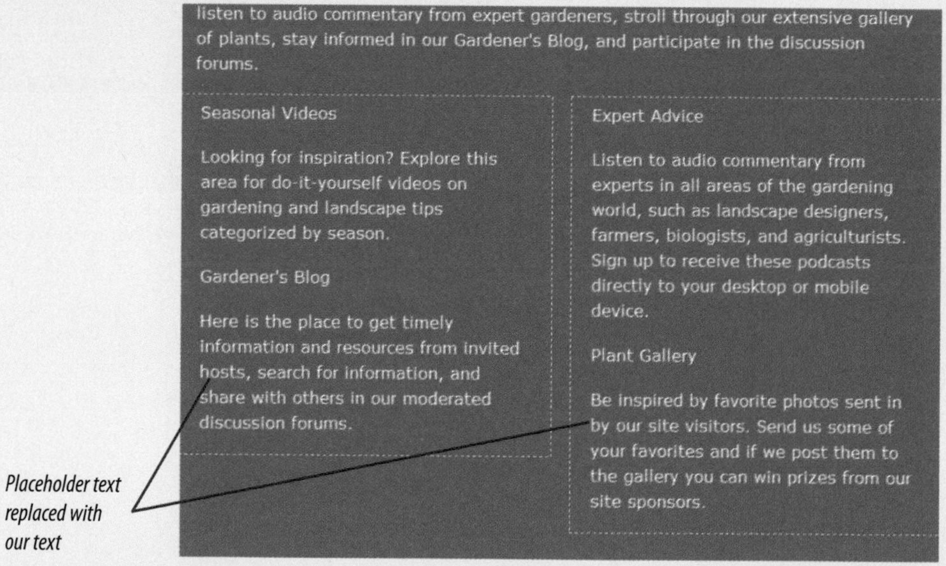

Placeholder text replaced with our text

Figures © Cengage Learning 2013

Working with Text

Figure 44 *Heading formats applied to headings*

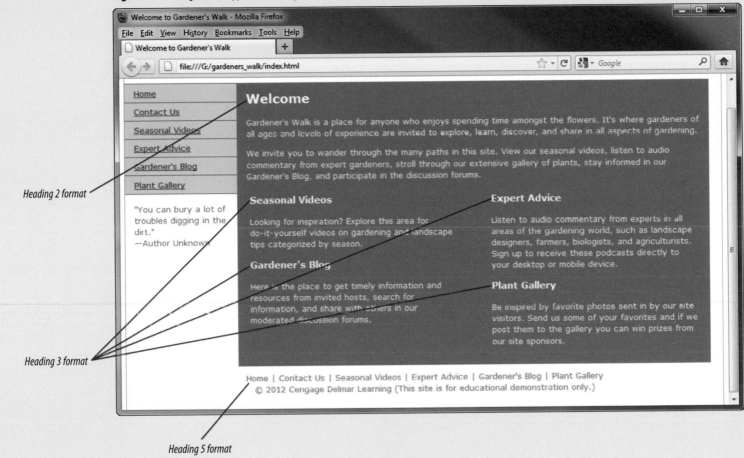

Figure © Cengage Learning 2013

Modify rules to enhance text presentation

You can add the following code to a container tag to create four identical rounded corners to the div, as shown in Figure 45. The larger the pixel value, the "more round" the corners.

border-radius: 10px;

You can also specify a different radius for each corner or a different shape for the corners. For instance, to create two rounded corners at the top with slightly different shapes, but square corners at the bottom, modify the code to:

border-radius: 21px 10px 0px 0px;

You can also use a unit of measure other than pixel, such as percentage (%) or em.

Figure 45 *Modifying the content rule to add rounded corners*

```
.content {
    width: 760px;
    float: right;
    background-color: #4A8217;
    padding-top: 10px;
    padding-right: 0;
    padding-bottom: 10px;
    padding-left: 0;
    margin-right: 20px;
    border-radius: 10px;
}
```

Code added to container rule

Figure © Cengage Learning 2013

Add a site search form with HTML5

1. We searched for some examples for an HTML5 site search form for our page using "HTML5 site search" as the search string.

2. We then went to Google and searched through the Google web elements at google.com/webelements for a search form.

3. We selected one of the free JavaScript forms from javascriptkit.com, as shown on our page in Figure 46. To see the code we used, go to the live gardenerswalk.com site and view the code in the head content for any of the pages. Be sure to include all of the code in the script if you decide to use it to adhere to their stated terms of use.

QUICK TIP

To view the source code in a browser, look for a command similar to View > View Source (Safari), Tools > Web Developer > Page Source (Firefox), or Tools > View source (Chrome).

Figure 46 *Search form added to the page*

Search text box

```
Search our site     Submit
(banner stretches across this block)

Home
Contact Us
Seasonal Videos
Expert Advice
Gardener's Blog
Plant Gallery

"You can bury a lot of
troubles digging in the
dirt."
—Author Unknown
```

Welcome

Gardener's Walk is a place for anyone who enjoys spending time amongst the flowers. It's where gardeners of all ages and levels of experience are invited to explore, learn, discover, and share in all aspects of gardening.

We invite you to wander through the many paths in this site. View our seasonal videos, listen to audio commentary from expert gardeners, stroll through our extensive gallery of plants, stay informed in our Gardener's Blog, and participate in the discussion forums.

Seasonal Videos

Looking for inspiration? Explore this area for do-it-yourself videos on gardening and landscape tips categorized by season.

Expert Advice

Listen to audio commentary from experts in all areas of the gardening world, such as landscape designers, farmers, biologists, and agriculturists. Sign up to receive these podcasts directly to your desktop or mobile device.

Gardener's Blog

Here is the place to get timely information and resources from invited hosts, search for information, and share with others in our moderated discussion forums.

Plant Gallery

Be inspired by favorite photos sent in by our site visitors. Send us some of your favorites and if we post them to the gallery you can win prizes from our site sponsors.

Home | Contact Us | Seasonal Videos | Expert Advice | Gardener's Blog | Plant Gallery
© 2012 Cengage Delmar Learning (This site is for educational demonstration only.)

Figure © Cengage Learning 2013

Test for CSS level 3 validation

1. To validate our style sheets, we went to jigsaw.w3.org/css-validator.

2. We clicked the **By file upload tab**.

3. We then clicked the **Profile list arrow**, then clicked **CSS level 3**.

4. We clicked the **Browse button**, located and selected our local style sheet file, then clicked the **Check button**, as shown in Figure 47.

5. Our results were displayed, as shown in Figure 48.

If you see any errors, read the documentation, which cites the line number and nature of each error. Correct them as necessary and retest the file until you don't have any errors.

Figure 47 *Validating the style sheet for CSS level 3*
Courtesy of w3.org

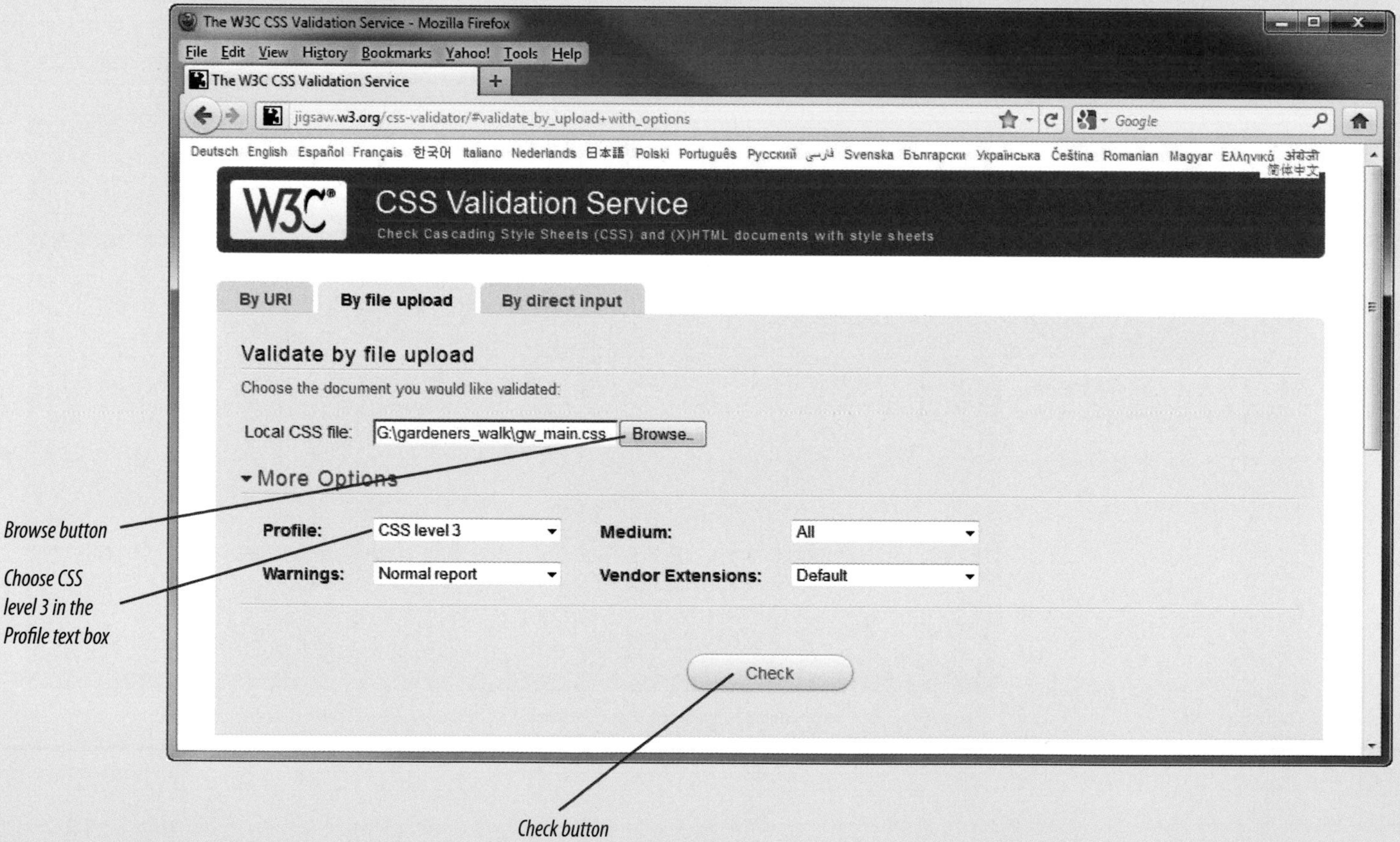

Browse button

Choose CSS level 3 in the Profile text box

Check button

Figure 48 *Viewing the validation results*

Courtesy of w3.org

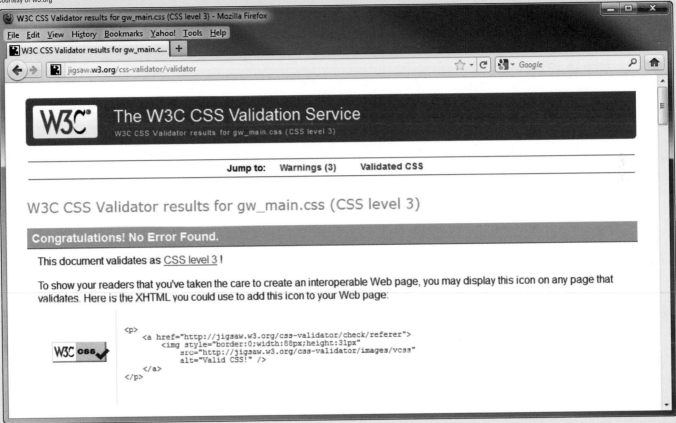

ADDING TEXT TO YOUR INTERACTIVE MEDIA PROJECT

Now that you've learned about fonts, type design, and style sheets, you're ready to incorporate text into your project. Using the wireframe you created in Chapter 3 as your guide, replace any existing placeholder text with your own headings and paragraph text.

1. If you're creating a website for your project, this is the time to create the style sheet that you'll use for each page. You can either create a new page and use the CSS Styles panel to create a new style sheet file, or you can use the File > New menu to create a blank CSS page. If you use the File > New menu, the new style sheet file will open in Code view. You can either type the code for new CSS rules in Code view, or, use the CSS Styles panel to add your rules.

2. Type, import, or copy and paste the text required for your project.

3. Apply rules from the project style sheet to all text blocks.

4. Use the CSS Validation Service to validate your style sheet as CSS3.

5. Preview your project in a browser to check for readability and appearance.

6. Refer to the design tips presented in this chapter to verify that you haven't violated an accepted design strategy.

USING WOFF FONTS

WOFF, which is discussed on page 5-13, is an interesting concept that you should learn more about. If you're in a classroom setting, work together in a group to answer the following questions. You'll probably want to begin your research on the W3C website.

1. Define WOFF and explain several benefits of using it.
2. Cite at least three websites that you can use to demonstrate WOFF fonts, such as the Microsoft website shown in Figure 49.
3. List two sources for locating WOFF fonts.
4. Write a list of steps that you would take to incorporate WOFF fonts into your project.
5. Will WOFF work on mobile devices?
6. Locate and watch a video about WOFF, and document the URL where it is published.

Figure 49 *Microsoft website demonstration of WOFF fonts*
Used with permission from Microsoft

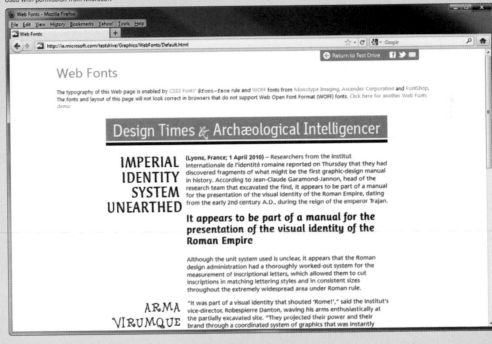

Even More to Explore

To explore some of the topics discussed in this chapter in more depth, see the References section at the end of the book. For links to additional web resources, visit the Even More to Explore link under Book Resources on Cengage Brain.

CHAPTER 6 INCORPORATING IMAGES

- Finding and Creating Images

- Applying Image Design Strategies

- Working with Images using Adobe Illustrator, Fireworks, Photoshop, Dreamweaver, and Flash

- How We Did It: Adding Images

- It's Your Turn: Adding Images to Your Interactive Media Project

- More to Explore: Using Creative Commons Licensing

CHAPTER 6 INCORPORATING IMAGES

Introduction

In the previous chapter, you explored type design principles and then applied them to the text in your interactive media project. Next, you styled your text using Cascading Style Sheets. When the majority of content takes the form of text, it's more interesting if images are used to enhance or illustrate the information. Well-designed media includes a balanced combination of text and images.

In this chapter we'll identify some good resources for finding images to add visual interest to your project. We'll add several images to our Gardener's Walk website and apply design principles that will maximize their effectiveness and impact. We'll also look at several ways to create your own images by drawing your own illustrations, using a digital camera to take photographs, and compositing multiple images to create one image.

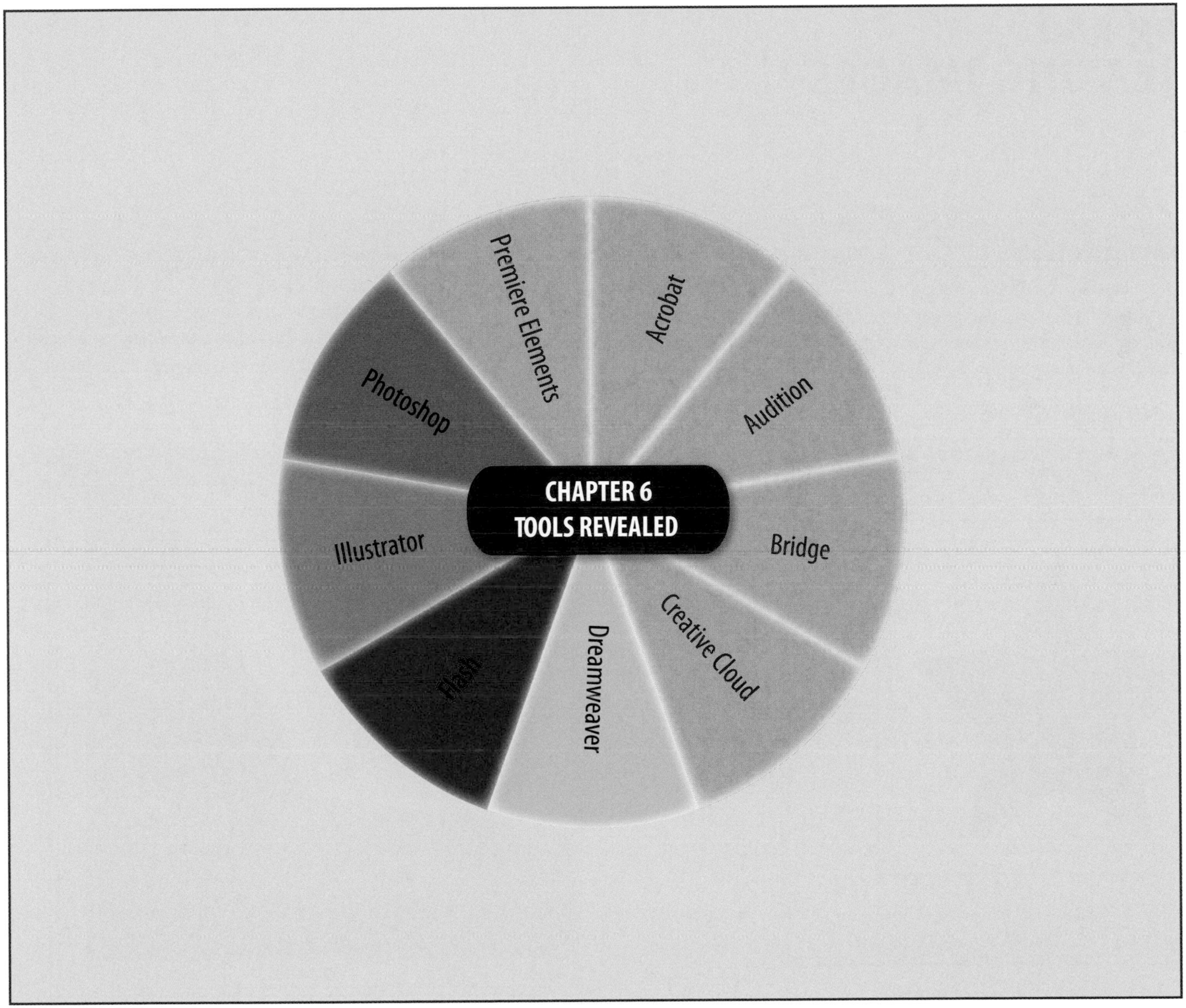
CHAPTER 6
TOOLS REVEALED
Premiere Elements
Acrobat
Audition
Bridge
Creative Cloud
Dreamweaver
Flash
Illustrator
Photoshop

Figure © Cengage Learning 2013

Finding and CREATING IMAGES

Overview of Available Tools

For creating original artwork, Adobe Illustrator is the tool of choice for most professional designers because it creates vector-based graphics. **Vector-based graphics** are scalable graphics that are built using mathematical formulas. The advantage of vector-based graphics is that they can be resized without losing image quality. For example, you can create a vector image of a business logo and reduce it to a size that will fit on a business card, or enlarge it to billboard size. Figures 1 and 2 compare a vector image at 100% and 400%. Notice that the larger image retains its quality. The star outline is smooth with no jagged edges.

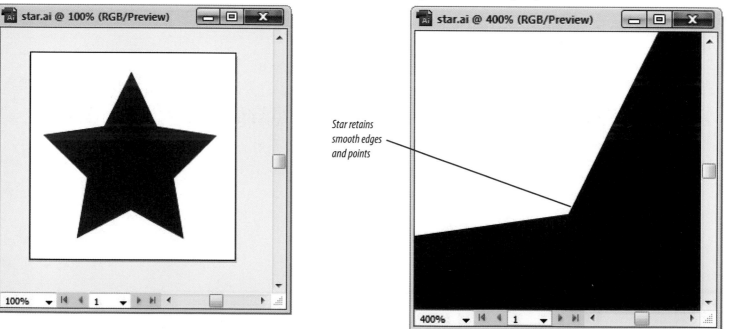

Figure 1 *Star created in Illustrator as a vector image*

Figure 2 *Star vector image magnified*

Star retains smooth edges and points

On the other hand, **Bitmaps**, or raster graphics, are built using a grid of pixels. Each color is "mapped" to a pixel on the grid. Figures 3 and 4 compare a bitmap image viewed at 100% and 300%. Notice that the image becomes blurry when the image is magnified. Although most images in media projects are bitmaps, these images often start off as vector graphics and are then converted to bitmaps. In fact, it's common practice to design and create images as vector graphics and then save a copy of them as bitmaps. That way, you can retain your original images for editing purposes, but have bitmap copies to use in your projects. Some types of bitmaps are suitable for Internet use and some for use in print. We'll explore and compare the different file types in the next section, Applying Image Design Strategies.

For image editing, Adobe Photoshop is the tool of choice for most professional designers. **Image editing** refers to changing the appearance of an image using processes such as resizing, enhancing color or contrast, or removing unwanted parts of images. Photoshop is also great for combining multiple images into one image, a process called **compositing**. Compositing is similar to

Figure 3 *Star image created in Photoshop as a bitmap or raster image*

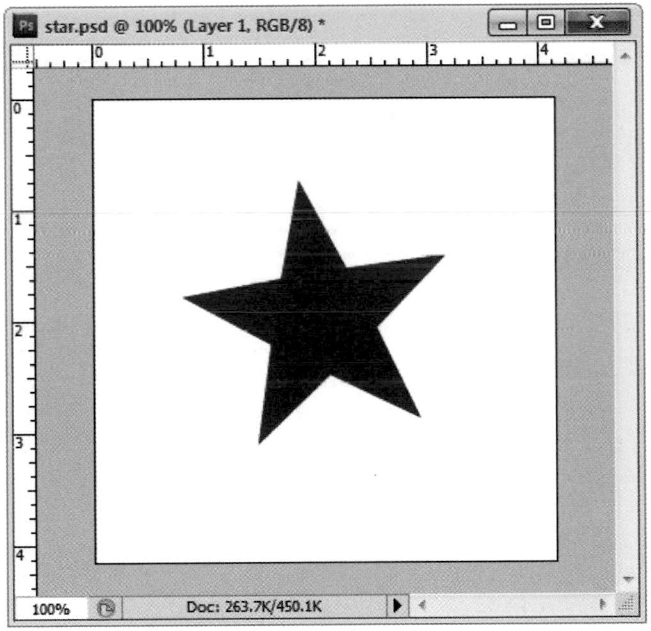

Figure 4 *Star bitmap image magnified*

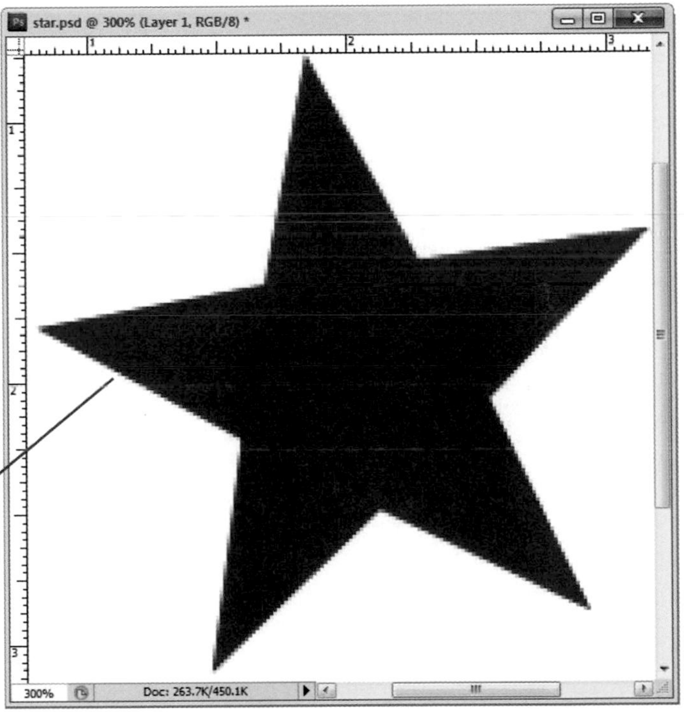

Enlarged bitmap image has jagged edges

making a collage with a selection of images. A great example of compositing is the design shown in Figure 5 that was created for a book cover. The design includes two images: an image of several referees and an image of a zebra. The black and white color scheme is consistent in both images, although the content is dramatically different. The book title includes the word "Revealed" so the image ties in with the title as the zebra, although slightly camouflaged, is "revealed."

Adobe Lightroom is a product in the Photoshop family that's used to manage and edit photographs. You can use Lightroom to create layouts, slide shows, and web galleries. Graphic artists work with the Lightroom and Photoshop applications individually or together. A technique known as **roundtrip integration** makes it easy to move images back and forth between the two applications. Take some time to explore Lightroom's editing and processing tools with your photographs to see how these features work with Photoshop. If you're a serious photographer, you'll probably find Lightroom to be an invaluable tool.

You learned about Adobe Bridge and its image management features in Chapter 1. Although you can use Windows Explorer (Win), Finder (Mac), or the Dreamweaver Files panel to organize your images, Bridge is by far the best tool. With Bridge, you can view images, color code image files, add metadata, and organize files into a logical folder structure.

Adobe Fireworks is the tool of choice for optimizing bitmap and vector graphics for the

Figure 5 *Example of compositing*

Using Good Graphic File Management Practices

Whatever tool you decide to use, it's a good practice to separate your working files from your project files. Before you edit them, save all original graphic files, especially photographs, with their original size, format, and settings. That way, if you decide you want to return an image to its original settings, you can easily locate and open the original file. For example, once you've reduced the size of an image, then saved and closed it, it's too late to return to the original size unless you saved the original copy. To protect them from accidental loss or overwriting, always place your original graphics files in a separate location; this could be a separate folder, an external hard drive, or an online storage location such as Carbonite (carbonite.com). Keep your project files folder as small as possible, with only the files you're currently using or plan to use. Files that you've experimented with, but have decided not to use, should be placed in a different folder that's clearly named to reflect its contents.

Figure © Cengage Learning 2013

Incorporating Images

Web or mobile devices. It also incorporates the Adobe text engine to produce clear, crisp type. Fireworks integrates well with other Adobe products; for example, you can import Photoshop and Illustrator files and export to the Flash software family. You can also copy and paste content between Fireworks and Dreamweaver.

Locating Images to Use in Your Project

Other than creating your own images, there are several great sources of high-quality images for your media projects. The Internet is a rich source of stock photos. **Stock photos** are available by paying either a per-image download fee, or a subscription fee that covers multiple downloads. Creative Commons

is another great image source. Creative Commons (see their website in Figure 6) is a non-profit organization that promotes the sharing of digital creativity through their legal and technical infrastructure. A Creative Commons license allows free use of an image according to terms that the license holder defines. An example of a site that

Figure 6 *Creative Commons website*
© Creative Commons–creativecommons.org

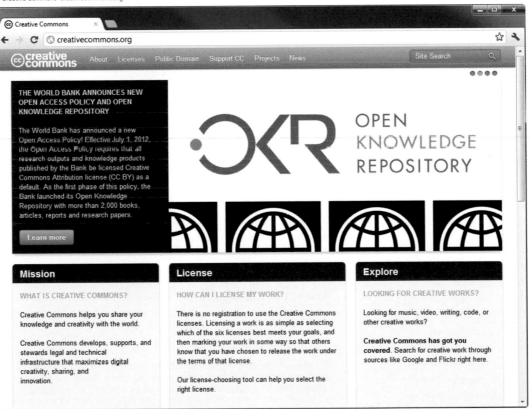

uses Creative Commons licensing is Flickr, a photo-sharing website. With over 100 million images posted on their site, Flickr is the Web's largest single source of Creative Commons licensed content. Google, YouTube, and Wikipedia are other examples of sites that use Creative Commons licensing.

QUICK TIP

iStockphoto at istockphoto.com and Getty Images at gettyimages.com are two of our favorite sources of stock photos.

Understanding Copyright Law

Copyright law is a topic that many people do not understand. The ease of access to information on the Internet, combined with the ease of copy and paste, leads many to the misconception that if they can copy it, they can use it. Nothing could be further from the truth. Learning about copyright law helps you understand when you can use protected content that has been created by others.

When you find a photo or other content that you would like to use, you should always assume that the work is protected by copyright or another category of intellectual property law. Websites that host content may have a licensing agreement associated with the files. A **licensing agreement** is the permission given by a copyright holder that conveys the right to use the copyright holder's work under certain conditions, such as paying a fee. A website generally has **terms of use** that govern how a user may use its content. Figure 7 shows the Library of Congress website policies on copyright, privacy, and publicity rights. To understand how you can legally use the information you find, always look for a "Terms of Use" or "Legal" link on a website you're using as a source.

When you consider using the work of others, you should be familiar with the concepts of intellectual property, copyright, trademark, fair use, derivative work, and public domain, all of which are described in the following sections.

Intellectual Property

Intellectual property is a product resulting from human creativity. Videos, podcasts, movies, music, art, and custom designs are examples of intellectual property. Intellectual property is divided into two categories: **industrial property**, such as patents, trademarks, or industrial designs; and copyright, such as books, plays, music, paintings, photographs, or poetry.

Figure 7 *Library of Congress legal statements of policy*
Library of Congress website – www.loc.gov

About Copyright and the Collections

Whenever possible, the Library of Congress provides factual information about copyright owners and related matters in the catalog records, finding aids and other texts that accompany collections. As a publicly supported institution, the Library generally does not own rights in its collections. Therefore, it does not charge permission fees for use of such material and generally does not grant or deny permission to publish or otherwise distribute material in its collections. Permission and possible fees may be required from the copyright owner independently of the Library. It is the researcher's obligation to determine and satisfy copyright or other use restrictions when publishing or otherwise distributing materials found in the Library's collections. Transmission or reproduction of protected items beyond that allowed by fair use requires the written permission of the copyright owners. Researchers must make their own assessments of rights in light of their intended use.

If you have any more information about an item you've seen on our website or if you are the copyright owner and believe our website has not properly attributed your work to you or has used it without permission, we want to hear from you. Please contact OGC@loc.gov with your contact information and a link to the relevant content.

View more information about copyright law from the U.S. Copyright Office.

Top

Privacy and Publicity Rights

Privacy and publicity rights reflect separate and distinct interests from copyright interests. Patrons desiring to use materials from this website bear the responsibility of making individualized determinations as to whether privacy and publicity rights are implicated by the nature of the materials and how they use such materials.

QUICK **TIP**

For more information, visit the World Intellectual Property Organization (WIPO) website at wipo.int/about-ip/en.

Copyright

A **copyright** protects the particular and tangible expression of an idea, but not the idea itself. If you wrote a book about a family that decides to move to a farm and become organic gardeners, your rights are protected from someone copying or using text from your book without permission. However, anyone can write a similar book about a family becoming organic gardeners. The original book is copyrighted, but not the general idea of the book. Typically, copyrights in the United States last for the life of the author plus 70 years. Other countries have similar laws, but some are different. You do not have to register a copyright with the U.S. Copyright Office; it automatically goes into effect when you create the work.

Trademark

A trademark protects an image, word, slogan, symbol, or design used to identify goods and services. Trademark protection lasts 10 years with 10-year renewal terms. If the trademark is in active use, it can last indefinitely.

QUICK **TIP**

For more information, visit the United States Patent and Trademark Office at uspto.gov.

Fair Use

The law does limit copyright protection. Fair use is an example of a limitation. **Fair use** allows limited use of copyright-protected work under certain circumstances. If challenged, the courts will decide, on a case-by-case basis, when fair use was correctly invoked. An example would be using a verse from a song in a presentation. To determine if fair use applies to a work, the courts consider the following factors:

- the purpose of its use
- the nature of the copyrighted work
- how much you want to use
- the effect on the market or value of the original work

Derivative Work

A **derivative work** is work based on another pre-existing work. A good example is a movie adaptation of a novel. Only a copyright holder can create a derivative work of his or her original work unless the rights are transferred or sold.

Public Domain

Work that is not protected by copyright is said to be in the **public domain**. Anyone can use it without charge for any purpose. Websites that contain work in the public domain may contain a statement to that effect. In general, content on federal government websites is in the public domain. If you're not sure that content you want to use is in the public domain, it's better to assume that it's not; this avoids the possibility of violating copyright laws. The burden is on you to "perform due diligence" (make a reasonable effort to learn if it is truly in the public domain) in determining whether you can use content without permission or must pay a fee.

Posting a Copyright Notice

The word "Copyright" or the copyright symbol © is no longer required to indicate copyright, nor does it automatically register your work. It does serve a useful purpose, however. When you post or publish it, you are clearly stating that this work is claimed by you and is not in the public domain. If someone violates your copyright, your case is made stronger by its presence. No one can claim that they thought they could use content because they did not see a copyright symbol © attached to the work or web page.

Obtaining Permissions

So what steps should you follow if you'd like to use content that is neither in the public domain nor covered by fair use? You must obtain a license or permission to use the content. The permissions process is specific to what you want to use and how you want to use it. The fundamentals, however, are the same. Your request should contain the following:

1. Your full name, address, and complete contact information.
2. A specific description of your intended use. You might include a sketch, storyboard, or wireframe to help illustrate your use in context.
3. A signature line for the copyright holder.
4. A target date for when you'd like the copyright holder to respond, especially when you're working under a specific deadline.

The copyright holder is under no obligation to respond to you, and if you do not receive a response, that's the equivalent of a "no."

Citing Your Sources

You must provide proper credit for content that you incorporate into your own work. You should always provide proper attribution for text you quote directly, summarize, or paraphrase. When you use media, giving attribution for it is also good practice, but it's never a substitute for claiming a fair use argument, purchasing a license, or obtaining permission. This applies not only to copyrighted content, but to unsigned content and to content that does not display a copyright notice.

Whenever you cite your sources, you should use commonly accepted sets of style rules, such as the American Psychological Association (APA) or Modern Language Association (MLA) style manuals. We're using the APA style to cite the sources listed at the end of the book.

QUICK TIP

The APA URL is apastyle.org.

An APA-style citation of web-based resources would include:

- Author's name (if known)
- Last edited date
- Title of resource
- Date of access
- URL

An example of APA style is:

> Meyer, D. 3D Design: Adding Richness to the Web Pages. Retrieved August 24, 2011, from http://www.webgranth.com/3d-design-adding-richness-to-the-web-pages

QUICK TIP

The Modern Language Association URL is mla.org.

An MLA-style citation of web-based resources would include:

- Author's name (if known)
- Title of document
- Title of complete work or website
- URL
- Date of publication
- Date of access

An example of MLA style is:

> Meyer, David. "3D Design: Adding Richness to the Web Pages." *webgranth.com/3d-design-adding-richness-to-the-web-pages*. Web. 24 August 2011.

When you cite your sources for images, sounds, or video, include the following:

- Name of the researching organization
- Date of publication
- Caption or description
- Brief explanation of what type of data is there and in what form it appears, in brackets
- Project name and retrieval information

Both APA and MLA styles have many conventions that depend on the type of source you're citing. Be sure to check the *Publication Manual of the American Psychological Association* and the *MLA Handbook for Writers of Research Papers* for more specific information. Proper attribution of all your sources is important in creating a well-documented work and in protecting yourself from legal liability.

Creating Your Own Images

Although there is a wealth of good sources for locating images to use in your projects, often it's easier to create your own. For instance, Annesa drew all of the original artwork for the illustrations in our project using Illustrator. She then exported them as JPGs, a file format that can be read on the Internet and with mobile devices. Once they were converted, they were no longer fully editable. To make significant changes, she'll have to go back to the original Illustrator files. Let's go over some pointers for several approaches to creating original images.

Drawing

If you have a talent for drawing and painting *and* can use digital tools to create your art, you are very fortunate. Some people are very talented artists, but struggle using computers. Some people can learn graphics software intuitively, but may not have the gift to draw or paint. If you can do both, you have a marketable skill set. Original illustrations truly set off media projects by providing a unique personality and presence. If you plan to use drawing and painting tools in a program such as Illustrator, consider purchasing a graphics tablet. A **graphics tablet** uses a digital pen for drawing rather than a mouse, and can be an invaluable tool. Figure 8 shows the Wacom Bamboo Create tablet. Tablets come with a variety of features and prices, so you can match a particular model to your specific needs. Bamboo Connect, Bamboo Capture, and Bamboo Create are the three Bamboo models you can choose from.

QUICK TIP

To visit the Wacom website and view tablet comparisons, go to wacom.com.

Compositing

As you learned earlier in this chapter, **compositing** is the art of combining visual elements from multiple files into one image file. If done skillfully, it looks natural, appearing to be an original image. Other times, compositing is done to intentionally show that the elements have been placed together unnaturally, such as a flower shown growing out of someone's head. Photoshop is an excellent tool to use for compositing. Its variety of precise selection tools and settings make it a snap to copy image areas, move them from one image to another, and reposition them after they're placed. New refinement tools allow you to automatically vary selection edges and select intricate areas such as grass.

Figure 8 *Wacom tablet*

The selection in Figure 9 was made with the Photoshop Quick Selection tool. The marquee shows the selected area that can now be moved into a different image file. Once you've moved a selection to the target image, you can resize, flip, rotate, or manipulate the image settings for just that selection, as shown in Figure 10.

Compositing is also used in video; just think of TV anchors in front of a blue or green screen in the studio. With this technology, weather maps or images of the news story can be displayed behind the anchor, as if the anchor were actually standing in front of the map or scene pictured.

Unless you're working with your own images, remember that you'll need to obtain a license or permission to use each image that makes up the composite. Even if you only use a small part of an image, you must still obtain permission.

Photography

It's easy to create stunning graphics using your own photographs. Whether you have a point-and-shoot camera or a state-of-the-art SLR (single-lens reflex) camera, you can capture great images. One of the main advantages of an SLR camera is that you can change the lens, allowing you to shoot objects that are either very close to you or very far away. You also have more advanced camera settings to use for creating artistic effects. With an SLR, you think for the camera, rather than the camera "thinking" for you. Although you can set an SLR camera to full automatic mode, that wastes the camera's power and capabilities.

Learning a camera's capabilities is important, but it's not quite enough. One of Sherry's favorite photographers is Tim Ernst, who is also a gifted photography instructor. In one of his workshops he told the story about a great photographer who went to a dinner party. The table conversation turned to his photography accomplishments, with several guests complimenting his work. The hostess then said, "Wow, you must have really great photography equipment to have become so accomplished!" As the photographer was leaving that night, he complimented the hostess on the great dinner and added, "Wow, you must have some really great pans!" The point being: you can have the best and most expensive equipment, but that doesn't mean

Figure 9 *Compositing using Adobe Photoshop*

Quick Selection tool

Selected image to move

Dotted line shows outline of selected image

Figure © Cengage Learning 2013. Images courtesy of Sherry Bishop

you'll be able to use it creatively. By the same token, a skillful photographer with a great eye for composition can use a point-and-shoot camera and take very nice photos.

When you use your own photos, you don't have to worry about copyrights or permissions unless you're photographing people. When you photograph people, you should obtain signed model releases. Sherry keeps several blank model release forms with her camera equipment in case she sees someone she would like to photograph during her travels. We used all of our own photos in the Gardener's Walk project. If you want to incorporate your own photos, it's also a good idea to take a class or two to learn basic camera fundamentals. In the next section, we'll go over some basic design strategies for improving the quality of your photos.

QUICK **TIP**

When photographing people, candid photos are often more expressive than posed photos.

Storing Images

Whether you're planning to draw illustrations, composite images, or take photographs, always store them in separate folders designated for original files. It's easy to transfer your digital images to a computer for storage. A high-speed card reader/writer that plugs into your USB port is an easy way to transfer photos. You simply insert your card in one end of the card reader and plug the other end into a USB port.

Figure © Cengage Learning 2013. Images courtesy of Sherry Bishop

A window opens, prompting you to designate the drive and folder where you would like to download your photos. Many cameras come with a cable to connect the camera with a USB drive for downloading images. Sherry always uses Bridge to download her photos, but you can use Windows Explorer or Mac Finder, or your camera may come with a proprietary program for downloading your photos. Most laptops now have slots for inserting camera cards, which eliminates the need for either special software or cables.

Figure 10 *Composited image*

Selection from other file has been moved, resized, and flipped horizontally

Caring for your camera and lenses

As with any electronic equipment, you need to take special care with your cameras and lenses. Protect them from being contaminated by moisture, dust, and dirt. When Sherry traveled on a photo safari to Kenya, she kept her camera bodies and lenses in zipped plastic storage bags when she wasn't using them. Extreme temperatures are another danger. You wouldn't think of leaving your camera in a freezer or hot oven, so don't leave it in your car when it's hot or cold outside. If you use a tripod, make sure it's a sturdy, heavy one so it won't tip over while you have your camera mounted.

Applying Image Design
STRATEGIES

Overview of Image File Types and Formats

As you select images for your interactive media project, be sure you choose an appropriate file type and resolution. Earlier in the chapter, we talked about the difference between vector and bitmap (raster) images. Table 1 lists the most common file formats used to create images. Since web content is viewed with back-lit screens, the standards are different from images that will be used in print. For printed images, a resolution of 300 ppi or dpi (pixels per inch or dots per inch) is a commonly used standard. Images that will be viewed on the Web only need a minimum of 72 ppi. Image editing programs, such as Photoshop, Illustrator, and Fireworks, let you choose from multiple file format and resolution settings, as shown in

TABLE 1: COMMON GRAPHICS FILE FORMATS			
Format (file extension)	Stands for	File type	Explanation
.jpg, .jpeg	Joint Photographic Experts Group	Bitmap	Can set image quality in pixels per inch (ppi), which affects file size. Supports millions of colors and is used for full-color images, such as photographs.
.png	Portable Network Graphics	Bitmap	Can be compressed for storage and quicker download without loss of quality. Supports variable levels of transparency and control of image brightness on different screens. Used for small graphics as well as complex photographs. Is the native Fireworks file format.
.gif	Graphics Interchange Format	Bitmap	Limited to 256 colors with low color quality and limited detail. Not suitable for printing. Small file size means faster transmission. Suitable for images with few colors, such as cartoons or icons. Supports transparency.
.tiff	Tagged Image File Format	Bitmap	For high resolution images, usually large file sizes. Used for printed images, scanning, and faxing.
.ai	Adobe Illustrator	Vector	Proprietary file format developed by Adobe Systems. Files can be resized without losing quality.

© Cengage Learning 2013

Figure 11. The blue star image in the figure was originally created in Illustrator with the .ai file extension. Then it was opened in Photoshop, where the Save for Web and Devices command on the File menu offers these format conversion choices. When you choose a file format that will reduce the size of the original file, the process is referred to as **optimizing** an image.

The resolution for photographs depends on the settings you choose on your camera before you take the photo. High-quality photographs must be large files to provide good quality for print, but are then optimized or compressed for viewing on the Web. **Compression** refers to the process of reducing the number of bits in a file to decrease the file size.

Figure 11 *File format choices for optimizing images in Photoshop*

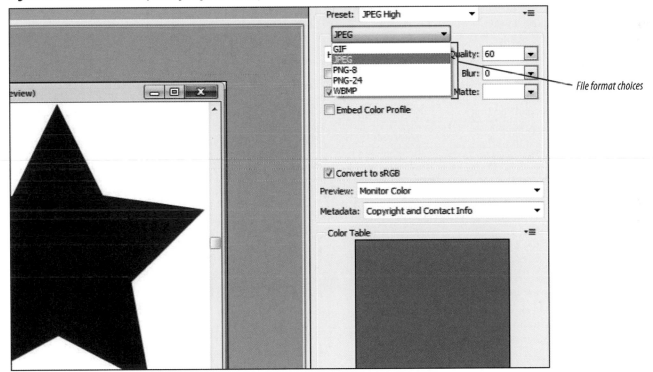

File format choices

Design Strategies for Creating Great Photos

The quality of a photograph is determined during three stages and all three stages are vital. These are:

1. When the picture is taken (camera settings used, file format, composition)
2. When the picture is processed (adjustments made in Photoshop or Lightroom)
3. When the picture is printed or viewed (quality of printer, paper type, printer settings, screen size and resolution if viewed electronically)

To create high-quality photographs, be aware of not only camera settings and editing techniques, but also of the principle of balance. Special effects can play an important role in the artistic expression of your ideas.

Camera Settings

First, let's briefly review some basic camera settings that affect Stage 1. The shutter speed determines how long the lens stays open to expose light and is measured in fractions of seconds, as shown in Figure 12. The F-stop (aperture) sets the exposure by adjusting the lens opening with a range of 3.5 to 22. The aperture size determines the amount of light exposure, with the lowest numbers letting in the most light. See Figure 13.

Besides affecting the light exposure, changes in the F-stop setting affect the depth of field, or how clear the subjects are at various distances from the camera lens. Generally, the smaller the F-stop, the longer the depth of field; the larger the F-stop, the shorter the depth of field.

Figure 12 *The relationship of shutter speed to light exposure*

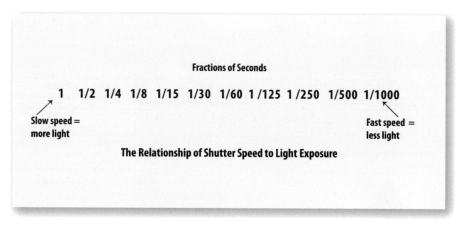

Figure 13 *The relationship of F-stop to light exposure*

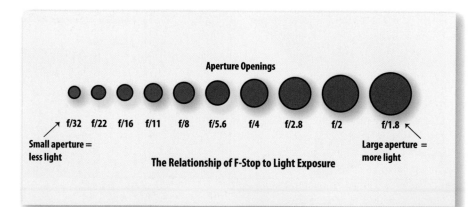

Incorporating Images

The image shown in Figure 14 has a short depth of field because the two birds are in focus, but the background is blurred. If the birds and background were both in focus, it would reflect a longer depth of field.

The composition of your photographs reflects your "photographer's eye" or visual interpretation of your subject. Techniques such as the use of creative lighting, unique perspective, level of horizon, and the rule of thirds greatly enhance your compositions. The **rule of thirds** divides an image into nine equal sections, like a tic-tac-toe grid. Focal points should occur at grid intersections, as shown in Figure 15. When you use the Crop tool in Photoshop, the crop selection is divided into the rule of thirds grid, providing a guide that helps you position a focal point in your photo near one of the grid intersections. **Cropping** refers to designating a rectangular area that you want to keep in an image, and removing the rest of the image. Never place a person in the "bull's eye" of your camera, or the exact center of the photo. It's much more pleasing to photograph subjects using the rule of thirds.

Image Editing

Once you've taken the photograph, you move to Stage 2, in which you edit the image using a photo editor. Some simple Photoshop features you can use include the Auto Contrast, Auto Color, and Auto Tone commands, but it is better to make each of these adjustments manually, fine tuning as you preview the changes you're making.

Figures © Cengage Learning 2013. Images courtesy of Sherry Bishop

Figure 14 *Image with short depth of field*

Background is blurred

Figure 15 *Rule of thirds using the Photoshop Crop tool*

Grid intersections

Rock (focal point) is at intersection of grid lines

Drag selection edges to adjust crop lines

Other photographic enhancement techniques include layering, masking, feathering, and color enhancement. **Layering** refers to arranging the order of image elements to place them in the background or foreground relative to other image elements. **Masking** means removing the edges of an image, similar to placing a matte over a picture before it's framed, as shown in Figures 16 and 17. You can use **feathering** to blur the edges of a mask to soften an image, as shown in Figure 18. **Color enhancement** can mean changing the hue, saturation, brightness, contrast, or color balance in an image. Color enhancement can also be applied using filters to apply color overtones. Photoshop has endless ways to edit images. Take the time to explore the menus—you'll be surprised how addictive it is!

Figure 16 *Image before a mask is applied*

Figure 17 *Image after a mask is applied*

Figure 18 *Mask with feathered edges*

Achieving Balance

You learned about the importance of balance in Chapter 3. As you place your text and images in a project, take a critical look at the symmetry of the page. Is it balanced? Are there too many images compared to text, or vice versa? Is any area of the page "heavy" or does the weight of the page elements seem evenly distributed across the page? Horizontal symmetry is achieved when the elements are balanced across the page. Vertical symmetry is achieved if the elements are balanced down the page. In diagonal symmetry, elements are spaced along an invisible diagonal line across the page. In radial symmetry, elements run from the center outward, like the petals of a flower. Sometimes an asymmetrical balance is more interesting, where the elements are off center or out of balance. Remember the rule of thirds not only for taking photos, but for arranging content that will be viewed on desktops or mobile devices.

Using Three-dimensional Effects

There has been tremendous growth in three-dimensional (3D) media during the last several years. 3D movies are experiencing renewed popularity. 3D televisions are now on the market. And of course, 3D objects are used extensively in most computer games. 3D technology "grabs" your attention and draws a viewer into the content, so it's not surprising that websites are incorporating more 3D elements into their pages.

A 3D effect can draw interest to a particular page feature, such as a navigation button or other clickable element, that the user would use to control the content. You can apply 3D effects to images or text simply by adding bevels or drop shadows. Many image editing programs have more complex 3D effects, such as the 3D Extrude and Bevel effect in Adobe Illustrator, pictured in Figure 19. 3D effects can be engaging if used sparingly, but overuse can make a site look unprofessional. Use them only if they serve a purpose.

Figure 19 *Image with 3D Extrude and Bevel effect applied*

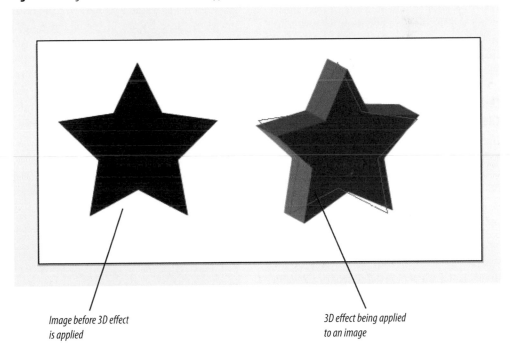

Image before 3D effect
is applied

3D effect being applied
to an image

Working with Images Using Adobe
ILLUSTRATOR, FIREWORKS, PHOTOSHOP, DREAMWEAVER, AND FLASH

Once you've created or located the images for your interactive design project, you're ready to adopt them to your project needs using Adobe tools. Let's look at how easy it is to create, optimize, edit, and import images using Adobe Illustrator, Fireworks, Photoshop, Dreamweaver, and Flash.

Creating and Optimizing Images with Illustrator and Fireworks

Illustrator and Fireworks are the premier tools for creating and editing vector graphics. After creating a vector graphic, you can save it as a bitmap for use on the web or in print. Remember to always preserve your original source file and make the edits to a copy of the original file.

When you create a new Illustrator document, you designate the width and height of the drawing, the orientation (landscape or portrait), the unit of measure for the rulers to display, and the color mode. The **CMYK Color Mode** (Cyan, Magenta, Yellow, and Black) is usually used for print projects, while the **RGB Color Mode** (Red, Green, and Blue) is usually used for projects that will be viewed on a screen.

A really great feature of Illustrator lets you convert a photograph (bitmap) into a vector image by tracing it. Figures 20 and 21 show a photo of a bird placed in Illustrator before and after it was traced to convert it to a vector image. Because it's now a vector image, you can resize it without losing image quality. You can also edit the tracing effects to adjust the number of colors used and the sampling rates. The **sampling rate** sets the resolution of the traced image. The higher the sampling rate, the more detailed the traced image will be.

Figure 20 *Photograph placed in Illustrator before tracing*

You can create a similar image in Fireworks if that's your preferred drawing tool. Fireworks has many commands that are related to optimizing images for the web, such as creating slide shows, adding mouse events, and setting Alt text.

Figure 21 *Photograph after tracing*

Figures © Cengage Learning 2013. Images courtesy of Sherry Bishop

Alt text is text that's attached to an image on a website, and used to describe the image. Alt text is read by screen readers and is one of the most basic tools for creating an accessible website; it provides an alternate way to present information for visually impaired users.

Editing and Optimizing Images in Photoshop

Photoshop can open most graphic file formats except for Illustrator files. When you open an Illustrator file in Photoshop, it imports the image as a PDF; you can then save it to a format of your choice. You can also open a file in Illustrator and export it to a different file format, such as a PNG, that Photoshop can read. You can then open and edit it in Photoshop. Photoshop will also open movie files, such as MOV, AVI, and MP4 files. After you've finished making your edits, you'll need to optimize the file if you plan to use it in a media project. Remember that optimizing a file reduces the number of bits in the file, reducing the overall file size.

Editing Images in Photoshop

Let's look at some of the Photoshop editing tools we talked about in Applying Image Design Strategies; making adjustments to contrast, color, and tone. These adjustments can help compensate for over- or underexposed images. One of the real advantages of using Photoshop is that it lets you layer objects to manipulate their position and relationship to the foreground,

background, and other objects. Figure 22 shows an image before any adjustments were made. The photo was underexposed when it was taken and it's too dark. Figure 23 shows the same image after adjustments were made to the contrast, color, and tone

Figure 22 *Image before adjustments*

Figure 23 *Image after adjustments*

Figures © Cengage Learning 2013. Images courtesy of Sherry Bishop

Incorporating Images

with the Auto Tone, Auto Contrast, and Auto Color commands on the Image menu. You can also make custom adjustments by using the Image > Adjustments command, then choosing your adjustment settings. This allows you to experiment with the settings rather than using auto adjustments.

Figure 24 shows the addition of a sea lion into the photo. The sea lion was selected from another file, then moved to the beach photo (this created a new layer) and resized.

To create the reflection, Sherry duplicated the sea lion, which created yet another layer. She then flipped the sea lion and moved it below the original sea lion, reduced the layer opacity (transparency), and then used the Blur and Erase Tools to blend the reflection into the sand.

Optimizing Images in Photoshop

In addition to the Photoshop editing tools discussed in Applying Image Design Strategies, one of the most basic factors to consider when working with digital images is image optimization. The goal of image optimization is to reduce a file to the smallest acceptable file size without compromising the image quality when it's viewed online. With high-resolution cameras, it's easy to forget how large the images can be. So before you use a high-resolution photo on a website or other multimedia project, be sure to reduce its resolution and file size.

Figure 24 *Image with sea lion and reflection layers added*

Reflection was created by duplicating and editing the sea lion layer

Opacity reduced

Two new layers

Original layer

Figure © Cengage Learning 2013. Images courtesy of Sherry Bishop

To optimize an image in Photoshop, use the File > Save for Web command and then choose your target file format and settings in the Save for Web & Devices dialog box, as shown in Figure 25. Remember to save the optimized file with a different name to prevent writing over your original file.

The difference in file sizes between original Photoshop files and optimized files is dramatic. For the example images, these were the file sizes after changing the file format and then optimizing the image:

Original PSD file:	72,412 K
Saved as JPEG:	6,809 K
Optimized:	75K

Bringing Images into Dreamweaver

To bring images onto a page in Dreamweaver, you can either use the Insert > Image command or copy and paste the image from Fireworks, Illustrator, Flash, or Photoshop. When you use the Paste command to paste an image into Dreamweaver, you'll be prompted to optimize the image and save it in your website images folder. Other options for inserting images include inserting image placeholders, inserting rollover images, and inserting Fireworks HTML.

Figure 25 *Save for Web & Devices dialog box in Photoshop*

Preset text box
File format text box

Optimized check box

Save button

Figure © Cengage Learning 2013. Images courtesy of Sherry Bishop

And don't forget to assign alternate text to all images in your project, including form objects, text displayed as graphics, button, and media files. By default, Dreamweaver prompts you to enter alternate text whenever you insert an image.

Using Image Placeholders

As you develop your project, you'll often want to use an image placeholder to indicate where you want to insert an image later. By assigning the exact dimensions to an image placeholder, you can place other page content around it without the fear of it shifting when you insert the actual image. The placeholder lets you visualize how the image will relate to the rest of the design, so you can make most of your design decisions early on. Open the Image Placeholder dialog box, shown in Figure 26, using the Dreamweaver Insert menu or Insert bar.

Using Rollovers for Navigation

Rollover images are images that change to a different image when the user moves the mouse pointer over them. Rollover images are excellent for creating navigation objects because they draw the user's eye to them and because they're intuitive—the user expects something to happen when they click them. Rollover images are a great way to add interactivity to a project.

To create a rollover image, you'll need two images that are the same height and width but different in appearance. An easy way to incorporate rollovers is to create rollover buttons, using a different background or text color for the two

images. For instance, one button would appear with a blue background and white text until the mouse pointer moves over it. With the pointer over it, it might change to a blue background with black text. The HTML code for the button includes a link to the page or location that it would open when clicked.

To insert rollover images in Dreamweaver, use the Insert > Image Objects > Rollover Image command or the Rollover Image button on the Insert bar. The Insert Rollover Image dialog box is shown in Figure 27. Use this dialog box to assign a name, link to the two images used in the rollover, add alternate text,

Figure 26 *Image Placeholder dialog box in Dreamweaver*

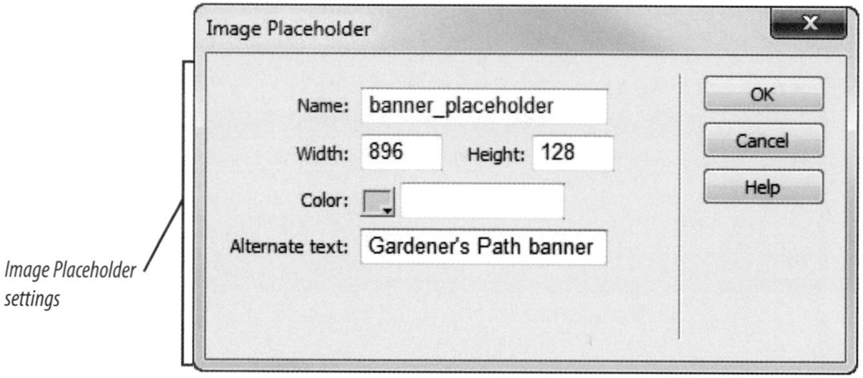

Image Placeholder settings

Figure 27 *Insert Rollover Image dialog box*

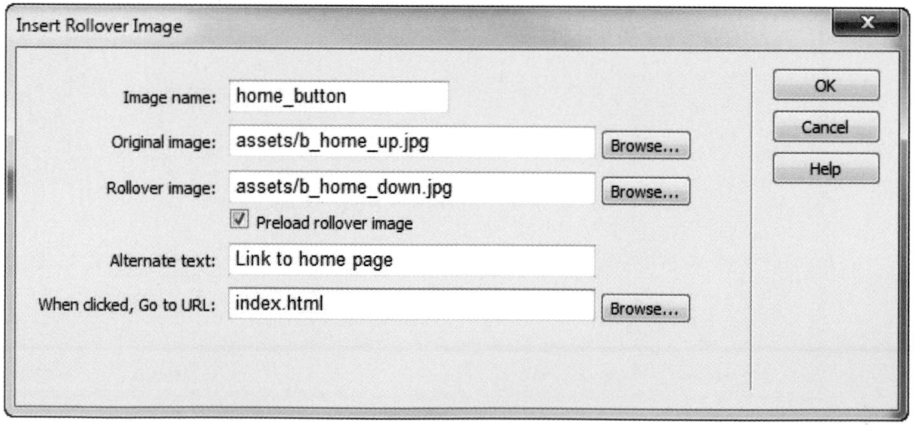

Incorporating Images

and assign a URL that will open when the rollover image is clicked.

A good alternative to using rollover images is using unordered lists, since rollover images don't work well on mobile devices with touch screens. Because list properties can be customized using CSS, this makes them an attractive alternative when designing for multiple devices. Since each device can have a separate style sheet, the list items can appear differently depending on the device being used to view them.

Using Background Images

Rather than inserting an image into a page element such as a div tag, you can set it as a background image. Figure 28 shows the CSS Rule Definition dialog box with an image being set as the background for a container,

Figure 28 *CSS Rule Definition dialog box*

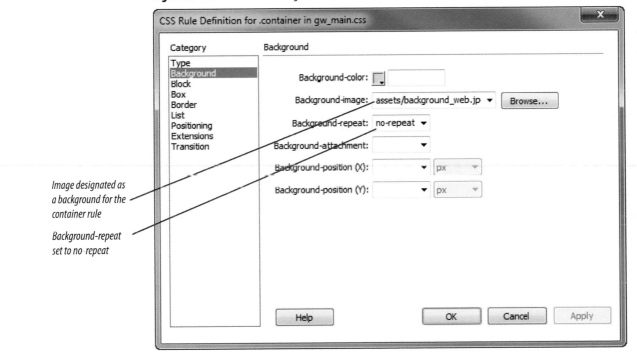

Image designated as a background for the container rule

Background-repeat set to no-repeat

Incorporating Images

as opposed to the image being inserted into the container. This lets you then type text over the image. In our project, we have a search form in the top right corner, so by using a background image, the search form will display on top of the image. Figure 29 shows our background image stretching across a page. This image incorporates flower designs across a solid white background that fills the page. The search form appears on top of the background image in the top right corner of the page.

A more substantial advantage, however, is that by setting an image as a background, you can use media queries to target different images to different devices. Recall that we discussed media queries in Chapter 2 as one of the best strategies for targeting multiple devices.

Figure 29 *Background image with form displayed on top of image*

This background image fills the page

This search form is displayed on top of the background image

Figure © Cengage Learning 2013

Incorporating Images

Importing Images into Flash

When you're ready to insert an image into a Flash movie, you use the File > Import menu. Your choices are Import to Stage, Import to Library, Open External Library, or Import Video. When you choose Import to Stage, the image is automatically placed in the Library. The Library is a panel that lists your image files, called **library items**, for a movie. When you choose Import to Library, the image is placed in the Library, but not on the stage. Open External Library will open a library that is not part of the open document. Import Video will import a video file. You can also copy and paste images from Dreamweaver, Photoshop, Illustrator, and Fireworks. When you copy and paste an image, the image will automatically be added to the library. The Preview window in the Library panel shows a preview of the selected library item, as shown in Figure 30. We'll spend more time with Flash in Chapter 9.

Figure 30 *Library panel in Flash*

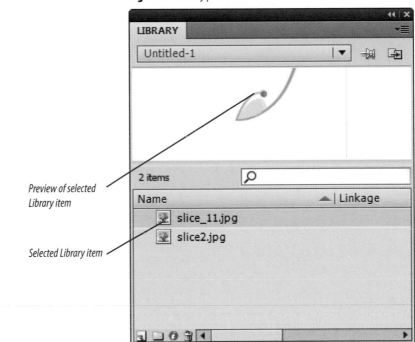

Preview of selected Library item

Selected Library item

ADDING IMAGES

Introduction

After you've gathered or created the images for your interactive media project, it's time to integrate them into the content. We'll use Adobe Dreamweaver to demonstrate the steps for placing images on web pages. If you're going to create a different kind of interactive media project, your steps will differ, depending on the program you're using. While working through the steps, you may choose to follow along and set up a practice site.

Adding Images

You can place images in containers on a page with a command on the Insert menu, or you can add them as a background image using CSS rules. We're going to use an image as a background for the container rule. By using it as a background image, rather than placing it, we're positioning ourselves to be able to change the background image for optimum viewing on multiple devices using media queries. The page we're now designing will be viewed on desktop or laptop screens. By adding an additional style sheet for each additional device we want to design for, we can change the background image being used. As the screen sizes get smaller, we'll specify smaller background images that fit on the smaller screens.

Using Lists to Create Rollover Buttons for Navigation

The page layout we selected when we first created the index page includes navigation links formatted as an unordered list. The default formatting for each link includes gray text that changes to white when the pointer rolls over it. The background for each "button" is light green, which changes to a darker green when the pointer rolls over it. We plan to change these links to buttons with dark green text and a gold background that changes to light green when the pointer rolls over them. We want to remove the underlines from the text and change each button border to white. We'll make these changes using the rules for the unordered list and list items.

Using an AP Div to Add an Image Layer

One type of div tag is an AP div. AP stands for absolutely positioned, so an **AP div tag** creates a container that has a specified, fixed position on a web page. The great advantage of an AP div is that it can be placed on top of another page element, such as another div; so you can use AP divs to overlap other page elements. They can also be coded to display according to set criteria, such as the date the page is being viewed.

By default, AP divs are placed in relation to the top left corner of a web page. This can be a problem if your page content is centered in the browser. Because the browser width is different on various screens, or as users resize their browser window to take up less or more of their screen, the AP div will shift in relation to the other page elements as it maintains its position from the top left corner of the screen. See Figures 31 and 32. It's much easier to show it than to try to explain it!

We wanted to place a graphic in the lower-right corner of the page to provide balance and to help carry the design through. We also wanted the graphic to appear on top of and straddling the content div and the right image div, so we decided that an AP div was the way to go. To anchor the AP div in place, we rearranged some of the HTML code to make the AP div placement relative to the main page container rather than the body tag.

Making a Template from a Page

Once we complete the home page, we want to use it as a template for the rest of the pages in the site. We'll create an editable region from the content div, where the content will change for the other pages. The banner, side images, and navigation buttons will be in locked areas so that they cannot be changed except in the template. This makes global changes a snap and promotes consistency across the pages. We decided to first remove the quote from the sidebar and place it, along with other quotes, on some of the other pages instead.

Figure 31 *AP div viewed in a browser*

AP div is not obstructing text
with current window size

Figure 32 *Same AP div viewed when the browser window is resized*

After the window is widened
the AP div shifts to the left
and obstructs text

Add images

1. Open the header rule in the CSS Styles panel, then add a Height property in the Box category, as shown in Figure 33.

   We used 170 pixels for the height value. This will give us some space to display the top of the image in the container tag as a banner. Increasing or decreasing the container height determines how much of the background image will show.

2. Edit the container rule by adding a background image, as shown in Figure 34.

   We set the Background-repeat value to no-repeat to stop the image from repeating across the page.

3. Edit the header rule Text-align property in the Block category to right, as shown in our example in Figure 35.

   This moves the search form to the right so it doesn't conflict with the background image design.

4. Edit the sidebar1 rule by removing the background color.

   Removing the background color on the sidebar will allow more of the background image to show.

Figure 33 *Adding a Height property for the header rule*

CSS Rule Definition for header in gw_main.css

Category   Box

Type
Background
Block
Box
Border

Width: ▼   px ▼   Float: ▼

Height: 170   ▼   px ▼   Clear: ▼

Height=170px

Figure 34 *Editing the container rule Background properties*

CSS Rule Definition for .container in gw_main.css

Category   Background

Type
Background
Block
Box
Border
List
Positioning

Background-color: ▢

Background-image: assets/background_web.jp ▼   Browse...

Background-repeat: no-repeat ▼

If your image is smaller than your container, use the no-repeat value

Browse to find the file you are using for a background image

Figure 35 *Editing the header rule Block properties*

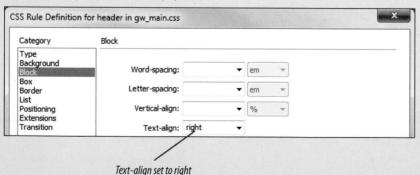

CSS Rule Definition for header in gw_main.css

Category   Block

Type
Background
Block
Box
Border
List
Positioning
Extensions
Transition

Word-spacing: ▼   em ▼

Letter-spacing: ▼   em ▼

Vertical-align: ▼   % ▼

Text-align: right   ▼

Text-align set to right

Figures © Cengage Learning 2013

Incorporating Images

5. Click the **Live view button** to preview the page and make sure the background is displayed correctly, as shown in our example in Figure 36. Then click the **Live view button** again to exit Live view.

Use lists to create rollover buttons for navigation

1. Edit the nav ul li rule to set a bottom border with the following property values:

   Style: **solid**
   Width: **2px**
   Color: **#FFF**

   These settings change the button borders to white with a slightly heavier width.

2. Edit the nav ul a, nav ul a:visited rule with the following property values:

   Font-family: **Arial, Helvetica, sans-serif**
   Font-size: **medium**
   Font-weight: **bold**
   Type Color: **#4A8217**
   Background-color: **#FCC165**
   Box Height: **22px**

   These settings change the font, background color, and height for the buttons.

3. Edit the nav ul a:hover, nav ul a:active, nav ul a:focus rule with the following property value:

   Background-color: **#BCF09E**

   This setting will change the background color of the link buttons to a light green when the pointer moves over or rests on top of them.

4. Edit the nav ul rule with the following property value:

   Type-color: **#4A8217**
   Border: **none**

Figure 36 *Using Live view to view background*

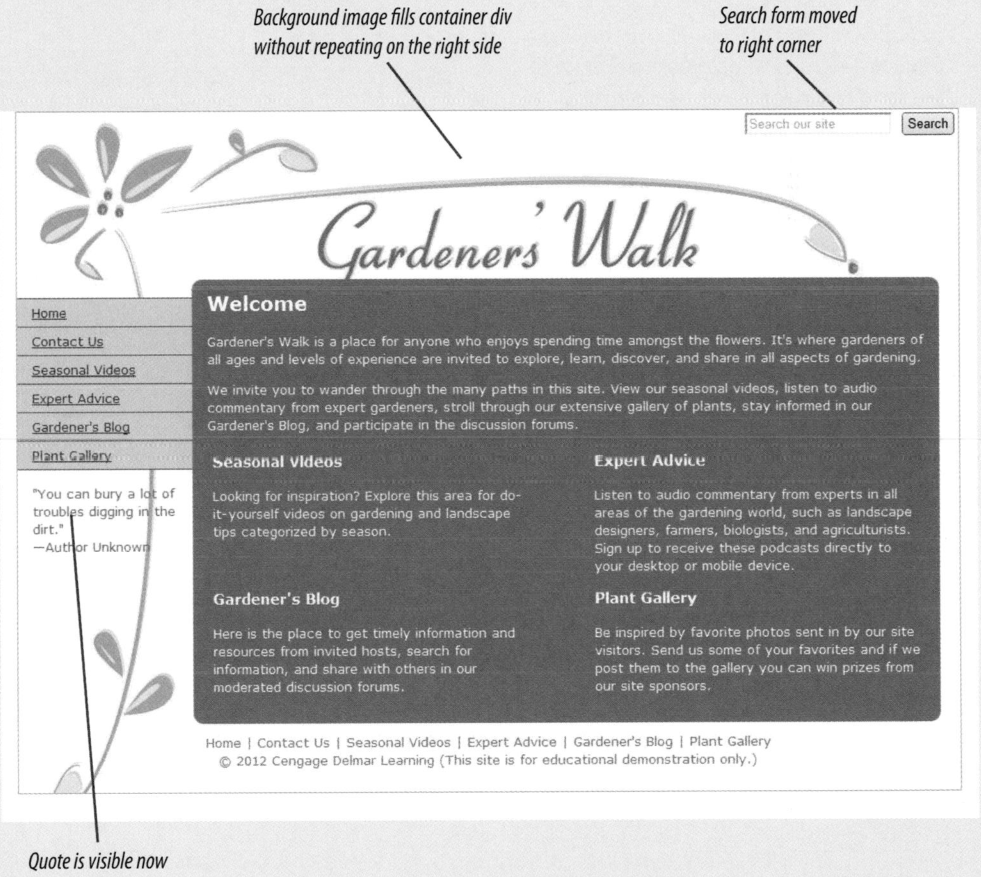

Background image fills container div without repeating on the right side

Search form moved to right corner

This setting changes the button text links to dark green and removes the default value of a top gray border for the unordered list.

Quote is visible now

5. Add a new rule named nav ul a:link with the following property values:

Text-decoration: **none**
Color: **#4A8217**

This removes the underline from the links in the list, but does not affect the rest of the links on the page. Unless there is a reason, such as creating a button design, it's wise to leave text links with the default underline to help users recognize them as links.

6. Select the Home link and use the Property inspector to link it to the index page.

We'll need some placeholder pages to use for linking the buttons until the other pages have been developed. When each page is developed, it will replace its placeholder page. To quickly create new, blank placeholder pages:

7. Right-click in the Files panel, click **New File**, then type a file name using the .html file extension. (We typed contact.html for the first placeholder page for the Gardener's Walk website.)

8. Repeat Step 7 to create the rest of the files that will be linked to the rest of your navigation buttons. (We used videos.html, advice.html, blog.html, and gallery.html to match our buttons.)

9. Select each button and link it to the respective page until all buttons are linked correctly.

10. Save your work, then use Live view or the browser to test each button, as shown in Figure 37.

TIP Since all but the index page are blank pages so far, you'll have to use the Back button to return to the index page each time until you create content for each page.

Figure 37 *Viewing the completed button links in Live view*

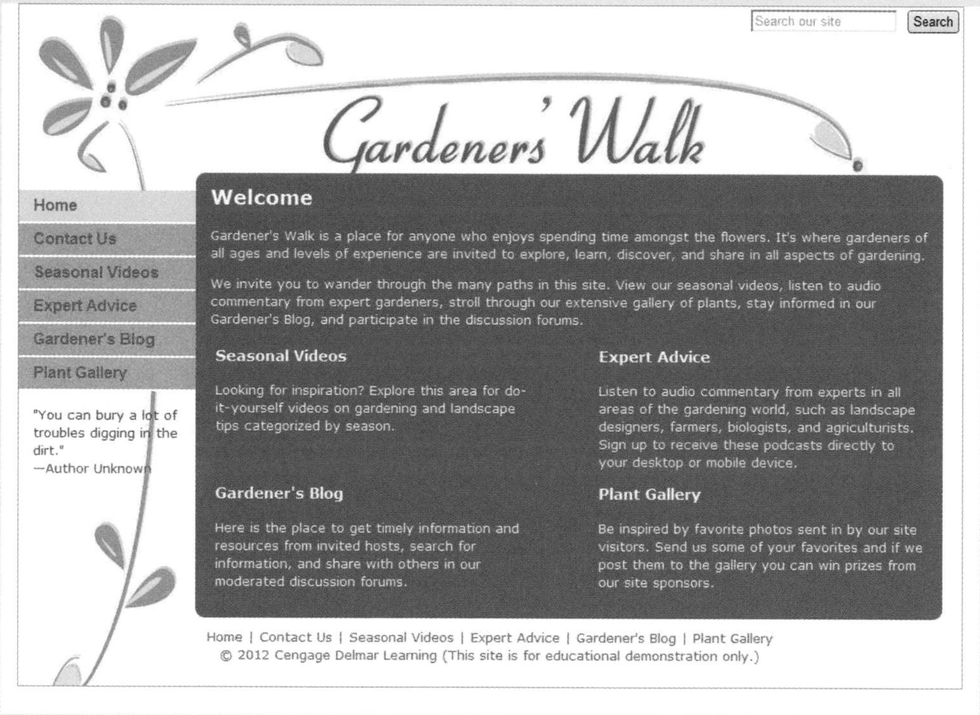

Incorporating Images

Use an AP div to add an image layer

1. Choose **Insert** > **Layout Objects** > **AP Div**.

   Your AP Div will appear on the page as a rectangle with a yellow or blue outline, with an AP div icon above the upper-left corner, as shown in Figure 38.

2. Drag the AP icon to the approximate position you would like to place the AP div on the page.

3. Click the **AP div icon** to select the AP div if necessary, then use the Property inspector to change the name in the CSS-P Element text box to a meaningful one (we used flower).

4. Use the Browse for File button to link the Bg image to an image file (we used a flower image).

5. Change the W value to match your image width (ours is 162px), then change the H value to match the image height (ours is 139px), as shown in Figure 39.

6. Save your file, preview it in a browser, then drag the browser window borders to resize the window.

   Notice how the AP div shifts position when the window is resized.

   You'll have to experiment with the exact position you want to use for the AP div. Before you spend too much time on it, go to Step 7 to add the code to prevent the AP div from shifting.

7. Use the CSS Styles panel to edit the container rule Position property to relative, then cut and paste the AP div code from its current position in the code to right under the opening tag for the container div code, as shown in Figure 40.

Incorporating Images

Figure 38 *AP div inserted on a page*

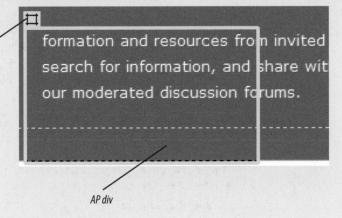

AP div icon

AP div

Figure 39 *Using the Property inspector to edit an AP div*

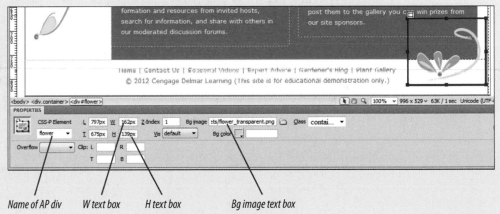

Name of AP div   W text box   H text box   Bg image text box

Figure 40 *Moving the code for the AP div under the opening tag for the container div code*

```
<div class="container">
<div id="flower"></div>
  <header>
```

If you see a green wavy line under the code, you can hover the mouse pointer over it to read a warning. This warning states that any AP divs that you nest, or create inside the original AP div tags may not display in the order you would expect. Since we don't plan to nest other AP divs within this one, it's not an issue for us.

8. Now you can fine-tune the placement of your AP div as you view the page in the browser, as shown in Figure 41.

As a final touch, we inserted some custom bullet images to each of the four paragraph headings.

TIP Remember to view your pages using several different browsers and browser versions.

Make a Template from a Page

1. Select the quote in the sidebar and delete it.

Our quote was in an <aside> tag. Since the tag is empty now, we deleted it.

2. With the index page open, choose **File** > **Save as Template**.

3. In the Save As Template dialog box, type the **file name** you want to use for your template (we used main_template), as shown in Figure 42, click **Save**, then click **Yes** in the Dreamweaver dialog box that opens.

4. Select the content div, click **Insert**, point to **Template Objects**, click **Editable Region**, then enter a name in the Editable Region dialog box. (We used main_content.)

When this template is used to create a new page, the only area where content can be added is in the content div.

Figure 41 *Viewing the finished page*

Figure 42 *Save As Template dialog box*

Type your template name

5. Delete the content in the content div, then save the template file.

On any pages that are created based on this template, the content div is now the only place to which content can be added, as shown in Figure 43. We'll use the template to create the other pages, saving us from having to duplicate the common content, such as navigation links, that will appear on each page.

Figure 43 *Viewing the template*

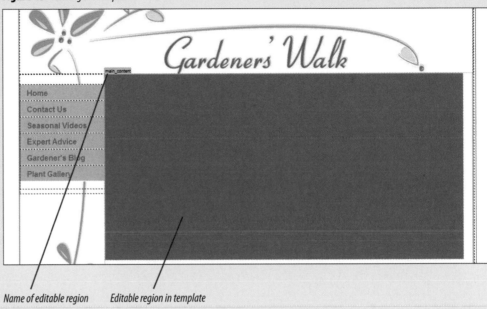

Name of editable region   *Editable region in template*

Incorporating Images

ADDING IMAGES TO YOUR INTERACTIVE MEDIA PROJECT

Now that you've learned about adding images to your content, you're ready to incorporate some images into your project. Use the wireframe you created in Chapter 3 as your guide to locate or create images that you can use throughout your project. This is a good time to create navigation buttons if you're going to use them for your navigation links.

1. Consult your wireframe to make a list of the images you'll need for your project.

2. If you're going to create some of the images or use original photographs, create and save the original files in a folder for that purpose, then edit a copy of each file to meet the size and dimensions required for the project. Remember to use the smallest file size available.

3. If you're creating a website for your project, save the images you'll use in the assets folder of the website.

4. If you plan to use images for your navigation links, create them and place them in your project images folder.

5. Place the images you have available, and use image placeholders for those you do not yet have. Remember to use alternate text for all images except for background images.

6. Preview any pages with images in several browsers and browser versions.

7. Refer to the image design strategies presented in this chapter to ensure that your images are in the correct file format, relevant to the rest of the content, optimized to reduce file size, and balanced on the pages.

USING CREATIVE COMMONS LICENSING

You learned about Creative Commons licensing in the Finding and Creating Images section, earlier in this chapter. Creative Commons licensed content is a great place to begin looking when searching sources for project images.

1. Go to the Creative Commons website at search. creativecommons.org and search for some images. For example, type "flower images" in the search text box, then click on one of the providers such as Flickr, as shown in Figure 44.
2. Choose three images that can be used for commercial purposes and print the licensing documentation for each image.
3. Choose two images that can be modified and print the licensing documentation for each image.
4. List four criteria that can be set for searches and explain when you would use each criterion.

5. Visit two websites that post creative content and compare the effort required finding two images with Creative Common licensing to the effort required in your search in Step 1.
6. Research the steps necessary to submit an original image for Creative Commons licensing and write a paragraph that explains the process.

Figure 44 *Creative Commons search page*
© Creative Commons–creativecommons.org

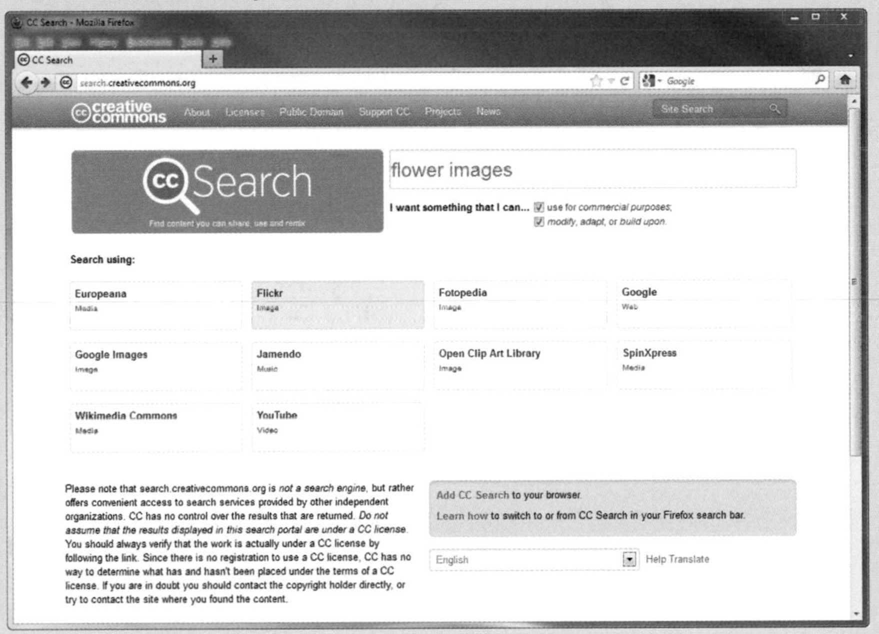

Even More to Explore

To explore some of the topics discussed in this chapter in more depth, see the References section at the end of the book. For links to additional web resources, visit the Even More to Explore link under Book Resources on Cengage Brain.

CHAPTER **7** ADDING
ANIMATION

- Getting Started with Animation
- Animation Design Strategies
- Working with Animation Using Adobe Flash CS6
- How We Did It: Adding Animation to a Flash Movie
- It's Your Turn: Adding Animation to Your Interactive Media Project
- More to Explore: Inverse Kinematics

CHAPTER 7

ADDING
ANIMATION

Introduction

In the previous chapter you learned basic design strategies for adding graphic elements to your pages. You then inserted images into each image placeholder and used image editing programs to optimize and enhance each image. In this chapter you learn how to create and integrate computer animation and motion graphics that you can use to enhance your project.

Animated graphics appeal to us in a way that static text or images cannot. In the not too distant past, animation over the Web was nothing more than flipping a few GIF images. In spite of its novelty, it was a slow and unsatisfying experience. Now as bandwidth has increased, along with the technologies for creating and viewing animation over the Internet, so has the demand for motion-enhanced media. With animation, you can create fade effects between photos to post on Facebook, enhance a web banner ad to attract more attention, or bring an online avatar to life.

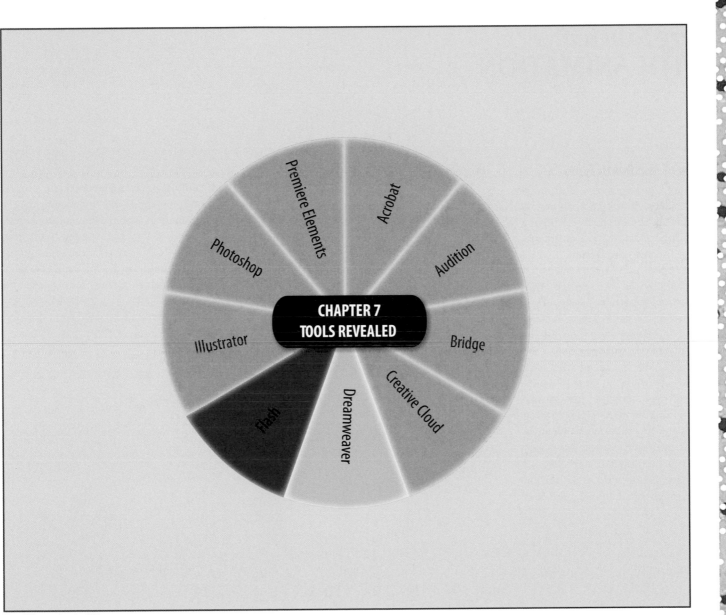

CHAPTER 7
TOOLS REVEALED

Premiere Elements

Acrobat

Photoshop

Audition

Illustrator

Bridge

Flash

Dreamweaver

Creative Cloud

Figure © Cengage Learning 2013

Getting Started
WITH ANIMATION

An Overview of Animation Types

Early animation techniques date all the way back to the 1800s. Traditional animators created the illusion of movement by moving a series of 2 dimensional (2D) hand-drawn illustrations in quick succession, like a flipbook. A later technique called cel animation was used in the earliest Walt Disney movies, and brought to life characters such as Pinocchio, Mickey Mouse, and the Seven Dwarfs. In **cel animation**, illustrations are hand drawn, representing snapshots of the trajectory of an action, and then played back on film frame-by-frame. Frame-by-frame animation portrays complex movements, like a person walking and talking, a dog wagging its tail, or any movement that alters shape in space and time. In **frame-by-frame animation**, an artist draws the contents of each frame (see Figure 1). Cel animation was a breakthrough in traditional animation

because it allowed parts of each illustration to be repeated from frame to frame by using celluloid for the foreground and simply superimposing the foreground elements over an opaque background, thus saving labor. A full-length feature film produced using cel animation would often require a million or more drawings to complete.

Although not as prevalent as cel animation, stop motion is another type of animation.

Stop motion could be thought of as a form of 3D animation. **3D animation** is the process of rotating, scaling, and **translating** objects, or moving them within 3-dimensional space along their x-, y-, and z-axes. With **stop motion**, a 3D object is moved in minute increments and recorded via camera or film. In takes about 24 frames to produce one second of realistic movement, so you can imagine how tedious it would be to move an

Figure 1 *Frame-by-frame illustrations for animation on the Gardener's Walk photo gallery page*

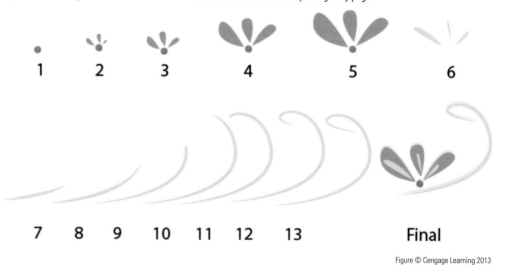

object in increments small enough to produce smooth motion. The many special effects in George Lucas's *Star Wars* utilized stop motion techniques at a time when the full power of computers was not yet realized. A wonderful example of the contemporary use of stop motion can be viewed in any of Nick Park's *Wallace and Gromit* movies.

By far the most influential innovation in the world of animation arts is the computer. Computers allow designers to create highly complex animations like those we might see in feature films. They enable designers to create sophisticated character animations and capture complex motions, using realistic cameras angles with pan and zoom effects. Designers can now infuse surfaces with simulations of reflecting and refracting light, and make natural looking objects, such as hair and plant life.

Animation can also be simple; for example, with a transitional fade from one image to another, or by sliding text onto a screen using a technique called tweening. **Tweening** is the process of recording two instances of a single object and having the computer calculate the images for the in-between frames. Tweening is the most basic digital animation technique and is used to create most of the simpler animation effects you see. Using tweening, you can alter an object's position, color, scale, rotation, and, in the case of a shape tween, its form (a process known as morphing).

Although the types of digitally-created motion are broad in scope, the fundamentals of animation remain the same. Animation combines an understanding of two concepts we experience every moment of our lives— time and space. In one second, our eyes can see a sequence of 10 to 12 still images. Perceiving more images within that second of time creates an illusion that the still images are in motion. Remember flipbooks? Each page of the book contains a still image, but when you quickly flip the pages the images appear to come to life.

In digital animation, this illusion of continuity is created using a unit of measurement called a **frame**, and the movement from frame to frame over time is the **frame rate**. It takes the movement of 24 to 32 frames per second (fps) to produce realistic movement. A higher frame rate produces smoother motion, while a lower frame rate creates a choppy effect, as you might see in old silent films.

When you work in computer animation programs, you usually create and edit animation using a visual timeline and motion editor that shows an editable graph of an animation's coordinates in space and time. See Figures 2 and 3 for examples of these elements in Flash.

However, in some programs you can also create animation by coding it in a scripting language. In Flash, for instance, you can use premade Code Snippets, even bypassing use of a visual editor. See the example of Flash ActionScript in Figure 4.

You'll get a chance to work with the Flash Timeline and an animation code snippet in the upcoming sections of this chapter.

QUICK TIP

Here are a few Flash sites with good animation examples (there are thousands more):

• DreamWorks Animation: dreamworksanimation.com
• Creative Commons: mirrors.creativecommons.org
• MillanNet Flash eCards: millan.net/anims/flash/flash.html

Popular 3D and 2D Animation Programs

Depending on the type of animation you want to achieve and the budget you have to work with, you can choose from a wide range of animation programs. Here's a list of the most popular programs and what they offer:

■ **3ds Max (Autodesk)** High-end 3D animation and modeling program used to produce special effects and character animations for video games and film; a popular program for industry designers and architects. Download a trial version from usa.autodesk.com/3ds-max. Cost: over $3,000

■ **Maya (Autodesk)** High-end 3D animation, modeling, and compositing program with a vast array of lighting and shading rendering effects; customizable for integration with third party software. Maya is one of the most popular programs for use in film, games, and television. To try it out, download a trial version at usa.autodesk.com/maya. Cost: over $3,000

■ **LightWave 3D (NewTek)** 3D animation, modeling and rendering program used in television, film, video games, and print graphics and visualization. 30-day free trial available from newtek.com/products/lightwave.html. Cost: over $1,000

■ **Flash (Adobe)** 2D animation and interactive content development for online delivery, gaming, and streaming video. Popular program for professional designers, developers, and animators.

Figure 2 *A timeline (Adobe Flash)*

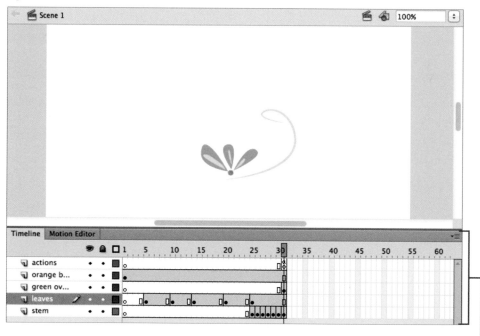

Timeline area

Figure © Cengage Learning 2013

30-day free trial available from adobe.com/products/flash.html. Cost: under $500

- **Toon Boom Studio (Toon Boom Animation)** 2D animation program ideal for students and hobbyists looking for an easy-to-use animation program. Visit: toonboom.com/products/toon-boom-studio. Cost: under $500
- **SWiSH Max 4 (SWiSHzone.com)** Program designed to create quick Flash-based animation effects. Details at: swishzone.com. Cost: under $250
- **CrazyTalk Animator (Reallusion)** 2D character animation and cartoon maker program with innovative character generation (using your own photos, for example) with puppet control and lip syncing. Visit: crazytalk.reallusion.com. Cost (standard version): under $100

Figure 3 *A motion editor (Adobe Flash)*

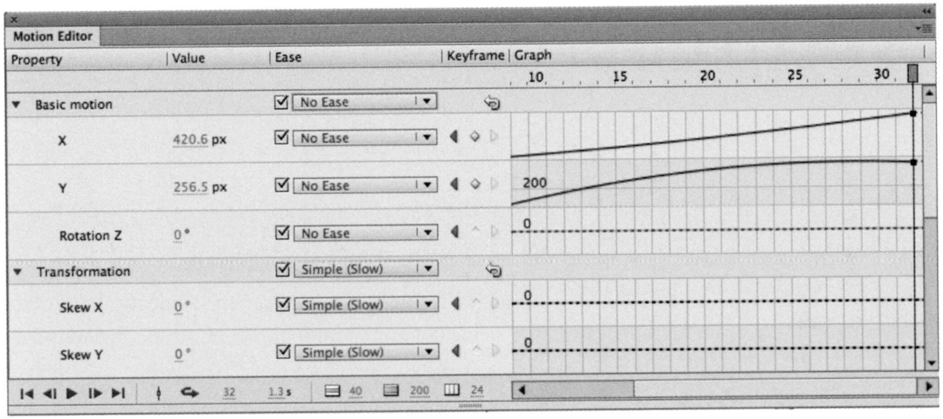

Figure 4 *Flash ActionScript for producing an animated alpha fade effect*

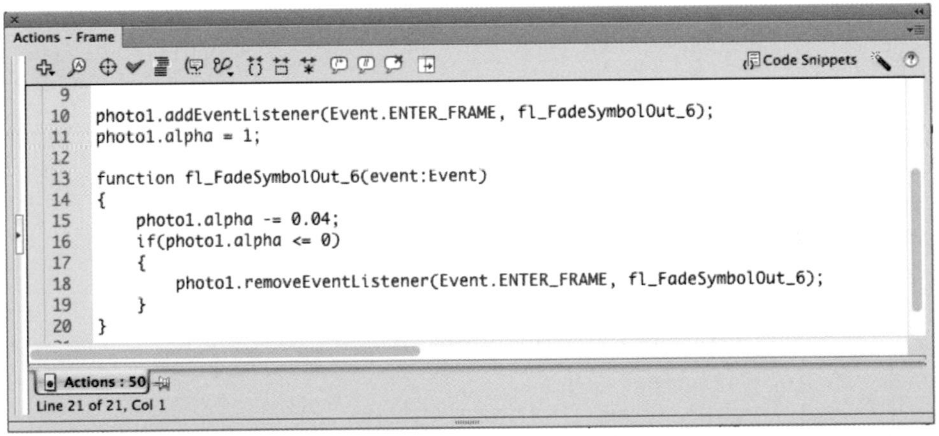

```
 9
10   photo1.addEventListener(Event.ENTER_FRAME, fl_FadeSymbolOut_6);
11   photo1.alpha = 1;
12
13   function fl_FadeSymbolOut_6(event:Event)
14   {
15       photo1.alpha -= 0.04;
16       if(photo1.alpha <= 0)
17       {
18           photo1.removeEventListener(Event.ENTER_FRAME, fl_FadeSymbolOut_6);
19       }
20   }
```

Adobe Edge: The HTML5-Compatible Animation Solution

As you learned in Chapter 4, Adobe is working on a web motion and interaction creation program called Adobe Edge. Edge content is designed to run smoothly on mobile devices and modern browsers utilizing HTML5, CSS3, and JavaScript. At the time of this book's printing, Edge is still in its trial phase; a preview of Edge can be downloaded here: success.adobe.com/en/na/sem/products/edge.html

Animation Design
STRATEGIES

Now that you have some background on the various styles of animation and the tools for achieving animated effects, let's cover some design strategies for making the most of your animated work.

Using Storyboards

Storyboarding is a useful way to help visually map out and organize the flow of your animation before you create it. And, like a wireframe, storyboarding provides a visual way to communicate your idea to others. A storyboard can be a highly complex rendering of drawings depicting the various poses of an animated character, including camera angles and scene transitions, or it can be a series of simple motion study sketches. See Figure 5.

You can find many excellent online examples of storyboards and templates to use. For example:

- Andy Lee Storyboards: andyleearts.com
- Studio 1151: www.mcli.dist.maricopa.edu/ authoring/studio/guidebook
- Video of storyboarding for movies: youtube .com/watch?v=t3mAHQuBqQI

Using Animation Physics

If you're interested in creating believable characters and object motion, spend some time studying and practicing established animation physics techniques. A great way to start is by exploring the tutorials on the Animation Physics website: animationphysics.com.

Figure 5 *A simple storyboard*

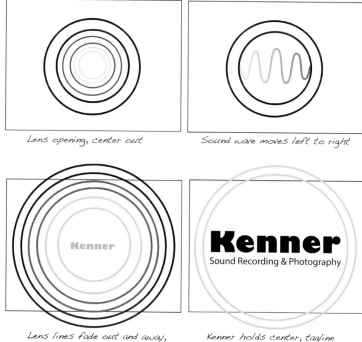

Lens opening, center out

Sound wave moves left to right

Lens lines fade out and away, Kenner zooms in.

Kenner holds center, tagline fades in below

Figure © Cengage Learning 2013

Apply Easing

Easing is a simple way to make motion appear more believable by subtly adjusting the timing at the beginning and/or end of an animation. For example, in Flash, when you apply a tween animation to an object moving from point A to point B, the default speed at which it moves is the same for every frame; a constant rate of speed. With an ease-in effect, the start of the motion slowly accelerates up to its constant defined speed. With an ease-out effect, the end of the motion slowly decelerates to its final resting point. Think of the motion of a car, for example, accelerating onto or decelerating off of a freeway ramp. You'll learn how to apply easing to a tweened object in the next section of this chapter.

Utilize Onion Skinning

Onion skinning is a feature in most 2D animation programs where you can view several frames at once. It's a wonderful tool to help you see the trajectory of your animation over time, so you can properly position or easily edit a series of keyframed objects. In Flash you can enable the onion skinning feature from the Timeline. See Figure 6, which demonstrates a motion tween with onion skinning turned on, showing the previous few frames of animation.

Sequence file names for faster import

If you'll be importing drawings or photos into your animation program from elsewhere, use a three- or four-digit naming system and proper file naming convention (no spaces, instead use underscores or dashes, and no unusual characters like $, %, or @) to ensure a compatible and sequential conversion. Lower numbers should have zeros placed before them (so that number 1, for example, appears before number 10). Programs like Photoshop and Adobe Bridge can help with the batch renaming process.

A numbering system like this one always sorts correctly and makes it easy to find what you need:

- frame_001.jpg
- frame_002.jpg
- frame_010.jpg

Figure 6 *Example of onion skinning on a motion tween*

However, a system like this one causes the objects to appear out of order in an alphabetized list, and will most likely lead to problems when you import or export it:

- image 1.jpg
- Image_02.jpg
- image__003.jpg

Don't Overdo It

We've all seen animated PowerPoint presentations that are more fluff than substance. Just because the options exist to swirl, spin, and bounce an object across a screen, they don't necessarily make the presentation more engaging. Avoid using animation unless it supports and enhances the purpose of your project.

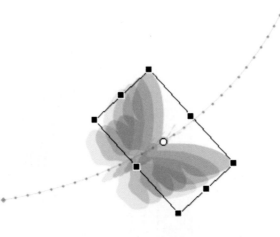

Figure © Cengage Learning 2013

Adding Animation

Working with Animation
USING ADOBE FLASH CS6

Animation in Flash is 2D animation: objects are animated in two dimensions (x and y, or horizontally and vertically). There is an exception: two tools, the 3D Rotation and 3D Translation tools, can be used to rotate or translate 2D movie clips along the z-axis, producing a simulated 3D perspective (see Figure 7).

2D animation is different from animation produced by 3D animation programs like Autodesk Maya or 3ds Max, where you can model and animate objects in three dimensions (x, y, and z). What might seem like 3D in Flash is actually a series of 2D images. For example, you can import a series of camera views of a 3D model from another source (like Swift3D or Plasma) and play back each position of it orbiting in space in Flash. Another option to simulate 3D movement is using ActionScript, which is essentially applying math to create a 3D effect.

The Flash Timeline

The Timeline is the heart of animation creation in Flash. It's the place where you organize your content into layers, and where you create, record, review, edit, and play back your animations, including tweened

Figure 7 *Rotating a rectangular shape using the Flash 3D Rotation Tool*

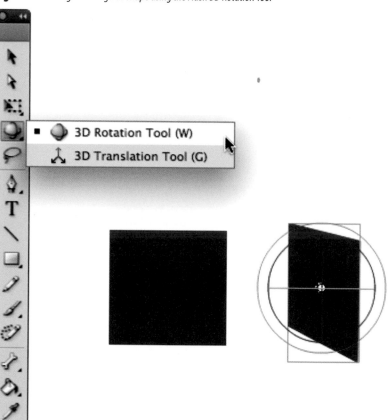

Adding Animation

and frame-by-frame animations. Learn the anatomy of the Timeline by reviewing the following list and Figure 8. For future reference, you can also review Timeline features by choosing Help > Flash Help from the program's menu bar.

The major components of the Timeline are layers, frames, and the playback head.

Refer to Figure 8 to identify each numbered item:

1. Layers in a document are listed in a column on the left side of the Timeline.
2. Hide, lock, or view objects as outlines on a layer. Click a black dot of a specific layer below the hide, lock, or outline icons to hide, lock, or view that object as an outline.

3. Create a New Layer, a New Folder, or Delete a layer by choosing one of the icons in the lower left part of the panel.
4. Frames contained in each layer appear in a row to the right of the layer name. There are four types of frames: keyframe, property keyframe, blank frame, and frame.

- **Keyframe:** A keyframe is indicated by a black dot on a frame. A keyframe records an object's point in time. To create a keyframe, choose Insert > Timeline > Keyframe.
- **Property Keyframe:** A property keyframe is indicated by a small, black diamond on a frame. A property keyframe defines the object's properties (rotation, scaling, etc.) that are associated with a motion tween.

- **Blank Keyframe:** A blank keyframe is indicated by an empty dot. A blank keyframe indicates there are no objects on that frame at that point in time. To create a blank keyframe, highlight a frame in the Timeline and choose Insert > Timeline > Blank Keyframe.
- **Frame:** A frame is colored gray on the Timeline. A frame holds, or freezes, an object's position on the Stage. The object is visible but not moving. To create a frame, highlight a frame in the Timeline and choose Insert > Timeline > Frame.

QUICK TIP

The shortcut key for setting a keyframe is F6. Press F5 to create a frame, and to create a blank keyframe, press F7.

Figure 8 *Parts of the Flash Timeline*

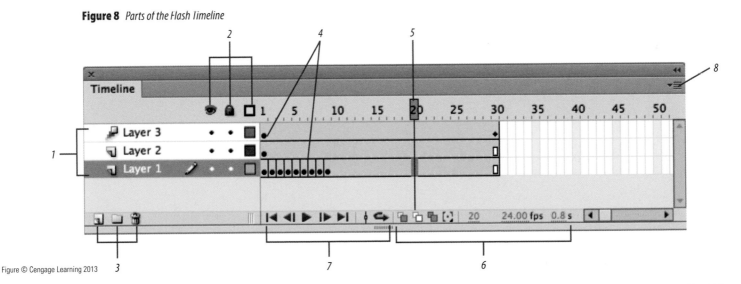

Adding Animation

5. The playhead (colored red) indicates the current frame displayed on the Stage.

6. The status area at the bottom of the Timeline has buttons to enable/disable Onion Skinning, and to edit multiple frames. It also shows the selected frame number, the current frame rate, and the elapsed time to the current frame.

7. The animation playback controller includes options to play, go to first frame, go to last frame, or step forward or back a frame.

QUICK TIP

By default, the frame rate for animations in Flash is set to 24 frames per second (fps). However, the final playback of a movie really depends on client-side factors, such as computer performance and Internet connection speed if the movie is viewed from the Web.

8. Options for how to view items in the Timeline are found in the Options menu in the upper right corner of the panel.

Creating a Simple Tween in Flash

Using tweens in Flash is an effective way to create movement while minimizing file size. Simple objects, such as text, logos, buttons, and bitmaps, are often tweened in Flash. Let's go over how to create a motion and color tween, adjust it using onion skinning, and apply an ease-out effect.

Figure 9 *Selecting the Essentials workspace*

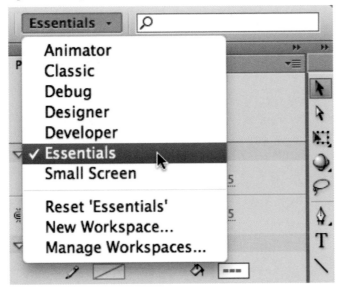

Figure 10 *Selecting the Text tool and its properties*

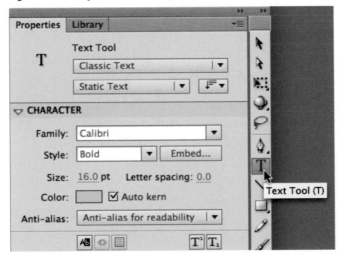

Adding Animation

Set up the basic tween

1. Open Adobe Flash.
2. Choose **File > New** and create a new ActionScript 3.0 document.
3. Be sure the workspace is set to the Essentials workspace. See Figure 9.
4. On the Tools panel on the right side of the screen, choose the **Text tool** and set the following options in the Properties panel. See Figure 10.

   Text engine: **Classic Text**
   Text type: **Static Text**
   Family: **your choice**
   Style: **your choice**
   Size: **16 to 45 point**
   Color: **your choice**

   Note that on the first frame of Layer 1 in the Timeline there is a blank keyframe (an empty circle shape). This indicates there is currently no object on this layer.

   (continued)

5. Click just inside the upper left corner of the white stage area, then type the word **TWEEN**. Now the first frame of Layer 1 has a keyframe (a black dot), indicating there's now an object on Layer 1 on the first frame of the Timeline. See Figure 11.

6. Choose the **Selection tool** in the Tools panel (see Figure 12) and select the text on the stage.

On the Menu bar choose **Modify** > **Convert to Symbol**. In the dialog box, name the symbol **tween**, and set the type to **Movie Clip**, as shown in Figure 13.

Any object you want to motion tween in Flash must be saved as a symbol. Symbols are reusable objects that are stored in the Flash library. Symbols on the Stage are called instances. Instances reference the attributes of the symbol in the library, resulting in minimal file size and easy editing. You can also give a name to an instance of a symbol, which then allows you to assign specific interactions to it using the Flash scripting language, ActionScript.

7. Click **OK** to close the dialog box.

8. Next, be sure the instance of the text symbol is selected on the stage, and choose **Insert** > **Motion Tween** from the Menu bar. A blue bar appears along Layer 1.

(continued)

Figure 11 *Placing the word **TWEEN** on the stage*

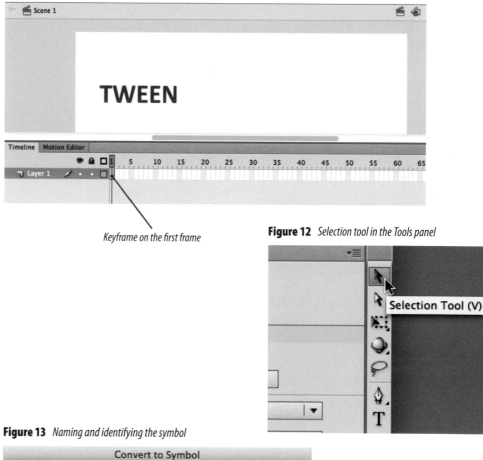

Keyframe on the first frame

Figure 12 *Selection tool in the Tools panel*

Figure 13 *Naming and identifying the symbol*

Adding Animation

Figure 14 *Extending the time of the motion tween to frame 36*

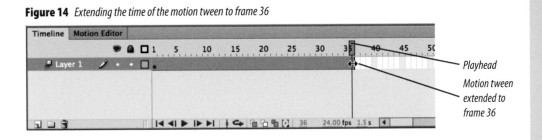

Playhead

Motion tween extended to frame 36

Figure 15 *Setting the next position of the object by dragging from upper left to lower right*

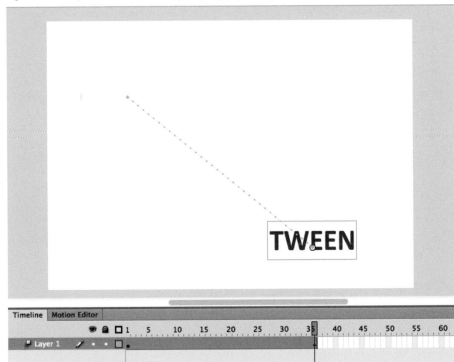

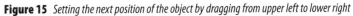

Figures © Cengage Learning 2013

Adding Animation

9. Drag the end of the blue bar to frame 36 (about 1.5 seconds of animation at the default Flash setting of 24 fps). See Figure 14.

10. Move the playhead (the red bar on the Timeline) to frame 36. Move the tween object to the lower right corner of the Stage. Frame 36 now shows a new keyframe recording the new position of the object at that point in time. See Figure 15.

11. Press **[Enter]** to play back the tween animation. Alternatively you can also choose the Play button at the bottom of the Timeline or Control > Play from the menu bar.

    You can also view the animation as a rendered SWF file by choosing Control > Test Movie > in Flash Professional.

12. Save your file.

Add an ease effect

1. To add an ease effect to the tween, click anywhere on the blue bar between the two keyframes on Layer 1 of the Timeline. This displays the properties for the motion tween in the Properties panel. See Figure 16.

2. In the Properties panel, set the ease to **70** by dragging to the right over the ease number (or click once on the number and enter the value).

3. Move the playhead to frame 1 on the Timeline and press **[Enter]** to play the animation. Notice that the animation decelerates at the end—this is called an ease out.

4. Try an ease in: Click anywhere on the blue bar between the two keyframes on Layer 1 to highlight the properties for the Motion Tween.

5. In the Properties panel, set the ease to -70 by dragging to the left over the ease number (or click once on the number and enter the value).

6. Move the playhead to frame 1 on the Timeline and press **[Enter]** to view the ease in effect.

Edit the motion path

1. Choose the **Selection tool** in the Tools panel.

2. Set the playhead to frame 1.

3. Place the mouse pointer over the middle part of the tween path until you see a small icon that looks like an arc. **Drag the path** to create a curve shape, similar to the one shown in Figure 17.

4. Press **[Enter]** to see the result.

Figure 16 *Motion Tween Properties*

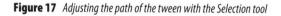

Ease option

Figure 17 *Adjusting the path of the tween with the Selection tool*

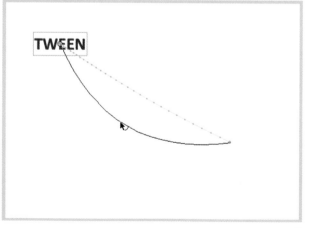

Figures © Cengage Learning 2013

Figure 18 *Adjusting the color of the TWEEN instance*

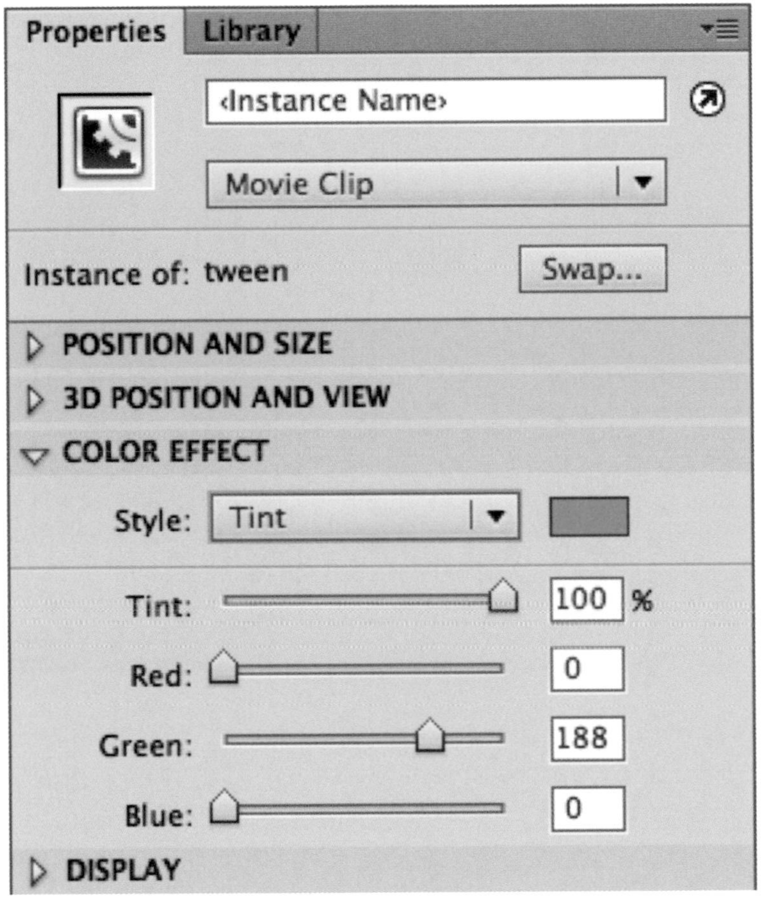

Animate color

1. Move the playhead to frame 20. Be sure the **Selection tool** is selected.
2. Click the instance of the TWEEN object on the Stage.
3. In the Properties panel for the instance, choose **Color Effect > Style: Tint**. Adjust the color sliders to create a new color choice for the TWEEN object. See Figure 18. Note the new property keyframe that appears at frame 20 on the Timeline.
4. Press **[Enter]** to see the new result.
5. Save the file if necessary and close the file.

Figure © Cengage Learning 2013

Create a frame-by-frame animation in Flash

Unlike tweening, where the computer calculates "in-between" frames, in frame-by-frame animation an artist draws the contents of each frame. Let's explore how this works by using the drawing tools in Flash to create a simple growing flower.

1. Open Adobe Flash and create a new ActionScript 3.0 document. Make sure the workspace is set to the Essentials workspace.

2. In the Tools panel, choose the **Brush tool**. See Figure 19.

3. Set the Brush color to a green color of your choice.

(continued)

Figure 19 *Choosing the Brush Tool*

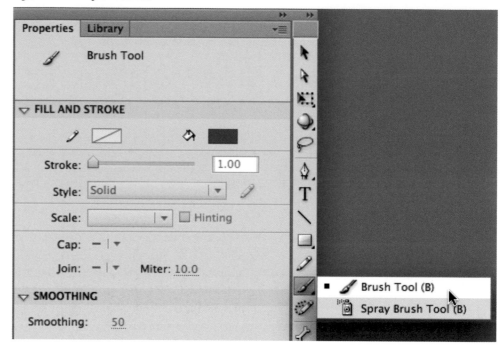

Figure 20 *Choosing a thicker brush size*

Figure 21 *Frames of a simple painting of a growing flower*

4. Choose a thicker Brush size by selecting a size from the brush options in the lower part of the Tools panel. See Figure 20. Note that these options only appear when the Brush tool is selected.

5. For the first frame of the animation, place a dot of green in the lower part of the Stage. Figure 21 shows an example of each drawing you'll create in steps 6 to 13 below.

6. Click **frame 2** of Layer 1 and choose **Insert > Timeline > Keyframe** to insert a keyframe. Paint a bit more of the green stem in this frame.

7. Click frame 3 and choose **Insert > Timeline > Keyframe** to insert a keyframe. Paint more of the green stem and a leaf. Don't worry about making the painting a masterpiece, but if you do want to undo a step choose Edit > Undo from the menu bar.

8. Add a keyframe to frame 4 and continue painting the stem.

9. Add a keyframe to frame 5 and continue painting the stem and another leaf.

10. Add a keyframe to frame 6, then Choose **Edit > Deselect All**.

11. Be sure the Brush tool is selected and, in the Properties panel, choose a new color for the flower part of the drawing.

12. Continue adding keyframes and paint the flower or flowers until complete.

13. Press **[Enter]** to play back the animation.

ADDING ANIMATION TO A FLASH MOVIE

In developing the animation effects in the Plant Gallery movie on the Gardener's Walk website, Sherry and Annesa used both the Timeline and ActionScript to create motion. Take a moment to view the Plant Gallery page of our demo interactive project at www.gardenerswalk.com/gallery.htm. The frames of the growing flower on the introduction screen were drawn in Illustrator. The drawings were imported into Flash sequentially by file name, and placed on individual keyframes.

However, the fade-in effect of each photo in the gallery was not produced on the Timeline (although it could have been using a simple color tween between each photo—adjusting the alpha value from 0 to 100%). Instead, we used a Flash code snippet. **Code snippets** are bits of ActionScript 3.0 code that are commonly used in interactive projects (for example, when hyperlinking to another web page, stopping and playing sound and video, and with animation effects like fading in and out of a movie clip symbol). Programmers can combine code snippets and can also use the Code Snippet panel to create and store custom snippets for later use. Here, we'll demonstrate how we created the Photo Gallery using a Flash code snippet, along with the process for placing the final Flash movie into a web page using Dreamweaver. You may choose to try the same effect in your interactive project or use it as a jumping-off point to add your own animated variations.

Preparing the photo layers for animation

1. In Photoshop, open three photos and crop them to the size that you'll need in the Flash movie. Optimize them for web viewing and save them in the JPEG format. Name each photo sequentially for easier importing and save them in the same folder. For example:

   gallery_001.jpg
   gallery_002.jpg
   gallery_003.jpg

   TIP To review how to optimize images for web delivery, see Chapter 6.

2. Open Flash. Create a new ActionScript 3.0 document. Set the document dimensions to the size of the photos.

3. Choose **File > Import > Import to Stage**, and browse for the first photo in the sequence. Click **Open**. A dialog box opens, asking if you would like to import the photos as a sequence. Click **Yes**. See Figure 22.

4. Move the playhead to **frame 1** of the **photos** layer, and click the photo on the Stage to select it. Choose **Modify > Convert to Symbol**, name it **photo1**, and then set the symbol to the Movie Clip type. (You need to convert objects to symbols so they animate properly). Follow this step for each photo in the sequence, naming each appropriately (**photo2** and **photo3**) in the Convert to Symbol dialog box.

5. View the Symbols library to ensure all photos are saved properly as symbols. See Figure 23.

Figure 22 *Importing images as a sequence*

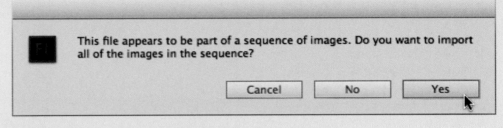

Figure 23 *Viewing saved symbols in the Library panel*

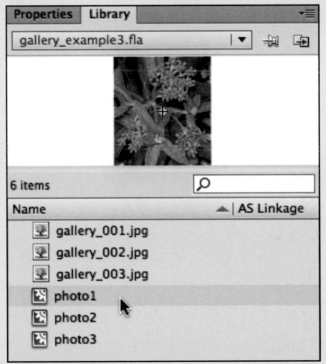

Figures © Cengage Learning 2013

Adding Animation

6. Scroll the Timeline to the right and set a frame on frame 250 using **Insert** > **Timeline** > **Frame**. See Figure 24.

7. Scroll the Timeline back to the left or click the **Go to first frame button** on the controller at the bottom of the Timeline. See Figure 25.

8. Create two new layers by clicking the New Layer icon twice in the lower left corner of the Timeline See Figure 26.

Figure 24 *Setting a frame on frame 250*

Figure 25 *Going to the first frame of the Timeline*

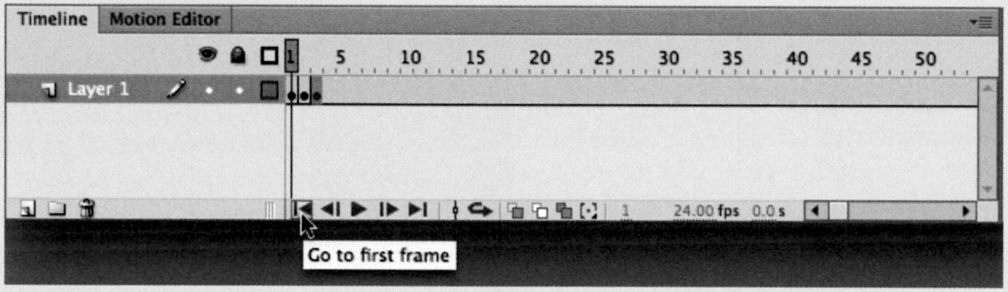

Figure 26 *Creating two more layers on the Timeline*

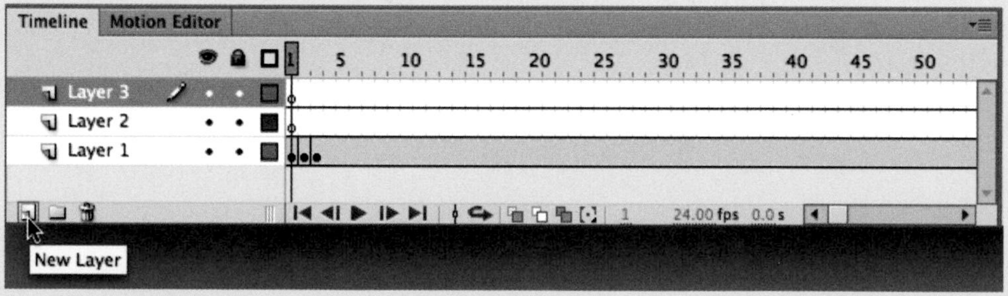

Adding Animation

9. Double-click the Layer 1 title and rename it **photo1**. Rename Layer 2 as **photo2** and rename Layer 3 as **photo3**. See Figure 27.

10. Click **frame 3** of the **photo1** layer to select it. Then drag the frame to the first frame of the **photo3** layer. See Figure 28.

11. Click **frame 2** of the **photo1** layer to select it, then drag the frame to the first frame of the **photo2** layer.

Figure 27 *Naming the new layers*

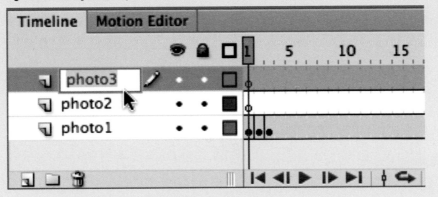

Figure 28 *Moving a frame to another layer*

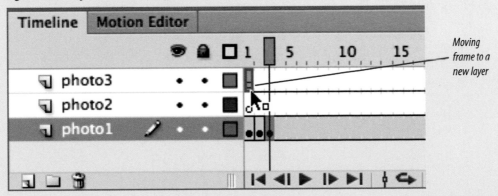

Moving frame to a new layer

12. Now, rearrange the layers so that each will fade out into another: Drag the **photo2** layer title down below the **photo1** layer title. Drag the **photo3** layer title below the **photo2** layer. See Figure 29.
13. Hide the **photo2** and **photo3** layers. See Figure 30.

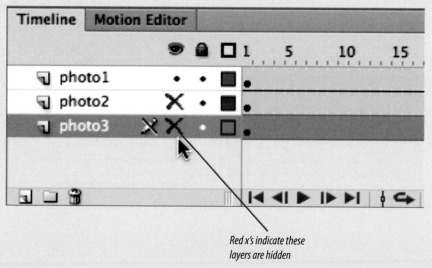

Figure 29 *Rearranging layers*

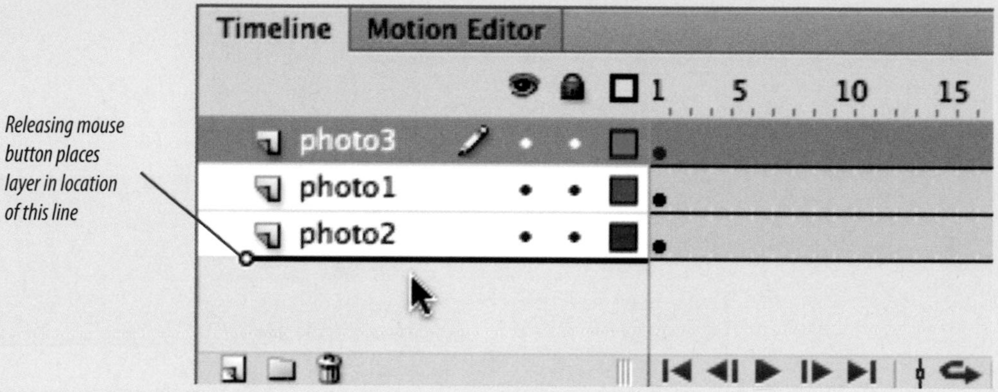

Releasing mouse button places layer in location of this line
Timeline
Motion Editor
1
5
10
15
photo3
photo1
photo2

Figure 30 *Hiding layers*

Timeline
Motion Editor
1
5
10
15
photo1
photo2
photo3
Red x's indicate these layers are hidden

Adding a code snippet

1. Move the playhead to **frame 50**, and click **photo1** on the stage to select it.

2. Choose **Window > Code Snippets**.

3. Open the Animation folder and double-click the **Fade Out a Movie Clip** snippet. See Figure 31.

4. The Set Instance Name dialog box opens. Name the instance **photo1** and click **OK**. See Figure 32.

An **instance name** identifies the specific instance so you can apply actions to it.

Figure 31 *Choosing a code snippet*

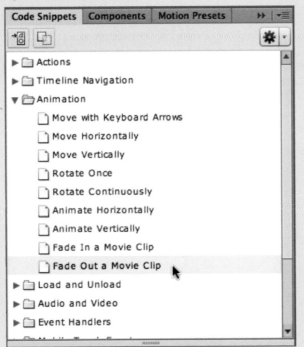

Figure 32 *Naming an instance*

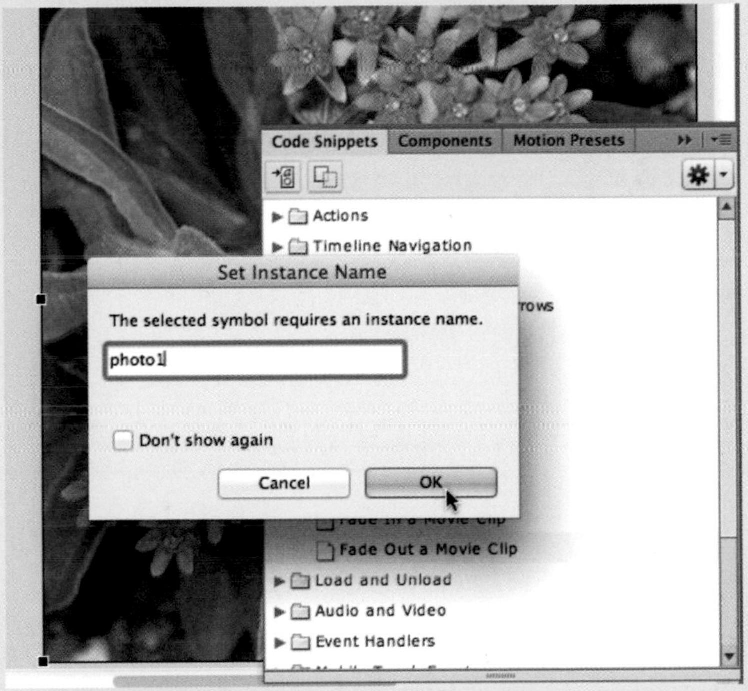

5. The Actions panel opens, displaying the code that the code snippet created. Figure 33 identifies some of the snippet code.

6. In the Actions panel, highlight the photo1 alpha value **0.01** and change it to **0.04**. Altering this number changes the speed of the fade. The larger the number the faster the fadeout. See Figure 34.

7. Close the Actions panel. Note in the Timeline that a new layer called **Actions** was created, and on frame 50 a little "a" indicates there is an action to be initiated at that point in time.

TIP If you need to view the code again for frame 50, select the frame and choose Window > Actions to open the Actions panel again.

8. Choose **Control > Test Movie > in Flash Professional** to see the first fadeout effect.

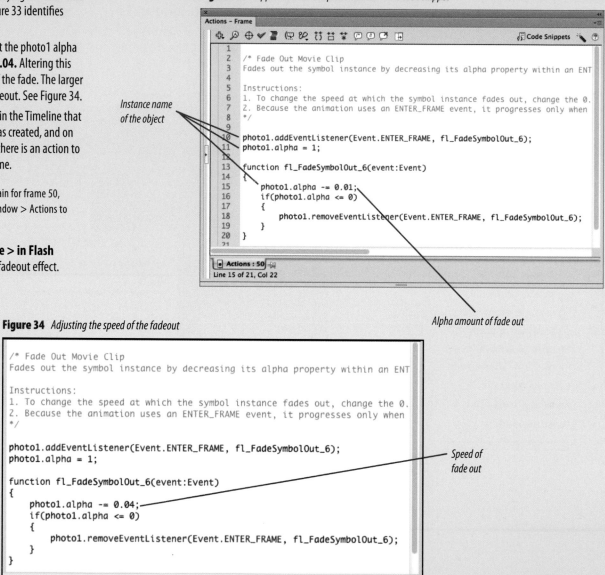

Figure 33 *Snippet name and alpha amounts in the code snippet*

Instance name of the object

Alpha amount of fade out

Figure 34 *Adjusting the speed of the fadeout*

```
/* Fade Out Movie Clip
Fades out the symbol instance by decreasing its alpha property within an ENT

Instructions:
1. To change the speed at which the symbol instance fades out, change the 0.
2. Because the animation uses an ENTER_FRAME event, it progresses only when
*/

photo1.addEventListener(Event.ENTER_FRAME, fl_FadeSymbolOut_6);
photo1.alpha = 1;

function fl_FadeSymbolOut_6(event:Event)
{
    photo1.alpha -= 0.04;
    if(photo1.alpha <= 0)
    {
        photo1.removeEventListener(Event.ENTER_FRAME, fl_FadeSymbolOut_6);
    }
}
```

Speed of fade out

Adding Animation

9. Unhide the **photo2** layer (by clicking the red X next to its layer name), and then hide the **photo1** layer.

10. Move the playhead to **frame 150**.

11. Select the **photo2** object on the stage.

12. Go to the Properties panel and in the Instance name area enter **photo2**. See Figure 35.

13. Choose **Window > Code Snippets**. Open the Animation folder if necessary and from the drop down menu, double-click the **Fade Out a Movie Clip** snippet. The Actions panel opens with the code for the fadeout effect. Note that the script refers to the instance name as **photo2**.

14. In the code, change the fadeout speed from **0.01** to **0.04**.

15. Close the Actions panel. Frame 150 on the Timeline now shows a small "a" to indicate there's an action to be initiated at that point in time.

16. Stop the animation: Select **frame 250** of the Actions layer, and choose **Insert > Timeline > Blank Keyframe** to insert a frame.

17. With Frame 250 selected, choose **Window > Actions** to open the Actions panel.

18. Type the script **stop();** in the Actions panel and press **[Enter]**. See Figure 36.

19. Choose **Control > Test Movie > in Flash Professional** to the see the two fadeout effects and the stop at the end.

20. Close the Actions panel, then name and save your file.

Figure 35 *Entering an instance name in the Properties panel*

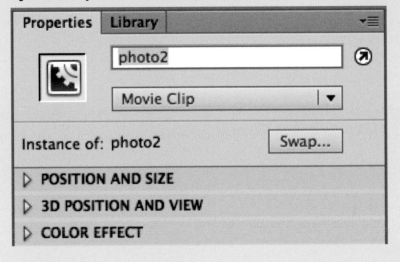

Figure 36 *Entering script to stop the Flash movie*

Adding Animation

Placing a Flash movie into a web page

1. If necessary, open the Flash animated movie file (the FLA file) that you created in the previous section.

2. Choose **File** > **Publish Settings**.

   The Publish Settings dialog box lets you select numerous output options for your Flash movie. The default output option is the **SWF format**— a compressed format that lets you run the movie using the Flash player application. The HTML Wrapper option creates an HTML document that includes the embed code necessary to retrieve the SWF file and view it properly in a browser. In our example, however, we'll have Dreamweaver create the embed code when we insert the SWF file into our existing Gardener's Walk photo gallery page.

3. Deselect the **HTML Wrapper** option in the Publish Settings dialog box and insert a name for the output file. Leave the remaining options at the default settings. See Figure 37.

4. Click the **Browse button** (the yellow folder), then save the file in the Assets folder for your project. Click **Publish**, then **OK** to exit the Publish Settings dialog box.

5. Close Flash, then open Dreamweaver and the HTML page on which you want to insert the Flash movie.

6. Click to place the insertion point at the page location where you'd like the Flash movie to appear.

   On the Menu bar, choose **Insert** > **Media** > **SWF** (see Figure 38) and navigate to the SWF file you saved in your project's Assets folder.

Figure 37 *Specifying the Publish Settings for the Flash movie*

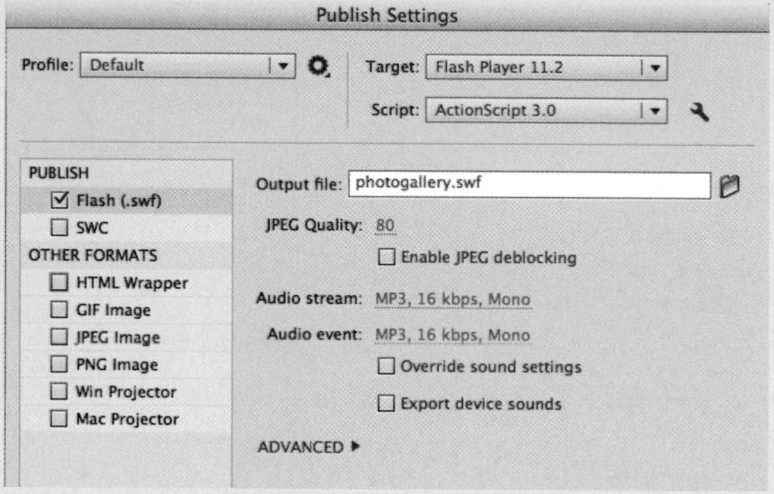

Figure 38 *Inserting the SWF file into the HTML page*

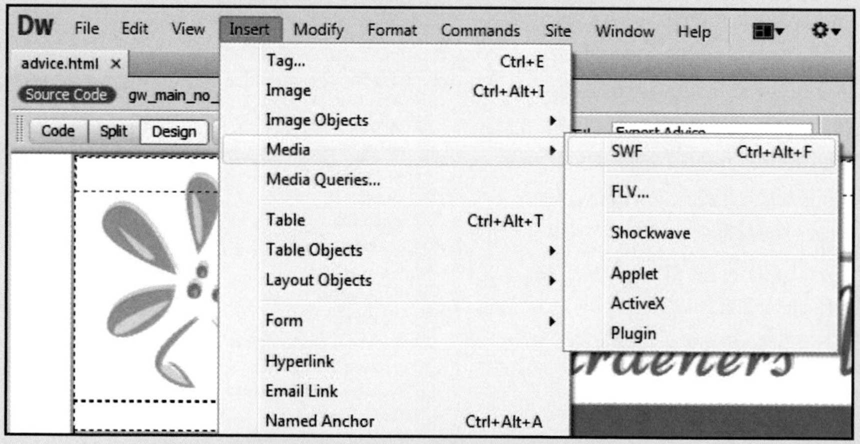

Adding Animation

7. In the Object Tag Accessibility Attributes dialog box, enter a descriptive title for the movie (see Figure 39), then click **OK**.

8. Save your work, then click the **Preview/Debug in browser** button to view the page and Flash movie in a web browser. See Figure 40.

Figure 39 *Setting an alternate (ALT) text tag for the SWF file*

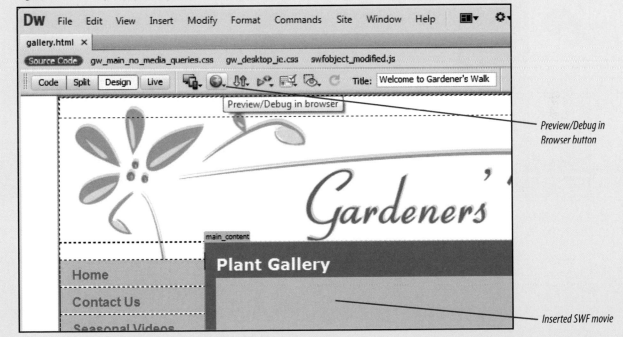

Figure 40 *Previewing the page in a browser*

Preview/Debug in Browser button

Inserted SWF movie

Figures © Cengage Learning 2013

TIP If you see the Get Adobe Flash Player notice (see Figure 41), this means that the published SWF file is saved in a different version of Flash Player than the one currently installed on your computer. By default, the embed code looks for the latest version of Flash Player, but you can change this in the Flash Publish Settings dialog box.

9. Close the browser window.

There may be situations when you'll want to examine the code for the embedded Flash file in the Web page code. To do this:

1. Choose the **Split View** option in Dreamweaver, then click the **Flash movie** on the page to select it.

Figure 41 *Get Adobe Flash Player notice*

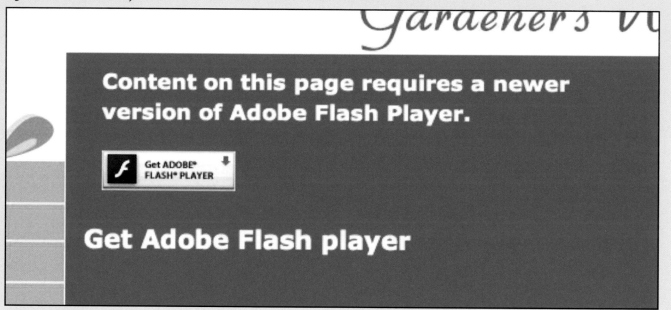

2. The object's embed code becomes highlighted in gray in the Code portion of the window. This is the code that renders the SWF file properly in the browser; it was created automatically when you inserted the SWF file into the page. See Figure 42.

Figure 42 *SWF embed code*

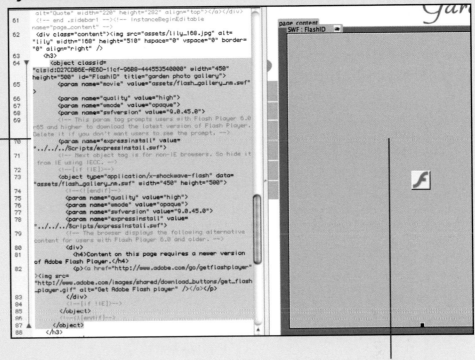

Highlighted code for
embedded SWF

Selected
SWF object

Adding Animation

ADDING ANIMATION TO YOUR INTERACTIVE MEDIA PROJECT

Now that you've learned some basic animation techniques, and explored the creation of some animated effects in Flash, you're ready to consider adding some animation to your own project.

1. Consider where in your project an animated effect might be most engaging—keep it simple, with a simple Flash banner, or a small movie of favorite photos or personal artwork.

2. Sketch a simple storyboard of each frame of the animation. Through a series of sketches, define the direction (right to left, up or down) of the object or objects to be animated or its various states of changing shape or color. Will the object or objects be animated with a tween, or using the frame-by-frame method?

3. Prepare the objects that will be animated. For example, if you will motion tween a series of photos, first set the dimensions and optimize the images in Photoshop, then save them with sequential file names. Import them into Flash and save each photo as a symbol. Or, if you're considering a frame-by-frame animation, draw each frame in a vector program like Illustrator or in Flash. Save each stage of the drawing as a symbol in Flash.

4. Using Flash, animate the objects using the tween or frame-by-frame steps you learned in this chapter.

5. Save the animation as a SWF file using the **File > Publish** commands, and then insert the SWF into your project.

INVERSE KINEMATICS

There's an incredibly cool feature in Flash, supported by ActionScript 3.0, called Inverse Kinematics (IK). Inverse kinematics lets you animate one or more objects using a jointed bone structure. You can easily apply motion to symbol instances and shapes so they move in true-to-life ways. For example, you can animate a character's arms, legs, and facial features to move in ways that, only a short time ago, were possible only with highly sophisticated software and equipment. This feature is a real boon for character animators. Try this:

1. Create a new Flash file (ActionScript 3.0).
2. Use the Oval tool and create a simple arm shape with three parts—upper arm, lower arm, and a hand. See Figure 43.
3. Select the Bone tool in the Tools panel. See Figure 44.

Figure 43 *Drawing the arm shape*

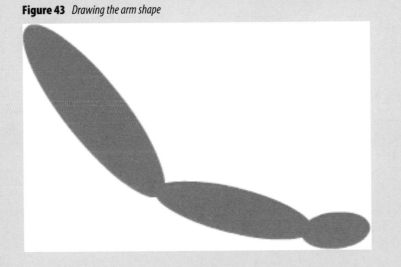

Figure 44 *Selecting the Bone Tool*

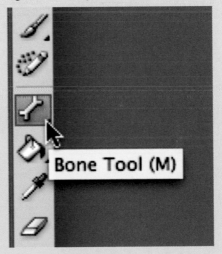

4. Click and drag the Bone tool from the shoulder down to the elbow—the top arm bone. Then, click and drag again from the end of the top arm bone to the wrist—the lower arm bone. Then click and drag from the end of the lower arm bone to create the hand. See Figure 45.

TIP To successfully connect the bones together, you must hold the mouse pointer over the end of each bone section until you see the bone tool turn white then click and drag to connect and create the next bone.

5. Notice in the Timeline that an "Armature" layer is created.

Figure 45 *Drawing the bone object*

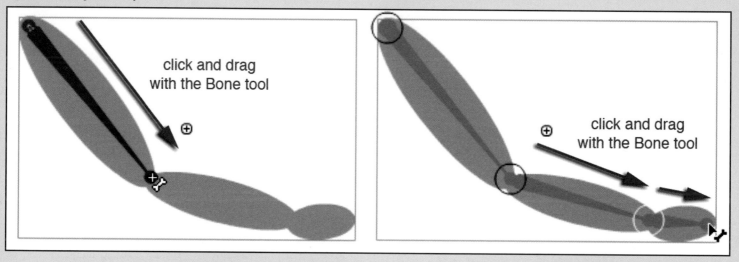

click and drag
with the Bone tool

click and drag
with the Bone tool

Adding Animation

6. Using the Selection tool, click the end node of the hand bone (the circle shape on the fingertips of the armature) and drag to articulate the full arm. See Figure 46.
7. Animate the arm—set keyframes (poses) of the arm and hand waving. See Figure 47.

Study more about IK in the Flash help files: Timelines and Animation > Inverse kinematics.

Figure 46 *Articulating the arm*

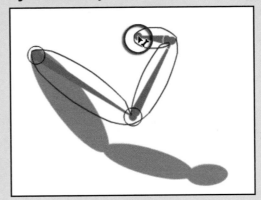

Figure 47 *Animating the armature*

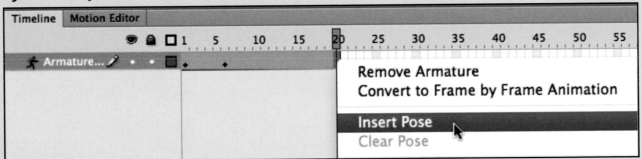

Figures © Cengage Learning 2013

INTERACTIVE MEDIA DESIGN
AND DEVELOPMENT WITH ADOBE CS6

CHAPTER **8** USING
AUDIO

- Digital Audio Overview

- Audio Design Strategies

- An Overview of the Podcasting Process

- Working with Audio Using Adobe
  Audition CS6

- How We Did It: Adding Audio to a
  Flash Movie

- It's Your Turn: Adding Audio to Your
  Interactive Media Project

- More to Explore: Embedding Sound in Flash

CHAPTER 8 USING AUDIO

Introduction

In the previous chapter you learned how to create and integrate animation as part of your interactive media project. Now, in this chapter, you discover how to use audio to enhance a user's interactive experience.

You don't need sophisticated sound equipment and a master's degree in sound engineering to successfully incorporate audio into your interactive media project. A general understanding of how sound is reproduced, and how to find, prepare, and publish sound for digital delivery, particularly online, can set you on the right track.

Adding audio to your media creation also has the significant benefit of providing an alternate learning modality for your user, especially if your project is intended to teach or inform. **Learning modalities** are ways in which people receive and retain information, such as through visuals, text, or sound. Each of us has preferred learning modalities, so content developers should provide information using various modalities in order to target the widest audience possible.

CHAPTER 8
TOOLS REVEALED

Premiere Elements

Acrobat

Photoshop

Audition

Illustrator

Bridge

Flash

Creative Cloud

Dreamweaver

Figure © Cengage Learning 2013

Digital Audio
OVERVIEW

To start, it's useful to understand how digital sound is reproduced. When you reproduce sound digitally, the quality of the sound is determined by its **sample rate**—the number of times audio is sampled per second. Sound is continuous, and it's not possible to capture and reproduce every bit of it. So instead, a digital recorder takes periodic **samples** at points over time. When these samples, which are like snapshots, are captured and played back quickly enough (with short intervals), the human ear perceives the series of samples as a continuous sound, without hearing the gaps between them. This is similar to the way humans perceive motion: the faster the playback of a series of still frames, the more continuous the motion appears. In digital audio, the more frequent the samples (i.e., a higher sample rate), the higher the quality of the reproduced sound, as shown in Table 1.

A sample is measured by the number of cycles in a sound's sine wave or waveform. See Figure 1. A single wave cycle (the range from one peak to another peak of a sine wave) in one second is known as a hertz. For example, at one sample per second, the sample rate would be expressed as 1 Hz. If you sample that sound a thousand times in one second, the sample rate would be one kilohertz (kHz). And, at a million times in one second, the sample rate would be one megahertz (MHz).

As with images, sound is represented on the computer by a series of 0s and 1s known as bits. Audio samples can also have different resolutions or dynamic range determined by **bit depth**—the number of bits that make up the complexity of a sound. Bit depths for audio can be 8 bit, 16 bit, 24 bit, and 32 bit. The higher a sound's bit depth, the higher its **fidelity**—that is, it will sound more like the original. For example, because it has a higher bit depth, music played from a CD will most likely have a higher sound quality than the same music heard via the Web. However, the sound on the CD will also be larger in file size.

Another property of sound that affects its quality is whether it's monaural or stereo sound. Amplifiers produce monophonic (mono) sound by transmitting a single channel to one or more speakers—even if two speakers are used, a mono signal will produce the same exact sound in each speaker. Mono sound produces a smaller file size and is suitable for speech recordings. Stereophonic (stereo) sound uses two or more independent audio channels, creating the sensation of a live band or orchestra. Music mixed with

TABLE 1: COMMON SAMPLE RATES FOR DIGITAL AUDIO	
Sample rate	Quality level
11,025 Hz	Poor AM radio (low-end multimedia), the lowest recommended quality for a short segment of music or voice recording
22,050 Hz	Near FM radio (high-end multimedia), good for web playback
32,000 Hz	Better than FM radio (standard broadcast rate)
44,100 Hz	Standard CD rate
48,000 Hz	Standard DVD
96,000 Hz	Blu-ray DVD

© Cengage Learning 2013

various instruments and effects is best saved as stereo—although a stereo file is larger than a comparable mono file, it better preserves the depth and subtleties of the recording.

So, a sound's sample rate and bit depth determine its sound quality (fidelity) and file size, as shown in Table 2. These factors are important to remember when you're determining the best sound solution for your interactive media project.

Finding Sound

Now that you have a basic understanding of what makes up a sound file, you can begin to find or record the sound that you want to use. There are various avenues to consider, depending on whether you need sound bites, background tracks, musical numbers, or voice recordings. Your choice will also depend on any concerns you may have about budget, time constraints, and usage rights.

Free Sounds

Just as you can find free fonts and images on the web, you can also find sound files at no charge. Do a search for "free sounds" and you'll find a wealth of information. Most of the audio on these sites is within the public domain, available under a Creative Commons license, or free to use if you credit the composer. However, for any file you obtain over the web, it's important to read the site's fine print to learn exactly how the audio can be used. If you're unsure, contact the site's webmaster or the creator of the

work. As you learned in Chapter 6, **Creative Commons (CC)** is the nonprofit organization that offers flexible copyright licenses for creative works. CC allows authors of music, film, photos, text, etc. to share their work under a specific license they can define on their website (see creativecommons.org). Two of Annesa's favorite repositories for

Figure 1 *Waveform of an audio file*

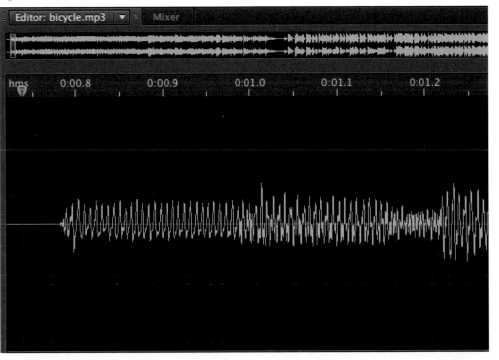

© Cengage Learning 2013

TABLE 2: APPROXIMATE FILE SIZES OF 1-MINUTE OF DIGITAL AUDIO			
	Sample Rate		
File Type	**44 kHz**	**22 kHz**	**11 kHz**
16 bit Stereo	10.1 MB	5.05 MB	2.52 MB
16 bit Mono	5.05 MB	2.52 MB	1.26 MB
8 bit Mono	2.52 MB	1.26 MB	630 KB

sound are Freesound at freesound.org and ccMixter at ccmixter.org. Both resources offer extensive collaborative databases of Creative Commons-licensed audio snippets, samples, or songs for mashing-up (blending parts of songs into a new song) and remixing.

Purchased Sounds and Music

There are also plenty of resources where you can purchase sounds and music for limited or unlimited use. Some of the more common sites are the same ones that also offer stock images and video footage, including iStockphoto, Getty Images, Digital Juice, and Footage Firm.

Producing Your Own

The best way to guarantee that sounds are royalty free and low cost is to produce your own sounds, voice recordings and music. Or, find a musician friend to help you out. That's what we did for our Gardener's Walk demo project. The acoustic music in the Flash photo gallery is part of a song composed by Annesa's friend, Ethan Lipton & his Orchestra. To make it official, we had Ethan sign a permission form and offered a small stipend for the use of part of the song specifically for our project. The Gardener's Walk site also features a phone interview on the Expert Advice page that Annesa conducted using freeconferencing.com. This handy service lets you create a free account that gives you access

to your own phone conference line, along with online administrative tools for recording and retrieving phone conversations. The only cost incurred is the long distance fee for the call itself. See the Audio Design Strategies section of this chapter for tips on producing successful voice recordings.

Preparing Audio

Once you have some audio to work with, the next items to consider are the tools you might use to edit your sound. You should also decide which file format will be best for the intended output. Table 3 lists programs that let you resample, clip, crop, equalize volume, mix multiple tracks, add effects to, and output your sound before embedding or linking it into your interactive media project framework.

We used Audition to edit the audio files for our Gardener's Walk project. You'll explore basic editing features in the Working with Audio Using Adobe Audition CS6 section of this chapter.

The type and compression scheme (called the **codec**, an acronym for encoder/decoder) of a particular format will make a big difference in the quality and file size of your sound. Just like images, sound can be compressed into various formats depending on its purpose. There are many formats out there, and these are a few common ones:

WAV (.wav): WAV is an uncompressed audio format, supported by both Windows and Macintosh. The sound quality and file size can vary widely depending on the sample size (the number of bits) and whether the sound file is stereo or mono. It's probably the most widely supported sound format for the Web.

AIFF or AIFF-C (.aiff, .aif, or .aifc): Audio Interchange File Format or AIFF is an uncompressed audio file format for Macintosh (AIFF-C is the compressed variant). As with WAV files, the sound quality and file size depend on the sample rate and whether the sound file is stereo or mono.

TABLE 3: AUDIO EDITING PROGRAMS			
Program	**Website**	**Platform**	**Description**
Audacity	audacity.sourceforge.net	Windows, Mac	Popular, low-end, cross-platform audio editor; and best of all, it's free
GoldWave	goldwave.com	Windows	Low end, about $50
Sony Sound Forge	sonycreativesoftware.com/soundforge	Windows	A professional audio solution, about $400
Steinberg Cubase	steinberg.net/en/products/cubase	Windows, Mac	For advanced music production, ranging from $100 to $500
Adobe Audition	adobe.com/audition	Windows, Mac	The premiere audio solution for recording, mixing, and editing sound. Cost is about $350.

© Cengage Learning 2013

MP3 (.mp3): MP3 is a standard cross-platform compressed audio format, and is widely used for delivering sound via the Internet.

AAC (.aac, .m4a, .mp4): Advanced Audio Coding. This compressed format is a successor of MP3, with improved quality and smaller file sizes. AAC is commonly used in MPEG-4 multimedia files, and can support features such as surround sound.

Ogg Theora (.OGG): An open source multimedia format for both audio and video, developed by Xiph.org. Supported by the HTML5 video and audio elements.

Publishing Audio

Once you've prepared your audio, you're ready to integrate it into your interactive media project. You can insert it in a web page using an embed tag; or for HTML5 the audio element tag; or you can link to it or embed it in a Flash movie. In the How We Did It section of this chapter, we'll show you the specific methods we used to publish audio in the Gardener's Walk Flash-based photo gallery, but here we'll look at the most common method—inserting audio into a web page.

Inserting Audio into a Web Page

The most common method for getting your audio on a web page is to link to it using an embed tag or, for HTML5 compatibility, the <audio> element. These tags also define specific players for the audio. See Figure 2 for examples of three different players, and Figure 3 for code examples of each one.

(In the HTML5 code, the second-to-last line will appear in a user's browser if it cannot support HTML5.) Just like with images, it's a good idea to put audio files in an assets folder within your site folder, so that everything remains properly linked together when you upload your project to a remote location.

Figure 2 *Example audio players*

Figure 3 *Code for the Dreamweaver generic audio player, Google audio player, and HTML5 controller*

Generic audio player (default player for Dreamweaver)

```
<embed src="your_file.mp3" width="200" height="20" autostart ="false">
</embed>
```

Google Reader MP3 Player

```
<embed type="application/x-shockwave-flash"
flashvars="audioUrl="your_mp3_file_URL"
src="http://www.google.com/reader/ui/3523697345-audio-player.swf"
width="400" height="27" quality="best">
</embed>
```

HTML5 audio controller (viewable on HTML5-supported browsers)

```
<audio controls="controls">
<source src="your_file.ogg" type="audio/ogg"/>
<source src="your_file.mp3" type="audio/mpeg" />
Your browser does not support the audio element.
</audio>
```

Insert audio into a web page

1. In Dreamweaver, place the insertion point on the page where you'd like the audio player to appear.

2. Choose **Insert** > **Media** > **Plugin** from the Menu bar. Search for your audio file.

3. By default, the plugin controllers for the audio will be set to 32 pixels wide and 32 pixels high. To see all the audio controls, select the plugin object on the page in Dreamweaver, and in the Properties panel, set the width to at least 125 pixels, and the height to 16 pixels. See Figure 4.

(continued)

Figure 4 *Setting properties for the audio controller plugin*

Audio player size settings   Selected audio player plugin

USING OGG AUDIO WITH HTML5

If you want your project to adhere to HTML5 standards, you'll want to hand-code the HTML5 elements shown in Figure 3 into your web page. You'll notice that the code calls two types of audio formats: Ogg and mp3. Ogg (also known as Ogg-Theora) is a lesser-known audio format that, at this time, must be used to view HTML5-compatible video in the latest Firefox and Opera browsers. Unfortunately, many audio editing programs do not offer Ogg conversion options. However, free online audio conversion tools are available, such as audio.online-convert.com/convert-to-ogg or media.io. For more information on creating HTML5-friendly audio, visit w3schools.com/html5/html5_audio.asp.

Figure © Cengage Learning 2013

Figure 5 *Audio controller on the Gardener's Walk site*

Audio controller
in browser

4. View the page in a browser to hear the sound and test the audio playback controls. See Figure 5.

5. So the audio doesn't start playing automatically, edit the source code to include the property autostart="false". It would look something like the code shown in Figure 6.

Figure 6 *Player code with autostart set to false*

```
<embed src="assets/audio/my_recording.mp3" width="200" height="20" border="1" autostart="false"></embed>
```

Figures © Cengage Learning 2013

Using Audio

Audio Design
STRATEGIES

Now that you have some idea of what it takes to get started using audio in your project, let's get into some specific strategies for the most effective design and delivery of your audio, keeping usability and accessibility in mind.

Start with the Best Recording You Can Get

Depending on the subject you're recording, your determination of a "best" recording could vary. If you're recording a rock concert, for example, you don't have much control over screaming fans, but perhaps it's a desired enhancement for the recording's auditory ambience. On the other hand, recording an interview for your upcoming podcast episode might involve a bit more work to ensure the best recording possible and to alleviate extensive editing later. Here are some suggestions for those types of recordings:

1. Eliminate background noise.
2. Use a headset style microphone. It doesn't need to be expensive, just one that leaves your hands free. It can be unidirectional with noise cancelling features, and if you're recording from your computer, one with a USB connection. A USB version tends to have a better frequency response, and can capture your voice more accurately than an analog two-plug version. Plantronics, Logitech, and Altec Lansing are reputable manufacturers of USB headsets.
3. For interviews or voice recordings, use a script, or prepare speaking points.
4. Record in sections.
5. Speak clearly and with dynamic voice inflection.
6. If you make a mistake, avoid stopping and redoing the whole recording; instead, pause and repeat the section. You can edit out mistakes, miscellaneous "ums," and breath sounds later.

Provide User Controls

Music and sounds can pique a wide range of emotions in people. Consider that moment when someone's cell phone goes off. A ring tone that might be music to one person's ears can be grounds for a public disturbance violation to someone else. Moreover, what you might think is the most awesome soundtrack for the background music of your site might not be so for your audience. On the flip side, sound can be a great enhancement to an interactive media experience, so don't avoid it entirely; just provide it in a context that lets users control when to stop, play, or change the volume at their leisure. Fortunately, standard audio embed tags include an end-user controller. Programs that support audio, like Flash, make it fairly easy to add stop, pause, and play buttons. Your job is to be sure those controls are always included and are easily accessible in your design.

Include a Transcript

Provide accessible, text-based transcripts for all voice recordings, particularly those for educational purposes—interviews, stories, news items, lessons, and the like. If you started with a script for your recording, you already have a head start. Transcription can be a tedious process, but there are some speech analysis tools available that can do an adequate job, though you'll need to clean up the text later. With each new version, the Adobe Premiere Pro Speech Analysis feature becomes more accurate in its transcription ability, and can save typing time. You can place your transcription in an HTML page, or provide a link to a downloadable PDF. As an example, view the PDF transcript of the Expert Advice interview on our demo site.

Watch File Size

As with images and video, it's important to optimize your audio files so they download in a reasonable time for the majority of Internet users and maintain good quality. Optimizing a sound file includes reducing its overall length to fit the needs of your project, looping the sound if possible, compressing it, and setting the correct bit depth and channel for the type of sound—voice only or instrumental music with or without vocals.

Avoid Gratuitous Sounds

Like animation and images, avoid including sound in your project unless there's a good reason for it. If it doesn't have a significant purpose or doesn't support and enhance the mood and theme of your project, don't use it.

An Overview of the PODCASTING PROCESS

As you consider audio for your interactive media project, be sure to consider podcasting, one of the most prevalent audio delivery methods on the Internet today.

Podcasting is a method of delivering syndicated content over the Internet. **Syndicated** refers to content that is sent to you automatically when new content is created, like subscribing to an email newsletter or magazine. While we most often experience podcasting as audio content, you can podcast all kinds of digital media, including PDF files, images, HTML pages, and video.

Podcasting is different from streaming audio in its distribution method and how the content loads. In general, users access streaming audio by navigating to its web location, clicking on a button to download it, and listening to it right away. With syndicated podcasted audio, the material is sent to you automatically when new content is created. This is done through an **RSS (Really Simple Syndication) feed**. An RSS feed is a standardized XML document that includes information on how the podcast should be published, including full or summarized text, plus authorship and date/time metadata.

Podcasting is appealing because it's automatically downloaded to your computer, easy to control, portable, and always available. Once you find the type of audio programs you like, you don't have to go looking for them; they come to you. It's like programming a TiVo digital video recorder to search for and record your favorite TV programs over a given period of time. Once you've set up an RSS feed, the content is automatically delivered to you. You can subscribe to a podcast feed, usually free of charge, using what's called a **podcatcher** or **podcast aggregator**. The best known podcatcher is iTunes, but there are many more. These programs enable you to aggregate (gather) feeds from many sites into one place. You can also subscribe by bookmarking the podcasts. Bookmarked podcasts will appear on your Bookmarks Toolbar. You click on the bookmark to view the latest downloaded podcast links.

Figure 7 *RSS feed subscriber icons*

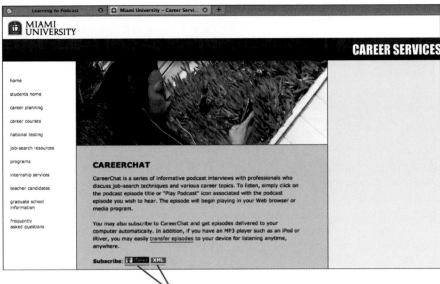

RSS feed subscriber icons

Using Audio

Subscribing to a podcast

1. Using the Firefox or Safari browser, go to Miami University's CareerChat: www.units.muohio.edu/careers/students/podcast.

2. Click the XML icon in the Subscribe area. See Figure 7.

   This takes you to a page with an index of the current podcasts and an option to subscribe using a bookmark (depending on the browser you are using the bookmark option could be in various locations on the page. For example in Firefox it's at the top of the page labeled Live Bookmarks and in Safari it's in the sidebar under Actions).

   (continued)

Select the application you'd like to subscribe with, and the podcasts will appear in the browser's bookmark bar, as shown in Figure 8. The list updates automatically when new podcasts become available. Alternatively, you can subscribe using your mail program, such as Microsoft Outlook or Mail.

(continued)

Figure 8 *Podcast subscription in the Firefox browser*

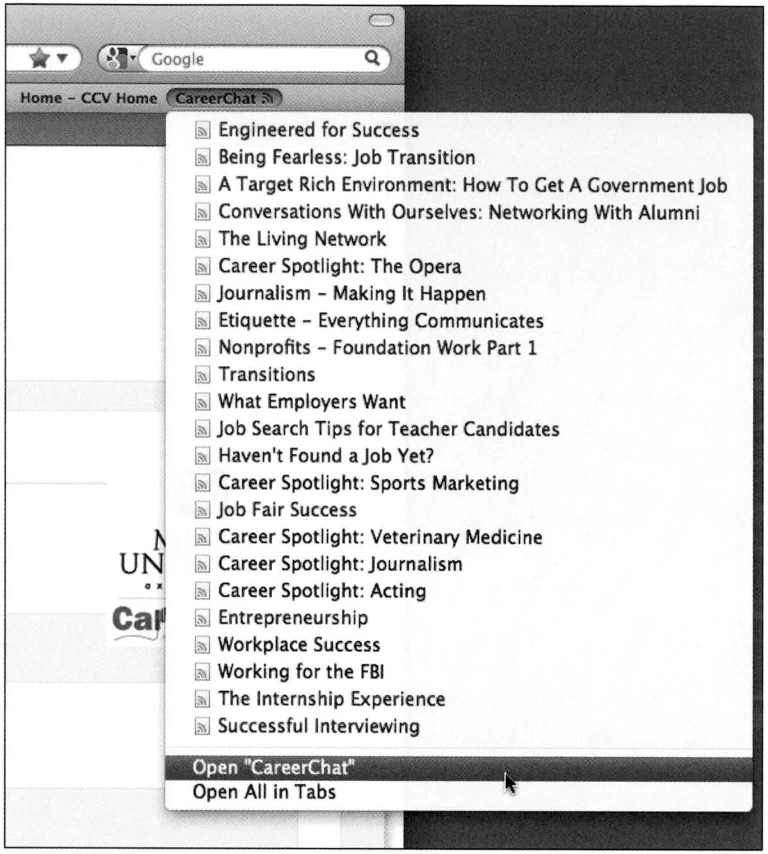

Figure 9 *Podcast listed in iTunes*

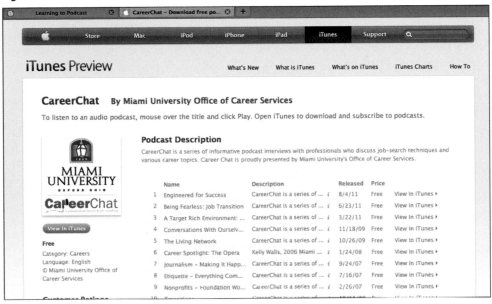

3. Return to the Miami University CareerChat site and choose the iTunes icon in the Subscribe area. This link takes you to the college's iTunes podcast area. If you have iTunes installed on your computer, you can then open iTunes and subscribe directly to the podcasts. See Figure 9.

Using Audio

Podcasting is easy to control. You decide when you want to receive a podcast by simply subscribing to it. If you don't want to listen anymore, you unsubscribe.

Podcasts are also portable because they're saved in the MP3 audio format, which preserves the sound quality of music and voice at a greatly reduced file size. This makes podcasts easy to download and transfer to an MP3 player where you can listen to them on-the-go and within your schedule.

Producing a Podcast

We can't cover all the details of how to produce a podcast in this chapter, but a general overview of the process is a good place to start. The process is the same as integrating other types of audio on the Web: make the content, edit the content, store the content, and access the content. See Figure 10.

In making and storing content, you must be sure to prepare the necessary metadata and RSS feed codes so the audio is published properly for various subscription tools. In general:

- When encoding and publishing your audio, be sure to create an **ID3 tag** so the file can be properly identified on the web. **ID3** is a metadata container most often used in conjunction with the MP3 audio file format. It allows information such as the title, artist, album, track number, and other information about the file to be stored in the file itself. To find the

Figure 10 *Podcasting process*

Using Audio

ID3 metadata settings in Audition, for example, choose Window > Metadata and select the ID3 tab on the Metadata panel. See Figure 11.

- Title podcasts with their name and date, such as podcastname-YYYYMMDD.mp3 or podcastname-episodenumber.mp3, so they'll be listed sequentially for the listener.
- Create an RSS feed to invite others to subscribe to your podcast. If you are XML- and HTML-savvy, you can code your own RSS feed or subscribe to a feed management service like Google FeedBurner(feedburner.google.com)which will create the RSS feed for you.
- Place a **chiclet** (a small icon adjacent to your podcast) on your web page to indicate the availability of an RSS feed. Do an image search for "RSS icons" and choose from an endless array of chiclets that can be used to hyperlink to your RSS feed document. The Gardener's Walk uses this icon:

QUICK TIP

Other great resources on how to podcast are available at: Apple in Education at apple.com/education/podcasting and PoducateMe at poducateme.com.

Figure 11 *ID3 tag settings in the Audition Metadata panel*

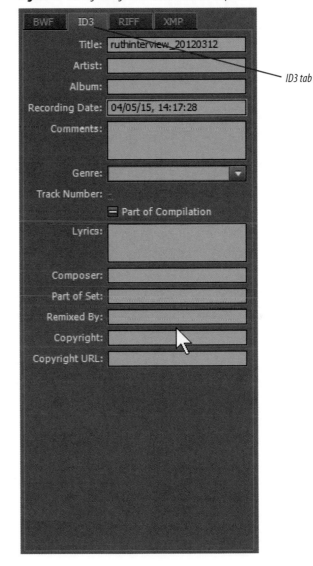

ID3 tab

Working with Audio Using ADOBE AUDITION CS6

The premiere program for working with audio is Adobe Audition. The program contains features for both novice and professional sound enthusiasts. In this section, you learn about a few of the basic features of the program, including how to record your voice, how to remove areas of a recording, adjust volume, create a fade in/fade out, and output the audio file. See Figure 12.

Figure 12 *Adobe Audition in action*

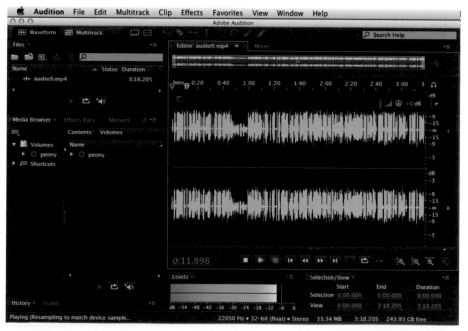

Using Audio

Figure 13 *Adobe Audition interface (Mac)*

Files panel   *Effects Rack panel*   *Editor panel*

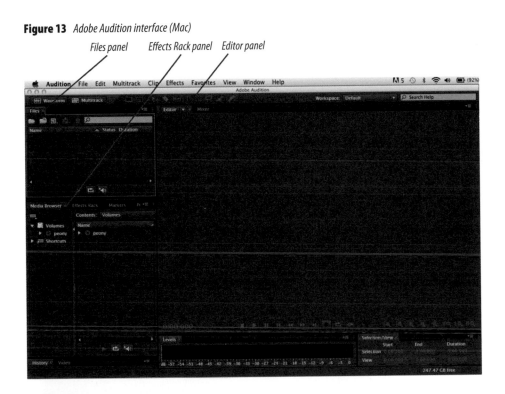

Figure 14 *Setting the workspace to Default*

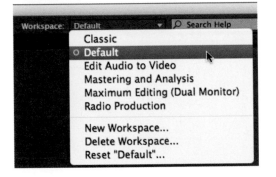

Using Audio

Record voice in Audition

1. Open Adobe Audition.

   If you're familiar with other Adobe products, you'll notice right away that the interface for Audition looks somewhat different. See Figure 13.

   The program window is divided into three panels: the Files panel, which lists the names of open files; the Editor panel, where you edit your files; and the Effects Rack panel, where you control special effects.

2. On the Menu bar, choose **Workspace** > **Default** to make sure the default workspace is selected. See Figure 14.

   (continued)

3. On the Menu bar, click the **Waveform button** (shown in Figure 15).

    The New Audio File dialog box opens.

4. Enter the following preferences for your voice recording, then click **OK**.

    a. Filename: **my_recording** (or whatever name you choose)

    b. Sample Rate: **44100 Hz**, standard sample rate

    c. Channels: **Mono**

    d. Bit Depth: **16** bits

    The recording title appears in the Files panel on the left. Before recording, check that the audio preferences are set to your recording device.

5. Choose **Edit > Preferences > Audio Hardware** (Windows), or **Audition > Preferences > Audio Hardware** (Mac).

6. Set the Default Input and Default Output to the settings you'll be using.

    For example, if you're recording using the microphone that's built into your computer, choose Built-in Input. On the other hand, if you have a headset, plug it in and Audition should recognize the device. Choose that device from the Default Output and Input areas.

7. Once your options are set, compare your settings to Figure 16, and then click **OK**.

    Now you're ready to record.

    (continued)

Figure 15 *Setting up options for a new file*

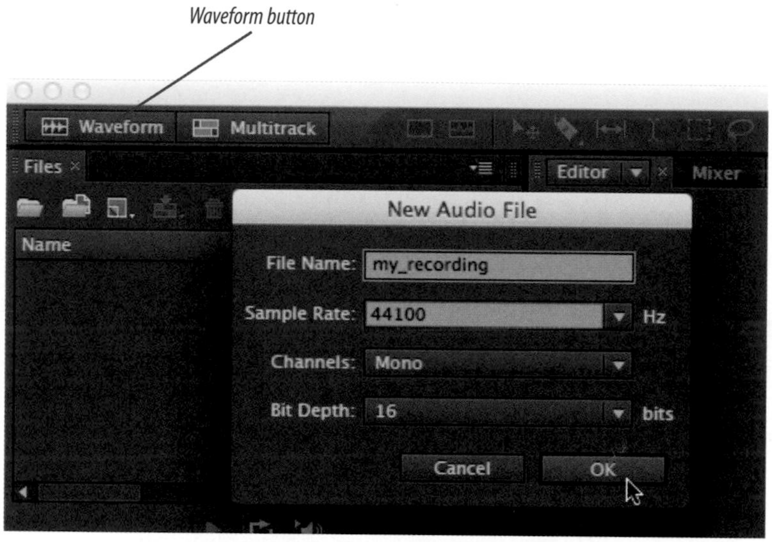

Figure 16 *Setting audio hardware preferences*

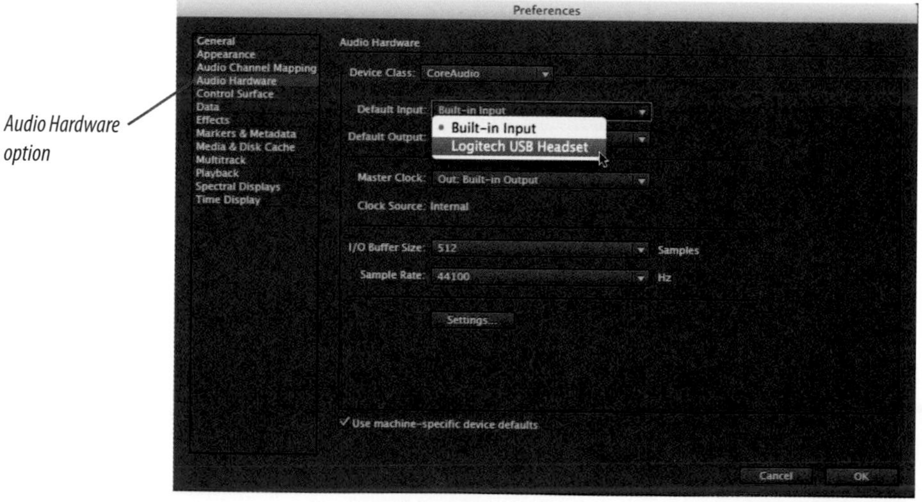

Figures © Cengage Learning 2013

Using Audio

Figure 17 *Audio control options in Audition*

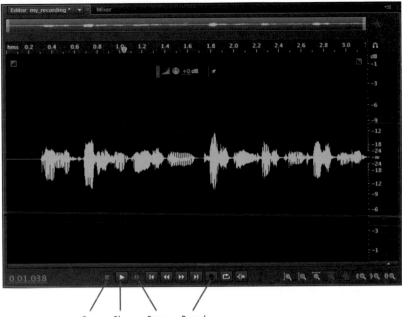

Stop   Play   Pause   Record

Figure 18 *Saving the file in an uncompressed format*

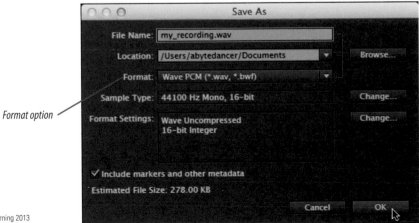

Format option

8. Click the red **Record button** in the bottom of the Editor panel and start talking.

   If your input device is working properly, you'll see the waveform of the sound as you speak.

9. Click the **Stop button** to stop recording, and the **Play button** to listen back. See Figure 17.

10. Choose **File** > **Save**, and save the file as an uncompressed WAV file. See Figure 18.

Export a sound file to MP3 format

Now, let's publish the file as an MP3, a compressed file format more suitable for Internet playback.

1. Choose **File** > **Export** > **File**.

   The Export File dialog box opens.

   (continued)

Figures © Cengage Learning 2013

Using Audio

2. Click the **Format list arrow** and click **MP3 Audio**. Create a name for your file and select a location to save it. See Figure 19.

3. Click **OK**.

   A warning appears, telling you that MP3 is a compressed file format and recommending that you first save an uncompressed version of the file. See Figure 20.

4. Click **Yes**.

   In Step 7 you already saved the file in an uncompressed format (WAV) for use as a backup.

5. Chose **File** > **Close All**.

Figure 19 *Export settings*

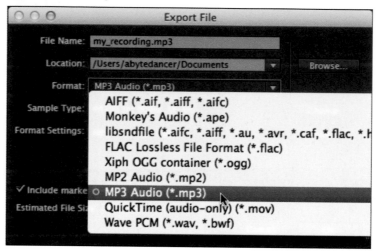

Figure 20 *Compressed file warning*

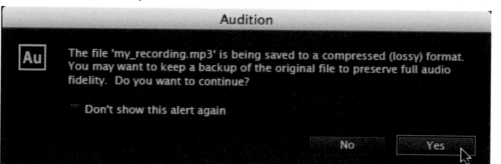

Figure 21 *Sound file in Files and Editor panels*

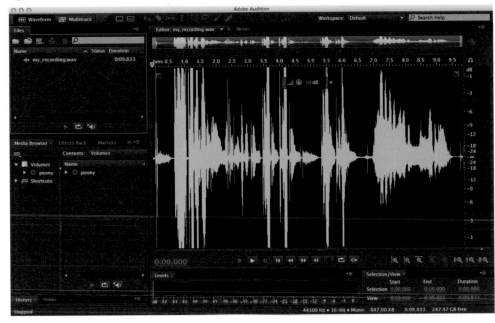

Figure 22 *Magnifying a section of an audio file*

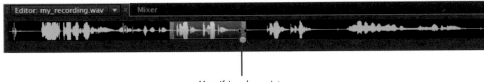

Magnifying glass pointer

Navigate the Timeline and remove audio

1. Open Adobe Audition, if necessary.

2. On the Menu bar, choose **Workspace** > **Default**.

3. Choose **File** > **Open** from the menu bar, and browse for the uncompressed (WAV) version of your audio recording.

   The recording name appears in the Files panel and its waveform appears in the Editor panel. See Figure 21.

4. Click the **Play button** on the controller at the bottom of the Editor panel and review your recording.

5. Navigate to the area of the recording you would like to remove. Make sure the Editor panel is selected (highlighted with a yellow border).

   TIP If the Editor panel is not selected, click anywhere in the panel.

6. In the Zoom Navigator at the top of the Editor panel, drag the right or left edge of the yellow bordered bar (the pointer becomes a magnifying glass, shown in Figure 22) to magnify the general area.

   (continued)

Figures © Cengage Learning 2013

7. Move the bar (the hand icon appears) to locate the specific area you would like to modify. See Figure 23.

   You might have to zoom in and then move the bar a couple times to find the area you want to edit.

TIP With the Editor panel selected, you can also zoom by amplitude, time, or point, using the controls in the lower right of the panel (see Figure 24) and/or using the scroll wheel, if your mouse has one.

8. To select the specific time range, select the **Time Selection tool** on the toolbar (see Figure 25) and drag in the Editor panel. To extend or shorten a selection, drag the selection edges. See Figure 26.

TIP Shift-click beyond the edges to quickly extend a selection to a specific location.

(continued)

Figure 23 *Locating a section of an audio file*

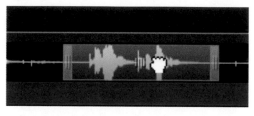

Figure 24 *Additional zoom features in the Editor panel*

Figure 25 *Time Selection tool*

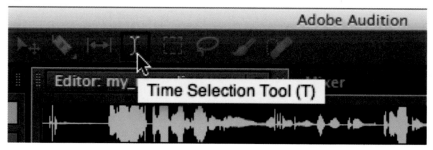

Using Audio

Figure 26 *Extending or shortening a selection*

Time Selection tool pointer

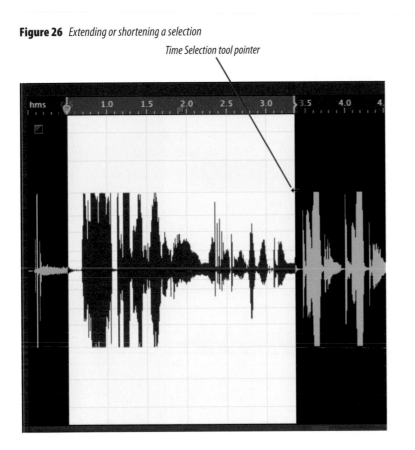

Figure 27 *Indicating where you want the file to start playing*

Current time indicator

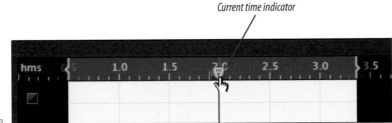

Using Audio

9. Click **Play** to play the section you've selected.

   As it's playing, you can continue to adjust the time selection to get the exact area you want to remove. To play a specific section within the selected area, move the current time indicator (the yellow marker that looks like a guitar pick) to the location and click **Play** again. See Figure 27.

10. To remove the section, do one of the following;

    ■ Press **[Delete]** on the keyboard.
    ■ Right-click (Win) or Ctrl-click (Mac) over the area and choose **Delete** from the shortcut menu.
    ■ Choose **Edit > Delete**.

If you make a mistake, choose Edit > Undo, or reverse your steps in the History panel (Window > History).

Adjust volume (amplitude)

1. With the Time Selection tool, navigate to and select the area on the waveform where you want to adjust the volume. To adjust the volume of the entire file, don't select anything.

2. In the HUD (heads-up display) gain control that floats above the panel, drag right or left over the Adjust Amplitude knob to reach your desired volume. See Figure 28.

TIP If you don't see the HUD, choose View > Show HUD.

Add a fade effect

Audition has three types of fade effects:

1. **Linear fades:** These create a volume change that continues at the same rate throughout the fade. These can sound abrupt, though, so you may want to try the other two fade types.

2. **Logarithmic fades:** These produce smooth volume changes, first slowly and then rapidly, or the reverse.

3. **Cosine fades:** These fades are shaped like an S-curve, with the volume changing slowly at first, then changing rapidly through most of the fade, and then slowly again at the end.

(continued)

Figure 28 *Adjusting the selection's volume using the HUD gain control*

Adjust Amplitude knob   HUD gain control

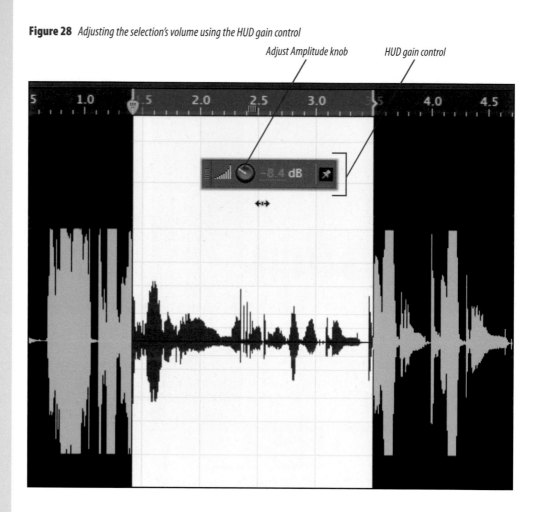

Using Audio

Figure 29 *Adding a fade effect*

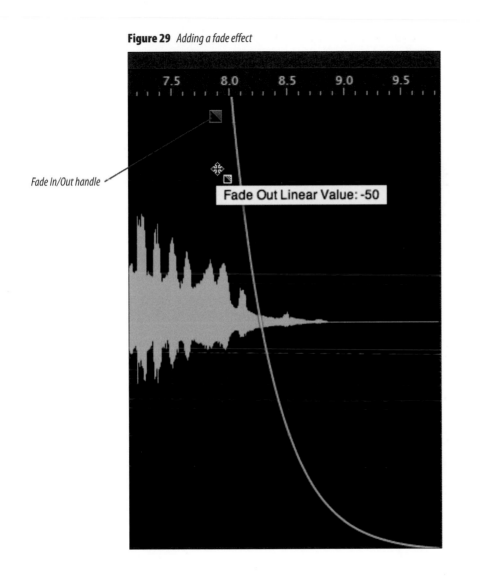

Fade In/Out handle

Figure © Cengage Learning 2013

Try each of the fade options:

1. Open an audio file in Audition, and select the **Editor panel**.

2. In the upper left or right of the waveform, drag the **Fade In** or **Fade Out handle** inward horizontally to create a linear fade. See Figure 29.

3. Play the audio to hear the fade.

4. Choose **Edit** > **Undo Fade** (or reverse your steps using the History panel).

5. Drag the Fade In or Fade Out handle inward, as you drag up or down to create a logarithmic fade.

6. Play the audio to hear the effect.

7. Choose **Edit** > **Undo Fade**.

8. Finally, make a cosine fade. Hold down [Ctrl] (Win) or ⌘ (Mac) as you drag the Fade In or Fade Out handle inward.

9. Play the audio to hear the effect.

10. Save the file in an uncompressed file format (such as WAV) and export another, compressed version for playback over the Internet (such as MP3).

ADDING AUDIO TO A FLASH MOVIE

Earlier in this chapter, we discussed how to integrate audio into a web page, as demonstrated on the Expert Advice page of our Gardener's Walk project. But we also incorporated audio within our Flash photo gallery on the Gallery page. See Figure 30. First, we asked permission to use part of a song composed by a band we know, and then output it in a compressed format using Audition. Next, we saved the compressed audio file in our project's assets folder, and in Flash we entered ActionScript code that calls this sound file into the photo gallery. We also used ActionScript to code the actions of the Play and Pause buttons for the sound. Adobe **ActionScript** is the object-oriented programming language of the Adobe Flash Platform and is essential for creating interactivity with Flash. We won't get into the specifics of ActionScripting in this book—you can refer to Jim Shuman's *Adobe Flash CS6 Revealed* book—but we will show you the steps and ActionScript used to import sound at runtime into a Flash movie.

As you work through these steps, you may choose to set up your own example in Flash, which you can then incorporate into your own interactive media project.

Figure 30 *ActionScript code to integrate audio into the Gardener's Walk Flash photo gallery*

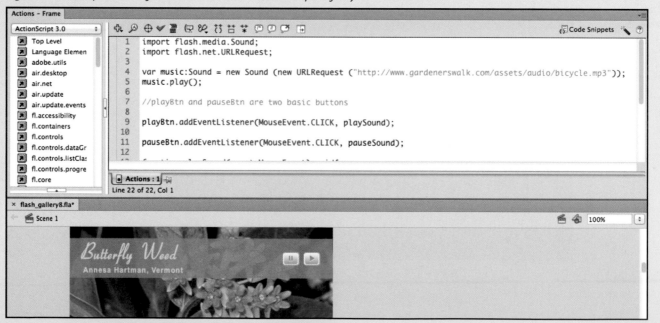

Figure © Cengage Learning 2013

Set up the movie file

1. Open Flash. Create a new ActionScript 3.0 document, as shown in Figure 31.

2. In the Timeline panel, rename the first layer **buttons**.

3. Go to **Window** > **Common Libraries** > **Buttons**, open the **playback rounded folder**, and drag both the **rounded green pause** and **rounded green play** buttons to the Stage. See Figure 32.

Figure 31 *Creating a new ActionScript 3.0 document in Flash*

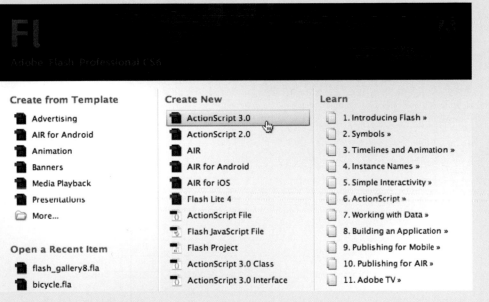

Figure 32 *Selecting premade button designs*

Using Audio

4. Click the **Play** button and, in the Properties panel, give it an instance name of **playBtn**. The instance name is the name that will be called in the ActionScript you'll create in the next section. See Figure 33.

5. Select the **Pause** button and give it an instance name of **pauseBtn**.

6. Choose **File** > **Save** to save your file.

Figure 33 *Setting an instance name for a button*

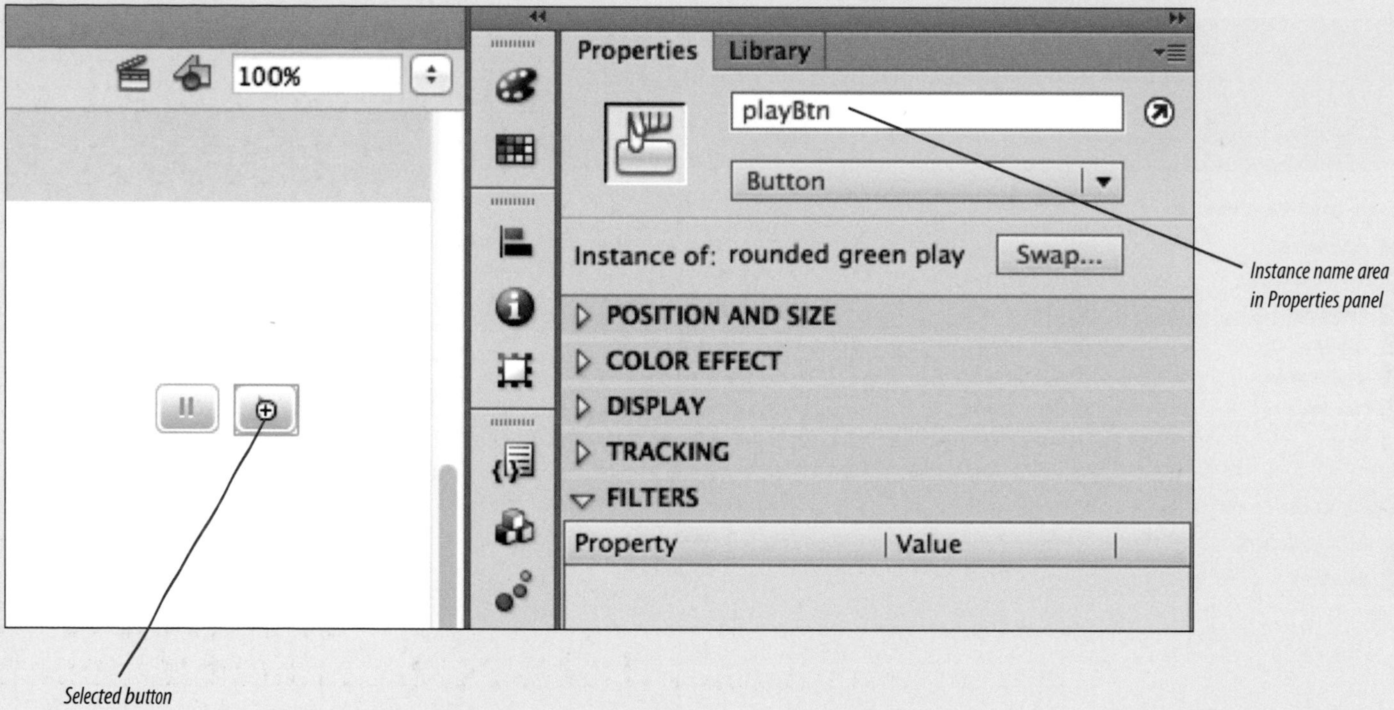

Instance name area in Properties panel

Selected button

7. Place your Flash file in a folder, and place your sound file in the same folder. You'll be linking to your sound file at this location in the next section. See Figure 34.

Figure 34 *Keeping your files together*

Add the ActionScript

1. In Flash, create a new layer and call it **actions**. See Figure 35.

2. Select the first frame of the **actions** layer, and choose **Window** > **Actions** to open the ActionScript panel.

3. Enter the code exactly as it appears in Figure 35. (This code is available to copy and paste from Free Stuff at Cengage Brain).

4. In the code, change the information between the green quotes in the URLRequest to the name and location of your sound file, relative to the Flash movie document.

5. Be sure that the instance names you created for the Play and Pause buttons (Steps 4 and 5 of Setting up the movie file) are also correct in the ActionScript. See lines 7 and 9 in Figure 36.

Figure 35 *Creating a new layer*

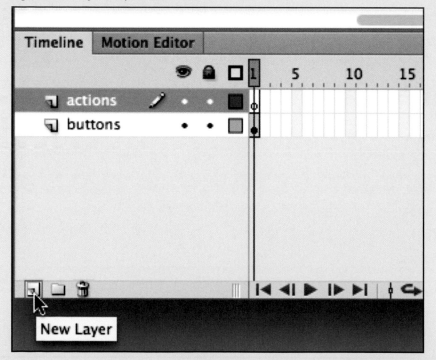

Using Audio

Tip If you plan to post this sound project to a remote location, you'll need to adjust the URLRequest to reflect the full URL of the location of your sound file. For example, when testing the sound in our photo gallery on our local computer, we set the URL to where it was located on our hard drive relative to the Flash movie. When we posted it to our final site space, we changed the URL in the code to reflect the sound file's new location (http://www.gardenerswalk.com/assets/audio/bicycle.mp3) and output a new SWF file. See Figure 37.

6. Choose **Control > Test Movie > In Flash Professional**, and test the buttons.

Figure 36 *Code for importing a music file at runtime, including actions for the play and stop buttons*

```
1   import flash.media.Sound;
2   import flash.net.URLRequest;
3
4   var music:Sound = new Sound (new URLRequest ("NAME_OF_YOUR_FILE.mp3"));
5   music.play();
6
7   playBtn.addEventListener(MouseEvent.CLICK, playSound);
8
9   pauseBtn.addEventListener(MouseEvent.CLICK, pauseSound);
10
11  function playSound(event:MouseEvent):void{
12  SoundMixer.soundTransform = new SoundTransform(1);
13
14      }
15
16      function pauseSound(event:MouseEvent):void{
17
18      SoundMixer.soundTransform = new SoundTransform(0);
19      }
20
21
```

Figure 37 *Adjusting the new URLRequest code to reflect the remote location of a sound file*

```
var music:Sound = new Sound (new URLRequest ("http://www.gardenerswalk.com/assets/audio/bicycle.mp3"));
music.play();
```

ADDING AUDIO TO YOUR INTERACTIVE MEDIA PROJECT

Now that you've learned the basics of how to find, prepare, and publish audio files, you're ready to incorporate audio into your own project.

1. Find some copyright-free audio or record your own.
2. Prepare your audio file for its intended output. Edit the audio, if necessary, edit the audio in an audio editor and save the file in the proper format for your project (review format options in the Preparing Audio section of this chapter). The MP3 format is the most common format used for interactive projects accessed over an Internet connection.
3. Next, locate the place in your project where you would like to include the audio. If you're inserting the audio on a web page, see instructions for Inserting Audio in a Web Page in the Publishing Audio section of this chapter. If you're inserting the audio in a Flash movie, see the How We Did It: Adding Audio to a Flash Movie section.
4. Refer to the transcription strategies presented in this chapter to ensure your audio meets usability and accessibility standards.

EMBEDDING SOUND IN FLASH

In the How We Did It section of this chapter, we showed how we added a sound file to our Flash movie using an action that calls the sound file from its URL link. This method is useful if you're using longer tracks of music. However, if you'd like to add a sound effect to a button, or a short looping track to part of an animated sequence, you can embed the sound directly into the final SWF file. Try this:

1. Create a new document in Flash.
2. Go to **Window** > **Common Libraries** > **Buttons**, open a folder, and drag a pre-made button to the Stage (or you can create your own button design).
3. Double-click the button to enter editing mode. Make a new layer called **sound.**
4. Highlight the sound layer and select the Over state frame. Place a keyframe (**Insert** > **Timeline** > **Keyframe**). See Figure 38.

TIP If you don't see the Up, Over, and Down states of the button, try choosing another premade button in the Common Libraries panel.

Figure 38 *Creating a keyframe to place a sound file*

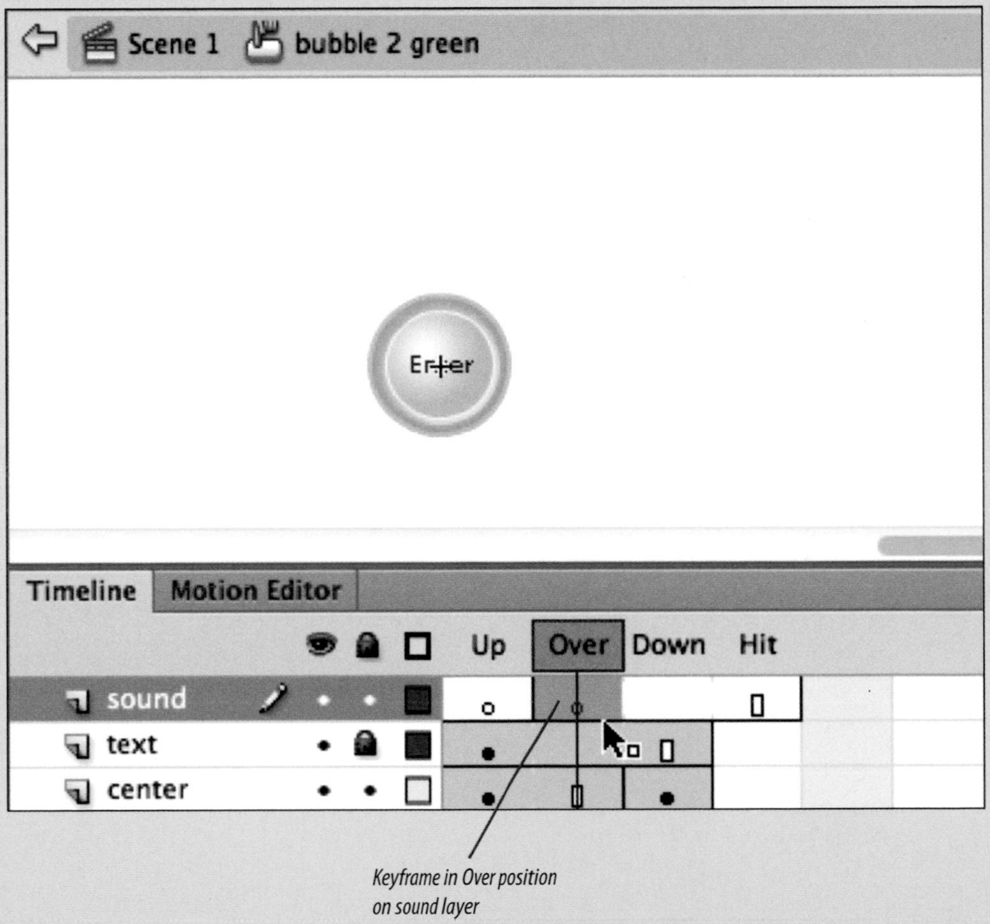

Keyframe in Over position on sound layer

Figure © Cengage Learning 2013

5. Choose **Window** > **Common Libraries** > **Sound**, and play the sounds until you find one you like. See Figure 39.

Tip You can also find your own short clip, such as on freesound.org, and save it to your computer. To place it in the Flash Library, choose File > Import > Import to Library, browse for the sound file and click Open.

Figure 39 *Playing sounds from the Library panel*

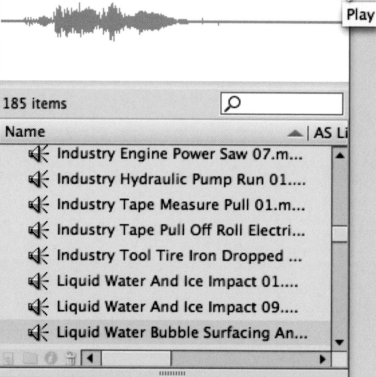

Using Audio

6. Be sure the keyframe is selected on the sound layer where you want to put the sound. Drag the sound you've chosen from the Library to the Stage. The waveform of the sound appears on the selected keyframe. See Figure 40.

7. Choose **Control > Test Movie > in Flash Professional** and place the mouse pointer over the button to hear the sound.

Figure 40 *Sound file waveform embedded on a keyframe*

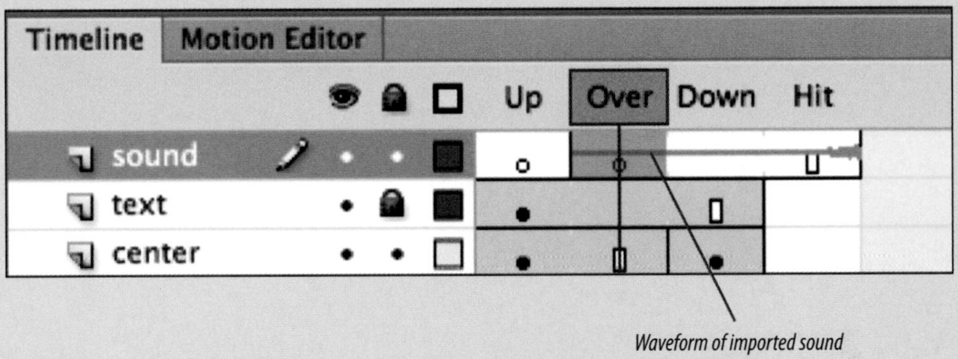

Waveform of imported sound

Even More to Explore

To explore some of the topics discussed in this chapter in more depth, see the References section at the end of the book. For links to additional web resources, visit the Even More to Explore link under Book Resources on Cengage Brain.

Figure © Cengage Learning 2013

Using Audio

CHAPTER **9** INTEGRATING
VIDEO

CHAPTER 9 INTEGRATING VIDEO

Introduction

In the previous chapter you learned how to use audio to enhance your interactive design. In this chapter, you learn to provide an even richer experience for your users by integrating video content. You explore the characteristics, tools, and design strategies that are used to create, edit, compress, and insert digital video clips, and you practice working with video in Adobe Premiere Elements and Flash.

As with audio, you don't need expensive video equipment, and extensive experience in video production, to successfully incorporate video into your interactive media project. Because of this low entry barrier, digital video has become a ubiquitous feature on the Web. YouTube (youtube.com), for example, is a revolutionary online platform where even the most novice videographer can post and share video clips, and millions of people can search and view them. As bandwidth expands and more people gain access to higher Internet connection speeds, the amount of video available online is increasing. People around the world can now take advantage of video-based online learning materials, real-time conferencing, marketing, and entertainment.

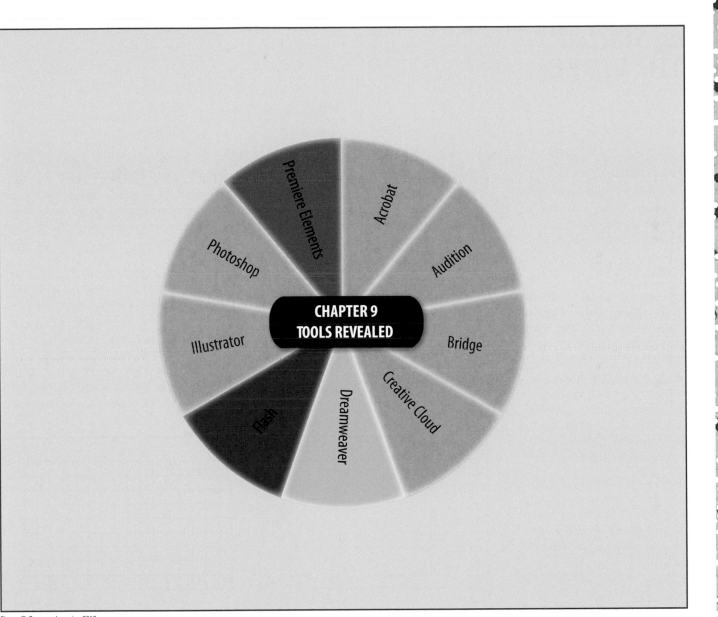

CHAPTER 9
TOOLS REVEALED

Acrobat

Audition

Bridge

Creative Cloud

Dreamweaver

Flash

Illustrator

Photoshop

Premiere Elements

Figure © Cengage Learning 2013

Getting Started
WITH VIDEO

Characteristics of Video

To use video most effectively in your interactive media projects, it helps to have an understanding of some basic video characteristics. This will help you better understand the processes for capturing, editing and publishing digitized video.

You've already learned about the basic components of video from previous chapters—bitmaps (Chapter 6) and audio (Chapter 8). Digital video is simply a series of bitmap images that, when played back, create the illusion of movement. And like a single bitmap image, the quality and overall file size of digital video is determined by its resolution, bit depth, and dimensions. Similarly, the sound quality of a video depends on the sound's sample rate and bit depth.

However, there are a few other characteristics specific to video. Frame rate, frame size, and bit rate also help determine a video's quality and file size, as well as its encoding process, the output of the video to its intended viewing device.

Frame Rate

As with animation, video frame rate is measured in frames per second (fps). The higher the frame rate, the smoother the video appears. Standard TV video runs at about 30 fps. For a film, the frame rate is 24 fps. For Web videos, average standard frame rates are 12–15 fps. Of course, higher quality video also demands more data, so the frame rate varies with connection speed. Someone with a slow Internet connection will likely see rates between 5 and 15 fps, while a user with a high-speed connection may see up to 30 fps.

Figure 1 *4:3 frame aspect ratio versus 16:9 aspect ratio*

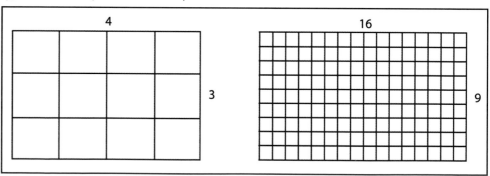

Aspect Ratios and Frame Size

A video's frame rate is linked to its aspect ratio and frame size. **Aspect ratio** defines the proportional width and height of a video. You've probably seen video where the aspect ratio is not quite correct—the imagery on the video is "squished" either vertically or horizontally. There are two standard aspect ratios for digital video, 4:3 and 16:9. In the 4:3 aspect ratio, the frame size can vary from small (320 × 240 pixels) to large (640 × 480 or 720 × 480 pixels). More common now, however, are video recording devices that will capture, or players that will display, video in the 16:9 wide-screen ratio. See Figure 1.

It's best practice to provide video in various file sizes to accommodate users with different Internet connection speeds, browsers, and devices (e.g. mobile, tablet, or desktop).

To determine a video's frame width and height, a general rule of thumb is to use multiples of 16. For example, the width of 512 is 16 × 32, and the height of 384 is 16 × 24. Table 1 lists common frame sizes for the two standard aspect ratios.

Bit Rate

Another factor to consider when working with video is bit rate. The **bit rate**, or data transfer rate, of a video controls the amount of data that the video streams or downloads over time. (Audio downloads are based on bit rates as well.) Bit rate is measured in **kilobits per second (kbps)**—a rate of data transfer equal to 1000 bits per second. You've most likely experienced the situation when the bit rate of a streaming video exceeds your connection speed: you must wait for the video to buffer, play, then buffer again. **Buffering** occurs when the rate at which data is being downloaded does not keep up with the rate at which a computer is processing it, so the computer must pause the playback while it downloads the next batch of data. In general, the larger a video's frame size, the higher its bit rate. You can set the bit

Figure © Cengage Learning 2013

Integrating Video

rates for your project's video and audio tracks during the encoding process. Table 2 shows a chart of a few video frame sizes, bit rates, and their average file size per minute of video.

Encoding/Compression

In video editing and production, **video encoding** is the process of preparing the video for output. It's in the encoding process where

TABLE 1: COMMON FRAME SIZES IN THE 4:3 AND 16:9 STANDARD ASPECT RATIOS		
Video Aspect Ratio	Internet Connection Speed	Frame Size
4:3	Low	320 x 240
4:3	High	512 x 384, 640 x 480
16:9	Low	256 x 144, 512 x 288
16:9	High	768 x 432, 1024 x 576, 1280 x 720

© Cengage Learning 2013

Mobile Device Output Settings

Settings for mobile devices will vary depending on the device. For example, the Premiere "Low Quality" video output dimensions for the Apple iPhone have a frame size of 400 x 224. Adobe Premiere Elements and Premiere Pro provide many output presets for the most common mobile devices. See Figure 2.

Figure 2 *Mobile output screen in Premiere Elements*

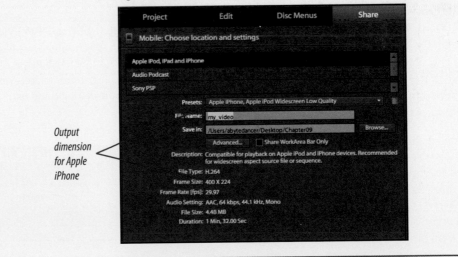

Output dimension for Apple iPhone

you set your video's frame rate, frame size and bit rate. These settings depend on where you plan to publish your video, such as on a DVD, online, or on a local computer. You can perform video encoding (also called video conversion) using a video editing program like Adobe Premiere Elements or Pro, Apple Final Cut Pro, or TechSmith Camtasia, and with more basic compression tools like QuickTime Pro, or the Adobe Media Encoder (AME), which comes with the Flash program.

Depending on the use, a video can be encoded using any number of **video codecs**—methods by which digital video data is compressed and decompressed—and many different formats. For example, video codecs used by the Flash video (FLV) formats are called VP6 or Sorenson Spark; for the current MPEG-4 standard it's H.264; and for WebM it's VP8. These formats and their codecs produce more highly compressed (optimized) video for online delivery than video in a standard DVD or HD format. In this chapter we'll work with video in the MP4 and FLV formats.

There are hundreds of video formats and new ones seem to spring up every year as video technologies improve, and the devices and browsers which support them change and evolve. Currently, browsers vary in their support of various video formats and codecs. For example, for video to play successfully on a majority of browsers (i.e. Chrome, Safari, Explorer, Firefox, and Opera), at least three different formats of video need to be published. It's important to be aware of current video formats, that they have different characteristics and compression schemes, and may or may not be supported by your favorite browser or device. For the most up-to-date information on this topic, the Web is your best resource. For a start, however, let's look at a few of today's common video file formats:

- **Microsoft Video for Windows (.AVI)** Most Windows-based applications save video in this format. It's supported by both the Macintosh and Windows platforms, but is not suitable for online delivery.
- **Apple QuickTime (.MOV)** Supported by both the Mac and Windows platforms and is a popular format for online delivery.
- **MPEG-4 (.MP4)** Part of the MPEG family of digital video compression standards, commonly used for online delivery and mobile output.
- **Adobe Flash Video (.FLV and .F4V)** Video format designed specifically for Internet delivery using the Adobe Flash Player.
- **WebM (.WebM)** An open source video format developed by Google and used for HTML5 video.
- **Ogg Theora (.OGG)** An open source multimedia format for both video and audio, developed by Xiph.org. Supported by the HTML5 video and audio elements.

Finding Video

Depending on your needs, budget, and time constraints, you can obtain video in several ways: you can look for copyright-free or public domain resources, purchase video through video repositories, or capture the video yourself.

Free and Purchased Video

Sources for pre-produced video are similar to those you learned about in Chapter 8 for audio. An online search will provide numerous avenues to explore. The Moving Image Archive site, for example, provides an extensive archive of public domain videos, free for download and use in scholarship and research.

TABLE 2: FRAME SIZE, BIT RATE AND FILE SIZE COMPARISONS		
Frame Size	**Bit rate**	**File size per minute of video**
320 x 240	400kbps	3 MB
480 x 360	700kbps	4 MB
720 x 540	1000kbps	7.5 MB

© Cengage Learning 2013

Producing Your Own Video

If you need polished, quality video and if budget allows, you can always hire a professional videographer. However, if you're willing to put in some effort, you should consider capturing your own video. The resources to do this are more readily available and economical than ever before. With a digital camcorder, a robust personal computer, and video editing software, you're on your way. For example, the video provided on the Gardener's Walk site was captured with an inexpensive Flip video recorder. It's not professional grade videography, but it works well enough for the intention of our project—to highlight videos sent in by gardeners from all walks of life.

QUICK TIP

Did you know that about 9 minutes of DV footage requires about 2 GB of hard drive space? Video files can get big fast, so it's best to have a robust computer system, with ample memory and storage.

See the Video Design Strategies section of this chapter for tips on successful video capture.

Preparing and Publishing Video

Once you have some video to work with, the next thing to consider is the tools you might use to edit your video and what output format will be best. The following video editing programs are common in today's market. Some programs also let you capture video on your computer screen.

- **Windows MovieMaker** (explore.live.com/windows-live-essentials-movie-maker-get-started) A basic video editing program compatible with Microsoft Windows. Cost: free

- **Apple iMovie** (apple.com/ilife/imovie) An easy-to-use video editing program compatible with Mac computers and iOS devices (**iOS** is the Apple mobile operating system for iPhone, iPad, and iPod touch.). Cost: included with purchase of a new Mac, or $5 for iOS

- **Apple QuickTime Pro** (apple.com/quicktime/extending/) Quicktime Pro is a low-cost, reliable and easy-to-use solution to convert your video media to different formats; however, its editing features are minimal. Cost: around $30

- **Adobe Premiere Elements** (adobe.com/products/premiere-elements.html) The light version of Adobe Premiere Pro, offering automated movie editing features, effects, and output options. Available for both Mac and Windows. Cost: around $100

- **Adobe Premiere Pro** (adobe.com/products/premiere.html) The Adobe professional video editing and publishing program. Available for both Mac and Windows. Cost: around $800

- **Apple Final Cut Pro** (apple.com/finalcutpro) The Apple high-end audio and video post-production program for professionals. Available for Mac. Cost: around $300

- **Adobe After Effects** (adobe.com/products/aftereffects.html) Used to create sophisticated motion graphics, video, and cinematic visual effects. Available for both Mac and Windows. Cost: around $1000

- **Adobe Captivate** (adobe.com/products/captivate.html) The Adobe elearning authoring program, which includes a high-end screen recorder program and presentation slide generator. Often used for the development of instructional videos, it is available for both Mac and Windows. Cost: around $800

- **TechSmith Jing** (techsmith.com/jing.html) A screen recording program for both Mac and Windows; with the free version you can capture up to 5 minutes of screen video. Jing video can be output to various formats or posted online at screencast.com, the TechSmith video hosting service, where you can post 2 GB of video for free. Cost for Pro version, per year subscription: around $15

- **TechSmith Camtasia** (techsmith.com/camtasia.html) Professional grade screen recorder and presentation creation program, compatible with Microsoft PowerPoint. Often used for the development of instructional videos, it is available for both Mac and PC. Cost: around $100

- **Telestream ScreenFlow** (telestream.net/screen-flow/overview-s.htm) A professional, easy-to-use screencasting program for the Mac; used to create software demos, tutorials, and presentations. Cost: around $100

Once you've recorded and edited your video, you're ready to integrate it into your interactive media project. You can integrate video in several ways. For example, you can link it to a web page using an object embed tag; in HTML5, you can use the video element; or you can embed the element into a Flash movie file. In the How We Did It section of this chapter we show you how we embedded our video into our Gardener's Walk project. In the More to Explore section, you can learn how to integrate video within Flash.

Video Design
STRATEGIES

Now let's get into some specific design and delivery strategies to make your video effective, usable, and accessible.

Storyboard

Planning your video shoot can help avoid extensive editing later. The first step is to create a storyboard, especially for longer videos. Your storyboard can be similar to what we covered in Chapter 7 on storyboarding for animation.

Start with the Best Recording You Can Get

As with recording audio, what might be considered a "best" recording can vary, and also depends on the subject you're filming. If you're making a video of a breaking news event, for example, you probably won't have much control over the lighting, pacing, or ambient sound. However, if you're performing a video interview, you can set up the interview environment to avoid unexpected distractions. One of Annesa's friends, for example, recently shot a wedding on a Flip video recorder that wasn't his best

work, simply because the wedding was conducted on a snowy, overcast morning, atop a mountain accessible only by a ski lift.

Here are some suggestions to help ensure good video recordings:

- **Use a camera with an audio output for a microphone.** Chances are having the option to use an external microphone to record a video's audio will produce a higher quality sound than relying on a camera's built-in speakers.
- **Minimize background noise.** Anticipate what noises could come up during the recording—for example, the sound of a clock tower or a passing train.
- **Do a camera test.** Run a mock shoot in the actual location, play it back, and identify what can make the recording better. This might include a different camera position, better lighting, background scenery, or a costume change; a checked polo shirt against a red backdrop, for example, might be distracting to the eye.
- **Use a tripod.** If at all possible, use a tripod to stabilize the camera, and to help create smooth panning and zooming effects.

Provide User Controls

Lucky for us, video players (also called "containers") like QuickTime Player, Flash Player, and Windows Media Player automatically include user navigation controls, such as the stop, play, and pause buttons. For Flash, you can also choose various designs, or skins. A **skin** is a graphic element that determines the type and design of playback controls your video will have. The controller can be placed over the video or below it. Also, you can often tweak the code that's used to embed these players within your design. For example, if you want the user to start the video, rather than having in start automatically, you can set the autoplay or autostart parameter value to "false," rather than "true."

Consider Video Length

If you decide to include video in your interactive media project, be mindful of its length. The length of a video directly correlates with its file size—the longer the video, the longer it will take to download if users view it on the Internet. In addition, Internet viewers notoriously have short attention spans, so if your video is intended to market a product, to demonstrate a concept, or to educate, it's important to find a length that will keep your end user engaged.

Wistia, a video hosting service, has done extensive tracking of video usage. Their studies have found that a shorter video is better, and that viewers are more likely to watch a shorter video to the end. About 85% of the people they tracked watched a 30-second video all the way to the end, compared to a completion rate of 50% for videos between 2 and 10 minutes.

Consider Captioning or Subtitles

When accessibility and Section 508 compliance is of utmost concern, consider adding captions or subtitles to your video. **Captions** assist the hearing impaired by providing a text equivalent of the audio portion of a video as it plays. Captioning can be a tedious but worthwhile process. Some video editing programs contain captioning features, or you can use a third party program. Adobe Premiere Pro now lets you attach a closed captioning data file to a video sequence and preview it within the program. TechSmith Camtasia allows you to import or create a text transcript directly in the program, and sync it directly to various points on the video.

There are also many third party programs that you can use to add captions or subtitles over your finished video project. A favorite is MAGpie, which is supported by the National Center for Accessible Media (NCAM). Its most recent version supports Windows and older versions of Mac OS X. Visit ncam.wgbh.org/invent_build/web_multimedia/tools-guidelines/magpie to download the program.

Figure 3 *Video example with captions*

Closed captioning button

QUICK TIP

Another wonderful resource on the basics of captioning is Caption It Yourself at dcmp.org/ciy. See Figure 3 for an example of captioning.

Use Transition Effects

Transitions are effects that allow you to blend or disguise the motion between cuts of video and title treatments. Without transitions, frames between video clips can jump awkwardly from one shot to the next, which can appear jarring to the viewer. Most video editing programs provide preset transitions that are easy to apply and make for a more polished and seamless visual experience.

Figure © Cengage Learning 2013

Editing Video Using
ADOBE PREMIERE ELEMENTS

The Adobe programs for working with video are Premiere Pro and Premiere Elements. Premiere Pro contains a full set of features for the intermediate and advanced videographer. To run properly, it requires ample hardware and RAM. It also requires a good dose of tinkering and study before you reach a point where you can easily maneuver around the program. Premiere Elements is a lighter version of Premiere Pro. For those new to video publishing, and who want to edit and format their videos quickly with minimal cost, Premiere Elements might be the better place to start.

We'll use Premiere Elements to demonstrate some of the basic steps in preparing a video, including importing a video clip, placing it on the timeline, trimming unwanted sections, adding a color and title effect, applying transitions, and outputting the final product. To get the most out of this tutorial, you'll need a short video clip loaded on your computer. Depending on what's available, you can capture the clip using a high-end digital video recorder, a Flip video camera, or even your cell phone if it supports video.

Figure 4 *Creating a new project from the Welcome screen*

Import a video clip

1. Open Adobe Premiere Elements, and from the Welcome Screen, click the **New Project** button. See Figure 4.

2. When the New Project dialog box opens, enter a name for your project, and designate a folder on your computer as the save location. See Figure 5.

   We'll leave the project settings at the default: NTSC-DV-Standard 48kHz.

   (continued)

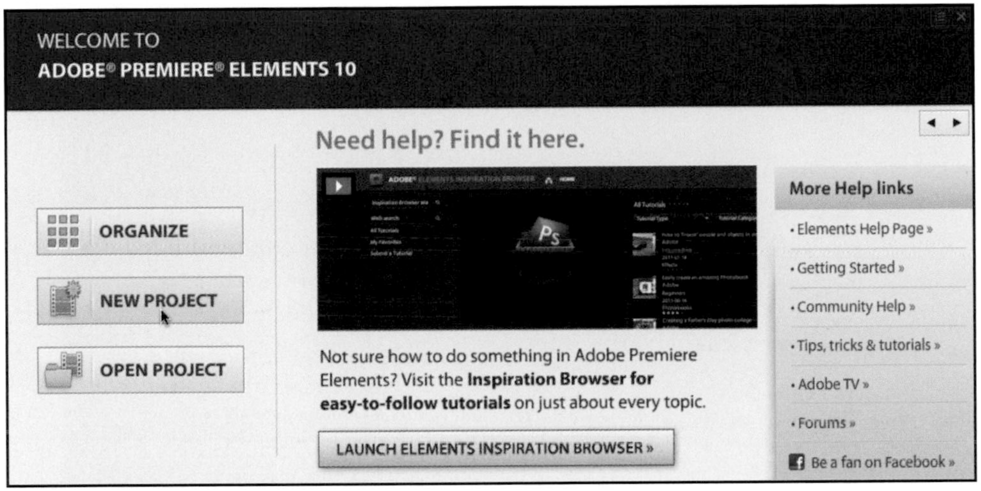

Figure 5 *Setting up your new project*

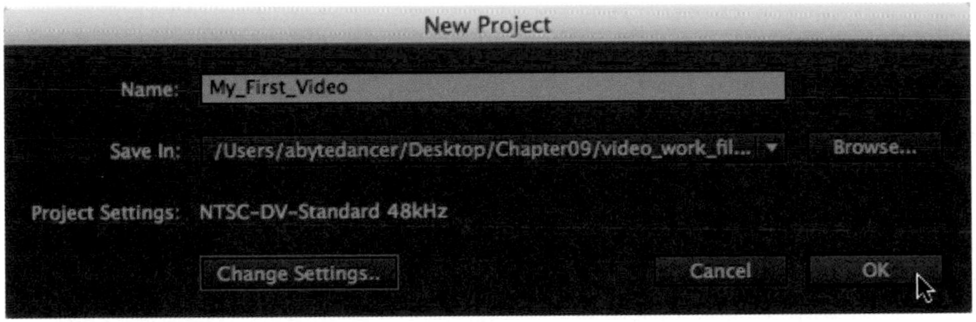

Figures © Cengage Learning 2013

Integrating Video

3. Click the **Change Settings button** in the New Project dialog box to see the various video format presets that are available. See Figure 6.

4. Click **Cancel** to close the Change Settings dialog box.

5. Click **OK** to close the New Project dialog box.

6. If you see a dialog box asking if you want to install a full set of themes and templates, click **No**.

The Premiere Elements interface looks similar to that of Adobe Audition, the audio editing

(continued)

Figure 6 *Available preset video formats*

Integrating Video

Figure 7 *Adobe Premiere Elements interface (Mac)*

Monitor panel

Tasks panel

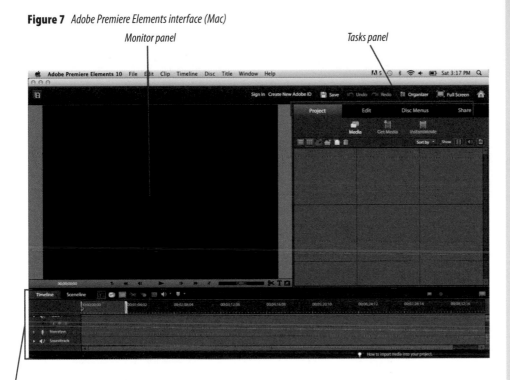

My Project panel
(Timeline and Sceneline)

program we explored in Chapter 8. Figure 7 shows each of the sections of the interface.

For all our basic tasks, Premiere Elements has three main panels: The Tasks panel, Monitor panel, and My Project panel, which includes the Timeline and Sceneline. The Tasks panel is the central location for adding, organizing and editing media, creating menus, and sharing finished projects. It's organized into four main task workspaces: Project, Edit, Disc Menus, and Share.

7. On the Menu bar, choose **File** > **Get Media from** > **Files and Folders**, and import the video clips you created.

(continued)

Integrating Video

The clips appears in the Project tasks panel. This area holds all media files that you might use in your video project. See Figure 8.

Now you're ready to put your video together, using the clips you've imported.

Figure 8 *Project tasks panel with movie clips*

Integrating Video

Figure 9 *Sceneline tab*

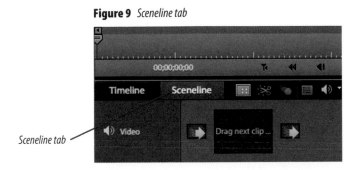

Sceneline tab

Figure 10 *Placing a video clip in the Sceneline*

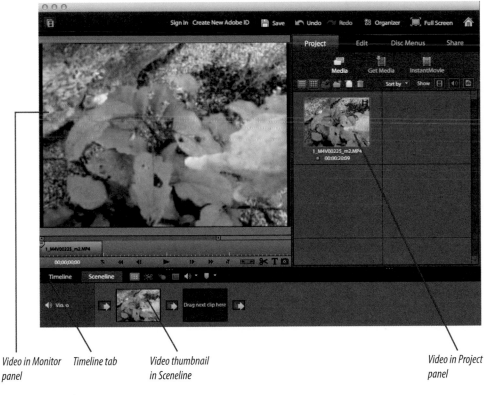

Video in Monitor panel   *Timeline tab*   *Video thumbnail in Sceneline*   *Video in Project panel*

Integrating Video

Place the video clips in the Sceneline

To assemble the pieces of your video in the order that you want them to appear, you place them in the My Project panel, which contains the Sceneline and Timeline. The **Sceneline** allows you to see and edit thumbnail views of your movie clips and transitional effects in the order in which they will play back. The **Timeline** allows you to view your movie clips over time and edit them frame by frame. Let's look at the Sceneline first.

1. In the My Project panel, click the **Sceneline tab**. See Figure 9.

2. Drag a clip you imported from the Project task area to the Sceneline.

   The clip appears in the Monitor panel, and a thumbnail of it appears in the Sceneline. See Figure 10.

3. Click the **Play/Pause Toggle button** on the controller at the bottom of the Monitor panel to preview the video.

   Notice the blue playhead (also called the current-time indicator) that progresses along the length of the video, right above the controller.

   (continued)

You can drag the playhead anywhere along this mini-timeline slider to quickly find another area in the video. If you press the Play/Pause Toggle button again, the video will start to play from the location marked by the playhead. See Figure 11.

Next, let's check out the video clip in the Timeline.

4. Click the **Timeline tab** in the My Project panel. See Figure 12.

In the Timeline, you can see separate representations of your video and audio track.

5. To enlarge the Timeline, move the mouse pointer over the boundary between the Timeline and controller until you see the divider pointer shown in Figure 13.

6. Drag upward to expand the Timeline area.

(continued)

Figure 11 *Video controller and playhead*

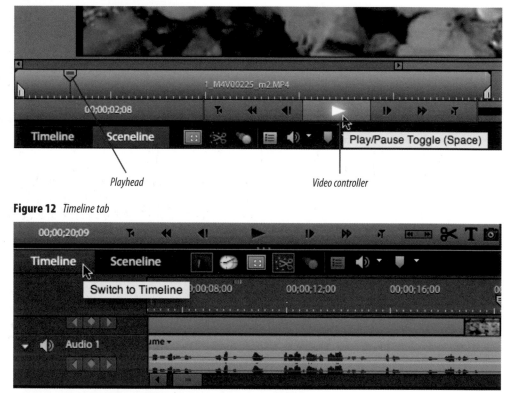

Playhead

Video controller

Figure 12 *Timeline tab*

Figure 13 *Enlarging the Timeline area*

Divider pointer

Figures © Cengage Learning 2013

Integrating Video

Figure 14 *Navigating the Timeline area*

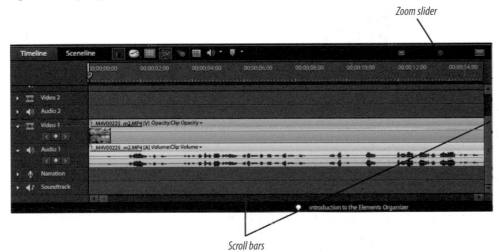

Zoom slider

Scroll bars

Figure 15 *Required project folders and files*

7. Next, adjust the scroll bars on the bottom and right of the Timeline until you see the sections of video (in blue) and audio (in green).

You can also magnify the area by adjusting the zoom slider in the upper right of the Timeline area. See Figure 14.

8. Save your file.

If you open the folder where you stored your video, you'll notice that Premiere Elements has created many new items. To ensure that your video project stays intact, it's important to keep all these folders and files in place. See Figure 15.

Figures © Cengage Learning 2013

Integrating Video

Trim the video in the Monitor panel

You'll most likely want to trim the beginning and end points of your video—areas that are usually shaky or blurry—and remove unwanted parts in the middle of your clip. There are several ways to trim video in Premiere Elements. Let's look at how to do this using the mini-timeline area of the Monitor panel.

1. Enlarge the Monitor panel area by dragging the divider bar between the Monitor panel and My Project panel. (Refer back to Figure 13.)

2. Click the **Sceneline tab**, and then select the video clip thumbnail in the Sceneline.

   A mini-timeline of the clip appears above the controller in the Monitor panel. The clip's filename, as well as In and Out points, become visible in the mini-timeline. See Figure 16.

   To trim the beginning of the video:

3. Move the playhead to the point on the mini-timeline where you want the good part of the video to start (you might need to play the video back a few times to find the right spot).

4. Drag the **In point handle** on the left end of the clip representation to the right, until it reaches the playhead location. As you drag, the area to the left of the playhead becomes highlighted, indicating the section that will be removed. See Figure 17.

   Don't worry if you don't get the trim selection just right; if necessary, click the Undo button at the top of the Premiere Elements window, above the Tasks panel. See Figure 18.

5. To trim the end of the video, move the playhead to the point on the mini-timeline where you

(continued)

Figure 16 *Mini-timeline in the Monitor panel*

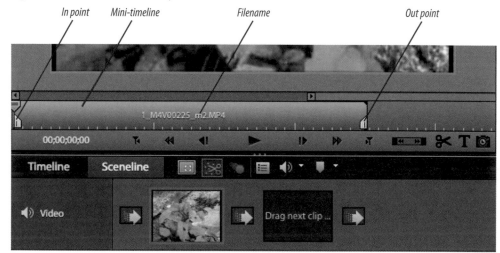

In point   Mini-timeline   Filename   Out point

Figure 17 *Highlighting a Timeline area for removal*

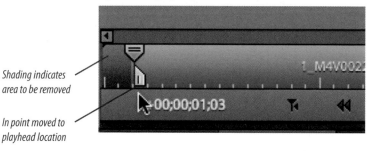

Shading indicates area to be removed

In point moved to playhead location

Figure 18 *Undo button*

Undo

Figures © Cengage Learning 2013

Integrating Video

Figure 19 *Split Clip button*

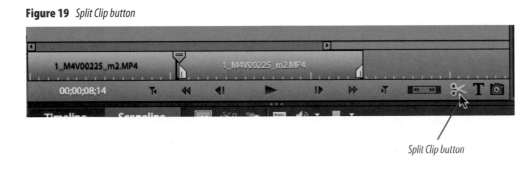

Split Clip button

Figure 20 *Highlighted area in the middle of the mini-timeline is removed*

want the video to end, then drag the Out point handle (on the right of the clip representation) to the left, until it matches the playhead location.

As you drag, the area that will be removed becomes highlighted.

6. To remove a section in the middle of the clip, drag the playhead on the mini-timeline to the frame where the unwanted material begins.

7. In the Monitor panel, on the controller bar, click the **Split Clip button** shown in Figure 19.

Notice that there are now two clip representations that replace the original in both the mini-timeline and the Sceneline.

8. Click inside the representation of the second clip in the mini-timeline to select it. Then drag its In point to the right, until it is past the unwanted material. (To easily identify the unwanted section, place the playhead at the end point of the unwanted material to mark how far to drag the In point handle).

TIP You can also select the first clip and edit it by setting a new Out point.

The unwanted material is removed from the beginning of the second clip (or end of the first clip, if you chose to edit that clip), and the gap created between the first and second clips is automatically closed. See Figure 20.

TIP Premiere Elements also has a feature called Smart Trim, which will analyze and highlight the low-quality parts of a clip, which you can then choose to remove or keep. To learn more about Smart Trim, consult the Help files under Help > Adobe Premiere Elements Help.

9. Save your file.

Figures © Cengage Learning 2013

Use video effects

The quality of your video depends on many factors, such as the type of recording device you used to capture the video, the video environment, and of course the eye and steady hand of the videographer. While it's best to set the stage so that the video you capture is of the highest quality while it's being recorded, Premiere Elements offers some effects to correct imperfections after the fact.

1. Click the **Edit tab** in the Tasks panel to view the available effects. See Figure 21.

2. Be sure your video clip is selected in the Sceneline (it will have a blue border around it).

3. Use the scroll bar on the right side of the Adjust area to view all the available effects.

4. Click the effect you'd like to apply to your video.

5. Click **Apply** in the lower right corner of the Tasks panel, to apply the effect.

   The Effect will be applied to the video clip in the Monitor panel.

6. Click the **Play/Pause Toggle button** on the controller to view the video with the applied effects.

   The effects applied will be listed in the Effects list in the upper part of the Edit tab. If you click more than one effect, it will be added to any previous effects you've applied.

   (continued)

Figure 21 *Edit effects*

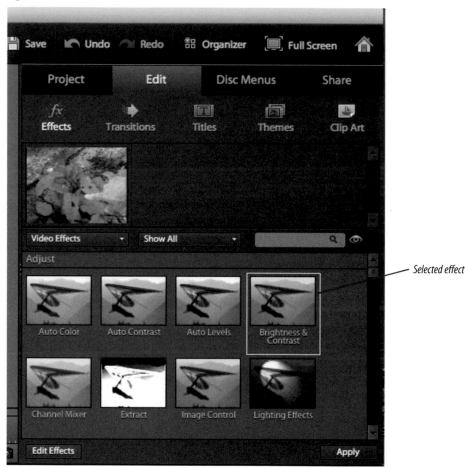

Selected effect

Figure © Cengage Learning 2013

Integrating Video

Figure 22 *Deleting an effect*

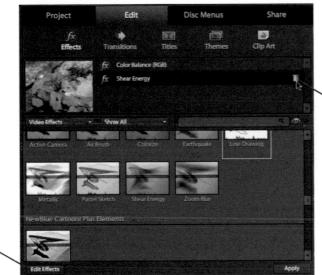

Delete button

Edit Effects button

Figure 23 *Effect editing options*

Integrating Video

7. To delete an effect, select it in the list and click the **Delete button** (the trashcan) to the right of the effect title. See Figure 22.

8. To edit an effect that's been applied to the selected clip, click the **Edit Effects button** in the lower left corner of the Edit tab in the Tasks panel. Figure 23 shows some of the options available for editing an effect.

9. Save the file.

Add a title treatment

Let's add a customized title treatment at the beginning of our video. We'll start by inserting a black video clip and then adding text to it.

1. Select the first clip in the Sceneline.

2. Click the **Project tab** in the Tasks panel, click **Media**, click the **New Item button**, then click **Black Video**. See Figure 24.

3. In the Sceneline, drag the new black video clip to the beginning of the movie. See Figure 25.

(continued)

Figure 24 *Media options for a new item*

Media >
New Item
button

Figure 25 *Moving the black clip*

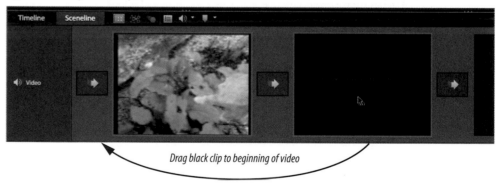

Drag black clip to beginning of video

Integrating Video

Figure 26 *Text tool*

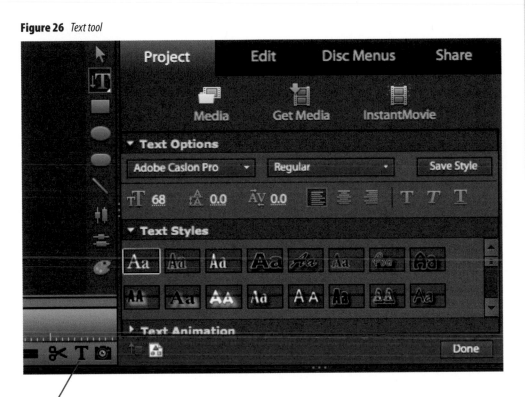

Text tool

4. Select the **Add default text tool** in the Monitor Panel (see Figure 26) to open the Text Options on the Project tab in the Tasks panel.

5. In the Add Text area of the blank video clip, select any existing text, and type your title.

6. To move the text, click the **Selection tool**, located on the Tools panel along the right side of the Monitor panel, and drag the text to a new location.

   Feel free to explore the other options in this area (the shape, alignment, and color tools) and also the various text options and styles in the text options area.

TIP You can also superimpose a title directly over a video clip: select the clip and then on the Project tab in the Tasks panel, click Media, click the New Item button, and then choose the Title option.

(continued)

7. To place an image on your title, click the **Add image button** at the bottom of the Project tab (see Figure 27) and browse your computer for an image you would like to use.

8. In the Monitor panel, click the **Selection tool** in the Tools panel, click the image to select it, then right-click the image and use the **Transform command** to scale or rotate the image as needed. See Figure 28.

Figure 27 *Adding an image*

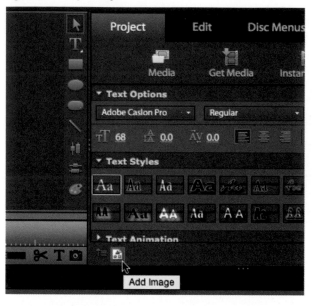

Figure 28 *Transforming the image*

Figures © Cengage Learning 2013

Integrating Video

Figure 29 *Setting a transition*

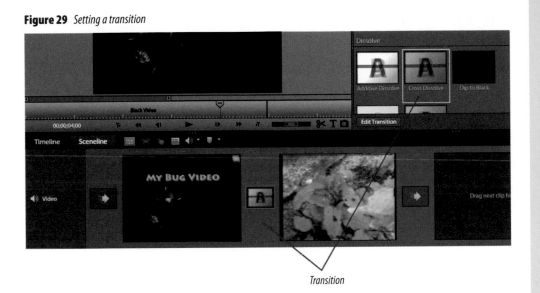

Transition

Add transitions

To give the video a more polished look, let's create a transition effect between the title clip and the beginning of the video, and another at the end of the video.

1. Go to the Sceneline if necessary.

2. Click to the **Edit tab** in the Projects task panel, then click the **Transitions button**.

3. Drag the **Cross Dissolve transition** to the arrow icon between the two clip thumbnails on the Sceneline. See Figure 29.

4. Drag the **Dip to Black transition** to the arrow between the last clip and the "Drag next clip here" thumbnail on the Sceneline.

(continued)

Integrating Video

5. To edit a transition, click the transition in the Sceneline, click the **Edit** tab in the Tasks panel, then click the **Edit Transition button** at the bottom of the panel. See Figure 30.

6. Choose **Timeline** > **Render Work Area** to see a full rendering of the effects.

7. Save your file.

Figure 30 *Edit Transition button*

Edit Transition
button

Figure 31 *Options for sharing a video*

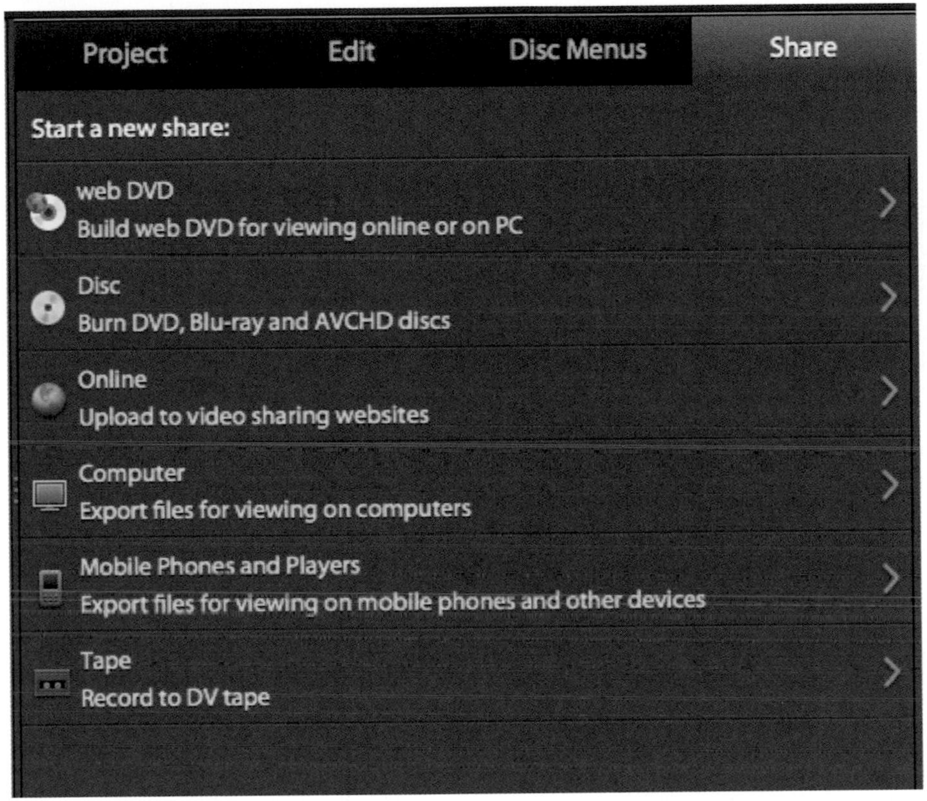

| Project | Edit | Disc Menus | Share |

Start a new share:

web DVD
Build web DVD for viewing online or on PC ›

Disc
Burn DVD, Blu-ray and AVCHD discs ›

Online
Upload to video sharing websites ›

Computer
Export files for viewing on computers ›

Mobile Phones and Players
Export files for viewing on mobile phones and other devices ›

Tape
Record to DV tape ›

Share the video

The final step in the video preparation process is to publish the video.

1. Click the **Share** tab in the Tasks panel. See Figure 31.

   The Share tab provides many options for publishing your video, depending on where it will be viewed (on a DVD or Blu-ray disc, on an online video sharing site like YouTube or Facebook, or on a computer or mobile device). For now, let's output the video so we can insert it into an HTML web page (more on how to do that in the How We Did It section of this chapter).

2. On the Share tab, choose the **Computer** option.

3. In the Computer output area, use the scroll bar on the right side of the window to view the various output options, which include Flash Video, MPEG, AVCHD (codec for playback of high definition video), QuickTime, a still image frame from the video, or just the audio track.

4. Click the **Adobe Flash Video** option.

(continued)

Figure © Cengage Learning 2013

5. Click the **Presets list arrow**, then choose **FLV - Web Large, NTSC Source (Flash 8 and Higher)**.

   This option will produce a video that's 640 x 480 pixels in size and that will run in Flash Player version 8 or later. Note the final file size in the lower portion of the Share tab. See Figure 32.

6. Select any text in the File Name text box, enter a new name, and save it in your project folder.

7. Click **Save** to render the video.

   Next, let's save our video in MPEG-4 (MP4)—a common format for web delivery, though it may produce a much larger file than the FLV option.

8. Click the **Computer** option on the Share tab, then click the **AVCHD tab** at the top.

9. Set the preset to **MP4-NTSC DV Standard**.

10. Create a filename, click **Browse** and locate your project folder, then save the file.

    For faster downloading, let's change the default size of the video to one with smaller dimensions.

11. Click the **Advanced** button.

(continued)

Figure 32 *Selecting an output option*

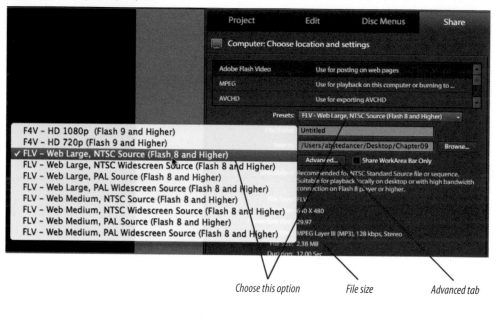

Choose this option   File size   Advanced tab

Integrating Video

Figure 33 *Customizing video export options*

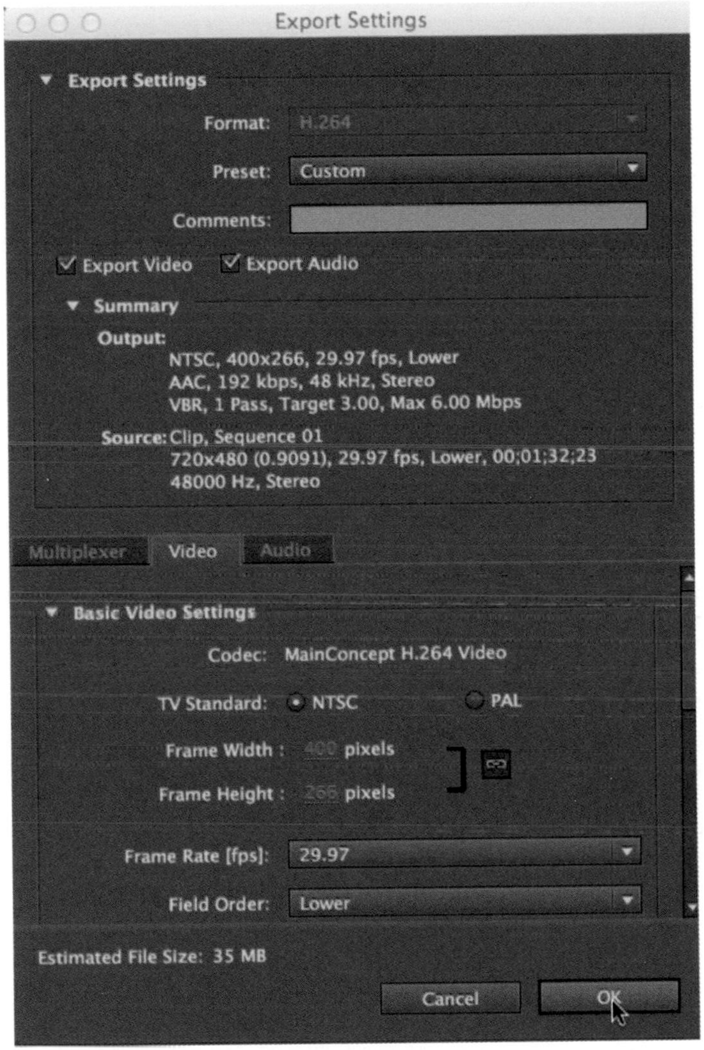

Figure © Cengage Learning 2013

Integrating Video

12. In the Export settings area, on the Video tab, change the Frame Width and Height to **400 x 266 pixels**. See Figure 33.

TIP To compress the video further, you can also lower the frame rate (try 15 fps for web delivery). On the Audio tab, you can reduce the frequency (if there's no music in your video, try 16 kHz) and choose Mono for the output channel.

13. Click **OK**, enter a name for the new preset and click **Save**.

14. Click **Save** again to render the video.

In the next section, we'll show you how to embed an MP4 video into a web page and in the More to Explore section, you learn how to insert an FLV into a Flash movie.

ADDING VIDEO TO A WEB PAGE

Like audio, a common method for getting your video on a web page is linking to it using an embed tag. We used Dreamweaver to embed our MP4 video on the Gardener's Walk seasonal video area. We'll show you how we did this. While you're working through these steps, you may choose to follow along and embed your own video within a web page you created. Then you might consider incorporating your own video into your specific interactive media project.

Insert an MP4 video using Dreamweaver:

1. In Dreamweaver, place the insertion point on the page where you'd like the video to appear.

2. Choose **Insert** > **Media** > **Plugin** from the Menu bar.

3. Search for your .mp4 formatted video file.

   It's best to put the video file in an assets folder, just like images, within your site folder, so that everything remains properly linked together when you load your project remotely.

4. By default the plugin controller for the video will be set to 32 pixels wide by 32 pixels high.

Figure 34 *Setting properties for the plugin video controller*

To see all of the video along with the video controls, click the plugin icon on the page, and in the Properties panel, set the width and height to the size of your video. In our example, the size was output to 400 x 266, but we added a bit more height so that the video controllers would be visible. See Figure 34.

Figure © Cengage Learning 2013

HTML5 Compatible Video

If you're building your project to adhere to HTML5, you'll want to manually insert the HTML5 video controller code into your web page, as shown in Figure 35. In this code you will notice two types of video formats are being called: .mp4 and .ogg. Ogg (also known as Ogg Theora) is a lesser-known format that, at the time of this writing, must be used to view HTML5 video in the Firefox and Opera browsers. Unfortunately, most video editing programs, including Adobe Premiere, do not currently offer Ogg conversion options. However, there are free online conversion tools available, such as Miro Video Converter at mirovideoconverter.com. For more information on creating HTML5-friendly video, visit w3schools.com/html5/html5_video.asp

Figure 35 *HTML5 code for inserting video*

Generic video controller (default player for Dreamweaver)

```
<embed src="your_file.mp4" width="400" height="280"></embed>
```

HTML5 video controller (viewable on HTML5-supported browsers)

```
<video width="400" height="280" controls="controls">
  <source src="your_file.mp4" type="video/mp4" />
  <source src="your_file.ogg" type="video/ogg" />
Your browser does not support the video element.
</video>
```

TIP Don't know the frame size of your video? Here's one way to find out: Right-click the video file and choose Properties (Win) or Ctrl-click the file and choose Get Info (Mac). In the Info box, open the More Info area.

5. View the page in your browser to see the video and test the playback controls. See Figure 36.

TIP If you don't see the video, you may need to download the latest version of QuickTime player. The MP4 format uses QuickTime to play video, so your browser must be able to support Apple QuickTime.

Figure 36 *MP4 video on the Gardener's Walk site*

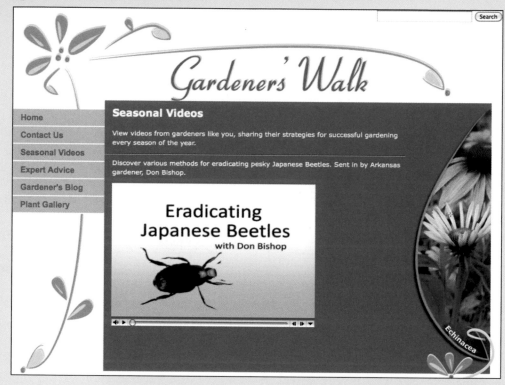

Integrating Video

ADDING VIDEO TO YOUR INTERACTIVE MEDIA PROJECT

Now that you've learned how to find, prepare, and publish video files, you're ready to incorporate video into your own project.

1. Find some copyright-free video or record your own.
2. Prepare your video file for its intended output. Edit the video, if necessary, in a video editor and save the file in the proper format for your project (review format options in the Characteristics of Video section of this chapter). MP4 and FLV are the most common formats used for interactive projects that will be viewed over an Internet connection.
3. Next, decide where you want to place the video in your project. If your project is a web page, see the How We Did It section of this chapter. If your video will appear within a Flash movie, see the More to Explore section in this chapter.
4. Refer to the design strategies presented in this chapter to ensure your video meets usability and accessibility standards.

EXTERNALLY LOADING VIDEO INTO A FLASH MOVIE

If you plan to create an interactive media project using only Flash, and would like to use video, explore the steps below on how to link and load the video file directly into your Flash movie. First, you'll set up your file structure as if you're preparing your movie and video to be uploaded to a website. You'll then use the Import Video wizard to load your FLV video from an external location.

Set Up the File Structure

Before starting Flash, set up a folder that will contain all the elements necessary to make your video presentation run properly on the Web.

1. In your lessons folder (or elsewhere on your computer) create a new folder and call it **My_Flash_Video**.
2. Place your FLV-formatted video in this new folder. (See the Sharing the Video section of this chapter for how to output your video into the FLV format.)

3. Now open Flash and create a new Flash file.
4. Choose **File** > **Save** and save your file as **my_flash_video.fla** in your My_Flash_Video folder.

Import the Video

1. Choose **File** > **Import** > **Import Video** to open the Import Video wizard.
2. Click **Browse** and locate the FLV video in your My_Flash_Video folder.

3. Click the **Load external video with playback component option button**, as shown in Figure 37.

TIP If you import a video file that Flash doesn't support, click the Launch Adobe Media Encoder (AME) button at the bottom of the Import Video wizard. AME will open, providing the option to convert the file to the FLV format.

4. Click the **Next button**.

Figure 37 *Import Video wizard*

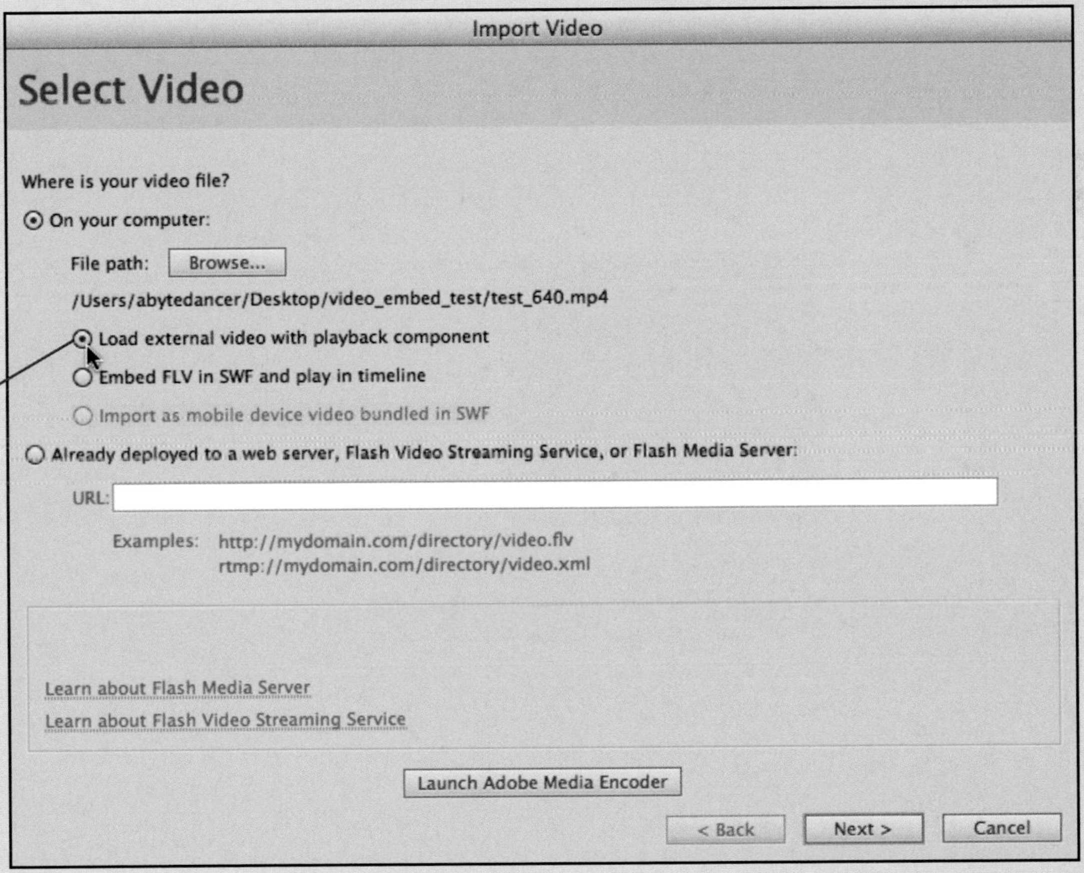

Import Video

Select Video

Where is your video file?

⊙ On your computer:

File path: [Browse...]

/Users/abytedancer/Desktop/video_embed_test/test_640.mp4

⊙ Load external video with playback component

Load option →

○ Embed FLV in SWF and play in timeline

○ Import as mobile device video bundled in SWF

○ Already deployed to a web server, Flash Video Streaming Service, or Flash Media Server:

URL: [   ]

Examples: http://mydomain.com/directory/video.flv
rtmp://mydomain.com/directory/video.xml

Learn about Flash Media Server
Learn about Flash Video Streaming Service

[Launch Adobe Media Encoder]

[< Back] [Next >] [Cancel]

5. In the Skin drop-down box, select **SkinUnderAll.swf**. Flash provides many premade skins. Some appear over the video, and others appear below it. Feel free to check out the different skin options, and then choose the SkinUnderAll.swf for this lesson. See Figure 38.

6. Read the notes in the Skinning section of the wizard, and then click the **Next button**.
7. Carefully read the information in the Finish Video Import section of the wizard.

This information reminds you how to configure your file structure so the video will play properly when loaded to a website. We won't load the content to a website, but it's good to know this information for when you eventually do.

Figure 38 *Import Video Skinning options*

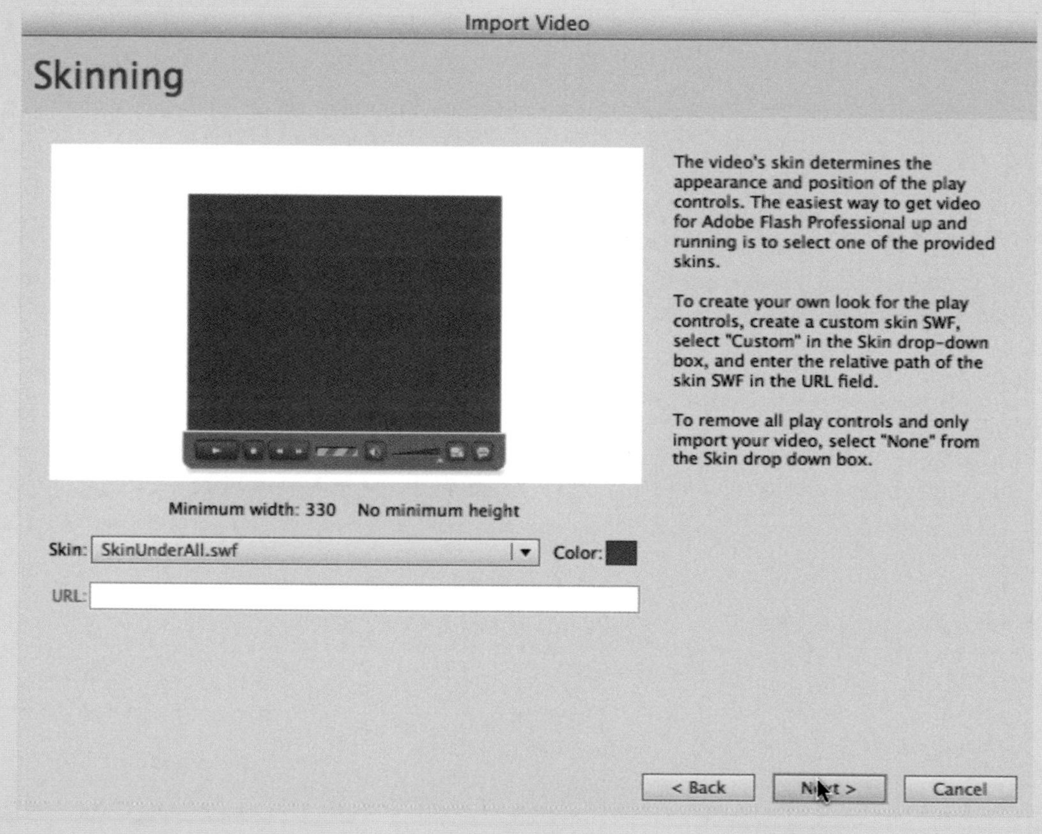

Import Video

Skinning

The video's skin determines the appearance and position of the play controls. The easiest way to get video for Adobe Flash Professional up and running is to select one of the provided skins.

To create your own look for the play controls, create a custom skin SWF, select "Custom" in the Skin drop-down box, and enter the relative path of the skin SWF in the URL field.

To remove all play controls and only import your video, select "None" from the Skin drop down box.

Minimum width: 330   No minimum height

Skin: SkinUnderAll.swf   ▼   Color:

URL:

< Back   Next >   Cancel

Figure © Cengage Learning 2013

8. Click the **Finish button**.
   The video appears on the Stage with the playback controls underneath it, reflecting the SkinUnderAll.swf skin you chose.
9. If the video is larger than the default Flash Stage area (550 x 400 pixels) choose **Modify** > **Document** to adjust the dimensions to match your video's frame size and position.
10. Choose **Control** > **Test Movie in Flash Professional** to play the video and test out the controls. See Figure 39.
11. Save your file.
    Well done!

Figure 39 *Viewing final movie in a browser*

Even More to Explore

To explore some of the topics discussed in this chapter in more depth, see the References section at the end of the book. For links to additional web resources, visit the Even More to Explore link under Book Resources on Cengage Brain.

Figure © Cengage Learning 2013

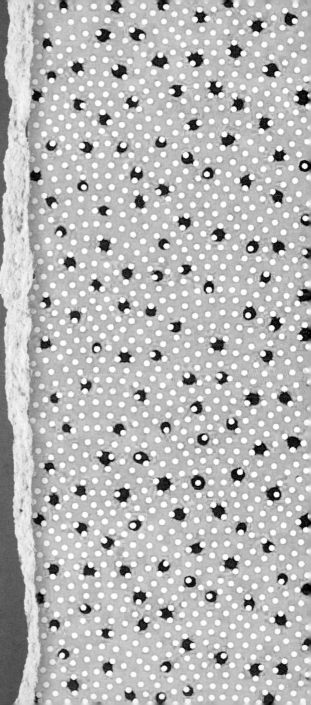

CHAPTER 10

FINE-TUNING, COMPLETING, AND PUBLISHING YOUR PROJECT

- Checking the Structure

- Final Testing and Fine-Tuning

- Getting It Out There

- How We Did It: Completing the Project

- It's Your Turn: Completing Your Interactive Media Project

- More to Explore: Designing Mobile Layouts

CHAPTER 10

FINE-TUNING, COMPLETING, AND PUBLISHING YOUR PROJECT

Introduction

Now that you've developed the various pieces of your interactive media project, and integrated them into your application framework, you're ready to fine-tune it and get it ready for prime time. To prepare your project for publishing, there are several tests you can use to evaluate it for accessibility and usability. Also be sure to optimize image and media files to reduce their sizes, and check that you've included transcripts of all audio and video content.

After you're satisfied that everything works correctly and meets current standards, it's time to present your work to your client for approval. Once you get the green light, you're ready to publish your work. Publishing can take many forms, depending on the type of project. For a website, you'll upload your files to web servers to make them available for viewing on the Internet. For video and audio projects, you'll transfer your files to CDs or DVDs, post them online, or both. For games, you'll transfer your files to DVDs or to websites for downloading.

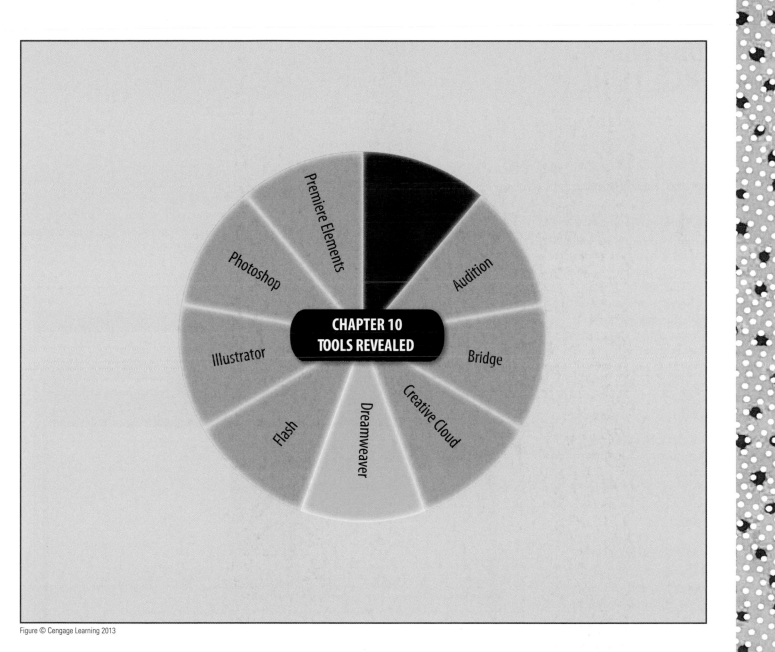

Figure © Cengage Learning 2013

Checking the STRUCTURE

Verifying the Final Navigational Structure

Your project's final navigational structure should show that your product is logically organized and easy to navigate. In Chapter 2, you considered your project's overall structure when you created the wireframe to serve as its blueprint. In Chapter 3, you considered your project's navigation structure and the links that would help create that structure. And in Chapter 4, you built your framework, creating a plan for the pages you would need, as well as the links to move between them. In Chapters 5 through 9, you added the pages to your project and developed the content for each page.

Now that you're preparing to launch your project, it's important to verify that the final product reflects your original intentions. To meet the expectations of your users, it must be easy to navigate, and everything must function correctly.

Finding and Repairing Broken Links

Links that don't work correctly and don't lead to their intended destination are called **broken links**. Broken links will irritate users, especially when they see the annoying Error 404 or Not

Found message. These messages mean that, though there's communication with the server, the server couldn't find the requested page. Sometimes users cause this error by incorrectly typing a URL, but often it means that the project designer or site administrator moved, renamed, or deleted a file without correcting the links to that page, or that they specified an absolute path where a relative path was needed. For an example of a more encouraging message when this occurs on the Federal Aviation Administration website, see Figure 1.

Figure 1 *Broken link message on FAA website*
Courtesy: National Transportation Safety Board

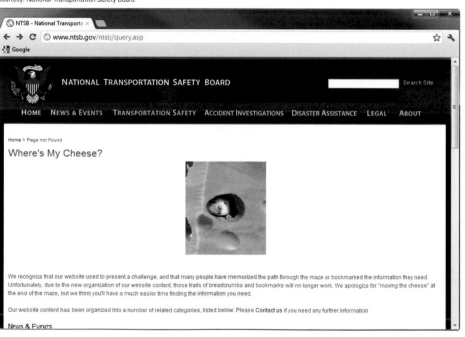

Locate and repair all project links to make sure they work correctly. Dreamweaver has a tool for checking internal links called the Link Checker, shown in Figure 2. You can find the Link Checker by using the Site > Check Links Sitewide command. The Link Checker can show broken links in an open document, in the entire site, or in selected files in a site. If the Link Checker finds a broken link, it will list the file with the broken link in the Files column and the link itself in the Broken Links column. Checking links to make sure they work is an ongoing and crucial task that you need to perform on a regular basis.

Although the Link Checker has an option to check external links, it only provides a list of them, along with the web page on which they're located. You need to periodically check your external links manually to make sure they work correctly.

Using Named Anchors for Navigating Long Pages

When a page is so long that users have to repeatedly scroll to find content, it's helpful to

Figure 2 *Link Checker options in Dreamweaver*

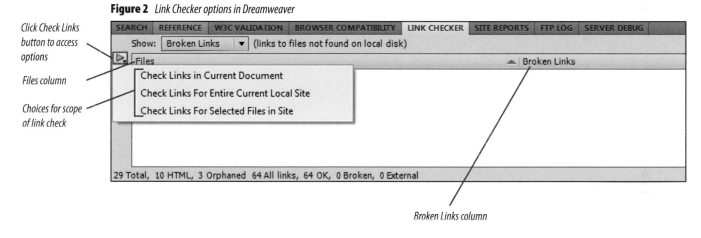

Click Check Links button to access options

Files column

Choices for scope of link check

Broken Links column

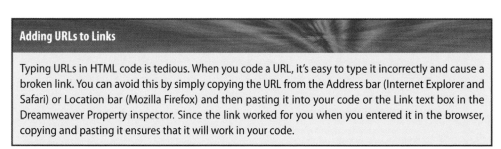

Adding URLs to Links

Typing URLs in HTML code is tedious. When you code a URL, it's easy to type it incorrectly and cause a broken link. You can avoid this by simply copying the URL from the Address bar (Internet Explorer and Safari) or Location bar (Mozilla Firefox) and then pasting it into your code or the Link text box in the Dreamweaver Property inspector. Since the link worked for you when you entered it in the browser, copying and pasting it ensures that it will work in your code.

provide named anchors with internal links. These enable users to "jump" to different parts of the page without scrolling. A **named anchor** is a specific location on a web page that has a descriptive name. An internal link uses a named anchor as a target to that location on the page. A **target** is the location on the page that a browser displays when users click the internal link. Good spots to place named anchors include the top of the page, the bottom of the page, or at the beginning of main paragraphs. Figure 3 shows a page on the USA.gov website where named anchors are used to link to different parts of the same page. A named anchor is preceded by a # sign in the HTML code.

Providing a User-friendly Navigation Structure

In addition to avoiding broken links and helping users quickly navigate content on long pages, there are several more strategies you can use to provide a user-friendly experience.

- **Use intuitive text for links**
  State the obvious. Don't make users guess where the links will take them.

- **Don't use the text "click here"**
  Speaking of the obvious, your links should be immediately recognizable as links so that users recognize them and know how to use them. You should never have to add directions for users to click on a link.

- **Add a set of plain text navigational links at the bottom of each page**
  This provides an alternative to flashier links that may require a plug-in that not all users have installed on their systems.

Figure 3 *Named anchors used on the USA.gov website*
USA.gov website – www.usa.gov

Links to named anchors

First named anchor

■ **Include a link to the home page on every page in the site**

This is especially important when users have found a page within your site as the result of a web search. In these cases, if the Back button is used, the user will leave your site. An obvious way to go to the home page helps keep users on your site.

■ **Use image maps**

An **image map** is an image that has one or more hotspots placed on top of it. A **hotspot** is a clickable area on an image that, when clicked, links to a different location on the same page or to another page. For example, you might provide a hotspot on a web page banner that links to the home page. When users move the mouse pointer over the hotspot, the pointer changes to a pointing hand, letting them know there's a link associated with that object. See Figure 4.

■ **Site maps**

Site maps serve as a "road map" or an index for a website. Sitemaps can provide a picture of the website content and how

Figure 4 *USA.gov site index, hotspot, and search text box*
USA.gov website – www.usa.gov

Link to site index

Pointer indicates presence of link

Links to content by category

Search text box

it's organized. The USA.gov website you saw earlier provides a site index of their content organized by government pages, departments, agencies, topics, audiences, and online services.

- **Site search**
  A site search allows your users to search for content quickly. Most people today are familiar with using search engines, so it's handy to include one internally. Google has a custom search tool that uses the Google database. The search tool also includes an option to search the entire Internet. Google Site Search is priced according to a search query limit. For a blog or personal site, the base price is $100.00 a year for a limit of 20,000 search queries per year. The price increases with higher numbers of queries.

  FreeFind at freefind.com provides a site search feature for small, personal sites, that's hosted on their servers. You can also use a search engine that resides on your host server, rather than a separate online service. For a simple site search, the HTML5 code that we used in Chapter 5 works very well and is easy to add.

Providing Access to External Documents

When preparing PDFs for use on a website, strive to make your documents as small as possible by using the settings in Adobe Acrobat to optimize the file size. You should also use as many accessibility features as possible in order to provide your content to all users. Include transcripts for all audio and video content and provide options that allow the user to control the playback of media.

Creating Accessible PDFs

Adobe Acrobat and Adobe Reader have made PDFs a common document format for presenting large amounts of information with both text and images, such as online bank statements, manuals, and tax forms. Acrobat and Reader include tools for making PDFs accessible to people with disabilities—and that actually benefit all users. These tools fall into two categories: features that *create* more accessible documents, and features that make it easier to read PDFs.

Acrobat is used to create accessible PDFs. Some of the tools that make a document more accessible include:

- using tags for document structure (Heading 1, Heading 2, etc.)
- converting an untagged PDF to a tagged PDF
- editing the reading order and document structure
- tools for creating accessible forms

Adobe Reader is used for reading PDFs. Some of the tools available in Reader to make documents more accessible include:

- saving text as accessible text for a Braille printer
- automatic scrolling

- keyboard alternatives to mouse actions
- displaying text in large type
- using text-to-speech conversion
- using screen magnifiers

You'll find options for downloading PDFs on many websites, such as the Internal Revenue Service (IRS) website shown in Figure 5. The IRS uses accessibility contractors and internal accessibility specialists to make their tax documents as accessible as possible.

Their techniques include using full text descriptions, Braille transcriptions, and large print formats.

Providing Transcripts for Accessibility

The first guideline for WCAG 2.0 is to "Provide text equivalents for every non-text element…." This includes images, sounds, standalone audio files (such as podcasts), and videos. We talked about transcripts in Chapter 9 when we added captions to a video on the advice page in the Gardener's Walk website. Transcripts can also feed more traffic to your site, because, unlike audio or video files, search engines can use them for indexing. You can also add captions that are synchronized with audio and video content. Captions are displayed on the screen while the content is playing. While helpful, they do not take the place of providing transcripts.

Figure 5 *Accessibility options for IRS tax documents*
Internal Revenue Service website – www.irs.gov

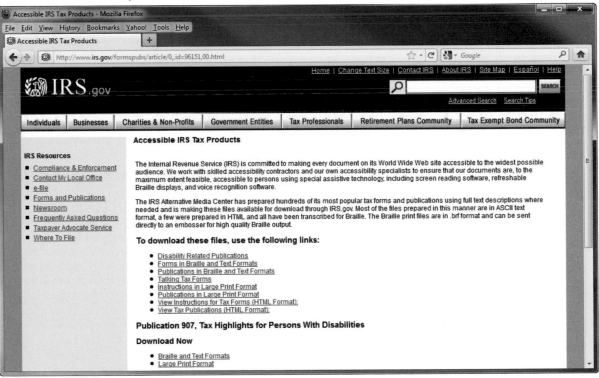

Final Testing and FINE-TUNING

Identifying and Correcting Errors

Before you can finally declare your project complete and present it to your client for approval and publication, you need to verify that it's free of any errors. Projects with errors look unprofessional, so be sure to check your spelling, grammar, and links at periodic intervals. And because it's much easier to make corrections as you go, most of the processes we'll describe here should be performed throughout the project, not just at the end.

Refer again to your wireframe and confirm that you've met all your goals and objectives, and that you've included the content necessary to meet those goals. Verify that you've provided accessibility to all users and that you've properly cited any outside content that requires permission for use, as you learned in Chapter 6.

Even when you do test continuously throughout project development, you'll want to run final tests before publishing. The following tests will help ensure that your project meets current standards of quality, accessibility, and usability. Some of these apply mainly to websites, but others apply to all types of projects.

- **Validate HTML markup**
  In Chapter 4 we talked about HTML5, the most current standard for HTML markup. Just as you can validate CSS code, you can validate HTML code. The W3C Validation Service allows you to upload files and validate them against several document types including HTML5. You can access the W3C service from their website, validator. w3.org, or by using the Dreamweaver Results panel W3C Validation tab, shown in Figure 6. Notice that errors are listed with red icons and warnings are listed

Figure 6 *Dreamweaver Results panel W3C Validation tab*

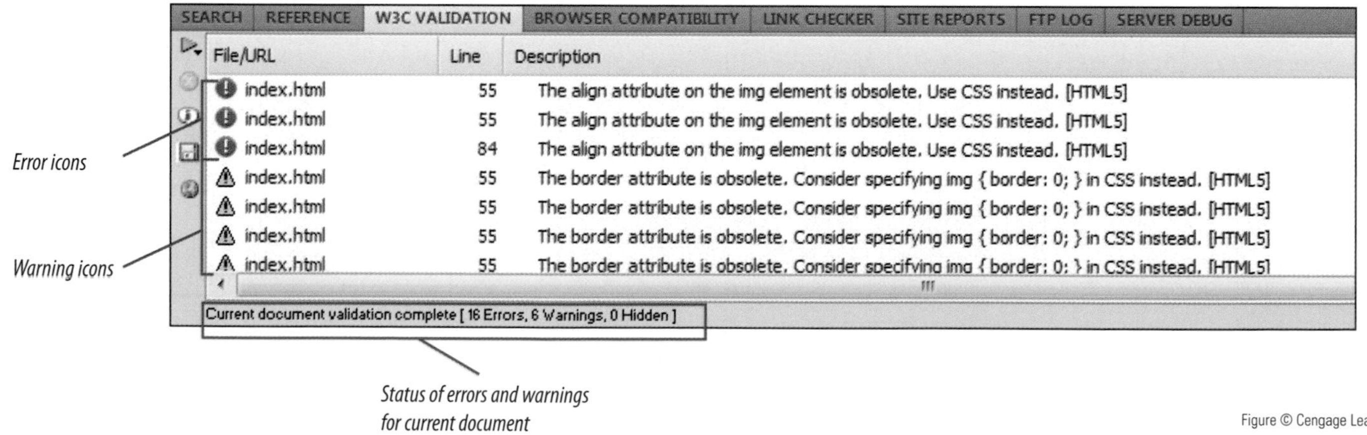

Error icons

Warning icons

Status of errors and warnings for current document

with yellow icons. Be sure to evaluate and correct any errors listed.

■ **Validate CSS markup**

In Chapter 5 we discussed the steps used to validate style sheets. Recall that we went to jigsaw.w3.org/css-validator then uploaded our CSS file and validated it against CSS level 3 standards. As you add to your style sheets, remember to validate them to ensure that your pages continue to meet current standards.

■ **Run site reports**

You can use the Reports command in the Dreamweaver Site menu to generate HTML reports for a current document, the entire current local site, selected files in a site, or a selected folder. You can also generate workflow reports when you're working with a team to identify files that have been checked out by others or recently modified. The Reports dialog box is shown in Figure 7.

■ **Test pages using multiple browsers and browser versions**

In Chapter 2 we discussed testing your pages using multiple browsers and browser versions. You can use the Preview/Debug in Browser button to access the browsers installed on your computer, as shown in Figure 8. If you click Edit Browser List, you can add additional browsers and designate which one will be at the top of the list. We also talked about using Adobe Browser Lab, which allows you

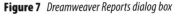

Figure 7 *Dreamweaver Reports dialog box*

Choices for scope of reports →

Figure 8 *Choices for previewing pages*

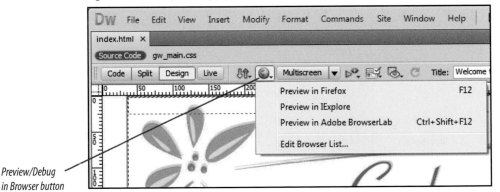

Preview/Debug in Browser button

to preview pages in browsers that aren't installed on your computer. You can also check Browser compatibility by using the Browser Compatibility tab in the Results panel.

■ **Test using multiple devices**

In Chapter 2 we also talked about testing your project using multiple devices, such as mobile or tablet devices. The Multiscreen preview button in Dreamweaver compares the page content as rendered on three different simulated screens such as a laptop, a smartphone, or a tablet. Remember that this feature works in combination with media queries, which specify the parameters for displaying pages on various devices. The Media Queries dialog box is one of the options listed in the Multiscreen Preview drop-down menu. As shown in Figure 9, this dialog box lets you specify a site-wide media query file, along with the supporting style sheets that are used to format the desktop, tablet, and mobile versions of the site. The code that's generated is shown in Figure 10.

Figure 9 *Dreamweaver Media Queries dialog box*

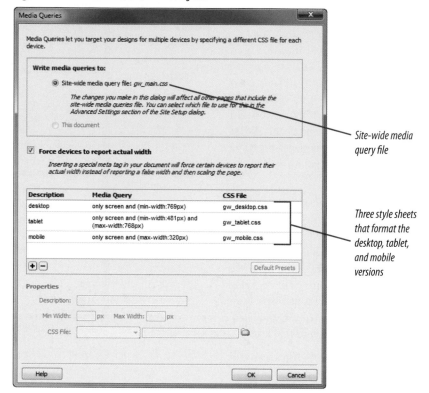

Site-wide media query file

Three style sheets that format the desktop, tablet, and mobile versions

Figure 10 *Code in site-wide media query file linking to three supporting style sheet files*

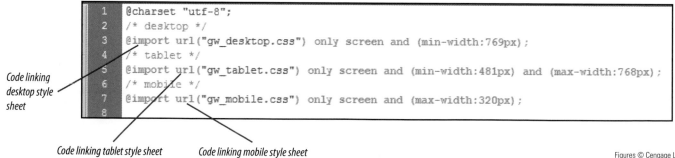

Code linking desktop style sheet

Code linking tablet style sheet   Code linking mobile style sheet

Figures © Cengage Learning 2013

Fine-Tuning, Completing, and Publishing Your Project

QUICK **TIP**

A word of caution about media queries: Internet Explorer versions 8 and below do not support media queries unless you add additional code to the head content.

■ **Gather feedback**

Feedback is vital to the development of a good interactive project. You learned about usability tests in Chapter 2 and about focus groups in Chapter 4. These are both great tools for gathering user feedback.

If you did not set up usability tests or focus groups during the development phases, it's not too late to conduct them now if time permits. If you have results from previously conducted usability tests or focus groups, compare the findings with your final project to verify that the proper adjustments were made in response to the feedback you received.

Another method of gathering feedback is to provide a way for users to send comments to a website administrator, such as the survey on the USA.gov website shown in Figure 11. Providing users the opportunity to send comments adds to the interactive experience and makes them feel like their feedback is important. However, popup surveys can be annoying to some users, so use them carefully. If you see that they are not being completed by most users, consider another option for gathering feedback.

Figure 11 *USA.gov website survey*
USA.gov website – www.usa.gov

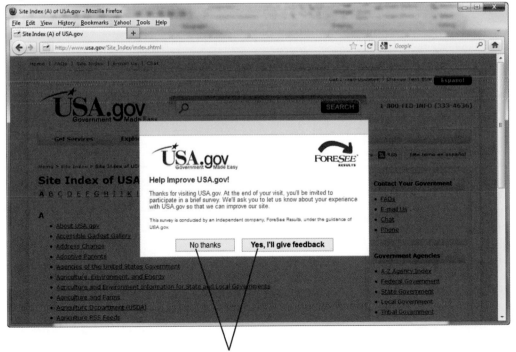

Links to accept or decline the survey

Getting It
OUT THERE

Setting Up Your Servers

After you've completed your project and tested it thoroughly, you're ready to take a test run. For a website, you can use a web server. A **web server** is a computer with software that enables it to host websites and is connected to the Internet with an IP (Internet Protocol) address. Some developers use a private **testing server** to test a site before publishing it to the live server, where it will be available to anyone. Before you can transfer your local files to a web server, you must obtain the necessary information to connect to it and upload your files. You add this information to Dreamweaver using the Site Setup dialog box.

Managing a Server

You can specify your remote server settings when you first create a site, or you can do it after you've completed the site and are confident that it's ready for public viewing. To specify a website's remote settings in Dreamweaver, click the Add new Server button in the Site Setup dialog box, add your server name, then choose a connection type. The most common connection type is **FTP**, which stands for File Transfer Protocol. If you choose FTP, you'll

need to specify a server address and folder name on the FTP site where you'll upload your site root folder. Your web hosting service will give you these settings. You can also use **SFTP**, which stands for Secure FTP. This option encrypts file transfers to protect your files, user names, and passwords. Figure 12 shows the Site Setup dialog box with example remote server settings added. When you have added all necessary information, click the Test button to verify that you can connect successfully to the server.

Figure 12 *Specifying remote server settings in the Site Setup dialog box*

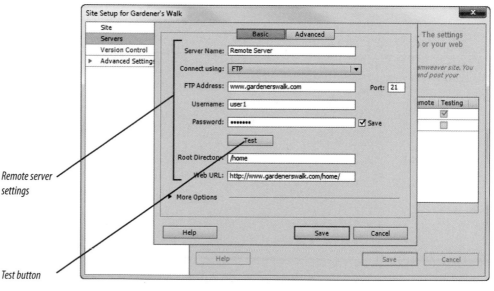

Remote server settings

Test button

Figure © Cengage Learning 2013

Transferring Files to and from a Remote Server

After you've set up your remote site, you **upload**, or copy your files from the local folder to the remote host. This is easy to do using Dreamweaver's built-in FTP capabilities. To transfer a copy of the files to the remote server, first view the site in Local view, select the files or folder you want to upload, and then click the Put File(s) button on the Files panel toolbar. To view the uploaded files on the remote server, either switch to Remote server in the Files panel or expand the Files panel to view both the Remote Site and the Local Site at once. To expand the Files panel, click the Expand to show local and remote sites button in the Files panel. The panel expands, as shown in Figure 13. (When the panel is expanded, the button becomes the Collapse to show only local or remote site button.) If you have both a testing server and a remote server set up, you can view each of them in the left pane by clicking the Testing Server button or the Remote Server button. Local folder icons are green in color, Testing Server folders are pink, and Remote Server folders are yellow.

Figure 13 *Files panel in expanded view*

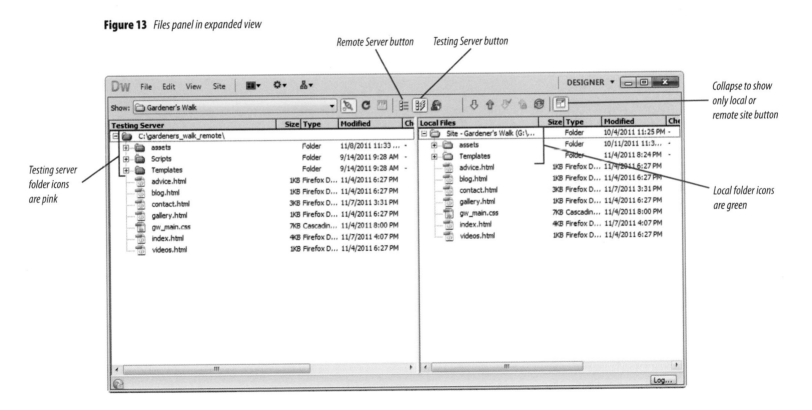

Figure © Cengage Learning 2013

Fine-Tuning, Completing, and Publishing Your Project

If a file you select for uploading requires additional files in order to function correctly, such as images or CSS files, a dialog box opens when you click the Put File(s) button and asks if you want those files (called **dependent files**) to be uploaded as well. When you click Yes, all dependent files will be uploaded to the appropriate folders in the remote site. When a file to be uploaded is located in a subfolder, that folder will be uploaded automatically. To upload the entire site, select the site root folder.

Two other file transfer options are downloading files and synchronizing files. To **download** means to copy files from the remote server to the local site folder. To download files from the remote server to the local folder, select the files or folder you want to download, then click the Get File(s) button. To **synchronize** means to compare the dates of all files in both the local and remote sites, then transfer only those files that have been changed. To synchronize files, use the Site > Synchronize Sitewide command to open the Synchronize Files dialog box shown in Figure 14.

If you're publishing a project other than a website, or are not using Dreamweaver to publish a site, you can use any FTP client to upload your files. One of our favorites is FileZilla at filezilla-project.org. FileZilla is open source software distributed under the terms of the GNU General Public License. The interface is easy to use and can be set up to quickly access multiple sites through the Site Manager or the Quickconnect button, as shown in Figure 15. Most interactive media projects today, such as games or mobile apps, can also be published

Figure 14 *Dreamweaver Synchronize Files dialog box*

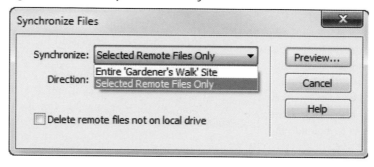

Figure 15 *FileZilla interface*
www.filezilla-project.org

Open the Site Manager list arrow

Quickconnect button

Figure © Cengage Learning 2013

Fine-Tuning, Completing, and Publishing Your Project

and sold electronically through sites such as iTunes, Amazon, Gamefly, and Best Buy.

Attracting Users

Even though you've designed, developed, and published a terrific site, that doesn't automatically mean you'll be overrun with users from day one. Here are some ways you can get your site listed by the top search engines and increase the traffic on your site:

Tips for Increasing Website Traffic

- **Register your site with several search engines**
  To register your site with a search engine, submit your URL for inclusion in the site index. For example, to submit a website to Google, you would use the link shown in Figure 16.

- **Include meta tags (page titles, keywords, and descriptions) for your pages**
  Take the time to craft appropriate titles, keywords, and descriptions. Use keyword phrases rather than single keywords to

Figure 16 *Google Submit Your Content page*
©2012 Google

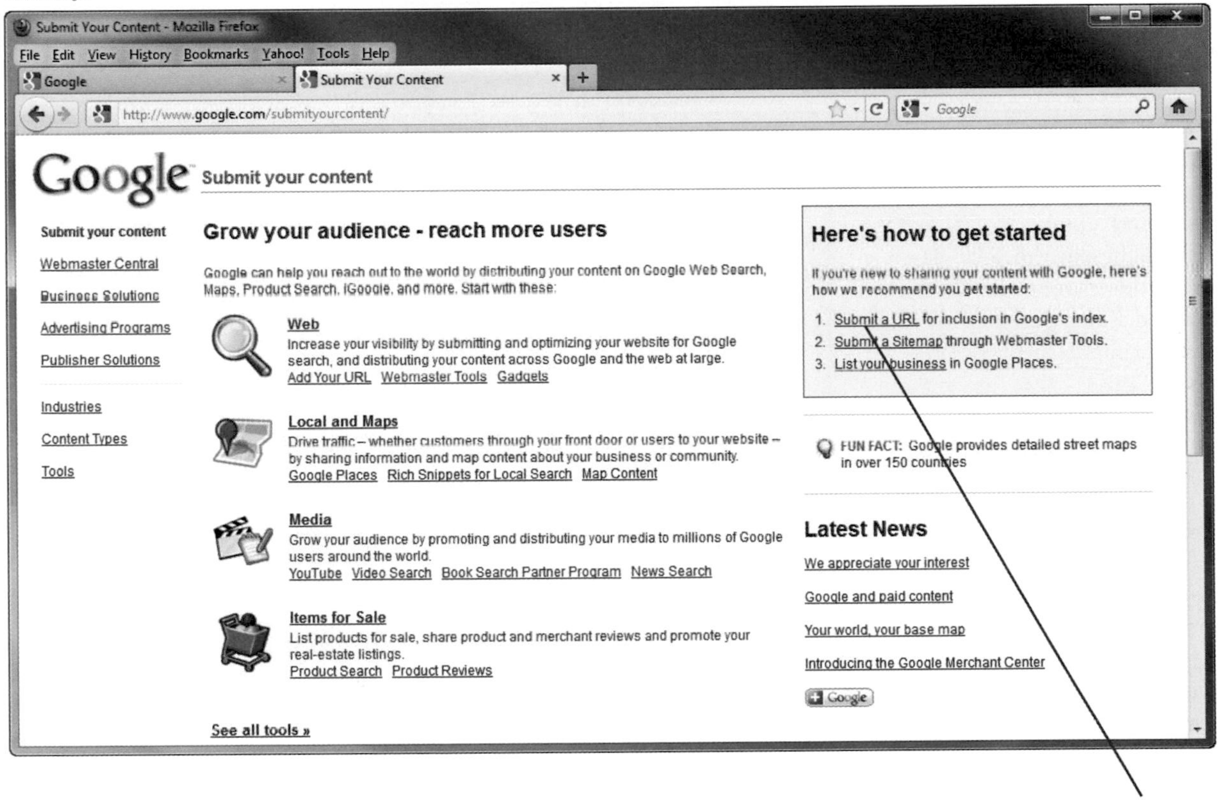

Link to submit URL

increase your chances of being listed. For example, use "white oak baskets" rather than "white, oak, baskets." The search engine will search for the phrase rather than each word separately.

- **Add alternate text to every image or media file**
Describe the image with words that would be used in a search for that type of image. The more descriptive, the better.

- **Add a site map**
A site map accomplishes two things: it's a navigational aid for users, and search engines use it to index your site content.

- **Include the most important information at the top of each page**
Search engines may choose to use the text at the top of the page in their page descriptions. Also, users may not take the time to read down a long page of text, so make sure the most important information is listed at the top. This is called "above the fold" in the newspaper business; the most important information is printed on the top half of the newspaper.

- **Use social networking sites to increase visibility**
Using services such as Facebook, YouTube, and Twitter gives your site much more exposure. Figure 17 shows an example of how the Walton Arts Center uses Twitter as one way to keep patrons updated with their current events and programs.

- **Consider using an SEO Services company**
Search Engine Optimization is a useful technique that aims to make a website more highly-ranked by search engines. For a professional website, you might want to hire an SEO Services company, such as Vizion Interactive at vizioninteractive.com. If you decide to go this route, be sure to thoroughly investigate prospective companies and ask for references.

Figure 17 *Walton Arts Center website with Twitter page*

Walton Arts Center website used by permission from Walton Arts Center – www.waltonartscenter.org

Fine-Tuning, Completing, and Publishing Your Project

Measuring Your Traffic

Once you begin welcoming users to your site, you'll want to know how many users are visiting each page, how long they're lingering, and where they're located around the world. The tools for gathering and measuring this information are called **Web analytics tools**. Google Analytics, shown in Figure 18, is one example of a web analytics tool. Besides being a great tool with many features, it's free. And there are many others from which to choose. Web analytics tools can tell you how well your site is laid out by counting the number of clicks users use to navigate the site. The tools can generate reports, export data, alert you to significant changes in data patterns, and track mobile websites.

Marketing Your Work

Other than publishing an interactive media project online as a website, there are several other ways to present projects to an audience or client. Electronic portfolios are one option. An electronic portfolio is a representative collection of an individual's work that showcases his or her range of talent, accomplishments, or services. A portfolio is typically published on the Web, but can also be presented using digital media such as a CD or DVD. Electronic portfolios are also known as e-portfolios or digital portfolios. They're used by many educational institutions to provide samples of their students' work, thus showing tangible evidence of their learning experience, achievements, and abilities. Portfolios provide a vehicle for self-expression and self-reflection and are vital tools for job applications. Electronic portfolios are also excellent ways to present samples of professional work to

Figure 18 *Google Analytics*
©2012 Google

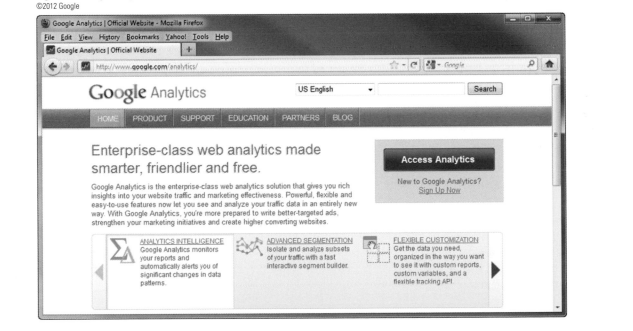

prospective clients or to present a prototype of a project to an existing client. They can be published online or burned to a CD or DVD. You should always have several copies of your electronic portfolio at hand, and maintain back-up copies of web-based portfolios.

Well-designed electronic portfolios should include the following:

- Your name and contact information
- Well-chosen projects that represent your best work
- Commentary with each project that describes specific features or goals
- A consistent look across the pages
- A table of contents or site map to outline the content
- A consistent, easy-to-use navigation system to move between the pages

- Reduced file sizes for images and other digital-media content
- A reflection of your personality, accomplishments, interests, and abilities

Creating Secure Pages for Data Transfer

If you're designing a website that includes online sales, such as an e-commerce website, you'll want to secure your pages via HTTPS to protect your customers' personal information from being accessed by unauthorized people. **HTTPS** stands for **HyperText Transfer Protocol with Secure Sockets Layer**. With HTTPS, data sent and received will be transferred as encrypted data, rather than as plain text. Data transferred as plain text is vulnerable to anyone who has the ability to intercept and read data. Credit card information is

especially vulnerable and should never be sent un-encrypted. When you're using a site with HTTPS, you can tell it's secure by looking at the URL. The URL for secure sites is HTTPS rather than HTTP. You don't have to make your entire site secure; only the pages that are used to transmit information from users have to be secure. To set up secure pages, contact your web host to verify that the web server supports SSL encryption.

Next, obtain a unique IP address. A unique IP address is not randomly assigned when users access your site; rather, it is a fixed address that never changes.

Lastly, obtain an SSL certificate, which can be purchased from a company such as VeriSign. When your site is protected with a VeriSign certificate, a VeriSign Trust Seal is displayed on the secure pages to further emphasize that the page is secure, as shown in Figure 19. However, if you don't need secure pages, but would like to show your users that your site identity has been confirmed and passed a malware scan, you can purchase the VeriSign Trusted seal without purchasing a SSL certificate. **Malware** is software that is downloaded, often without your knowledge, and whose purpose is to damage your computer files or steal your data.

Figure 19 *VeriSign SSL certificate information*

Information about page security

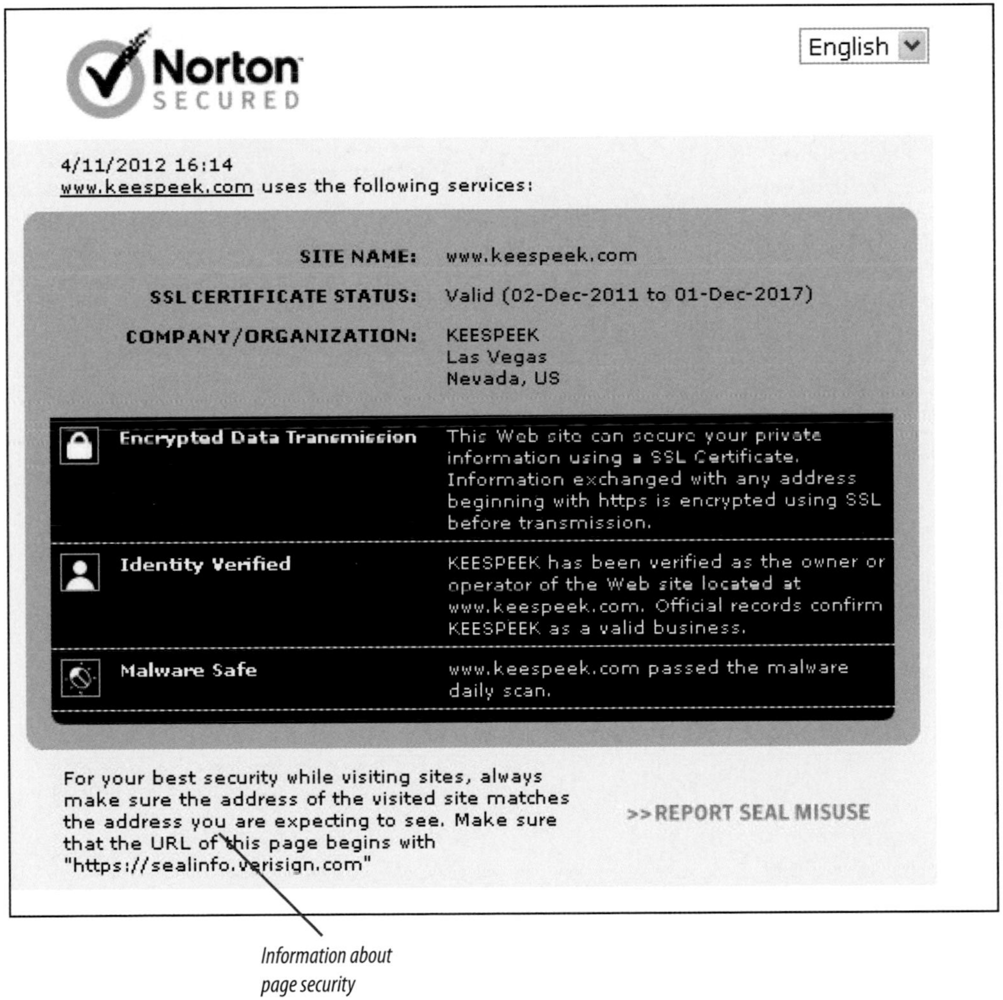

COMPLETING THE PROJECT

To fine-tune our project and prepare it for publication, we'll complete all page content and verify that all internal links in the Gardener's Walk website work correctly. We need each page to have accessible, plain text alternatives to the navigation button links. Since we used a template to create our pages, we'll add these links to the bottom of the template, and then we'll update the pages in the site to place the links on each page. We also have a PDF file that we'll need to optimize before we post a link to it on the expert advice page. And we'll use WordPress to create a simple blog that will be accessed via the Blog link.

Next, we'll use the Dreamweaver report tools to identify and correct any HTML5 and CSS3 errors so our pages comply with the most current standards. And once we're satisfied with the site and have all files ready to go, we'll use Dreamweaver to upload the site to our remote server.

If you're going to create a different kind of interactive media project, your steps for checking for errors and publishing your project will differ. While you're working through these steps, you may choose to follow along using a practice site. Even if you're not creating a website, you can use your FTP client to publish your project to the Web.

If you have another type of project, such as a video, game, or podcast, you might only need to burn it to a CD or a DVD. If you're creating a presentation, consider using Prezi at prezi.com. This site allows you to create and store interactive presentations. You can register for three types of licenses: Public, Enjoy, and Pro. The Public license is free, and the other licenses are available on a 30-day trial basis before you purchase them. Prezi also has a feature called Prezi Meeting that allows you to hold live conferences with colleagues as you build content collaboratively.

Create alternate plain text links

On our Gardener's Walk site, we had previously placed the text for the links at the bottom of the template, but had not yet created the links to the respective pages.

1. Open the main page template and scroll down to the text links at the bottom of the page.

2. Select each link and then use the **Point to File button** on the Properties panel to link each page in the Files panel to its corresponding text link in the template, as shown in Figure 20.

3. Save your file, then click **Yes** to close the Dreamweaver dialog box asking if you want to update all documents that use this template.

4. Click the **Close button** to close the Update Pages dialog box.

Remember that because the template is saved inside a templates folder, and not the site root folder, the paths for these links will be preceded by two dots and a slash (../). If you're not using a template, the path will simply be the filename.

Figure 20 *Using the Point to File button to link a file to a text link*

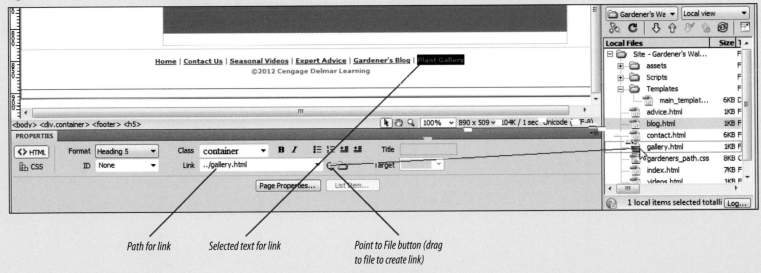

Path for link

Selected text for link

Point to File button (drag to file to create link)

Fine-Tuning, Completing, and Publishing Your Project

Update all page content

This is the time to add any last-minute updates to your pages. There are several ways to accomplish this.

If you're using a template for every page

If you have partially completed pages:

1. Open a partially completed page, copy the content unique to that page, then close the page.

2. Create a new file based on the main template (see Figure 21), then save it with the filename of the page you just opened and closed.

This replaces the original file with a new one that's based on the template.

3. Paste the content into the new file's main content editable area.

TIP Be sure you've copied the content before you save over the existing file. To be safe, first rename the original file before you save over it, then delete it after you've created the new page based on the template. For example, rename your index.html page index2.html. Then create a new page based on the template,

paste the content from index2.html, and save the new file as index.html. Finally, delete the index2.html file after you're satisfied with your work.

4. Save the file.

5. Repeat for each partially completed page in the site.

If you're waiting for last-minute information and have pages with no content (placeholder pages):

1. Create a new page based on the template, as shown in Figure 21.

Figure 21 *Dreamweaver New Document dialog box*

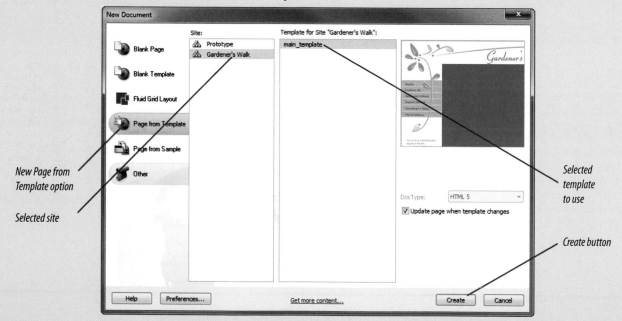

New Page from Template option

Selected site

Selected template to use

Create button

2. Save it using the filename of one of your blank pages, replacing the placeholder file.

The page does not yet have content, but it does have all the template items, such as the banner and navigation buttons.

3. Add content unique to the new page in the main content editable area, as shown in Figure 22.

4. Save the file.

5. Repeat to replace each placeholder page in the site.

If you're not using a template for every page

1. Create or import a new page with an appropriate file name to use as a main link.

2. Save the page.

3. Add all page content, including all links to other pages, and then resave the page.

4. Repeat for each and every new page.

You can see this is quite a bit more work than using a template.

Figure 22 *Creating a new page based on a template*

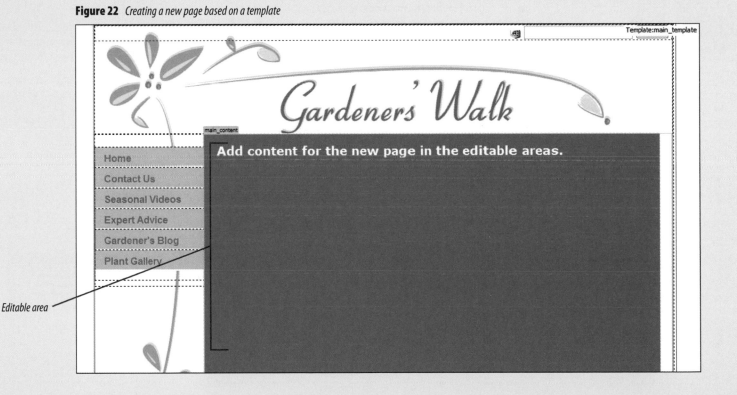

Editable area

Run site reports

There are several reports that are important to run before you finally publish a site.

Verify that all links work correctly

Dreamweaver has a simple report function which verifies that all internal links—links to the other pages in your website—work correctly. For example, if you accidentally use an absolute path to a file on your computer (e.g., a PDF intended to be downloaded from the site), rather than a relative path, the link will not work correctly

when you publish the site. Because a user's browser won't be able to find a file located on your computer, it's very important to use relative links for all internal links.

1. With a page open, click **Site** on the Menu bar, then click **Check Links Sitewide**.

2. Click the **Check Links button** in the Results panel, then click **Check Links for Entire Current Local Site**.

3. Check the panel to see if any broken links are listed, as shown in Figure 23.

4. If any broken links are listed, look them up using the code references and repair them.

Check browser compatibility

1. With a page open, click the **Browser Compatibility tab** in the Results panel.

2. Click the **Check Browser Compatibility button** in the Results panel, then click **Check Browser Compatibility**.

3. If you see a bug, such as the one listed in Figure 24, read the documentation to determine what action to take.

   In our case, the Z-Index bug warns of a potential problem for any child containers of the div with the transparent flower. However, since this particular div does not have a child container, it won't be a problem.

4. Use the Adobe Browser lab to view your pages using several different browsers.

Figure 23 *Link Checker panel showing no broken links*

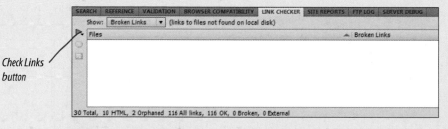

Check Links button

Figure 24 *Browser Compatibility panel with one bug documented*

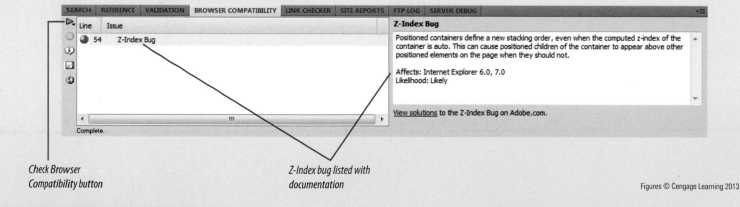

Check Browser Compatibility button

Z-Index bug listed with documentation

Validate HTML5

1. Click the **Validation tab** in the Results panel, click the **W3C Validation button**, then click **Validate Current Document (W3C)**, as shown in Figure 25.

2. If any errors or warnings are found, read the descriptions to determine how to correct them.

In our case, we originally used the Property inspector to align images, when this should have been done using CSS. To correct this, we removed the align tags from each image in the template. We then updated the img rule in the style sheet to add the vertical-align property (vertical-align: top;).

3. Correct your errors and warnings and run the validation again until you have no more errors or warnings listed, as shown in Figure 26.

Figure 25 *Validation panel listing seven errors*

W3C Validation button

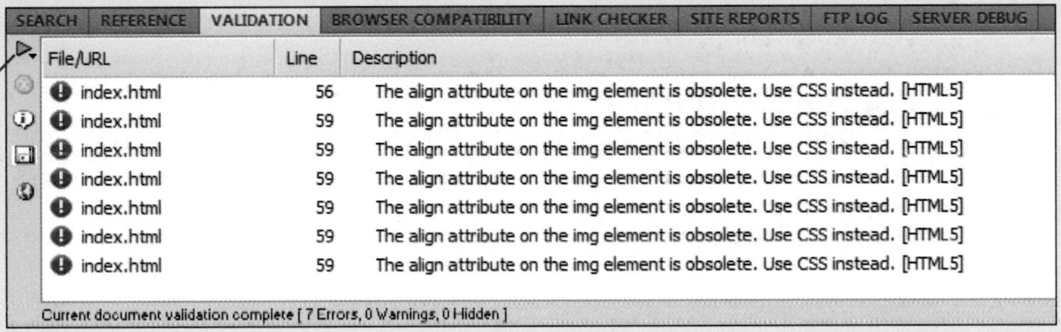

| SEARCH | REFERENCE | VALIDATION | BROWSER COMPATIBILITY | LINK CHECKER | SITE REPORTS | FTP LOG | SERVER DEBUG |

File/URL	Line	Description
index.html	56	The align attribute on the img element is obsolete. Use CSS instead. [HTML5]
index.html	59	The align attribute on the img element is obsolete. Use CSS instead. [HTML5]
index.html	59	The align attribute on the img element is obsolete. Use CSS instead. [HTML5]
index.html	59	The align attribute on the img element is obsolete. Use CSS instead. [HTML5]
index.html	59	The align attribute on the img element is obsolete. Use CSS instead. [HTML5]
index.html	59	The align attribute on the img element is obsolete. Use CSS instead. [HTML5]
index.html	59	The align attribute on the img element is obsolete. Use CSS instead. [HTML5]

Current document validation complete [7 Errors, 0 Warnings, 0 Hidden]

Figure 26 *Validation panel showing all errors corrected*

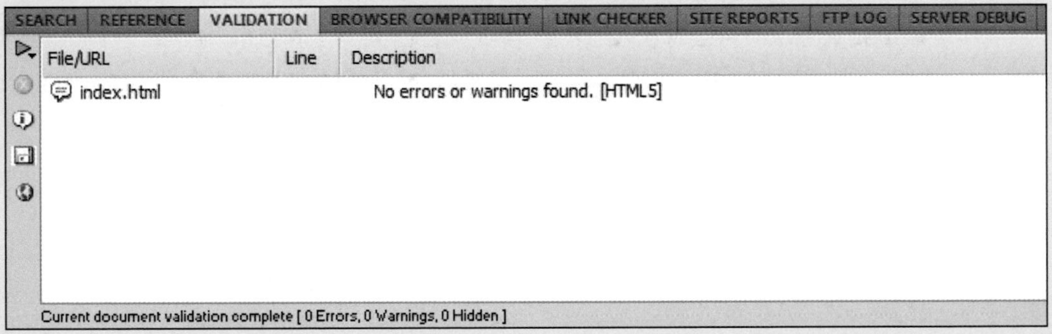

| SEARCH | REFERENCE | VALIDATION | BROWSER COMPATIBILITY | LINK CHECKER | SITE REPORTS | FTP LOG | SERVER DEBUG |

File/URL	Line	Description
index.html		No errors or warnings found. [HTML5]

Current document validation complete [0 Errors, 0 Warnings, 0 Hidden]

Validate CSS3

1. Open your browser and go to jigsaw.w3.org/css-validator.

2. Click the **By file upload tab**, then use the **Browse button**, as shown in Figure 27, to select your local style sheet file.

3. Click **More Options**, select the **CSS Level 3** profile if necessary, then click the **Check button**.

   The Validator results will appear, showing that no errors were found. If errors are found, you would need to locate and correct them, then try validating the style sheet again.

Figure 27 *Validating your CSS file*
Courtesy of w3.org

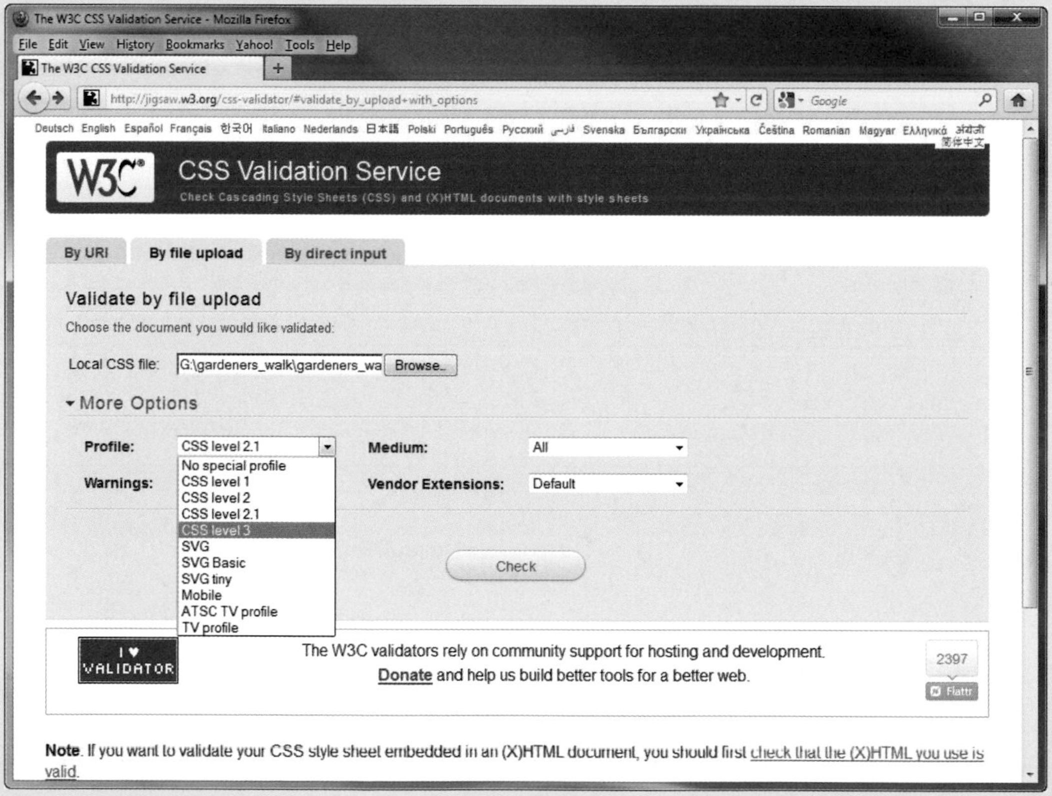

Fine-Tuning, Completing, and Publishing Your Project

Check for missing alt text and page titles

1. In Dreamweaver, click **Site**, then click **Reports**.

   The Reports dialog box opens.

2. Click the **Report on list arrow**, then click **Entire Current Local Site**.

3. Click to add checkmarks to both the Missing Alt Text and Untitled Documents check boxes, as shown in Figure 28, then click **Run**.

   If you see any items listed, take steps to correct the missing tags.

Figure 28 *Dreamweaver Reports dialog box*
Courtesy of w3.org

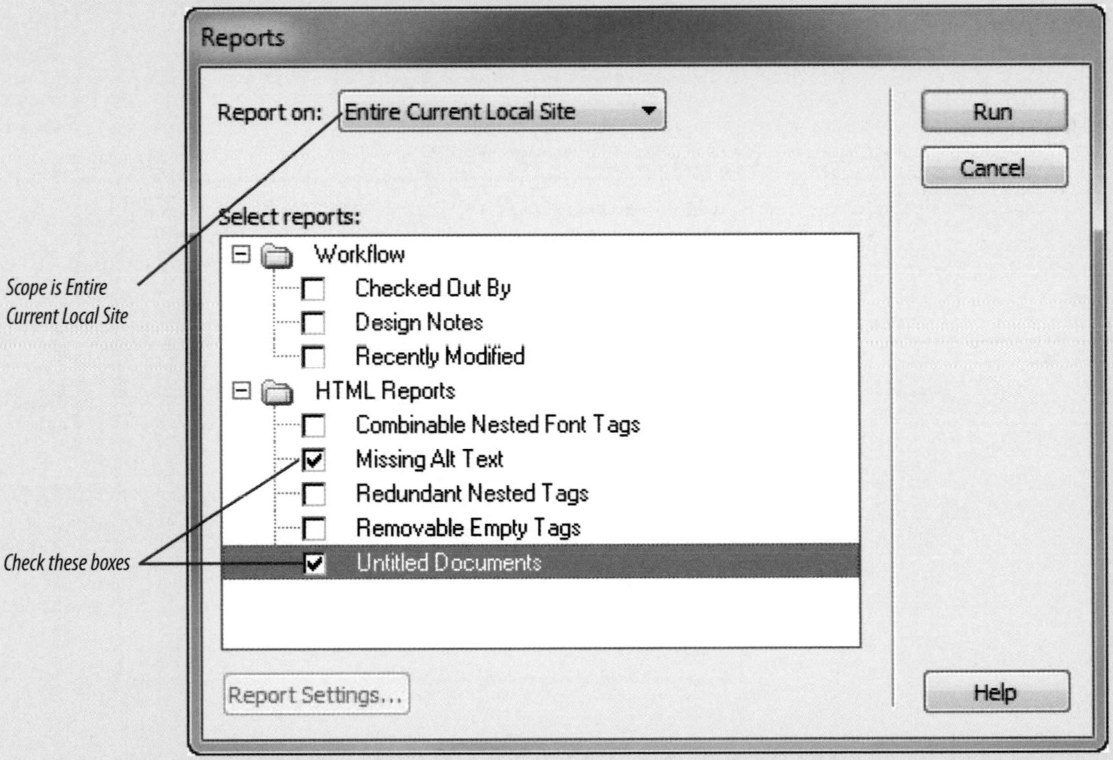

Scope is Entire Current Local Site

Check these boxes

Reports

Report on: Entire Current Local Site

Run

Cancel

Select reports:

☐ Workflow
　☐ Checked Out By
　☐ Design Notes
　☐ Recently Modified
☐ HTML Reports
　☐ Combinable Nested Font Tags
　☑ Missing Alt Text
　☐ Redundant Nested Tags
　☐ Removable Empty Tags
　☑ Untitled Documents

Report Settings...

Help

Prepare external documents
Check a PDF for Accessibility

We've mentioned some of the features of Adobe Acrobat that you can use to create more accessible documents for posting online. On the Expert Advice page of the Gardener's Walk website, we included a PDF transcript of an interview with Ruth Marx. We wanted to make sure it passed accessibility guidelines for PDFs, so we ran a report and studied the results.

1. Open Adobe Acrobat, click **Advanced** on the Menu bar, point to **Accessibility**, then click **Full Check**.

   The Accessibility Full Check dialog box opens, as shown in Figure 29.

2. Make sure both the Create Accessibility Report and Include repair hints in Accessibility Report check boxes are checked, then click **Start Checking**.

   If the PDF contains errors, a dialog box will notify you that they're listed in the report.

3. Click **OK** to close the dialog box, then view the Accessibility Report in the navigation pane, as shown in Figure 30.

Figure 29 *Accessibility Full Check dialog box in Adobe Acrobat*

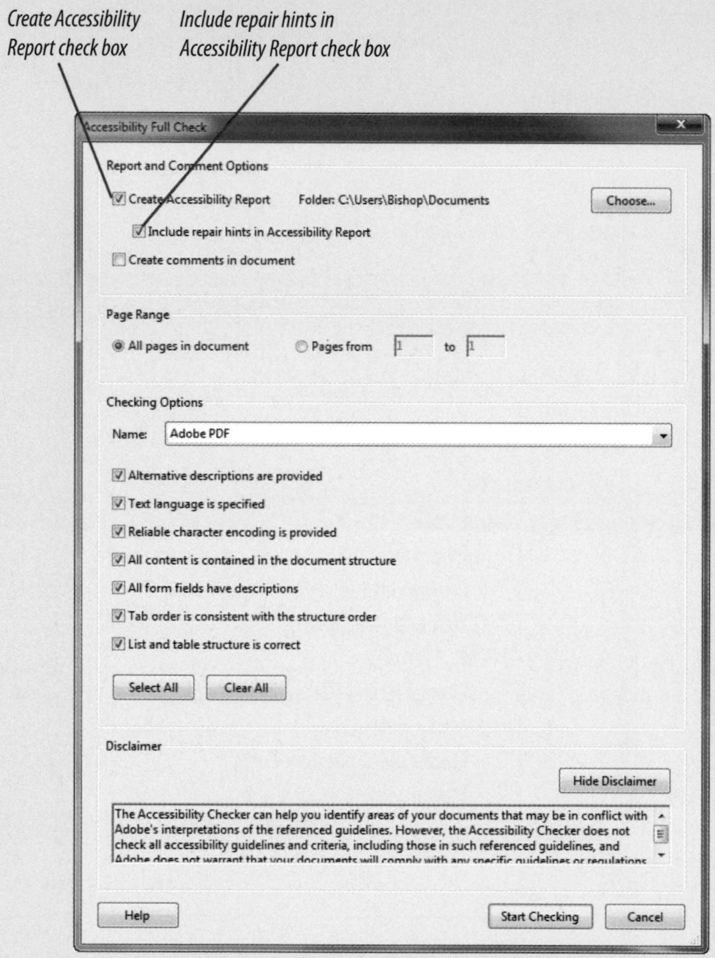

Create Accessibility Report check box

Include repair hints in Accessibility Report check box

Figure 30 *Accessibility Report*

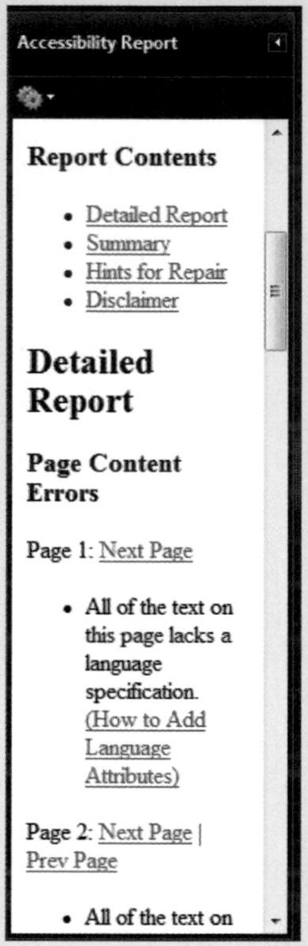

Transfer files

Before you transfer your files to a remote server, you can test your site using a local server. You can set up your computer or another location on your local area network for use as a local server. To do this, create a folder on your hard drive, external drive, or network, then use the Site Setup dialog box to add a new server. Assign it a name, then select Local/Network in the "Connect using" drop-down menu. Browse to add the path to your folder in the Server Folder text box, then click Save. Figure 31 shows a local folder we set up

Figure 31 *Setting up a local server to test a website*

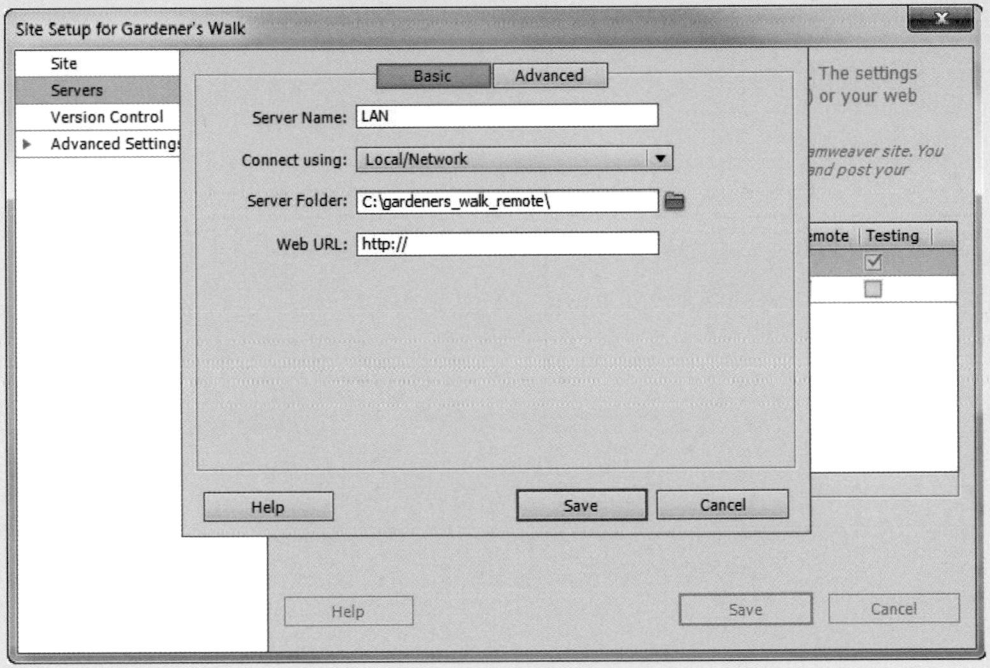

to test our website project. Figure 32 shows a remote server we used to publish our site.

After you've tested your FTP connection, you can upload your files from the Files panel in Dreamweaver or by using an FTP program such as FileZilla. To use the Files panel in Dreamweaver:

1. Click the **Expand to show local and remote sites button** in the Files panel.

2. Click the **Connects to remote host button** if you don't see the remote site folders and files listed on the left side (Remote Server pane) of the expanded Files panel.

Figure 32 *Setting up a remote server to transfer files*

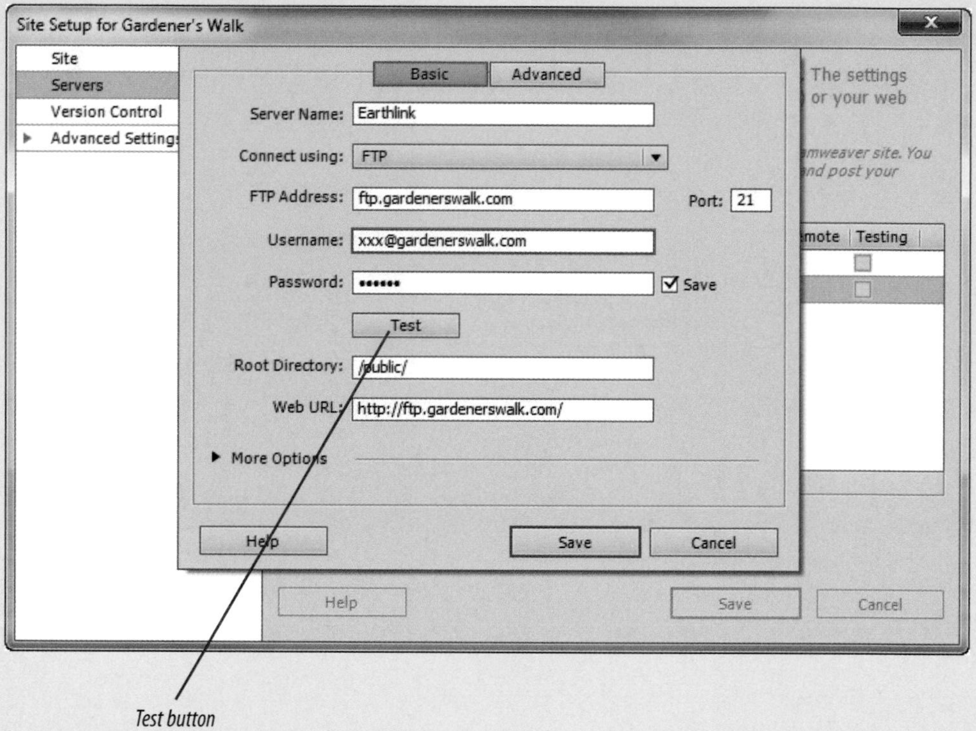

Test button

Fine-Tuning, Completing, and Publishing Your Project

3. Click to select the **file** or **folder** you want to upload in the Local Files pane (right side).

4. Click the **Put file(s) to [your server name] button**, as shown in Figure 33.

5. Click the **Collapse to show only local or remote site button** to collapse the Files panel

You don't have to expand the Files panel to transfer files. You can use the Put and Get buttons in the collapsed Files panel, though you won't be able to see both sets of files (remote and local) simultaneously.

Figure 33 *Uploading files with Dreamweaver*

Get file(s) button   Put file(s) button   Collapse to show only local or remote site button

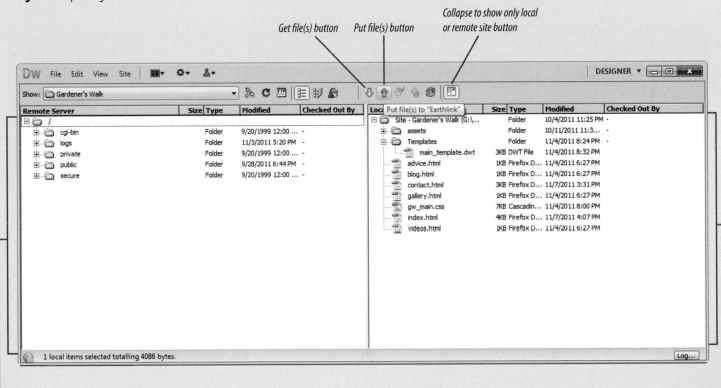

Remote Server pane

Local Files pane

Create and link to a blog

There are several ways to create a blog. You can create a blog that is an entity in itself, or you can create one to use as a website component. We chose to use WordPress.com to create our blog, linking to the blog URL with the Blog button. Although this will take users out of our site, we'll also create a link on the blog that they can use to return to the site. Of course, they could also use the Back button on the browser, but it's nice to avoid that: if they happened to open the blog first (before they had accessed our site) the Back button would take them to whatever site they had previously visited before finding our blog.

WordPress is open source software. There's no charge to use it unless you decide to use some of the optional services that require fees. The first decision you need to make is whether you want to use WordPress.org or WordPress.com to create your blog. When you use WordPress.org, you download the WordPress software, set up a web server, create a database, and then design your blog. This method requires some coding knowledge, but gives you total control over the design and management of your blog. The blog is hosted on your web server.

The second option is to use WordPress.com, where you create an account, use a wizard to set up your blog, pick and choose options such as applying a theme, and then publish the blog. When you use this method, the blog is hosted at wordpress.com, it's extremely simple to set up and manage, and requires no coding skills. For ease of use, we chose to use WordPress.com, but for a large business or commercial site you would probably choose WordPress.org. These are the steps to follow if you choose to set up a site on WordPress.com:

1. Open your browser and go to wordpress.com.

2. Click the **Start a blog button**.

3. Fill in the blanks for your Blog Address, Username, Password, and E-mail address, then click the **Create Blog button**.

   The next step is to activate your account. You'll receive an email with activation instructions, so be sure you type your email address correctly.

4. After you activate your account, and go to your blog (your URL will be http://[yourusername].wordpress.com/) where you'll see the welcome page.

Take the time to watch the short video explaining the basics of WordPress. It only takes a few minutes and is very informative.

5. Explore the Dashboard and begin experimenting with themes. You'll find the list of available themes on the Appearance menu.

The **Dashboard** is the first screen you see as an administrator. Your blog visitors will not see this page. It serves as a quick overview of everything relating to your blog, just as the dashboard of a car gives you an overview of your car's status. You can see your posts, read comments others have posted, edit your settings, and check your site stats.

6. Compose your first post and click the **Publish Post** button.

Your site is now live and ready for you to start posting and attracting users.

At this point, we linked our WordPress URL to the Blog button on our template. Since we won't be maintaining this example blog, we restricted access to it in order to avoid confusing viewers who might find it and think it's an actual blog site. Our blog is shown in Figure 34. If you click our Blog link, you'll see a WordPress login page. Click the Back button to return to the website.

Figure 34 *WordPress dashboard*
Courtesy of WordPress.com

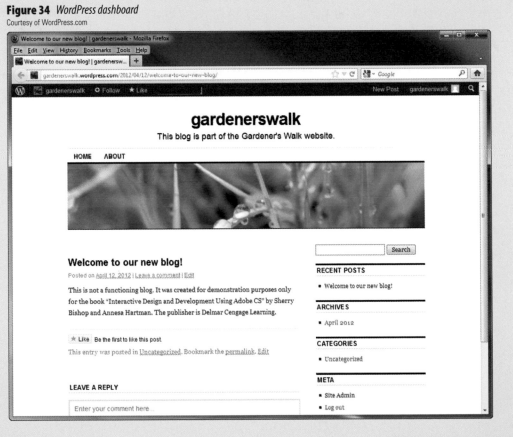

COMPLETING YOUR INTERACTIVE MEDIA PROJECT

Well, we've come to the end of the book. You're now ready to put the pieces of your project together and take them for a test drive. We hope you've gained the knowledge necessary to produce a robust interactive media project that you're proud of, whether it's a website, interactive game, mobile app, or any other media adventure. Some of the steps that follow will not be applicable to projects other than a website. If so, you can skip those steps, but see if you can relate a similar step to your project.

1. Consult your wireframe and verify that you've completed each project element.
2. Run the following tests:
   - Verify that all internal and external links work correctly.
   - Validate your style sheet against CSS3 standards.
   - Validate each HTML page against HTML5 standards.
   - Run site reports for missing titles and missing alt tags.
   - Check your site for compatibility using as many browsers and/or devices as possible.
3. Correct any errors or warnings you find listed in the reports in Step 2.
4. Include a set of plain text links at the bottom of each page.
5. Include a link to the home page from each page.
6. Add transcripts as an alternative to all audio/video components.
7. Present your site to your client or team members for feedback and approval.
8. Upload your files to your web server and obtain feedback.
9. Register your site with at least two search engines.

DESIGNING MOBILE LAYOUTS

It's not enough anymore to design a project that works and looks great only for users with a standard computer monitor. Users now expect to be able to access your site using multiple mobile devices. In this assignment you'll explore options for converting your pages to a format that will display correctly on a tablet and a mobile phone. One option is to use the Dreamweaver Media Query function. Even if you didn't design a website for your media project, you'll still be interested in how your project will function on multiple mobile devices. Take a look at it on your cell phone and a tablet. If it doesn't look exactly like you intended, do some digging to find possible solutions for improving the user's mobile experience.

1. If you're using Dreamweaver, click the **Multiscreen list arrow** on the Document toolbar, then click **Multiscreen Preview**.

    This shows your page as it will appear on a Phone, a Tablet, and a Desktop, as shown in Figure 35. Notice that users will have to scroll horizontally on both a phone and a tablet. This is not acceptable, so we'll use media queries to solve this design problem.

2. Click the **Media Queries button**.

    The Media Queries dialog box opens, where you can target your design to multiple devices by assigning a different style sheet for each device.

3. If you want to tackle this, create a style sheet that you'll use for a desktop, a tablet, and a mobile phone, using minimum width settings and a separate CSS file for each page. (To create a new style sheet, click the **New CSS Rule button** in the CSS Styles panel, choose a Selector type, enter a selector name, select **New Style Sheet File** in the Rule Definition drop-down menu, then choose your settings.)

Figure 35 *Multiscreen Preview before using media queries*

Figure © Cengage Learning 2013

4. Using your new style sheets, modify the container styles to fit the content within the device width so that a scroll bar isn't necessary. Save the style sheets with names that reflect their purpose, such as incorporating the word "mobile", "desktop", and "tablet" in the file names, as shown in Figure 36.

5. Now for the challenging part. Cut any styles from the main style sheet file that will have to be adjusted to fit in your alternate screen widths. Paste them into each of the new style sheet files and adjust the code to fit the screens. This is a trial and error process that takes time, but the results are worth the effort.

Figure 36 *Media Queries dialog box*

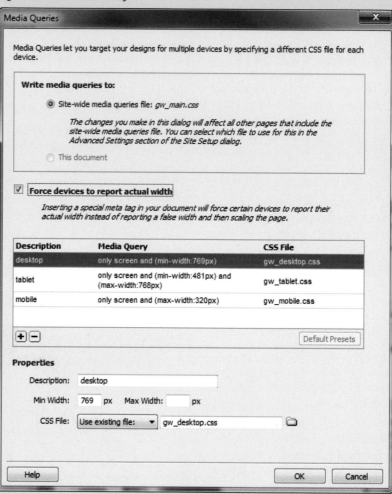

Figure © Cengage Learning 2013

Fine-Tuning, Completing, and Publishing Your Project

6. Use the Multiscreen Preview to see how the page now fits on a mobile, tablet, and desktop device, as shown in Figure 37.

   You'll probably have some adjustments to make before you're pleased with the results. For links to the style sheets we used, visit the Even More to Explore link under Book Resources on Cengage Brain.

Figure 37 *Multiscreen Preview after using media queries*

Even More to Explore

To explore some of the topics discussed in this chapter in more depth, see the References section at the end of the book. For links to additional web resources, visit the Even More to Explore link under Book Resources on Cengage Brain.

Figure © Cengage Learning 2013

A

3D animation
A type of animation where objects are scaled, rotated, and translated within 3-dimensional space. *See also* Translation.

AAC
A compressed format that is a successor of MP3, with improved quality and smaller file sizes; commonly used in MPEG-4 multimedia files.

Absolute path
A type of path used to reference external links; includes a protocol such as http:// followed by the complete URL. *See also* Relative path.

Accessibility
Describes the availability of a product to as many people as possible.

Active User
One who actively handles web content through interactive functions.

Adobe Acrobat
A program designed to convert, edit, manage, and deliver content in the Portable Document Format (PDF) format.

Adobe ActionScript
The object-oriented programming language of the Adobe Flash Platform; essential for creating interactivity with Flash.

Adobe Audition
An audio production program for recording, editing, and mixing sound.

Adobe Bridge
A centralized media content manager that organizes digital assets across the Adobe product line.

Adobe BrowserLab
A tool that can be accessed through Dreamweaver to test your site in multiple browsers; it is an online service that provides viewing, diagnostic, and comparison tools.

Adobe Creative Cloud
An Adobe initiative introduced in 2011 to give users a virtual space where they can download desktop and tablet applications, access creative services, and publish and share work.

Adobe Creative Suite (CS)
A collection of interactive media applications made by Adobe Systems for both the Macintosh and Windows platforms.

Adobe Dreamweaver
A design, authoring, and editing software application for creating standards-based HTML websites and mobile apps.

Adobe Flash
An authoring tool for creating animation and interactive multimedia content to be viewed using Adobe Flash Player.

Adobe Flash Video (.FLV and .F4V)
A video format designed specifically for Internet delivery using Adobe Flash Player.

Adobe Illustrator
A program for creating distinctive vector artwork using sophisticated drawing tools, brushes, and special effects.

Adobe Photoshop
A program for working with pixel-based imagery and photographs; includes extensive photo editing capabilities, painting and drawing tools, and special effects.

Adobe Premiere Elements
A program for editing and publishing video.

Adobe Premiere Pro
The Adobe professional-grade video editing program.

Adobe Reader
A free application that is used to read PDFs.

Adobe Version Cue
An application that provides a way to collaborate with team members, manage security, back up data, and use metadata to search files.

AIFF or AIFF-C
Acronym for Audio Interchange File Format; an uncompressed audio file format for Macintosh (AIFF-C is the compressed variant).

Alt text
Descriptive text attached to an image in a web page's HTML code; important for visually impaired users and search engines.

ARPANET
A government-financed research project established in 1969 to test the networking of the first major computer systems; precursor of today's Internet.

Aspect Ratio
Defines the proportional width and height of a video.

Assets
Related files in a website such as images and video files.

Authoring tool
Software, or collection of software components, that authors can use to create or modify web content.

AVI (Microsoft Video)
Common video format for most Windows-based applications; not suitable for online delivery.

——————— **B** ———————

Balance
A design principle referring to the symmetrical, asymmetrical or radial relationships between different objects.

Bamboo Project Management Suite
A project management tool.

Bit depth
The number of bits that make up the complexity of a sound.

Bit rate
The amount of data over time used to stream (download) multimedia.

Bitmap images
Images created with a grid of pixels. *See also* Raster images.

Blogs
Websites where the site owner regularly posts commentaries and opinions on various topics.

Blurbs
Short extensions of a headline that provide more details.

Broken links
Links that cannot find a destination file.

Budget
A list of itemized expenditures that will be needed to complete a project.

Buffering
When the data download rate does not keep up with the computer's processing rate, and the computer must pause playback while it downloads the next batch of data into an area of memory called a buffer.

——————— ———————

Captions
Assist the hearing impaired by providing a text equivalent of the audio portion of a video as it plays.

Cascading Style Sheet (CSS)
A file that efficiently formats web page content by using sets of attributes; provides a consistent presentation for content across a website.

Cel animation
A labor-saving form of traditional animation where illustrations are repeated from frame to frame by using celluloid to superimpose foreground elements over an opaque background.

Channels
Groupings of common content, similar to folders, with descriptive names such as "CSS" or "Dreamweaver."

Chiclet
A small icon adjacent to a podcast on a web page, used to indicate the availability of an RSS feed.

Child page
A page at a lower level in a web hierarchy relative to the pages it is linked to.

Class type
A CSS selector type that is used to format any HTML element.

Clean HTML code
Code that efficiently does what it's supposed to do without errors or unnecessary instructions.

Cloud
Online storage space accessed through the Internet, as opposed to storage on your own computer system.

Cloud computing
A networked, browser-based method for creating and sharing content, where you access storage space over the Internet.

CMYK Color Mode
A color mode used for print projects; uses the colors cyan, magenta, yellow, and black.

Code snippets
Prepackaged pieces of code.

Codec
Acronym for encoder/decoder, the method by which digital video data is compressed and decompressed.

Color
Describes the visual property of what we see when an object encounters light.

Color enhancement
Changing the hues, saturation, brightness, contrast, or color balance in an image.

Comments
Notes added to a page's HTML code and do not appear on the page when viewed in a browser.

Compositing
The art of combining visual elements from multiple files into one image file.

Compound type
In CSS, a selector that combines multiple rules to format a selection.

Compression
The process of reducing the number of bits in a file to decrease the file size.

Content Management Systems (CMS)
Applications used to publish, edit, and maintain websites; generally used for blogs and sites that need to be updated frequently. *See also* Drupal, Joomla!, and WordPress.

Contrast
A design principle that implies the juxtaposition of opposing elements.

Copyright
The intellectual property category that covers books, plays, music, painting, photographs, or art.

Creative Commons (CC)
A nonprofit organization that offers flexible copyright licenses for creative works.

Crop
To designate a rectangular area of an image that you want to keep by removing the rest of the image.

CSS layout blocks
Page elements created with <div> tags that include code for determining the placement, size, and appearance of the block and its content.

———————— **D** ————————

Data version control
The process of keeping track of and protecting the latest versions of your data.

Deliverables
Products that will be provided to a client at the completion of a project.

Dependent files
Files that are needed to correctly display the content of a web page, such as sound or image files.

Derivative work
Work based on other pre-existing work.

Description
A meta tag consisting of a short paragraph that describes the content and features of a website. *See also* Keywords.

Device agnostic
Refers to content that's accessible regardless of whether it's viewed on a desktop monitor, a tablet, or a mobile device.

Device fonts
Fonts provided by a user's computer or device; determined by a specific font name.

Digital scent
Technology that allows a user to "receive" smell through the Internet.

Document versioning
Refers to managing the changes made to a document as each new version is saved; multiple versions can be accessed for comparison and editing.

DOM
Acronym for Document Object Model; defines a standard to access and modify HTML documents.

Dominance
A design principle applied to one or more design elements to emphasize important information.

Download
To copy files from a remote server to a local folder.

Drupal
A free and open source content management system used for blogs, RSS feeds, and menus.

Dynamic text
Text that changes in response to a variable. *See also* Static text.

———————— **E** ————————

Easing
Making motion more believable by adjusting the timing at the beginning and/or end of an animation.

Editing
Changing content.

Embedded style
See Internal style.

Enriched text
Text with formatting applied specifically for e-mail messages.

External links
Links to web pages or files outside of a website.

External Style Sheet
CSS style sheet rules saved in a separate file. *See also* Internal Style Sheet.

———————— **F** ————————

Fair use
A limitation of the copyright law that allows limited use of copyright-protected work under certain conditions.

Feathering
Blurring the edges of a mask to soften an image.

Fidelity
A term used to describe the quality of a sound.

File Transfer Protocol (FTP)
The process of uploading and downloading files to and from a remote site.

Focus group
A marketing tool in which a group of people is asked for feedback about a product or product idea.

Font families
Groups of similarly designed type sets.

Font outlines
Characters broken down into shapes.

Fonts
The complete character sets of a single style in a particular typeface, such as Times New Roman.

Formatted text
Text that has formatting, such as bold, applied.

Formatting
Changing the appearance of content.

Frame
A unit of movement in digital animation.

Frame rate
The rate of movement from frame to frame over time.

Frame-by-frame animation
A kind of animation in which the artist draws the complete contents of each frame, representing snapshots of the trajectory of an action.

Framework
Basic files and folders that form the structure and organize the content for a project.

Free software
Software that can be downloaded and used at no cost.

FTP
See File Transfer Protocol.

——————— **G** ———————

Gamut
The color space or range that can be reproduced or interpreted by a particular device (e.g., the human eye, a printer, a computer monitor).

Gesture recognition
Technology that enables humans to interact directly with a computer screen via the motions or gestures of one's fingers or a pen-like stylus, instead of a mouse.

Glyphs
Character shapes on a page or screen.

Goal
A specific ambition that is measurable and attainable.

Gradation
A design principle that describes a change from one color to another.

Graphical User Interface (GUI)
A visually oriented computer interface, with windows, menus, clickable buttons, icons, and images.

Graphics tablet
A drawing tablet that uses a digital pen for drawing instead of a mouse.

Greeking
See Lorem ipsum.

GUI
See Graphical User Interface.

——————— **H** ———————

Harmony
A design principle that denotes the visually satisfying effect of combining similar, related elements, such as adjacent colors on a wheel or similar shapes.

HCI
See Human-computer interaction.

High-fidelity wireframes
Interactive and multidimensional diagrams used in the design of an interactive media project. *See also* Wireframe.

Hotspot
A clickable area on an image that, when clicked, links to a different location on the same page or to another page.

HTML
Acronym for Hypertext Markup Language, the authoring language used by web browsers.

HTML5
The latest version of HTML (HyperText Markup Language), the language used to create web pages.

HTML DOM
See DOM.

HTTPS
Acronym for HyperText Transfer Protocol with Secure Sockets Layer; used for transferring sensitive information.

Human-computer interaction (HCI)
The study of how human beings interact with computers.

Hyperlinks
See Links.

Hypertext
A system of embedding links in text to connect to other, related, text.

Hypertext mark-up language (HTML)
The authoring language used by web browsers.

——————— **I** ———————

ID type
A CSS rule that is used to redefine a single HTML tag.

ID3
A metadata container used in conjunction with the MP3 audio format.

Image editing
Changing the appearance of an image using processes such as resizing, enhancing color or contrast, or removing unwanted parts of images.

Image map
An image that has one or more hotspots placed on top of it.

Image placeholder
A graphic used in a document until final artwork is ready to be added.

Industrial property
The intellectual property category that covers patents, trademarks, or industrial designs.

Inheritance
A CSS governing principle that allows for the properties of a parent container to be used to format the content in a child container.

Inline styles
CSS rules saved in the body of the HTML code for a page; used to style a specific tag or object.

Input text
Text that users enter in a form field.

Integration
The act or process of forming, coordinating, or blending something into a functioning, unified whole.

Intellectual property
A product resulting from human creativity. *See also* Copyright.

Interactive media design and development
The design and development of content that is presented in a digital environment; can encompass many multimedia elements (text, images, animation, video, audio) and is an experience one can interact with, participate in, or simply view.

Internal links
Links to web pages within the same site.

Internal style
A CSS rule that is saved either in the head or body section of a web page.

Internal Style Sheet
Style sheet rules saved in the head content of a web page. *See also* External Style Sheet.

Internet
An infrastructure of networked computers.

Internet Service Provider (ISP)
A company that provides access to the Internet and/or website hosting services.

——————— **J** ———————

Jakob Nielsen
A familiar name in the web design community; a leading web usability researcher and consultant.

Jargon
Language specific to particular groups or professions.

Joomla!
Open source content management system used to create small and medium-sized websites.

——————— **K** ———————

Kerning
Refers to the spacing between two characters of a font. *See also* Tracking.

Keywords
Descriptive words contained in meta tags; used by search engines when indexing a site, they do not appear in the browser window or title bar. *See also* Description.

Kilobits per second (kbps)
A rate of data transfer equal to 1000 bits per second.

——————— **L** ———————

Layering
Arranging the order of image elements to place them in the background or foreground in relation to other image elements.

Leading
The space between two lines of type.

Learning modalities
Describe ways in which someone receives and retains information, such as through visuals, text, or sound.

Library items
Items, such as images, that are used to create a file, such as a Flash file.

Licensing agreement
Permission given by a copyright holder that conveys the right to use their work under certain conditions, such as through the payment of a fee.

Line
An edge or boundary in a drawing or design.

Linear game
A game that moves from one sequence to the next. *See also* Non-linear game.

Links
Text or images that are used for navigating between web pages and websites; also called hyperlinks.

Live server
The server where a website will reside when it is published.

Local site folder
A folder where all website files and folders are stored. Also known as a root folder.

Lorem ipsum
Placeholder text that helps you approximate the look of text in your layout until the actual copy is ready. Also called "dummy" text or greeking text.

Low-fidelity wireframes
Very simple wireframes, often created using Adobe Illustrator, Adobe Fireworks, or Microsoft PowerPoint. *See also* Wireframe.

M

Mainframes
First built in the 1960s and 70s, large, cabinet-like computers that housed a central processing unit and memory.

Malware
Software that is downloaded, usually without your knowledge, and whose purpose is to damage your computer files.

Masking
Removing the edges of an image, similar to placing a matte over a picture before it is framed.

Media queries
CSS3 attributes that specify which styles a device should use to display a website.

Meta tags
HTML codes that reside in the head section of a web page and include information about the page, such as keywords and descriptions.

Metadata
Information about a file such as keywords, descriptions, and copyright information.

Microsoft Project
A project management tool.

Microsoft SharePoint
A collaboration tool for sharing information.

Missing fonts
Fonts that an application is unable to locate and apply to text.

Mosaic
The first graphical web browser, developed by Marc Andreessen in 1993.

MP3
A standard, cross-platform compressed audio format, widely used for delivering sound via the Internet.

MPEG-4 (.MP4)
Part of the MPEG family of digital video compression standards, commonly used for online delivery and mobile output.

N

Named anchor
A specific location on a web page that has a descriptive name; allows for linking directly to that location on the page. *See also* Target.

Native app
An application that only runs on one platform, processor, or device. Also called Native software. *See also* Web apps.

Needs assessment
The process of determining and addressing the actual needs of your end user, rather than relying on assumptions or personal preference.

Non-linear game
A game that allows movement back and forth between sequences. *See also* Linear game.

O

Objective
A specific action, the purpose of which is to accomplish a larger goal.

Ogg Theora (.OGG)
An open source multimedia format for both video and audio; developed by Xiph.org and supported by the HTML5 video and audio elements.

Onion skinning
A feature in most 2D animation programs that allows you to view several frames at once; useful to help see the trajectory of an animation over time, for proper positioning or easy editing of a series of keyframed objects.

Open source
Describes software for which the original source code is freely available and which may be redistributed with or without modification.

Optimize an image
To reduce the file size of an image while maintaining satisfactory quality.

P

Parent page
A page at a higher level in a web hierarchy relative to the pages linked to it.

Participant
One who authors or contributes web content.

Passive viewer
One who passively consumes web services and information.

Path
The series of folders that are used to designate a file location.

PDF
See Portable Document Format.

PHP: Hypertext Preprocessor
An open source, server-side scripting language used to create websites.

Plain text
Text with no formatting applied.

Platform agnostic
Content that should be accessible and attractive regardless of the operating system on which it appears.

Podcasting
A method of delivering syndicated content, usually audio or video, over the Internet.

Podcatcher (or, Podcast aggregator)
A program used to gather (aggregate) podcast feeds from many sites into one place.

Points
A measurement used to designate font sizes; 72 points is equal to one inch in height.

Portable Document Format (PDF)
An open-standard (publicly available) file format that provides an electronic image of text, or text and graphics, that can be read on any computer that has the Adobe Reader program installed.

PostScript
A page description language that stores typeface glyphs as outlines and shapes, rather than as fixed-resolution bitmaps.

Printer-friendly pages
Pages that duplicate formatted content so they will print correctly.

Project management
The process of planning, organizing, and managing resources to complete a defined project.

Proprietary software
Software owned by an individual or company. You must purchase a license to use it, but the license does not allow you to legally copy or distribute it.

Prototype
A model built to help conceptualize, test, or evaluate a project.

Public domain
Describes a work that is not protected by copyright and that is available to use legally without permission or restrictions.

Public domain images
Images that are free for personal or professional use, without restriction.

Publish a website
To transfer all local website files to a web server for access over the Internet.

Q

QuickTime (MOV)
Video format supported by both the Mac and Windows platforms; a popular format for online delivery.

R

Raster images
Also known as bitmaps, images that are built using a grid of pixels, and that are not scalable.

Redundant backups
A backup system that backs up the same data to multiple locations.

Relative path
A type of path that references web pages or media files within the same website. *See also* Absolute path.

Remote site files
Files that have been transferred to a web server.

Repetition
A design principle that describes the repeating of elements, which may include a degree of variation.

Resources
Assets that could include your computer system, technical expertise, available staff, and access to materials and content.

RGB color mode
Colors used for projects to be viewed on a screen that are created with red, green, and blue.

Rich text
Text to which formatting has been applied; often refers to a Microsoft proprietary file format also known as RTF (Rich Text Format), developed to facilitate document exchange across computer platforms.

Rollover buttons
Sets of buttons that change appearance when the user points to, presses, or clicks them.

Rollover images
Images that change to a different image when the user moves the mouse pointer over them.

Root folder
See Local site folder.

Roundtrip integration
The ability to easily move back and forth between two applications.

Royalty-free images
Images that can be used legally with certain restrictions, such as attaching a statement crediting the image's owner.

RPG
Acronym for Role-Playing Game, such as *Dungeons & Dragons*.

RSS
Acronym for Really Simple Syndication, which describes the standard for the automatic distribution (syndication) of web content.

RSS feed
Acronym for Really Simple Syndication, which describes a standardized XML document that includes information on how a podcast should be published, including full or summarized text, authorship and date/time metadata; an RSS feed is used to distribute changing content on a regular basis. *See also* RSS.

Rule of thirds
A design principle stating that, if an image is divided into nine equal sections, focal points should occur at the grid intersections.

Rules
Sets of CSS formatting attributes.

————————— S —————————

Sample rate
The number of times audio is sampled per second.

Sampling rate
Determines the resolution of an image; the higher the sampling rate, the more detailed the image will be.

Sans-serif fonts
Block-style characters often used for headings and subheadings. *See also* Serif fonts.

Scope
The range a project encompasses when all of the project goals and objectives are defined:
what will be included and perhaps what will be excluded.

Scope creep
A change to the range a project encompasses, caused by impromptu changes to or additions of content, without corresponding increases in the schedule or budget.

SCORM
Sharable Content Object Reference Model. A set of technical standards for e-learning software products.

Semantic markup
Coding that conveys meaning to other computer programs, such as search engines.

Semantic web
A term that refers to the way page content can be coded to convey meaning to other computer programs, such as search engines.

Semantics
The meanings of words. *See also* Syntax.

SEO
Acronym for Search Engine Optimization, a set of techniques designed to get top search engines to list your site.

Serif fonts
Ornate characters with small extra strokes, or "tails," at the beginning or end of each character. *See also* Sans-serif fonts.

SFTP
Acronym for Secure File Transfer Protocol, a connection that uses an encryption process to protect files, user names, and passwords.

Shape
A closed line that encloses an area.

Site usability test
A test in which you ask unbiased people, who are not connected to the design process, to use and evaluate a site.

Skin
A graphic element that determines the type and design of video or audio playback controls.

Slang
Similar to jargon, but considered to be very informal.

Stakeholders
Anyone with an interest in a project.

Statement of purpose
A statement that clearly states the reason why a project is being developed.

Static text
Text that does not change. *See also* Dynamic text.

Stock photos
Photos that you can purchase, either by the image, or by a subscription fee that covers multiple image downloads.

Stop motion
The type of animation in which a 3D object is moved in minute increments and recorded via camera or film.

Storyboard
Similar to a wireframe; often used in planning animation or video projects, but can also be used for website projects.

SWF format
A compressed media format that plays using the Flash player application.

Synchronize
To compare the dates of all files in both a local and remote site, then transfer only copies of files that have changed since the previous synchronization.

Glossary

Syndicated
Describes content that is sent to you automatically when new content is created, such as a subscription to an email newsletter or magazine. *See also* RSS.

Syntax
The relationships of words in text. *See also* Semantics.

————————— **T** —————————

Tag type
A CSS rule that is used to redefine an HTML tag. *See also* ID type.

Target
The location on the page that a browser displays when a user clicks an internal link. *See also* Named anchor.

Templates
Pages with editable and protected (non-editable) regions that are used to create new pages with consistent design elements and common content.

Terms of use
Rules that govern how a user may use the contents of a website.

Testing server
A computer used to test a site before publishing it to the live server.

Text Layout Framework (TLF)
A framework used to deliver multilingual, print-quality typography for the web.

Texture
Describes an object's surface—how it might feel if we were to touch it.

Timeline
A chronological representation of dates and times from project inception to project completion.

Tracking
The spacing between characters in a block of text. *See also* Kerning.

Translation
The moving of objects within 3-dimensional space along their x-, y-, and z-axes. *See also* 3D animation.

Tree diagram
A visual way to define hierarchical relationships.

Tweening
The process of recording two instances of a single object and having the computer calculate the images for the in-between frames.

Type
Text with characteristics included, such as a font name, size, color, or style.

Typefaces
Designs like Times New Roman or Arial that type designers create.

Typography
The art of placing and arranging type. It includes choosing properties such as typefaces, styles such as bold and italics, size, color, alignment, spacing, and other formatting choices that affect text appearance.

————————— **U** —————————

Unity
A design principle that describes the artful combining of related design elements with the idea being expressed.

Universal usability
A principle describing the goal of enabling all citizens to succeed using communication and information technology in their tasks.

Upload
To copy files from a local folder to a remote host.

URL
Acronym for Uniform Resource Locator, the address of a web page.

Usability
Refers to how easy a product is to learn and use.

User profile
A description of the characteristics of a target audience.

User scenario
A written or drawn storyboard of who a typical user of an interactive experience might be. Also called a user profile.

————————— **V** —————————

Value
The relationship of the light and dark parts in an image, sometimes referred to as tone, shade, or brightness.

Vector-based graphics
Scalable images built using mathematical formulas.

Video codec
The method by which digital video data is compressed and decompressed.

Video encoding
The process of preparing video for output.

————————— **W** —————————

WAV
An uncompressed audio format, supported by both Windows and Macintosh.

Web
Short for World Wide Web, a protocol for information distribution based on hypertext, a system of links to connect text to other, related text.

Web analytic tools
Tools for gathering and measuring information about site usage.

Web apps
Web applications, such as web mail, accessed through web browsers where the program and data files are not stored on a local computer system.

Web Open Font Format (WOFF)
A system developed by the Mozilla Foundation, in concert with several other organizations, to use as a standard format for text on the World Wide Web.

Web server
A computer that is connected to the Internet with an IP (Internet Protocol) address, so that it is available for viewing on the Internet.

WebM (.WebM)
An open source video format developed by Google and used for HTML5 video.

Widget
A term that refers to a part of a GUI (Graphical User Interface) that allows the user to interface with the application and operating system.

Wireframe
A document or series of documents that illustrates the relationship and flow of content within an interactive experience.

Wizard
In authoring tools, an interface that lets you choose from lists of choices or fill in blanks to customize predesigned content.

WOFF
See Web Open Font Format.

WordPress
A general purpose content management system that began as open source blogging software.

World Wide Web Consortium (W3C)
An organization that provides the Web Content Accessibility Guidelines (WCAG) 2.0 as the standard for designing sites accessible to users of all abilities.

Chapter 1

Bellis, M. Inventors of the Modern Computer. Retrieved July 8, 2011, from http://inventors.about.com/library/weekly/aa043099.htm

Gaudiosi, J. (2011). Global Video Game Industry Sales Expected to Top $112 Billion by 2015. Retrieved July 8, 2011, from http://www.gamerlive.tv/article/global-video-game-industry-sales-expected-top-112-billion-2015

Heller, S. and Fernandes, T. (2010). *Becoming a Graphic Designer: A Guide to Careers in Design*, 4th Edition. John Wiley & Sons, Inc.

Kilker, J. What Is Interactive Media Design? [video] Retrieved June, 2011, from http://www.youtube.com/watch?v=Jq_9INEovFc

Kopplin, J. (2002). An Illustrated History of Computers. Retrieved July 8, 2011, from http://www.computersciencelab.com/ComputerHistory/History.htm

Maragos, N. (2006). Game Industry Revenue Expected To Double By 2011. Retrieved July 8, 2011, from http://www.gamasutra.com/php-bin/news_index.php?story=8205

Ozcan, O., Yantac, A., & O'Neil, M. (2009). Breaking the rules in interactive media design education. *Digital Creativity*, 20, 115–124.

Park, J. Y. (2007). Empowering the user as the new media participant. *Digital Creativity*, 18, 175–186.

Chapter 2

Browser Display Statistics. Retrieved December 19, 2011, from http://www.w3schools.com/browsers/browsers_display.asp

Seigel, B. (2011). A Comprehensive Website Planning Guide. *Smashing Magazine*. Retrieved July 1, 2011, from http://www.smashingmagazine.com/2011/06/09/a-comprehensive-website-planning-guide/

Chapter 3

Amazon Strategic Plan. *Scribd.com*. Retrieved February 23, 2012, from http://www.scribd.com/doc/24854038/Amazon-Strategic-Plan

Example of a Strategic Plan Model - Amazon. *Strategy-Keys.com*. Retrieved July 17, 2011, from http://www.strategy-keys.com/Strategic-Planning-Samples---Amazon-part-1.html

A Guide to Disability Rights Laws. U.S. Department of Justice. (2005). Retrieved July 22, 2011, from http://www.ada.gov/cguide.htm

Section508.gov. Resources for understanding and implementing Section 508. Retrieved July 22, 2011, from http://www.section508.gov

Turczyn, C. What Is This Thing Called Hello Kitty? *PopCult Magazine*. Retrieved July 17, 2011, from http://www.popcultmag.com/criticalmass/books/kitty/hellokitty2.html

Web Content Accessibility Guidelines (WCAG) Overview. W3 Web Accessibility initiative. Retrieved July 22, 2011, from http://www.w3.org/WAI/intro/wcag.php

Wroblewski, L. (2002). *Site-Seeing: A Visual Approach to Web Usability*. New York: Hungry Minds, Inc.

Chapter 4

Authoring Tools, Social Media. W3C. Retrieved July 10, 2011, from http://www.w3.org/standards/agents/authoring

Ford, J.L. Jr., and Stanek, W. R. (2010). *Increase Your Web Traffic in a Weekend, Sixth Edition*. Course Technology PTR, Cengage Learning.

HTML5 Tag Reference. *W3Schools*. Retrieved October 15, 2011, from http://www.w3schools.com/html5/html5_reference.asp

Komarov, A. (2009). iPhone Apps Design Mistakes: Over-Blown Visuals. *Smashing Magazine*. Retrieved November 12, 2011, from http://www.smashingmagazine.com/2009/07/21/iphone-apps-design-mistakes-overblown-visuals/

Pimmel, K. (2011). Making It a Mobile Web App. *Smashing Magazine*. Retrieved July 12, 2011, from http://www.smashingmagazine.com/2011/01/26/making-it-a-mobile-web-app/

SCORM Explained. Rustici Software. Retrieved July 12, 2011, from http://scorm.com/scorm-explained

Top Ten Search Engines – Top Ten SEs. SEO Consultants Directory. Retrieved July 12, 2011, from http://www.seoconsultants.com/app/webroot/search-engines/

Widget. *Webopedia*. Retrieved July 12, 2011, from http://www.webopedia.com/TERM/W/widget.html

RSS. *Webopedia*. Retrieved July 10, 2011, from http://www.webopedia.com/TERM/R/RSS.html

Chapter 5

Bringhurst, B. (2011). Design Decisions for Digital Publishing Apps. *InDesign Docs*. Retrieved on November 13, 2011, from http://blogs.adobe.com/indesigndocs/2011/02/design-decisions-for-digital-publishing-apps.html

Follett, A. (2010). Review of Popular Web Font Embedding Services. *Smashing Magazine*. Retrieved on July 30, 2011, from http://www.smashingmagazine.com/2010/10/20/review-of-popular-web-font-embedding-services/

Galineau, S., Daniels, S., Berry, J. and Duggan, M. Web Fonts. Retrieved August 14, 2011, from http://ie.microsoft.com/testdrive/Graphics/WebFonts/Default.html

The History of Type. *Independent Lens*. Retrieved July 31, 2011, from http://www.pbs.org/independentlens/helvetica/type.html

Kyrnin, J. 10 Tips for Good Web Writing. *About.com*. Retrieved August 4, 2100, from http://webdesign.about.com/od/writing/a/aa031405.htm

Macris, A. (2010). Publisher's Note: What Grade is Your Content Comprehension? *The Escapist*. Retrieved August 2, 2011, from http://www.escapistmagazine.com/articles/view/columns/publishers-note/7536-Publisher-Note-What-Grade-is-Your-Content-Comprehension

Miller, M. J. (2011). Why Adobe is Deflating Flash: HTML5. *Forward Thinking*. Retrieved February 19, 2012, from http://forwardthinking.pcmag.com/none/290436-why-adobe-is-deflating-flash-html5

@font-face Browser compatibility. Mozilla Developer Network. Retrieved July 30, 2011, from https://developer.mozilla.org/en/CSS/@font-face#Browser_compatibility

Muchmore, M. (2011). Adobe Edge, Flash Replacement Hedge, Gets Interactivity. *PCMag.com*. Retrieved February 19, 2012, from http://www.pcmag.com/article2/0,2817,2394025,00.asp#fbid=1WG8ufYUhiy

Potter, M. (2011). A Web Developer's Guide to Adobe InDesign. *Smashing Magazine*. Retrieved November 13, 2011, from http://www.smashingmagazine.com/2011/06/23/a-web-developer-s-guide-to-adobe-indesign-2/

Redshaw, K. Using MS Word Readability Statistics for Web Writing. Retrieved August 2, 2011, from http://www.kerryr.net/webwriting/tools_readability.htm

van Duyne, D. K., Landay, J. A., and Hong, J. I. (2006). *The Design of Sites: Patterns for Creating Winning Web Sites*. (Second Edition). Prentice Hall.

Writing Web Content. Retrieved on August 4, 2011, from www.usability.gov/pdfs/chapter15.pdf

Chapter 6

Meyer, D. 3D Design: Adding Richness to the Web Pages. *Webgranth*. Retrieved August 24, 2011, from http://www.webgranth.com/3d-design-adding-richness-to-the-web-pages

Who Uses CC? Creative Commons. Retrieved August 18, 2011, from http://creativecommons.org/who-uses-cc

What is Intellectual Property? World Intellectual Property Organization. Retrieved August 18, 2011, from http://www.wipo.int/about-ip/en/

Chapter 7

Nusair, D. Intro to Animation Techniques: An Insight Into the Three Main Types of Animation. *About.com*. Retrieved August 28, 2011, from http://movies.about.com/od/animatedmovies/a/animated-techniques.htm

Rainsberger, M. (2010). Motion Graphics and 2-D Animation: 10 Tips for a Clean Workflow. *Noupe*. Retrieved September 4, 2011, from http://www.noupe.com/how-tos/motion-graphics-and-2-d-animation-10-tips-for-a-clean-workflow.html

Chapter 8

eLesson Markup Language Glossary. http://www.elml.ch/website/en/html/website_glossary.html

Find Icons. Retrieved August 20, 2011, from http://findicons.com/

Geoghegan, M., and Klass, D. (2005). *Podcast Solutions: A Complete Guide to Podcasting*. [Google eBook]. Friends of Ed, Pap Edition.

Firke, B. Mono Vs. Stereo Audio. *eHow.com*. Retrieved August 15, 2011, from http://www.ehow.com/about_6695146_mono-vs-stereo-audio.html#ixzz1UgLZIU60

Sound Formats for the Internet. Virginia Commonwealth University, Office for Information Technology - Instructional Development Center. Retrieved August 15, 2011, from http://www.vcu.edu/mdcweb/selfstudy/monographs/formats.htm

Sound Systems: Mono versus Stereo. Mc Squared System Design Group, Inc. Retrieved August 15, 2011, from http://www.mcsquared.com/mono-stereo.htm

HTML5 Audio. *W3Schools*. Retrieved March 4, 2011, from http://www.w3schools.com/html5/html5_audio.asp

--------- **Chapter 9** ---------

Agarwal, A. (2011). What's the Optimum Length of an Online Video. *Digital Inspiration*. Retrieved September 15, 2011, from http://www.labnol.org/internet/optimum-length-of-video/18696/

HTML5 Video. *W3Schools*. Retrieved March 30, 2011, from www.w3schools.com/html5/html5_video.asp

Reinhardt, R. (2007). Optimal frame Dimensions for Flash video. Adobe Developer Connection. Retrieved September, 15 2011, from http://www.adobe.com/devnet/flash/apps/video_sizes.html

Viewing Habits [Tagged post]. *Wistia*. Retrieved September, 2011, from http://wistia.com/blog/tag/viewing-habits/

--------- **Chapter 10** ---------

Cutts, M. (2009). Add Custom Search to any site in two minutes. *Matt Cutts: Gadgets, Google, and SEO*. Retrieved September 9, 2011, from http://www.mattcutts.com/blog/add-custom-search-to-any-site/

Henry, S. L., Transcription Services. *uiAccess*. Retrieved on September 8, 2011, from http://www.uiaccess.com/transcripts/transcript_services.html

Henry, S. L., Transcripts on the Web: Getting People to Your Podcasts and Videos. *uiAccess*. Retrieved September 12, 2011, from http://www.uiaccess.com/transcripts/transcripts_on_the_web.html

INDEX

proprietary software, 2–17
Proto, 3–6, 4–11
ProtoShare, 3–6
prototypes, 2–10
public domain, 6–9
publishing, 2–20
    audio, 8–7
    video, 9–7
    websites, 4–21

QuickTime Player, 9–8
QuickTime Pro, 9–6

raster graphics, 6–5
readability, text, 5–14
Readability Statistics dialog box, Microsoft Word,
    5–14
Readability Test Tool, 5–14
Reader, 5–8
    reading PDFs, 10–8—9
Real Simple Syndication (RSS), 4–10, 8–12
recording voice, Adobe Audition CS6, 8–19—21
redundant backups, 2–19
regular backup systems, 2–19
relative paths, 4–15—16
remote site files, 4–21
removing audio, Adobe Audition CS6, 8–25
repetition, 3–19
Reports dialog box, Dreamweaver, 10–11
Research-Based Web Design and Usability
    Guidelines, 3–10

resources, 2–5
RGB Color Mode, 6–20
rich text, 5–2
rollover buttons, 5–15
rollover images, Dreamweaver, 6–24—25, 6–28,
    6–31—32
roundtrip integration, 6–6
royalty-free images, 2–11
RPGs, 4–12—13
RSS (Real Simple Syndication), 4–10, 8–12
rules (CSS), 5–16
    applying to text in Dreamweaver, 5–23
    creating in Dreamweaver, 5–20—21
    editing in Dreamweaver, 5–20—22
    modifying, 5–34, 5–38

samples, audio, 8–4
sampling rate, 6–20
Sanrio, 3–9
sans-serif fonts, 5–12
Save As Template dialog box, Dreamweaver,
    6–34
Save for Web & Devices dialog box, Photoshop,
    6–23
Sceneline, Adobe Premiere Elements, 9–15—16
Schneiderman, Ben, 3–15
Schuman, Jim, 8–28
scope, projects, 2–4
scope creep, 2–4
SCORM (Sharable Content Object Reference
    Model), 4–18

search engine(s)
    optimization, 4–18—19
    registering websites with, 10–17
Search Engine Optimization (SEO), 10–18
search text boxes, 5–34, 5–35, 5–39
Section 508 of the Rehabilitation Act of 1973,
    3–14—15
Secure FTP (SFTP), 10–14
Selection tool, Illustrator, 5–28
semantic markup, 4–6—7
Semantic Web, coding for, 4–16—17
SEO (Search Engine Optimization), 10–18
sequencing file names, animation, 7–9
serif fonts, 5–12
servers, 10–14—17. *See also* web servers
    live, 4–21
    managing, 10–14
    remote, transferring files to and from,
        10–15—17, 10–31—33
    setting up, 10–14
    testing, 4–21, 10–14
SFTP (Secure FTP), 10–14
Shape tools, Illustrator, 5–26
Sharable Content Object Reference Model
    (SCORM), 4–18
Shutterstock, 2–11
single-lens reflex (SLR) cameras, 6–12
site maps, 10–7—8, 10–18
site reports, 10–11, 10–26
site search(es), 10–8